P9-EMJ-930

The Ultimate INSTANT POT Cookbook

Foolproof, Quick & Easy
800 INSTANT POT Recipes
for Beginners and Advanced Users

Simon Rush

Copyright © 2019 by Simon Rush

ISBN: 978-1699451953

In no way is it legal to reproduce, duplicate, or transmit any part of this document by either electronic means or in printed format. Recording of this publication is strictly prohibited, and any storage of this material is not allowed unless with written permission from the publisher. All rights reserved.

The information provided herein is stated to be truthful and consistent, in that any liability, regarding inattention or otherwise, by any usage or abuse of any policies, processes, or directions: contained within is the solitary and complete responsibility of the recipient reader. Under no circumstances will any legal liability or blame be held against the publisher for any reparation, damages, or monetary loss due to the information herein, either directly or indirectly. Respective authors own all copyrights not held by the publisher.

Legal Notice:

This book is copyright protected. This is only for personal use. You cannot amend, distribute, sell, use, quote or paraphrase any part or the content within this book without the consent of the author or copyright owner. Legal action will be pursued if this is breached.

Contents

INTRODUCTION 10

BRUNCH & SIDE DISHES 11

1. Mango & Walnut French-Style Toast 11
2. Cheesy Grits with Crispy Pancetta 11
3. Carrot & Nut Cakes 11
4. Summer Garden Quiche 11
5. Lazy-Morning Eggs in Hollandaise Sauce 11
6. Simple Softboiled Eggs 11
7. Nut & Apple Breakfast 12
8. Shiitake Mushroom Oats with Garlic 12
9. Ground Beef & Egg Casserole 12
10. Sweet Corn & Onion Eggs 12
11. Butternut Squash & Carrot Egg Casserole 12
12. Three-Meat Mozzarella Quiche 12
13. One-Pot Colby Cheese, Ham & Eggs 12
14. Crunchy Pancetta & Egg Burgers 13
15. Sausage & Cheese Frittata 13
16. Parsley Pork Breakfast Biscuits 13
17. Sausage and Kale Casserole with Eggs 13
18. Fennel & Potato Salad 13
19. Tasty Onion Frittata with Bell Peppers 13
20. Savory Lemon Zesty Toast 14
21. Onion & Potato Frittata 14
22. Heavenly Coconut Pancakes 14
23. Quick Cilantro Salmon 14
24. Party Dark Chocolate Bread Pudding 14
25. Pear, Coconut & Pecan Porridge 14
26. Sunday Paprika Potatoes with Herbs 14
27. Nutmeg Cauliflower Potato Mash 15
28. Red Cabbage with Coconut 15
29. Black-Eyed Pea & Sweet Potato Bowl 15
30. Quick Ginger-Carrot Puree 15
31. Strawberry & White Chocolate Porridge 15
32. Inviting Potatoes & Snow Beans 15
33. Spicy Broccoli with Peas & Potatoes 15
34. Winter Squash & Cauliflower Bowl 16
35. Sweet Potatoes with Zucchini 16
36. Steamed Tabasco Potatoes 16
37. Minty Barley Bowls 16
38. Brussel Sprouts with Onions & Apples 16
39. Smoked Paprika Spiced Squash Hash 16
40. Creamy Blue Cheese Broccoli 16
41. Steamed Artichokes with Parsley Aioli 17

42. Mushroom Pâté 17
43. Savory Nutmeg Yam Mash 17
44. Grapefruit Potatoes with Walnuts 17
45. Gnocchi with Zucchini & Tomatoes 17
46. Savory Baby Spinach & Carrot Side 17
47. Rutabaga Salad with Honey Dressing 17
48. Perfect Mediterranean Asparagus 18
49. Lemony Grana Padano Broccoli 18
50. Golden Beets with Green Olives 18
51. Garlic Red Potatoes 18
52. Cherry Tomato & Summer Squash Delight 18
53. Meat-Free Lasagna with Mushrooms 18
54. Heavenly Spinach with Ricotta Cheese 18
55. Prune & Peach Barley 19
56. Savory Tomato Bell Peppers 19
57. Portobello Mushroom & Leek Delight 19
58. Thyme & Frascati Cauliflower 19
59. Eggs Florentine Casserole 19
60. Thyme Potato & Cannellini Bean Pottage 19
61. French Toast 19
62. Creamy Potatoes with Pancetta Crisps 20
63. Mustard & Sweet Zucchini 20
64. Homemade Asian-Style Tomato Chutney 20
65. Cucumber, Pepper & Quinoa Salad 20
66. Savory Mushroom & Squash Platter 20
67. Red Cabbage & Bell Pepper Side 20
68. Sweet Potatoes with Brussel Sprouts 20
69. Grandma's Cabbage with Apples 21
70. Tasty Potato & Carrot Mash 21
71. Bok Choy & Tomato Side 21
72. Ginger Mustard Greens with Bacon 21
73. Eggplant Caponata 21
74. Pumpkin Spice Oatmeal 21
75. Vanilla Sweet Potato Oatmeal 21
76. Date & Coconut Granola 22
77. Chili Pancetta Hash 22
78. Cheese, Egg & Sausage Casserole 22
79. Apple Oatmeal 22
80. Pumpkin Granola 22
81. Easy Monkey Bread 22
82. Savory Faro Breakfast 22

BEANS & GRAINS 23

83. Pink Beans with Pancetta & Tomatoes 23
84. Bean Soup with Pork & Vegetables 23
85. Two-Bean & Chickpea Stew 23
86. Lima Bean & Spinach Stew 23
87. Black Bean & Quinoa Stew 23
88. Kidney Bean & Shiitake Spread 23
89. One-Pot Beef with Beans 24
90. Mushroom & Cheese Buckwheat 24
91. Garbanzo Beans & Mixed Vegetable Stew 24
92. Grana Padano Grits with Ham & Eggs 24
93. Picante Red Bean & Corn Dip 24
94. Curry Pinto Beans 24
95. Homemade Bean Dip 24

96. Honey Quinoa with Walnuts 25
97. Italian Sausage with Beans & Chickpeas 25
98. Best Black Bean Chili 25
99. Tiger Prawns with Red Lentils 25
100. Rosemary Butter Beans 25
101. Buckwheat with Vegetables & Ham 25
102. Fresh Fig & Banana Barley 25
103. Vegan White Bean & Avocado Salad 26
104. Favorite "Ever" Cornbread 26
105. Pearl Barley & Black Olive Salad 26
106. Easy Barley Pilaf with Cashews 26
107. Split Pea Beef Stew 26
108. Fennel White Bean Stew 26

109. Barley & Potato Soup.......................26
110. Spelt & Red Beans with Mushrooms.......................27
111. Paprika Lima Bean Dip with Pancetta.......................27
112. Peach & Golden Raisin Porridge.......................27
113. Spicy Mashed Pinto Beans.......................27
114. Cheesy Bulgur with Spring Onions.......................27
115. Yellow Lentil Dip.......................27
116. Black Bean & Green Chili con Queso.......................27

117. White Beans with Tuna.......................28
118. Hazelnut Banana & Date Millet.......................28
119. Apple & Brazil Nut Porridge.......................28
120. Papaya & Honey Quinoa.......................28
121. Couscous with Cherries & Macadamia.......................28
122. Creamy Chicken with Quinoa.......................28
123. Serrano Pepper Bulgur.......................28
124. Bulgur with Vegetables.......................28

PASTA & RICE 29

125. Cheesy Sausage & Pepperoni Linguine.......................29
126. Creamy Turkey & Cauliflower Tortellini.......................29
127. Vegetable Lasagna with Mushrooms.......................29
128. Rotini with Beef & Monterey Jack Cheese.......................29
129. Penne with Sage & Pancetta.......................29
130. Chicken with Farfalle & Enchilada Sauce.......................29
131. Ziti Pasta with Pork Balls & Vegetables.......................30
132. White Wine Pasta Bolognese.......................30
133. Tuna & Artichoke Egg Noodles.......................30
134. Zucchini & Beef Lasagna.......................30
135. Kale Pesto Tagliatelle with Green Beans.......................30
136. Traditional Italian Peperonata.......................30
137. Sausage with Fusilli Pasta & Cheese.......................31
138. Dill Mackerel & Pasta Stew.......................31
139. Ramen Noodles with Beef Meatballs.......................31
140. Penne with Mixed Peppers & Beans.......................31
141. Pork with Brown Rice.......................31
142. Meatless Mexican Rice.......................31
143. Apricot Wild Rice Pudding.......................31
144. Burgundy Beef Rice Stew.......................32

145. Risotto with Green Peas & Mushrooms.......................32
146. Chili Rice with Vegetables.......................32
147. Beef & Rice Stuffed Cabbage Leaves.......................32
148. Saucy Basmati Rice.......................32
149. Chicken with Carrot & Brown Rice.......................32
150. Swiss Chard, Zucchini & Mushroom Rice.......................32
151. Rosemary Salmon Soup with Rice.......................33
152. Cheesy Shrimp Risotto.......................33
153. Basmati Rice with Pumpkin.......................33
154. Chicken & Veggie Gumbo.......................33
155. Wild Rice with Three-Color Bell Peppers.......................33
156. Cheesy Porcini Mushroom Risotto.......................33
157. Simple Celery Jasmine Rice.......................34
158. Arroz con Leche with Prunes.......................34
159. Date & Almond Rice Pudding.......................34
160. Chorizo & Cheese Rice.......................34
161. Sweet Rice Pudding with Hazelnuts.......................34
162. Sausage Pilaf with Sun-Dried Tomatoes.......................34
163. Spanish Rice with Chicken Legs.......................34

FISH & SEAFOOD 35

164. Creamy Shrimp Risotto.......................35
165. Healthy Salmon with Broccoli.......................35
166. Carrot & Onion Crabmeat.......................35
167. Prawn & Tuna Skewers with Soy Sauce.......................35
168. Traditional Catfish Chowder.......................35
169. Herby Clams in White Wine.......................35
170. Mediterranean Cod.......................36
171. Sunday Crab Legs with White Wine.......................36
172. Gruyère Cheese & Lobster Pasta.......................36
173. Best Crab Patties.......................36
174. Egg Noodles with Tuna & Peas.......................36
175. Parsley Haddock with Potatoes.......................36
176. Ginger Lime Salmon.......................36
177. Tasty Trout with Spiralized Vegetables.......................37
178. Drunken Mussels.......................37
179. Nut Crusted Tilapia.......................37
180. Smoked Paprika Squid with Green Beans.......................37
181. Rosemary Salmon with Spinach.......................37
182. Simple Basil & Haddock with Capers.......................37
183. Clams a la Marinera.......................37
184. Salmon with Parsley-Lemon Sauce.......................38
185. Salmon Loaf with Cucumber Sauce.......................38
186. Canned Tuna Casserole.......................38
187. Poached Trout with Pomegranate.......................38
188. Delicious Cod with Cherry Tomatoes.......................38
189. Greek Kakavia Fish Soup.......................38

190. Tomato Beans with Tuna.......................39
191. Easy Citrus Fish.......................39
192. Seafood Paella with Broccoli.......................39
193. Buttered Trout.......................39
194. Steamed Salmon with Caper Sauce.......................39
195. Bell Pepper & Salmon One-Pot.......................39
196. Halibut with Mango Sauce.......................39
197. Paprika & Garlic Shrimp.......................40
198. Eggplant & Tilapia Curry.......................40
199. Dilled Salmon with Fennel & Lemon.......................40
200. Steamed Pollock.......................40
201. Homemade Grits with Shrimp.......................40
202. Basil Infused Salmon with Chickpeas.......................40
203. Dill & Potato Salmon Chowder.......................40
204. Spicy Coconut Salmon Curry.......................41
205. Fennel-Scented Fish Stew.......................41
206. Wild Rice & Salmon Soup.......................41
207. Bell Pepper & Zucchini Salmon.......................41
208. Jalapeño Seafood Jambalaya.......................41
209. Garlic & Chili Prawns.......................41
210. Manhattan-Style Clam Chowder.......................42
211. Sweet & Sour Shrimp.......................42
212. Creole Seafood Gumbo.......................42
213. Garlic & Chili Crab Legs.......................42
214. Steamed Tilapia with Radicchio Salad.......................42
215. Salmon & Asparagus Frittata.......................42

POULTRY 43

216. Chicken in Roasted Red Pepper Sauce.......................43
217. Caraway Chicken with Vegetables.......................43
218. Hot Chicken & Leek Cassoulet.......................43

219. Chicken with Green Beans & Potatoes.......................43
220. Thyme Chicken with Red Currant Sauce.......................43
221. Colby Cheese Chicken Drumsticks.......................43

222. Garlicky Chicken with Mushrooms 44
223. Creamy Chicken with Tomato Sauce 44
224. Parsley & Carrot Chicken Stew.................................... 44
225. Lemony Chicken with Thyme & Garlic.......................... 44
226. Coq Au Vin.. 44
227. Ginger & Scallion Chicken.. 44
228. Chicken with Baby Carrots & Mushrooms 45
229. Chicken in Honey & Habanero Sauce.......................... 45
230. Tuscan Turkey Breast with Beans 45
231. Oregano Chicken with Garlic & Tomatoes 45
232. Chicken with Green Chilies 45
233. Serrano Chili Chicken 45
234. Adobo Chicken in Roasted Pepper Sauce 46
235. Creamy Chicken Legs 46
236. Juicy Chili Orange Wings.. 46
237. Cajun Chicken with Snow Beans 46
238. Italian Chicken Breasts... 46
239. Sweet Chicken Drumsticks 46
240. Saucy Chicken Teriyaki... 46
241. Chicken Jambalaya 47
242. Simple Sage Whole Chicken....................................... 47
243. Herb Chicken with Potatoes & Green Beans 47
244. Sweet & Spicy Chicken Thighs.................................... 47
245. Sage Drumsticks with Red Sauce 47
246. Thyme Chicken Soup 47
247. Chicken Garam Masala 47
248. Paprika Chicken in White Wine Sauce.......................... 48
249. Lime Chicken with Pesto Sauce 48
250. BBQ Chicken Wings with Shallots 48
251. Hot Chicken Wings with Sage..................................... 48
252. Chicken with Vegetables & Salad 48
253. Asian-Style Chicken Thighs.. 48
254. Garlic Basil Chicken with Carrots................................ 48
255. Mushroom & Green Onion Chicken 49
256. Chili Chicken Breasts with Bell Peppers 49
257. Herby Chicken Thighs... 49
258. Dijon Chicken with Mushrooms & Kale 49
259. Curry Chicken with Edamame 49
260. Cheesy Potatoes with Chicken Sausage 49
261. Chicken Tikka Masala 50
262. Garlicky Chicken Wings with Herbs............................. 50

263. Cumin Chicken with Salsa Verde 50
264. Cheesy Chicken Piccata with Olives............................ 50
265. Mediterranean Chicken 50
266. Teriyaki-Style Chicken Thighs..................................... 50
267. Chicken with Brown Rice 51
268. Picante Chicken Thighs... 51
269. Spicy Chicken Soup 51
270. Chicken Alfredo 51
271. Spicy Roasted Whole Chicken 51
272. Slow-Cooked Honey-Mustard Chicken 51
273. Basil Chicken Casserole... 52
274. Thai Chicken 52
275. Chicken Cordon Bleu 52
276. Maple Barbecued Chicken 52
277. Chicken Marrakesh... 52
278. Thyme & Bell Pepper Chicken 52
279. Marsala Wine Chicken with Mushrooms 53
280. Chicken & Mushrooms in Wine Sauce 53
281. Honey Garlic Chicken... 53
282. Sweet & Spicy Chicken Mole 53
283. Chipotle Chicken with Chives & Avocado.................... 53
284. Jamaican-Style Jerk Chicken...................................... 53
285. Herby Chicken with Tomatoes 54
286. Winter Chicken Hotpot.. 54
287. Parmesan Chicken with Rice....................................... 54
288. Cashew Flavored Chicken 54
289. Chicken with Spicy Honey-Orange Sauce 54
290. Garlic & Paprika Chicken 54
291. Jalapeño Chicken with Herbs...................................... 55
292. Orange Glazed Chicken.. 55
293. Spinach & Gnocchi Chicken Sausage Pot................... 55
294. Chicken Stew with Potatoes & Barley 55
295. Apple & Honey Chicken Drumsticks............................ 55
296. Shallot Turkey with Apricot Gravy 55
297. Juicy Turkey with Mushrooms 56
298. Homemade Duck & Snow Pea Soup............................ 56
299. Sriracha Pulled Turkey with Ale Beer 56
300. Buffalo Turkey & Squash Casserole 56
301. Turkey with Broccoli & Carrots.................................... 56
302. Onion Apple Goose 56

PORK 57

303. Pork Chops with Broccoli 57
304. Lemon & Cinnamon Braised Pork 57
305. Italian-Style Pancetta & Potato Casserole................... 57
306. Quick Pork Chops with Brussels Sprouts.................... 57
307. Pork & Shallot Frittata 57
308. Tasty Pork with Carrots & Shallots.............................. 57
309. Spicy Pork Sausage Meatloaf..................................... 58
310. Pork Tenderloin in Sweet Ginger Sauce...................... 58
311. Fall Pork Stew.. 58
312. Pear & Cherry Pork Tenderloin.................................... 58
313. Juicy & Tender Pork Loin 58
314. Tender BBQ Ribs 58
315. Juicy Sweet Pork Ribs.. 59
316. Pork Shoulder in BBQ Sauce...................................... 59
317. Grandma's Veggie Ground Pork.................................. 59
318. Herby Pork Butt with Potatoes.................................... 59
319. Rich Parsnip & Mushroom Pork................................... 59
320. Savoy Cabbage with Pancetta.................................... 59
321. Pork with Shallots & Mushrooms 59
322. Sauteed Spinach With Bacon & Chickpeas.................. 60

323. Flavorful Pork Roast in Beer Sauce 60
324. Pork and Sauerkraut Goulash 60
325. Pork Steaks with Apricot Sauce.................................. 60
326. Pork in Tomato Buttermilk Sauce 60
327. The Best Ever Pineapple Pork Meatballs 60
328. Pork Rib Chops with Carrots & Parsnips...................... 60
329. Mango Pork Roast with Dijon Mustard 61
330. Peach Short Ribs 61
331. Green Chili Pork.. 61
332. Balsamic Pork Tenderloin 61
333. Orange Cinnamon Ribs 61
334. Pork Chops with Veggies.. 61
335. Chorizo with Bell Peppers & Onions 62
336. Cuban Mojo Pork 62
337. Pork Meatballs with Sour Mushroom Sauce 62
338. Garlicky BBQ Pork Butt 62
339. Pork with Prune Sauce 62
340. Pork Chops with Shallots & Carrots 62
341. Juicy Chorizo Sausage with Tater Tots........................ 62
342. Basil Pork Meatballs 63

343. Delicious Pork Loin with Turnips & Apples 63
344. Curried Pork Stew with Green Peas 63
345. Tarragon Pork with Mushroom Sauce 63
346. Jalapeño Pork Stew 63
347. Grandma's Sweet Pork Roast 63
348. Orange Pork Carnitas 64
349. Mint & Cilantro Infused Pork 64
350. BBQ Pulled Pork 64
351. Chorizo Sausage Sandwiches with Gravy 64
352. German Pork with Cabbage & Tomatoes 64
353. Sweet Shredded Pork 64
354. Oregano Pork with Egg Noodles 65
355. Garlicky Sweet Pork with Rice 65
356. City Pork with Celery & Carrots 65
357. Korean-Style Pork 65
358. Pork & Rice Stuffed Peppers 65
359. Spicy Pork Chops 65
360. Green Onion Pork Ribs 66
361. Saucy Mustard Pork 66
362. Pork Ribs with Wine Pecan Sauce 66
363. Creamy Ranch Pork Chops 66
364. Pork Chops in Onion Sauce 66
365. Sweet & Sour Pork 66
366. Winter Pork Belly with Red Cabbage 66

367. Cheesy Pancetta Penne with Green Peas 67
368. Effortless Pork Chops 67
369. Pork Chops in Honey & Apple Sauce 67
370. Sherry Pork Chops with Artichoke Hearts 67
371. Moo-Shu Wraps 67
372. Pork Chops Teriyaki Style 67
373. Fruit-Stuffed Pork Loin 68
374. Mango Pork Sandwiches 68
375. Pulled Pork Mexican-Style 68
376. Mediterranean Pork Roast 68
377. Ribs with Plum Sauce 68
378. Honey-Dijon Pork Chops 68
379. Mediterranean Pork Meatballs 69
380. Thyme & Green Onion Pork Chops 69
381. Pork Loin with Mustard Sauce 69
382. European Stew 69
383. Pork Stew with Sun-Dried Tomatoes 69
384. Spiced Pork Ribs 69
385. Sausage with Beer & Sauerkraut 70
386. Pork Goulash with Spaghetti 70
387. Greek-Style Pulled Pork 70
388. Chili Pork with Pinto Beans 70
389. Peppered Pork Tenderloin with Rice 70
390. Jalapeño Pork with Pico de Gallo 70

BEEF & LAMB 71

391. Chili Beef Brisket with Chives 71
392. Mount-Watering Beef Ribs with Shiitakes 71
393. Thyme Creamy Beef Roast 71
394. Holiday Beef Meatloaf 71
395. Sweet Ginger Beef Ribs 71
396. Garlic Balsamic Steak 71
397. Sirloin Steak with Gorgonzola Cheese 72
398. Beef Sloppy Joes with Coleslaw 72
399. Sunday Beef Garam Masala 72
400. Beef Sausage & Bean Tagliatelle 72
401. Beef & Sauerkraut German Dinner 72
402. Saucy Corned Beef Brisket 72
403. Beef with Lemon-Grapefruit Sauce 73
404. Beef Roast with Red Potatoes 73
405. Mustardy Beef Steaks with Beer Gravy 73
406. Thyme Pot Roast with Potatoes 73
407. Grandma's Beef with Apple & Vegetables 73
408. Stewed Beef with Vegetables 74
409. Beef with Chestnuts & Pearl Onions 74
410. Mom's Rump Roast with Potatoes 74
411. Ground Beef with Zucchini Noodles 74
412. Quick & Easy Beef Meatloaf 74
413. Whiskey-Glazed Meatloaf 74
414. Homemade Beef Minestrone 75
415. Rosemary Flank Steak 75
416. Sticky Ginger Ale Short Ribs 75
417. One-Pot Fennel & Parsnip Beef 75
418. Tasty Beef with Carrot-Onion Gravy 75
419. Easy Beef & Rice Kaiser rolls 75
420. Provençal Meatballs with Cheese Sauce 76
421. Brussel Sprout & Beef with Red Sauce 76
422. Yummy Beef with Vegetables 76
423. Chipotle Beef with Wild Rice 76
424. Beef Spaghetti Bolognese 76
425. Chipotle Beef Curry 76
426. Juniper Beef Ragu 77

427. Spicy Beef with Chickpeas 77
428. Cajun Beef Ribeye 77
429. Beef & Pancetta Bourguignon 77
430. Mexican-Style Ropa Vieja 77
431. Caribbean Beef Roast 77
432. Italian Beef Stew with Root Vegetables 78
433. Tasty Beef with Rotini Pasta 78
434. Picante Beef Stew with Barley 78
435. Beef with Garlic & Honey 78
436. Zucchini Rump Steak 78
437. Smoked Beef Steak 78
438. Dinner Ribs with Beets & Potatoes 79
439. Beef with Pearl Onions & Mushrooms 79
440. Cheesy Beef Tortilla Pie 79
441. Barbecued Brisket with Tagliatelle 79
442. Beef & Vegetable Casserole 79
443. Cilantro Vegetable Beef Soup 79
444. Country Beef Stew with Sweet Potatoes 80
445. Curried Beef Stew with Green Peas 80
446. Burrito Beef 80
447. Malaysian Beef Curry 80
448. Stewed Beef Oxtails 80
449. Speedy Meatballs 80
450. Shiitake & Baby Carrot Beef Stew 81
451. Beef Paprikash 81
452. Beef & Rutabaga Stew 81
453. Herby Beef Stroganoff 81
454. Korean Beef Brisket 81
455. Parsley Buttered Beef 81
456. Tarragon Beef & Prune Casserole 82
457. Easy Beef Stew 82
458. Zucchini & Potato Beef Stew 82
459. Beef & Bean Goulash 82
460. Chipotle Shredded Beef 82
461. Polish-Style Beef & Cabbage Pot 82
462. Parsley Beef Roast with Mushrooms 83

463. Beef Stew with Tomatoes 83
464. Beef & Jalapeño Curry 83
465. Beef & Cavolo Nero Pot 83
466. Saucy Beef Short Ribs........................ 83
467. Melt-in-Your-Mouth Beef with Vegetables 84
468. Beef Brisket with Vegetables................. 84
469. Winter Beef with Vegetables 84
470. Beef Soup with Red Potatoes & Pancetta 84
471. Beef Sausage & Spinach Stew 84
472. Savory Beef Roast in Passion Fruit Gravy...... 84
473. Beat Lamb Stew with Kale & Peaches........... 85

474. Lamb Shanks in Port Wine.................... 85
475. Effortless Lamb with Green Onions............ 85
476. Herby Lamb with Vegetables 85
477. Lamb & Bok Choy Curry..................... 85
478. Lamb Stew................................. 85
479. Lamb & Mushroom Ragout 86
480. Lamb Roast with Turnips 86
481. Lamb with Green Onions 86
482. Thyme Braised Lamb 86
483. Chili Lamb with Carrots & Celery 86
484. Lamb Cacciatore............................ 86

VEGETARIAN & VEGAN 87

485. Cauliflower "Risotto" with Mushrooms.......... 87
486. Vegetable & Peanut Pilaf..................... 87
487. Mom's Carrots with Walnuts & Berries 87
488. Lemon Asparagus 87
489. Grana Padano Green Risotto 87
490. Savory Spinach & Leek Relish 87
491. Parmesan Zoodle Soup....................... 87
492. Chickpea & Bean Hummus 88
493. Vegan Shepherd's Pie 88
494. Broccoli, Cauliflower & Zucchini Cakes 88
495. Garden Vegetable Spaghetti 88
496. Herby Vegetables 88
497. Cottage Cheese Deviled Eggs 88
498. Tahini Tofu with Cauliflower & Potatoes........ 89
499. Niçoise-Style Ratatouille..................... 89
500. Chipotle Soybeans 89
501. Emmental Baked Eggs 89
502. Turmeric Vegan Sausage Casserole............ 89
503. Monterey Jack Vegetable Casserole 89
504. Blue Cheese Potatoes 90
505. Penne with Pepperoncini Sauce 90
506. Basil Buttered Corn on the Cob 90
507. Quick Veggie Meal.......................... 90
508. Cheesy Spinach with Eggs 90
509. Creamy Leek Potatoes....................... 90
510. Tempeh Stir-Fry with Sherry & Parsley 90
511. Cheesy Pumpkin Chutney 91
512. Peas, Sweet Potatoes & Spinach Pot 91
513. Simple Sweet Potatoes 91
514. Sweet Tomato Sauce......................... 91
515. Zucchini Pomodoro Pasta..................... 91
516. Mushroom & Bell Pepper Bruschettas 91
517. Spinach & Feta Pie Sandwiches............... 91
518. Vegan Burrito Bowls 92
519. Kalamata & Zucchini Toast................... 92
520. Pumpkin & Lentil Dhal 92
521. Scallion & Tofu Bowl........................ 92
522. Garlic Kale Hummus......................... 92
523. Simple Herby Potatoes 92
524. Pecan & Mashed Potato Bake 92
525. Veggie Flax Patties 93
526. Winter Root Vegetable Pot 93
527. Snow Pea & Raisin Salad..................... 93
528. Catalan Vegetable Samfaina 93
529. Green Chili Buttered Corn 93
530. Awesome Candied Potatoes 93
531. Gingery Sweet Potato & Kale Bowl............. 94

532. Spicy Red Lentils with Yogurt 94
533. Tasty Mac & Cheese......................... 94
534. Tomato & Broccoli Casserole 94
535. Cannellini Beans Ragout..................... 94
536. Oregano & Parmesan Zucchini Noodles 94
537. Apples in Cranberry Sauce................... 94
538. Morning Blueberry Oatmeal with Peaches 95
539. Brussel Sprouts & Apple Lunch 95
540. Vegetable Medley with Brazil Nuts............ 95
541. Bolognese Sauce Vegan-Style 95
542. Spicy Eggplants 95
543. Carrot & Zucchini Spirals with Avocado 95
544. Mint & Parmesan Zucchini 95
545. Easy Vegetable Roast 96
546. Yellow Split Peas with Cilantro & Spinach...... 96
547. Lime & Ginger Eggplants 96
548. Paleo Crusted Veggie Quiche................. 96
549. Balls of Zucchini in Ginger Sauce 96
550. Mango Okra Gumbo.......................... 96
551. Garlic Mushrooms with Wine & Parsley 96
552. Cilantro Cauli Rice with Carrots & Kale 97
553. Mozzarella Broccoli with Hazelnuts 97
554. Spaghetti Squash with Kale & Broccoli.......... 97
555. Palak Paneer 97
556. Green Chili & Cheese Frittata 97
557. Fennel & Zucchini with Mushrooms............ 97
558. Curry Spaghetti Squash...................... 98
559. Green Beans with Fresh Garlic 98
560. Cauliflower Mac & Cheese 98
561. Vegan Broccoli with Tahini Sauce 98
562. Poblano Pepper & Sweet Corn Side Dish 98
563. Mushroom & Eggplant Mix 98
564. Stewed Vegetables.......................... 98
565. Mirin Tofu Bowl............................ 99
566. Quick Indian Creamy Eggplants 99
567. Lemon Artichokes 99
568. Heavenly Black Bean & Bell Pepper Chili 99
569. Power Green Minestrone Stew with Lemon 99
570. Vegetable One-Pot.......................... 99
571. Garlic Green Peas with Zucchini............... 99
572. Jalapeño Tofu Stew with Vegetables 100
573. Braised Red Cabbage & Cherry Stew 100
574. Pinto Bean & Sweet Potato Chili.............. 100
575. Brown Rice and Kidney Beans Casserole....... 100
576. Raclette Soup with Tortillas 100
577. Ricotta Stuffed Potatoes 100

SOUPS, STEWS & CHILIS...101

578. Basil Cherry Tomato Soup 101
579. Tuscan Vegetable Tortellini Soup.................. 101
580. Mom's Vegetable Soup................................... 101
581. Moroccan Chicken Soup 101
582. White Bean & Pancetta Soup 101
583. Winter Squash & Chickpea Soup 101
584. Sage Zucchini & Navy Bean Soup 102
585. Chicken Enchilada Soup 102
586. "Eat-me" Ham & Pea Soup 102
587. Apple-Butternut Squash Soup 102
588. Japanese-Style Tofu Soup.............................. 102
589. Cheddar Cheese & Broccoli Soup 102
590. Curry Zucchini Soup 102
591. Lentil & Bacon Soup 103
592. Oregano Pearl Barley & Chorizo Soup 103
593. Thyme Potato & Pumpkin Cream Soup 103
594. Spiced Sweet Potato Soup 103
595. Greek Chicken Soup with Olive Tapenade 103
596. Pumpkin & Pearl Barley Soup 103
597. Udon Noodle Chicken Soup........................... 104
598. Beer Cheese Potato Soup 104
599. Beef, Potato & Carrot Soup 104
600. Coconut Pumpkin Soup 104
601. Cabbage & Carrot Soup with Bacon 104
602. Smoked Turkey & Bean Soup 104
603. Mexican Chicken & Corn Chowder................ 105
604. Cheesy Tomato Soup 105
605. Nutmeg Chicken Gnocchi Soup 105
606. South American Chicken & Lentil Soup.......... 105
607. Lentil Soup with Persillade Topping 105
608. Turmeric Chicken & Broccoli Soup................ 105

609. Vegetable Soup with Parsley Croutons 106
610. Hearty Sausage Soup..................................... 106
611. Spicy Haricot Vert & Potato Curry................. 106
612. Cheeseburger Soup.. 106
613. Tradicional Indian Chicken Curry.................. 106
614. Pork & Canadian Bacon Soup........................ 106
615. Simple Pumpkin Soup 107
616. Red Lentil Soup.. 107
617. Red Cabbage & Beet Borscht......................... 107
618. Chorizo & Black Bean Stew with Potatoes...... 107
619. Spanish Pisto Manchego 107
620. Basil Lentil & Barley with Mushrooms 107
621. Beef & Portobello Stew 108
622. Harissa Potato & Spinach Stew...................... 108
623. Yummy Lamb Stew 108
624. Chicken & Mushroom Stew with Spinach 108
625. Rosemary Beef Stew 108
626. Mushroom Lentil Stew 108
627. Rosemary Butternut Squash Stew 108
628. Leftover Turkey Stew 109
629. North African Chicken Stew 109
630. Spicy Chicken & Mixed Vegetable Stew 109
631. Turnip & Chickpea Stew 109
632. Fall Bean Chili... 109
633. Chickpea & Spinach Chili.............................. 109
634. Beef Stew with Carrots & Parsnips................. 110
635. Lamb Shanks & Root Vegetable Stew............. 110
636. Beef Stew with Bacon & Avocado.................. 110
637. Mediterranean Vegetable Stew 110
638. Caribbean Black-Eyed Pea Stew 110
639. Ground Beef & Tomato Chili......................... 110

SNACKS & APPETIZERS 111

640. Jamón Serrano & Parmesan Egg Muffins 111
641. Bacon & Cheese Eggs with Chives................111
642. Duck Legs with Serrano Pepper Sauce 111
643. Italian-Style Mushrooms with Sausage...........111
644. Mayonnaise & Bacon Stuffed Eggs................111
645. Mushroom & Sesame Pâté...............................111
646. Lemony Carrot Sticks with Nuts.................... 112
647. Hot Buffalo Chicken Balls 112
648. Herby Cipollini Onions................................. 112
649. Pumpkin Hummus... 112
650. Party Egg Custard... 112
651. Smoked Paprika Potato Chips 112
652. Cheese Fondue 112
653. Best Bacon Wrapped Mini Smokies............... 113
654. Bacon Asparagus Wraps................................ 113
655. Hot Chicken Dip... 113
656. Cauliflower Popcorn 113
657. Party Mix 113
658. Hard-Boiled Eggs... 113
659. Cheesy Potato Hash Brown 113
660. Jalapeño Chicken Dip.................................... 113
661. Spinach Dip.. 114
662. Crispy Sweet Potato Sticks 114
663. Reuben Dip.. 114
664. Cannellini Bean & Chili Salad 114
665. Buffalo Chicken Wings with Cheese Dip........ 114
666. Eggplant Caviar.. 114
667. Celery & Chicken Casserole 114

668. Cheesy Hamburger Tortillas 115
669. Garlic Buttered Almonds 115
670. Sausage & Cream Cheese Dip 115
671. Rolled Chicken with Asparagus & Prosciutto.. 115
672. Sticky Sweet Chicken Wings 115
673. Spicy-Sweet Meatballs.................................. 115
674. Beef Ribs Texas BBQ Style 115
675. Sticky BBQ Chicken Drumsticks................... 116
676. Teriyaki Chicken in Lettuce Wrap.................. 116
677. Pizza Marguerite with Cauliflower Crust 116
678. Orange Tofu & Broccoli Cups........................ 116
679. Cheesy Sausage with Potatoes 116
680. Dijon Deviled Eggs 116
681. Colby Asparagus with Anchovy Dressing....... 117
682. Yummy Smoked Sausage Bites...................... 117
683. Thyme Tomato Dip Sauce 117
684. Potato Balls with Walnut-Yogurt Sauce 117
685. Camembert Root Vegetable Mix 117
686. Potato & Parsnip Mix.................................... 117
687. Mashed Garlic Cauliflower Dish.................... 118
688. Pineapple & Soda-Glazed Ham...................... 118
689. Cheese Sweet Corn 118
690. Garlicky Potato & Rutabaga Mash.................. 118
691. Zesty Carrots with Pistachios........................ 118
692. Zucchini & Potato Patties.............................. 118
693. Swiss Chard Crisps with Orange Juice............ 118
694. Basil Infused Avocado Dip............................ 118

DESSERTS 119

695. Chocolate-Strawberry Bars 119
696. Delightful Tiramisu Cake 119
697. Homemade Raspberry Compote 119
698. Silky Lemon Cheesecake with Blueberries..... 119
699. Holiday Almond Cake 119
700. Lemony Berry Cream 119
701. Pineapple Chocolate Pudding................... 120
702. Poppy Seed & Lemon Bars 120
703. Savory Blueberry Curd............................. 120
704. Tasty Honey Pumpkin Pie 120
705. Authentic Spanish Crema Catalana........... 120
706. Pumpkin Custard 120
707. Sweet Milk Balls 121
708. Ice Cream Topped Brownie Cake.............. 121
709. Butter-Lemon Pears 121
710. Christmas Banana Bread 121
711. Lemon & Cinnamon Poached Pears........... 121
712. Party Cinnamon & Yogurt Cheesecake 121
713. Simple Poached Apricots.......................... 121
714. Almond Butter Bars................................. 122
715. Party Cherry Pie 122
716. Raisin Chocolate Cookies 122
717. Apple Coconut Dessert............................ 122
718. Speedy Nectarines with Blueberry Sauce 122
719. Awesome Chocolate Lava Cake................. 122
720. Orange Crème Caramel 122
721. Scrumptious Stuffed Pears 123
722. Easy Peach Cobbler 123

723. Hazelnut & Apple Delight........................ 123
724. Simple Cranberry Peach Biscuits............... 123
725. Pineapple Upside Down Cake 123
726. Apple Cacao Dessert 123
727. Summer Berry Cobbler 124
728. Pumpkin Cake 124
729. Apricots & Pecans with Mascarpone 124
730. Quinoa Energy Bars 124
731. Chocolate Pudding Cake 124
732. Walnut Fudge.. 124
733. Mom's Banana Cake 125
734. Vanilla & Fruit Compote 125
735. Coconut Stuffed Apples........................... 125
736. Grandma's Pear & Peach Compote 125
737. Blueberry Clafoutis 125
738. Classic Vanilla Cheesecake 125
739. Orange Cheesecake 126
740. Fruit Mix with Almonds 126
741. Cinnamon-Flavored Apple Sauce.............. 126
742. Apple & Cinnamon Cake 126
743. Tasty Apple Risotto 126
744. Mango Tarts.. 126
745. White Chocolate Cake in a Cup 127
746. Quick Rum Egg Custard........................... 127
747. Coconut White Chocolate Fondue............. 127
748. Beery Chocolate Cups 127
749. Peanut Pear Wedges................................ 127
750. Cinnamon & Raisin Muffins 127

MY 50 FAVORITE RECIPES 128

751. Cheesy Mushroom Cakes 128
752. Creamy Pumpkin & Ginger Soup 128
753. Colorful Pasta with Pine Nuts 128
754. Cheesy Mushroom Risotto 128
755. Jalapeño Haddock with Samfaina 128
756. Broccoli & Potatoes with Gruyere 129
757. Minestrone al Pesto with Cheese Bread 129
758. Crunchy Cod with Quinoa........................ 129
759. Habanero Beef Tortilla Tart 129
760. Saucy Seafood Penne with Chorizo 129
761. Herby Cavatappi Pasta Siciliana 130
762. Garlic Tilapia in Tomato-Olives Sauce 130
763. Easy Mac´n´Cheese with Sriracha Sauce...... 130
764. Canadian-Style Succotash with Fish 130
765. Chili Chicken Carnitas 130
766. Mashed Potatoes & Celeriac with Chives 130
767. Shrimp Paella with Andouille Sausage 131
768. Italian-Style Chicken............................... 131
769. Carrot & Potato Crispy Chicken 131
770. Salmon with Hot-Garlic Sauce.................. 131
771. Chicken Wings in Hot Sauce 131
772. Chicken Meatballs in Tomato Sauce 132
773. Green Onion & Walnut Salmon Pilaf........... 132
774. Egg Noodles with Sausage & Pancetta 132
775. Paprika & Leek Chicken Pilaf.................... 132

776. Mexican-Style Green Chili Chicken 132
777. Spicy Baby Back Ribs 132
778. Saucy Turkey with Green Peas.................. 133
779. Mushroom & Potato Beef Stew................. 133
780. Jalapeño Chicken Quesadillas with Kale 133
781. Pork with Mushrooms & Tomato Sauce 133
782. Easy Mango-Teriyaki Chicken................... 134
783. Beef Sloppy Joes with BBQ Sauce 134
784. Pearl Onion & Squash Beef Stew.............. 134
785. Hispanic Chicken & Rice 134
786. Beef Stew with Fennel & Red Wine 134
787. French Cheesy Beef Baguettes.................. 135
788. Empanadas Filled with Beef & Olives 135
789. Bacon & Mozzarella Egg Bites 135
790. Pork Ragu with Rigatoni 135
791. Spaghetti Carbonara with Broccoli 135
792. Guajillo Chili Beans with Bacon................ 136
793. Serrano Ham & Cheese Cups 136
794. Lemon Apple Pies 136
795. Grandma's Vanilla Cheesecake 136
796. Cinnamon Plum Clafoutis 136
797. Cinnamon Berry Cobbler 137
798. Banana Bread with Frangelico Liqueur........ 137
799. Berry Mascarpone Cake 137
800. Classic Caramel-Walnut Brownies............. 137

RECIPE INDEX 138

Introduction

This book is the only guide you'll ever need to start your adventure with the Instant Pot, and 800 recipes included in this book will keep you entertained for a long time if you want to try them all.

For those who are new to this marvel of cooking technology, the Instant Pot is a multi-functional electric pot, which you can use as a slow cooker, pressure cooker, rice or yogurt maker, steamer, or sauté pan. No wonder it's been taking the world by the storm in the recent decade.

As our lives get busier and busier, we take on more and more responsibilities. There are never-ending distractions and buzzing entertainment all around us. We've become desperate for anything that would let us cut out a slice of time from a hectic daily schedule and use it in some better way. That's why the Instant Pot's multifunctionality is not the only advantage it has to offer.

It's a great cooking device that saves you hours every week. Imagine someone gives you an extra three hours in the sauna at the end of every week. Who wouldn't want that? Instant Pot also gives you the freedom to cook your meals and do whatever you need or want to do in the meantime. Don't fancy using multiple pots and risking a house burn down? No problem! Thanks to this smart kitchen robot, you can go clean your home, go to the gym or even go to work for an entire day while your food (and your house!) remain in one piece. All of that without compromising on taste and quality.

One of many other benefits Instant Pot offers is that it keeps your meals warm for up to ten hours. So that's another few minutes saved right there if reheating meals is not what particularly enjoy doing. Plus if you cook for the whole family, the cooking pot (the inner pot) is big enough to fit in multiple portions easily. The best thing about it? You can fill up the pot to the brim, and it will still take the same amount of time to cook it all up.

I wrote this book to help you enjoy your daily meals while remaining active in our fast-paced world. No matter if you're a solo-eater, or if you cook for your family or friends — you'll always find dozens of recipes to satisfy everyone. With every recipe comes the cooking time and you can rest assured it will probably less than a drive to the local fast-food. Cooking with an Instant Pot is not a sacrifice, and you won't be left with a pile of dirty dishes in your sink. After you finish eating, all you need to do is to clean up the inside of the cooking chamber.

So embark on this journey with excitement! Don't be afraid of experimenting, and forget being a perfect cook. It's all about fun at the end of the day, isn't it? Save your precious time and spend it creating lots of beautiful moments with the closest ones. Or alone - it's up to you. All the best!

Note! The cooking times in the recipes do not include the time for the Instant Pot to come to pressure! In the recipes, you will be asked to press the button Manual. On some Instant Pot models, this button is labelled as Pressure Cook. Please note that they are interchangeable with one another.

Brunch & Side Dishes

Mango & Walnut French-Style Toast

INGREDIENTS for 6 servings

1 ½ tsp cinnamon
¼ tsp vanilla extract
6 bread slices, cubed
4 mangos, sliced
2 tbsp brown sugar
1 tbsp white sugar
½ cup milk
¼ cup walnuts, chopped
3 eggs
¼ cup cream cheese, softened
2 tbsp cold and sliced butter

DIRECTIONS and total time: approx. 40 minutes

Grease a baking dish and arrange half of the bread cubes. Top with half of the mango slices. Sprinkle with half of the brown sugar. Spread cream cheese over the mangos. Arrange the rest of the bread cubes and mango slices on top. Sprinkle with brown sugar and top with walnuts. Cover with butter slices.

In a bowl, whisk together eggs, white sugar, milk, cinnamon, and vanilla. Pour the mixture into the baking dish. Place a trivet inside the pot and pour 1 cup water. Lower the dish onto the trivet. Cook on Manual for 30 minutes at High. Do a quick pressure release.

Cheesy Grits with Crispy Pancetta

INGREDIENTS for 4 servings

3 slices pancetta, diced
1 ½ cups grated Emmental
1 cup ground grits
2 tsp butter
Salt and black pepper to taste
½ cup milk

DIRECTIONS and total time: approx. 25 minutes

Select Sauté and fry the pancetta until crispy, about 5 minutes. Set aside. Add grits, butter, milk, ½ cup water, salt, and pepper to the pot and stir. Seal the lid and select Manual at High for 10 minutes. Once the timer has ended, do a quick pressure release. Open the lid and add Emmental cheese and give the pudding a good stir. Serve the cheesy grits into serving bowls topped with the crisped pancetta.

Carrot & Nut Cakes

INGREDIENTS for 8 servings

¼ cup olive oil
½ cup milk
½ cup walnuts, chopped
1 tsp apple pie spice
1 cup carrots, shredded
3 eggs
½ cup apple sauce
1 cup ground hazelnuts

DIRECTIONS and total time: approx. 30 minutes

Pour 1 cup water into your Instant Pot and fit in a trivet. Place olive oil, milk, eggs, apple sauce, hazelnuts, and apple pie spice in a large bowl. Beat the mixture well with an electric mixer until it becomes fluffy.

Fold in the carrots and walnuts. Pour the batter into silicone muffin cups and arrange them on the trivet. Seal the lid, and cook on Manual at High for 15 minutes. When ready, do a quick pressure release. Remove the muffins, and let cool for a few minutes before serving.

Summer Garden Quiche

INGREDIENTS for 4 servings

1 carrot, shredded
1 tomato, chopped
½ cup collard greens
¼ cup milk
¼ onion, diced
½ bell pepper, diced
1 tsp basil
Salt and black pepper to taste
¼ tsp paprika
8 eggs

DIRECTIONS and total time: approx. 40 minutes

Pour 1 cup water into the Instant Pot and lower a trivet. Place eggs, milk, salt, pepper, basil, and paprika in a large bowl. Whisk until well combined and smooth. Add veggies to the mixture and stir well to combine.

Grease a baking dish with some cooking spray and pour in the egg mixture inside. Place the baking dish on top of the trivet. Seal the lid and cook on Manual at High for 20 minutes. Do a natural pressure release for about 10 minutes. Remove quiche, slice and serve!

Lazy-Morning Eggs in Hollandaise Sauce

INGREDIENTS for 4 servings

4 bread slices, chopped
4 eggs
½ cup arugula, chopped
Salt and black pepper to taste
4 slices cheddar cheese
1 ½ oz Hollandaise sauce

DIRECTIONS and total time: approx. 30 minutes

Place a trivet in your Instant Pot and pour 1 cup water. Divide the bread pieces between 4 ramekins. In a bowl, whisk the eggs and mix with arugula. Season with salt and pepper. Divide this mixture among the ramekins. Cover them with aluminum foil and place on the trivet. Select Manual and set the time to 8 minutes. Lock the lid and turn the valve to close. When cooking is over, do a quick pressure release. Remove the ramekins and discard the foil. Top with a slice of cheddar cheese and a bit of hollandaise sauce to serve.

Simple Softboiled Eggs

INGREDIENTS for 4 servings

4 eggs
2 cups water

DIRECTIONS and total time: approx. 15 minutes

Pour the water into your Instant Pot and insert a trivet. Place the eggs on the trivet. Seal the lid and cook on Manual for 4 minutes at Low. When ready, do a quick pressure release. Prepare an ice bath and drop the eggs in until they cool off a bit. Peel the eggs and enjoy!

Nut & Apple Breakfast

INGREDIENTS for 1 serving

½ cup milk
3 tbsp ground almonds
3 tbsp ground Brazil nuts
1 apple, grated

1 tbsp butter
2 tbsp flaxseed
A pinch of cinnamon
¼ tsp vanilla extract

DIRECTIONS and total time: 15 minutes

Place all ingredients in your Instant Pot, and give the mixture a good stir to combine. Seal the lid, and cook on Manual at High for 5 minutes. When ready, release the pressure quickly. Serve in bowls.

Shiitake Mushroom Oats with Garlic

INGREDIENTS for 4 servings

8 oz Shiitake mushrooms
2 cups chicken broth
½ onion, diced
2 tbsp butter

1 cup steel-cut oats
½ cup Monterey Jack, grated
2 sprigs thyme
1 garlic clove, minced

DIRECTIONS and total time: 30 minutes

Slice the mushrooms. On Sauté, melt butter and stir-fry onion, garlic, and mushrooms for 5 minutes until soft. Stir in oats and cook for another minute. Pour in ½ cup water and broth and mix in thyme sprigs. Seal the lid and cook on Manual for 20 minutes. Quick-release the pressure. Ladle into serving bowls and sprinkle with grated Monterey Jack cheese.

Ground Beef & Egg Casserole

INGREDIENTS for 4 servings

1 lb ground beef
6 eggs, beaten
¾ cup leeks, sliced
¾ cup kale, chopped

1 winter squash, shredded
1 garlic clove, minced
2 tbsp olive oil
Salt and black pepper to taste

DIRECTIONS and total time: 30 minutes

Warm olive oil on Sauté. Add leeks and garlic and cook for 2 minutes. Add in beef and cook for 8 more minutes until browned; transfer to a bowl. Add the remaining ingredients and stir well to combine. Pour 1 cup of water in the pot and lower a trivet. Put the egg and beef mixture into a greased baking dish and place on top of the trivet. Seal the lid, select Manual for 10 minutes at High. When ready, release the pressure quickly. Serve hot with roasted garlic bread.

Sweet Corn & Onion Eggs

INGREDIENTS for 2 servings

4 eggs
1 tomato, chopped
1 onion, diced
½ cup sweet corn

¼ tsp garlic powder
A pinch of cayenne pepper
Salt and black pepper to taste
1 cup water

DIRECTIONS and total time: 15 minutes

Pour water in your Instant Pot and lower a trivet. Beat the eggs along with garlic powder, cayenne, salt and pepper. Add tomatoes, corn, and onion; stir to combine. Pour the mixture into a greased baking dish. Place the baking dish on top of the trivet and seal the lid. Cook on Manual at High for 8 minutes. After the beep, do a quick pressure release. Remove to a plate and serve.

Butternut Squash & Carrot Egg Casserole

INGREDIENTS for 4 servings

2 cups butternut squash, shredded
8 eggs
½ cup milk
1 cup carrots, shredded

½ tbsp olive oil
½ tsp dried parsley
Salt and black pepper to taste
¼ tsp paprika
¼ tsp garlic powder

DIRECTIONS and total time: 20 minutes

Heat olive oil on Sauté. Add in carrots, butternut squash, herbs, and spices, stir well to combine, and cook the veggies for about 2-3 minutes. Beat together the eggs and milk in a bowl. Pour the mixture over the carrots and stir to incorporate well. Seal the lid, press Manual for 7 minutes at High. When ready, do a quick pressure release and open the lid. Serve warm.

Three-Meat Mozzarella Quiche

INGREDIENTS for 4 servings

6 eggs, beaten
1 cup sausages, cooked
4 pancetta slices, crumbled
2 green onions, chopped

½ cup milk
4 ham slices, diced
1 cup mozzarella, shredded
Salt and black pepper to taste

DIRECTIONS and total time: 25 minutes

Lower a trivet in your Instant Pot and pour in 1 cup water. In a bowl, combine eggs, milk, salt, and pepper. Mix the sausages, cheese, pancetta, ham, and onions in a greased baking dish and pour the egg mixture over. Place the baking dish on the trivet. Seal the lid and cook on Manual for 15 minutes at High. When done, do a quick pressure release. Let cool before serving.

One-Pot Colby Cheese, Ham & Eggs

INGREDIENTS for 4 servings

6 small potatoes, shredded
6 large eggs, beaten
1 cup Colby cheese, shredded

Salt and black pepper to taste
1 cup ham, diced
2 tbsp olive oil

DIRECTIONS and total time: 20 minutes

Heat olive oil on Sauté and cook potatoes for 6 minutes. Pour in 1 cup water. In a bowl, mix ham, cheese, and eggs and add to the pot. Seal the lid and cook on Manual for 10 minutes. Do a quick pressure release.

Crunchy Pancetta & Egg Burgers

INGREDIENTS for 4 servings

4 buns	Salt and black pepper to taste
4 eggs	1 tsp olive oil
8 pancetta slices	4 tbsp Muenster cheese, grated

DIRECTIONS and total time: 30 minutes

Heat oil on Sauté and cook pancetta until crispy, about 2-3 minutes per side. Remove to a paper towel to drain the excess grease. Put a trivet and 1 cup water in the pot. Crumble the pancetta in ramekins and crack the eggs on top. Season with salt and pepper.

Sprinkle with Muenster cheese, cover with foil and place the ramekins on the trivet. Seal the lid and cook for 15 minutes at High on Manual. When ready, do a quick pressure release. Assemble the burgers by cutting the buns in half and placing the mixture in the middle.

Sausage & Cheese Frittata

INGREDIENTS for 4 servings

6 eggs, beaten	1 tbsp olive oil
1 cup Monterey Jack, shredded	½ cup milk
2 sausages, sliced	2 green onions, chopped
1 cup water	Salt and black pepper to taste

DIRECTIONS and total time: 30 minutes

Warm olive oil in your Instant Pot on Sauté and cook sausages for 4 minutes. Whisk the remaining ingredients together in a bowl, except for the green onions, and mix in the sausages. Transfer to a greased baking dish. Pour in the water and lower a trivet. Place the dish on top of the trivet. Seal the lid and cook for 10 minutes on Manual at High. When done, do a quick release. Serve sprinkled with green onions.

Parsley Pork Breakfast Biscuits

INGREDIENTS for 4 servings

1 lb ground pork	1 shallot, chopped
4 biscuits	1 garlic, minced
2 tbsp apple cider	½ tsp sage
1 cup milk	½ tsp rosemary
½ cup flour	1 tbsp fresh parsley, chopped
2 tsp butter	Salt and black pepper to taste

DIRECTIONS and total time: 30 minutes

Melt butter on Sauté, add pork, and cook until browned. Add shallot and garlic and cook for another 2 minutes until soft. Stir in cider, sage, and rosemary. Seal the lid and cook for 20 minutes on Manual at High. Release the pressure quickly. Whisk together the flour and milk, and pour over the pork. Seal the lid again. Cook on Manual at High for 5 minutes. Release the pressure quickly. Serve over biscuits, sprinkled with parsley.

Sausage and Kale Casserole with Eggs

INGREDIENTS for 4 servings

8 oz pork sausages, cooked	1 cup kale, chopped
1 tbsp olive oil	1 red potato, shredded
6 eggs	1 tsp garlic, minced
¾ cup leeks, sliced	1 tbsp chopped parsley
Salt and black pepper to taste	1 cup water

DIRECTIONS and total time: 30 minutes

Place veggies in a greased baking dish and set aside. Set to Sauté your Instant Pot and warm oil. Sauté garlic, kale, and leeks for 2 minutes. Beat eggs in a bowl and pour them over the veggies. Stir in pork sausages and potato. Pour water in the pot and insert a trivet. Lower the baking dish on the trivet. Cook on Manual for 15 minutes at High. Do a quick pressure release. Sprinkle with chopped parsley and serve sliced.

Fennel & Potato Salad

INGREDIENTS for 6 servings

½ cup chopped scallions	1 ½ lb potatoes
1 fennel bulb, chopped	½ cup mayonnaise
1 carrot, chopped	½ tbsp vinegar
½ yellow onion, diced	Salt and black pepper to taste
4 hard-boiled eggs, sliced	½ tsp paprika

DIRECTIONS and total time: approx. 20 minutes

Wash the potatoes thoroughly, scrub them, and place inside your Instant Pot. Pour in 2 cups water and seal the lid. Select Manual and set the timer to 10 minutes at High. When ready, do a quick pressure release. Transfer the potatoes to a bowl and let cool slightly.

When safe to handle, peel the potatoes and chop them. Season with salt, paprika, and black pepper. Place potatoes in a bowl along with carrots, fennel, onion, and scallions. In a bowl, whisk together mayo and vinegar, and sprinkle over salad. Arrange eggs on top.

Tasty Onion Frittata with Bell Peppers

INGREDIENTS for 2 servings

4 eggs	¼ tsp garlic powder
¼ cup bell peppers, diced	Salt and black pepper to taste
¼ cup onions, diced	A pinch of ginger powder
2 tbsp milk	1 cup water

DIRECTIONS and total time: 20 minutes

Pour water in your Instant Pot and insert a trivet. In a bowl, beat eggs along with milk, ginger, salt, pepper, and garlic powder. Add in onions and bell peppers and stir well to combine. Pour the mixture into a greased baking dish and place on the trivet. Seal the lid, select Manual, and cook for 10 minutes at High. When the timer is off, release the pressure quickly. Serve sliced.

Savory Lemon Zesty Toast

INGREDIENTS for 4 servings

Zest of 1 lemon	1 ¼ cups milk
¼ cup sugar	½ tsp vanilla extract
2 large eggs	½ loaf Challah bread, cubed
3 tbsp butter, melted	A pinch of sea salt

DIRECTIONS and total time: approx. 35 minutes

Whisk together all ingredients, except for the bread, in a large bowl. Dip bread in the bowl and coat with the mixture. Arrange coated bread pieces in a baking pan. Add a trivet and pour in 1 cup water. Lower the pan onto the trivet. Seal the lid and set the time to 25 minutes on Manual at High. When ready, do a quick pressure release. Remove and serve.

Onion & Potato Frittata

INGREDIENTS for 4 servings

6 large eggs, beaten	Salt and black pepper to taste
1 tomato, chopped	2 tbsp flour
¼ cup milk	1 onion, chopped
1 tbsp tomato paste	1 garlic clove, minced
1 tbsp olive oil	4 oz potatoes, shredded

DIRECTIONS and total time: approx. 30 minutes

Mix eggs, milk, and oil in a bowl. Add in flour, onion, garlic, and potatoes and stir. Pour the egg mixture into a greased baking dish. Fit a trivet in your IP and pour in 1 cup water. Put the baking dish onto the trivet and select Manual. Set timer to 18 minutes at High. When ready, do a quick pressure release. Serve sliced.

Heavenly Coconut Pancakes

INGREDIENTS for 4 servings

1 cup flour	1 ½ cups milk
1 tsp coconut extract	1 cup ground cashews
2 tbsp honey	½ tsp baking soda
4 eggs	2 tbsp castor sugar

DIRECTIONS and total time: approx. 25 minutes

Whisk together eggs and milk in a bowl. Except for castor sugar, gradually stir in the remaining ingredients. Preheat your Instant Pot by pressing Sauté and spray the inner pot with cooking spray. Spread in a ladle of batter and cook for 5 minutes, turning once halfway through cooking. Repeat until the batter is exhausted. Serve sprinkled with castor sugar.

Quick Cilantro Salmon

INGREDIENTS for 2 servings

2 slices smoked salmon	Salt and black pepper to taste
2 eggs	1 tbsp paprika
1 tsp cilantro, chopped	1 cup water

DIRECTIONS and total time: approx. 10 minutes

Pour water in your Instant Pot and lower a trivet. Grease 4 ramekins with cooking spray. Place a slice of smoked salmon at the bottom of each ramekin. Crack an egg on top of the salmon. Season with salt and pepper, and sprinkle with cilantro and paprika. Arrange the ramekins on top of the trivet and seal the lid. Set on Manual at High for 5 minutes. When the timer goes off, release the pressure quickly. Serve warm.

Party Dark Chocolate Bread Pudding

INGREDIENTS for 4 servings

3 ½ cups bread, cubed	3 oz dark chocolate, chopped
¾ cup half-and-half	½ cup milk
1 tsp butter, melted	¼ cup + 1 tbsp sugar
2 tbsp lemon juice	1 tsp almond extract
Zest of 1 lemon	A pinch of salt
3 eggs	1 cup water

DIRECTIONS and total time: approx. 30 minutes

Beat the eggs along with ¼ cup sugar in a bowl. Stir in half-and-half, lemon juice, zest, almond extract, milk, and salt. Add in bread to soak for 5 minutes. Stir in dark chocolate. Pour water in your IP and fit in a trivet. Grease a baking dish with butter. Pour in the batter. Sprinkle the remaining sugar on top. Lower the baking dish on the trivet. Seal the lid and cook on Manual at High for 18 minutes. Do a quick pressure release.

Pear, Coconut & Pecan Porridge

INGREDIENTS for 2 servings

1 cup ground pecans	2 pears, diced
2 oz coconut flakes	1 cup milk

DIRECTIONS and total time: 10 minutes

Place all ingredients in your IP and stir well to combine. Seal the lid, and cook on Manual for 3 minutes at High. Do a quick pressure release. Pour into bowls and serve.

Sunday Paprika Potatoes with Herbs

INGREDIENTS for 2 servings

1 lb potatoes, quartered	1 garlic clove, minced
1 tbsp paprika	3 tbsp butter, melted
1 tbsp parsley, chopped	Salt and black pepper to taste
1 tbsp basil, chopped	1 cup water

DIRECTIONS and total time: approx. 15 minutes

Pour water in your IP and lower a trivet. Place potatoes in a baking dish that fits into the pot. Sprinkle with herbs and garlic, and drizzle with butter. Place the baking dish on top of the trivet and seal the lid. Select Manual and set time to 6 minutes on High. When done, do a quick release. Sprinkle with paprika to serve.

Nutmeg Cauliflower Potato Mash

INGREDIENTS for 4 servings

1 cauliflower head, cut into florets	1 tbsp rosemary
4 medium potatoes, peeled	¼ cup milk
2 tbsp butter	A pinch of nutmeg
	Salt and black pepper to taste

DIRECTIONS and total time: approx. 20 minutes

Place potatoes and cauliflower in your Instant Pot. Add water just enough to cover. Seal the lid, press Manual, and set the timer to 8 minutes on High. Once it goes off, release the pressure quickly. Drain potatoes and cauliflower and transfer to a bowl. Grab a potato masher and mash them well until there are no more lumps. Stir in the remaining ingredients until the mixture is thoroughly combined. Serve warm or chilled.

Red Cabbage with Coconut

INGREDIENTS for 4 servings

2 tbsp olive oil	1 carrot, sliced
½ cup desiccated coconut	1 tsp garlic, minced
3 tbsp apple cider vinegar	Salt and black pepper to taste
1 red cabbage, shredded	1 tsp ground cumin
1 onion, sliced	¼ tsp turmeric powder

DIRECTIONS and total time: approx. 30 minutes

Warm olive oil on Sauté, add onion, carrot, and garlic, and cook for 5 minutes. Stir in cabbage, cumin, turmeric, salt, and pepper for 5 minutes until tender. Pour in ½ cup water and seal the lid. Press Manual and set the timer to 5 minutes at High. Do a quick pressure release. Stir in vinegar and coconut, and serve.

Black-Eyed Pea & Sweet Potato Bowl

INGREDIENTS for 6 servings

1 lb sweet potatoes, cubed	¼ tsp dried sage
¾ lb fresh black-eyed peas	¼ tsp dried basil
1 tsp turmeric, minced	1 ½ cups chicken stock
1 tsp garlic, minced	1 tbsp olive oil

DIRECTIONS and total time: approx. 25 minutes

Heat oil on Sauté and add garlic and turmeric; cook for a minute. Add potatoes and pour in the stock. Seal the lid, select Manual, and set time to 10 minutes at High. Do a quick pressure release. Stir in the peas and seal the lid again. Cook on Manual for 4 minutes at High. Do a quick pressure release. Drain potatoes and peas and transfer to a bowl. Stir in basil and sage to serve.

Quick Ginger-Carrot Puree

INGREDIENTS for 4 servings

1 tsp ginger powder	1 ½ lb carrots, chopped
Salt and black pepper to taste	¼ cup whipping cream

DIRECTIONS and total time: approx. 15 minutes

Pour 1 cup water in your IP, place carrots in a steamer basket, and lower the basket inside the pot. Seal the lid, cook on Manual for 4 minutes at High. Do a quick release. Transfer the carrots to a food processor. Add in the rest of the ingredients. Process until smooth.

Strawberry & White Chocolate Porridge

INGREDIENTS for 4 servings

⅛ cup cane sugar	1 cup frozen strawberries
1 cup steel-cut oats	A pinch of sea salt
3 tbsp white chocolate chips	

DIRECTIONS and total time: approx. 20 minutes

Put all ingredients, except for chocolate, in your IP. Pour in 3 ½ cups water and stir well to combine. Seal the lid and cook on Manual for 12 minutes at High. Do a quick pressure release, stir in the chocolate to serve.

Inviting Potatoes & Snow Beans

INGREDIENTS for 6 servings

½ lb snow beans, chopped	½ tsp ginger powder
1 ½ lb potatoes, chopped	¼ tsp hot paprika
1 tsp garlic, minced	2 tbsp olive oil
1 onion, diced	Salt and black pepper to taste

DIRECTIONS and total time: approx. 25 minutes

Heat olive oil on Sauté. Add onion and garlic and cook for 3 minutes until softened. Add potatoes and cover them with water. Seal the lid, select Manual for 5 minutes at High. Do a quick pressure release. Stir in the snow beans, and seal the lid again. Cook for 3 more minutes on Manual at High. Do a quick release. Season with ginger, paprika, salt, and pepper. Serve warm.

Spicy Broccoli with Peas & Potatoes

INGREDIENTS for 6 servings

2 tomatoes, diced	Salt and black pepper to taste
2 ¼ cups green peas	½ tsp paprika
2 lb broccoli florets	½ tsp cayenne powder
2 garlic cloves, minced	¼ tsp red pepper flakes
1 lb potatoes, cubed	½ tsp onion powder
2 tbsp butter	½ cup vegetable stock

DIRECTIONS and total time: approx. 30 minutes

Put the potatoes in your Instant Pot and cover with water. Seal the lid, select Manual, and cook for 8 minutes at High. When ready, do a quick pressure release. Drain and set aside. Clean the pot and melt butter on Sauté. Cook garlic and spices for 1 minute. Stir in vegetable stock, broccoli, green peas, and tomatoes and cook for 7-8 minutes until tender. Mix in potatoes and season with salt and black pepper. Serve warm as a side dish.

Winter Squash & Cauliflower Bowl

INGREDIENTS for 6 servings

6 cups cauliflower florets
2 lb winter squash, cubed
2 tomatoes, diced
2 cups peas
1 tsp garlic, minced

1 cup scallions, chopped
3 tbsp olive oil
4 cups vegetable stock
Salt and black pepper to taste
2 tbsp thyme, chopped

DIRECTIONS and total time: approx. 25 minutes

Heat oil on Sauté, add scallions and garlic and cook for about 3-4 minutes. Add in winter squash, cauliflower, tomatoes, and stock. Seal the lid and cook at High for 6 minutes. Do a quick pressure release. Stir in peas and cook for 5 minutes on Sauté. Serve topped with thyme.

Sweet Potatoes with Zucchini

INGREDIENTS for 4 servings

1 lb sweet potatoes, diced
2 zucchinis, chopped
1 tbsp tomato puree
1 garlic clove, minced
1 onion, diced

2 cups chicken stock
¼ tsp cayenne pepper
1 tsp Italian seasoning
Salt and black pepper to taste
2 tbsp olive oil

DIRECTIONS and total time: approx. 20 minutes

Heat oil on Sauté. Add onion and garlic and cook for about 3 minutes. Stir in the remaining ingredients and seal the lid. Select Manual and set timer to 10 minutes at High. When done, do a quick pressure release. Serve.

Steamed Tabasco Potatoes

INGREDIENTS for 4 servings

1 lb potatoes, quartered
1 tbsp tabasco sauce

Salt and black pepper to taste
2 tbsp extra-virgin olive oil

DIRECTIONS and total time: approx. 15 minutes

Pour 1 cup water in your Instant Pot and insert a steamer basket. Place potatoes in the basket, seal the lid, press Steam, and set the cooking time to 8 minutes at High. When the timer goes off, do a quick pressure release. Drain the potatoes and place them on a serving plate. Drizzle with tabasco sauce and olive oil, sprinkle with salt and black pepper, and serve warm.

Minty Barley Bowls

INGREDIENTS for 4 servings

1 cup pearl barley
2 tbsp maple syrup
1 tsp vanilla extract

A pinch of salt
10-12 mint leaves
1 tbsp slivered almonds

DIRECTIONS and total time: approx. 20 minutes

Put 2 cups water, salt, and barley in your Instant Pot. Stir to combine well. Seal the lid and cook on Manual for 12 minutes at High.

When ready, do a quick pressure release. Open the lid and fluff with a fork. Mix in vanilla and maple syrup. Divide between serving bowls and top with mint leaves and almonds to serve.

Brussel Sprouts with Onions & Apples

INGREDIENTS for 4 servings

1 lb Brussel sprouts, shredded
1 cup diced onions
1 cup apples, chopped
1 tbsp cornstarch

1 ½ cups veggie stock
1 tbsp canola oil
Salt and black pepper to taste
¼ tsp cumin

DIRECTIONS and total time: approx. 35 minutes

Heat the oil on Sauté, add onions and apples, and cook for about 6-7 minutes. When softened, add the rest of the ingredients, except for cornstarch. Seal the lid, and select Manual. Set the timer to 15 minutes at High. Do a quick pressure release. Whisk together the cornstarch and 2 tbsp water. Stir in the mixture inside the pot. Cook on Sauté until the sauce thickens, 3 minutes.

Smoked Paprika Spiced Squash Hash

INGREDIENTS for 4 servings

1 lb squash, grated
1 tsp smoked paprika
1 tbsp butter

1 tbsp corn oil
Salt and black pepper to taste
½ small onion, sliced

DIRECTIONS and total time: approx. 35 minutes

Melt butter and oil on Sauté. Cook onion and squash for 3 minutes until soft. Season with salt, pepper, and smoked paprika, and transfer to a baking dish. Press the squash with a spatula. Place a trivet in your Instant Pot and pour in 1 cup water. Lower the dish onto the trivet and seal the lid. Cook at High on Manual for 15 minutes. Release the pressure quickly, and serve warm.

Creamy Blue Cheese Broccoli

INGREDIENTS for 4 servings

1 broccoli head, cut into florets
2 tbsp lemon juice
6 tbsp olive oil
2 tsp red pepper flakes

6 oz blue cheese
1 tsp nutmeg
½ cup whipping cream
Salt and black pepper to taste

DIRECTIONS and total time: approx. 15 minutes

Combine the lemon juice and broccoli in your Instant Pot and cover with water. Seal the lid, and cook for 2 minutes on Manual at High. Release the pressure quickly, and transfer to a plate. Discard the liquid and clean the pot. Heat 2 tbsp of oil on Sauté. Add red pepper flakes and cook for about a minute. Add broccoli and cook for 1 minute uncovered; then remover to a bowl. In a food processor, pulse blue cheese, nutmeg, whipping cream, remaining olive oil, salt, and pepper until smooth. Pour over broccoli and serve.

Steamed Artichokes with Parsley Aioli

INGREDIENTS for 4 servings

4 artichokes, trimmed
1 lemon, juiced
2 cloves garlic, crushed
Sea salt to taste
½ cup mayonnaise
2 tbsp parsley, chopped

DIRECTIONS and total time: approx. 15 minutes

Pour 1 cup of water in your Instant Pot and insert a trivet. Arrange the artichokes on top, and season with sea salt. Seal the lid, select Manual and cook for 8 minutes at High. Once ready, do a quick pressure release. In a bowl, whisk mayonnaise, lemon juice, garlic, parsley, and some salt. Plate the artichokes and serve with garlic-parsley aioli.

Mushroom Pâté

INGREDIENTS for 6 servings

1 cup dry Porcini mushrooms, soaked and liquid reserved
1½ lb Portobello mushrooms, sliced
1 tbsp chopped fresh thyme
2 onions, sliced
Salt and black pepper to taste
3 tbsps butter

DIRECTIONS and total time: approx. 35 minutes

Melt butter on Sauté. Add in onions and cook for 3 minutes until soft. Add Portobello mushrooms to the pot; sauté them until golden brown, for about 4 minutes. Pour in reserved mushroom liquid and soaked mushrooms and adjust the seasoning. Seal the lid, select Manual, and cook for 10 minutes at High. Do a quick release. Blend the ingredients with an immersion blender until smooth. Serve cool, topped with thyme.

Savory Nutmeg Yam Mash

INGREDIENTS for 6 servings

4 garlic cloves, minced
¾ cup milk
2 tbsp butter
2 lb yams, chopped
Salt and black pepper to taste
A pinch of nutmeg
A pinch of dried thyme
2 tbsp chopped chives

DIRECTIONS and total time: approx. 20 minutes

Place yam chunks in your IP and cover with water. Seal the lid, press Manual, and cook for 10 minutes at High. Release the pressure quickly. Drain the yams and place in a bowl. Mash with a masher to your desired consistency. Add in remaining ingredients, except for the chives, and mix well. Serve topped with chives.

Grapefruit Potatoes with Walnuts

INGREDIENTS for 6 servings

12 small potatoes, chopped
¾ cup walnuts, chopped
1 cup mayonnaise
Juice of 1 lemon
2 tbsp olive oil
¼ tsp turmeric powder
Salt and black pepper to taste
1 grapefruit, chopped

DIRECTIONS and total time: approx. 20 minutes

Place potatoes in your IP and cover with water. Seal the lid, select Manual, and cook at High for 10 minutes. Quick-release the pressure and drain the potatoes. Add grapefruit and walnuts. Whisk the remaining ingredients in a bowl and pour over the potatoes. Serve.

Gnocchi with Zucchini & Tomatoes

INGREDIENTS for 4 servings

1 lb potato gnocchi
2 zucchinis, diced
1 cup leeks, white parts only
1 cup bell peppers, chopped
1 sprig dry rosemary, crushed
Salt and black pepper to taste
½ tsp garlic powder
2 tsp olive oil
20 oz canned diced tomatoes
Grated Parmesan for garnish

DIRECTIONS and total time: approx. 20 minutes

Heat oil on Sauté and cook leeks for 3 minutes. Stir in zucchini and bell peppers and cook for 2 minutes. Add in tomatoes, rosemary, 1 cup water, garlic, salt, and pepper. Throw in gnocchi and stir. Seal the lid and cook on Manual for 8 minutes at High. Do a quick pressure release. Serve topped with Parmesan cheese.

Savory Baby Spinach & Carrot Side

INGREDIENTS for 6 servings

10 oz chopped baby spinach
3 carrots, sliced
½ onion, chopped
½ cup broth
1 tbsp olive oil
4 garlic cloves, minced
1 tbsp orange juice
Salt and black pepper to taste

DIRECTIONS and total time: approx. 15 minutes

Heat oil on Sauté, add onion, garlic, and carrots and cook for 5 minutes. Stir in the remaining ingredients. Seal the lid and cook for 10 minutes on Manual at High. Release the pressure quickly, plate, and serve.

Rutabaga Salad with Honey Dressing

INGREDIENTS for 4 servings

2 cups arugula
2 small rutabagas, sliced
4 tbsp olive oil
1 tbsp lemon juice
Salt to taste
1 tsp honey
½ tsp Dijon mustard
¼ cup walnuts, chopped
¼ cup crumbled feta cheese
1 cup water

DIRECTIONS and total time: approx. 15 minutes

Pour 1 cup water in your IP and fit in a trivet. Brush rutabaga with some olive oil and arrange on a baking dish. Place on the trivet. Seal the lid and cook on Manual at High for 5 minutes. When ready, quick release the pressure and let cool. In a bowl, whisk remaining olive oil, lemon juice, honey, and mustard. Place arugula in a salad bowl and top with rutabaga, walnuts, and feta cheese. Drizzle with the dressing and serve.

Perfect Mediterranean Asparagus

INGREDIENTS for 4 servings

1 lb asparagus, trimmed
1 garlic clove, minced
½ shallot, finely chopped
2 tbsp chopped parsley
1 cup water
2 tbsp olive oil
1 tbsp lemon juice
Salt and black pepper to taste

DIRECTIONS and total time: approx. 10 minutes

Pour the water in your Instant Pot and insert a trivet. Arrange the asparagus on the trivet. Seal the lid, and cook for 2 minutes on Manual at High. Once done, release the pressure quickly. In a bowl, whisk olive oil, lemon juice, salt, and pepper. Toss in the asparagus to coat and arrange on a serving platter. Scatter shallots and parsley on top to serve.

Lemony Grana Padano Broccoli

INGREDIENTS for 4 servings

2 cups broccoli florets
¼ cup grated Grana Padano
1 tbsp lemon juice
2 tbsp butter, melted
A pinch of salt
1 cup water

DIRECTIONS and total time: approx. 10 minutes

Pour the water and add broccoli in your IP. Seal the lid and cook at High on Steam for 3 minutes. When ready, release the pressure quickly and transfer to a bowl. Add in butter, lemon juice, and salt and toss to combine. Sprinkle with Grana Padano cheese to serve.

Golden Beets with Green Olives

INGREDIENTS for 4 servings

4 golden beets
2 tbsp olive oil
10 green olives
1 tsp garlic, minced
2 tbsp balsamic vinegar
Salt and black pepper to taste

DIRECTIONS and total time: approx. 30 minutes

Place beets in the pressure cooker and cover with water. Seal the lid and cook on Manual for 15 minutes at High. Release the pressure quickly. Let the beets cool. Whisk together olive oil, garlic, balsamic vinegar, salt, and pepper in a bowl. Peel and slice the beets and combine with the dressing. Top with olives to serve.

Garlic Red Potatoes

INGREDIENTS for 4 servings

2 lb red potatoes
4 tsp butter
1 cup vegetable stock
2 tsp garlic, minced
1 ½ tsp dried rosemary
Salt and black pepper to taste

DIRECTIONS and total time: approx. 35 minutes

Heat butter on Sauté and add potatoes, garlic, and rosemary. Sprinkle with salt and pepper and cook for 7 minutes, stirring occasionally until nice and soft.

Stir in vegetable stock and seal the lid. Cook for 10 minutes on Manual at High. Release pressure quickly.

Cherry Tomato & Summer Squash Delight

INGREDIENTS for 6 servings

16 oz summer squash, chopped
1 lb cherry tomatoes
2 small onions, chopped
2 garlic cloves, minced
2 tbsp olive oil
2 tbsp basil, chopped
Salt and black pepper to taste

DIRECTIONS and total time: approx. 20 minutes

Heat oil on Sauté, add in onions and garlic and cook for 3 minutes until soft and translucent. Stir in tomatoes and summer squash. Cook for 2 minutes until soft, and pour in 1 cup water. Seal the lid and cook for 5 minutes on Manual at High. Do a quick pressure release, and stir in basil. Season with salt and pepper to serve.

Meat-Free Lasagna with Mushrooms

INGREDIENTS for 6 servings

¼ cup chopped basil + some more for garnish
2 cloves garlic, minced
2 lb dry lasagna noodles
2 cups pasta sauce
2 cups cottage cheese
1 tsp red pepper flakes, crushed
Salt and black pepper to taste
1 tbsp cumin
2 cups mushrooms, sliced

DIRECTIONS and total time: approx. 35 minutes

Grease a springform pan with cooking spray. Place lasagna noodles at the bottom and spread the pasta sauce evenly on top. Then place a layer of cottage cheese and sprinkle roughly with mushrooms. Season with garlic, herbs and spices and repeat the process until you run out of products. Cover with aluminum foil. Place a trivet in your Instant Pot and pour in 1 cup water. Place the pan on the trivet and seal the lid. Cook for 25 minutes on Manual at High. Do a quick pressure release. Garnish with basil to serve.

Heavenly Spinach with Ricotta Cheese

INGREDIENTS for 4 servings

18 oz spinach, chopped
1 ricotta cheese, crumbled
1 onion, chopped
2 garlic cloves, minced
2 tbsp butter
2 tbsp cornflour
1 tsp cumin
1 tsp grated ginger
Salt and black pepper to taste
½ cup chicken broth

DIRECTIONS and total time: approx. 20 minutes

Melt butter on Sauté and cook onion, ginger, and garlic for 2 minutes. Stir in spinach, cumin, salt, and pepper and cook for 2 minutes. Pour in chicken broth. Seal the lid and cook for 3 minutes on Manual at High. Do a quick pressure release. In a bowl, whisk cornflour with ½ cup of the cooking liquid and pour in the pot. Stir on Sauté for 2-3 minutes. Top with ricotta cheese to serve.

Prune & Peach Barley

INGREDIENTS for 4 servings

2 prunes, sliced	2 tsp olive oil
1 cup barley	½ tsp cardamom
2 peaches, diced	1 cup water
1 cup milk	2 tbsp honey

DIRECTIONS and total time: approx. 20 minutes

Combine barley, milk, olive oil, cardamon, and water in your IP. Seal the lid and cook on Manual for 13 minutes at High. Quick-release the pressure and stir in prunes and peaches. Drizzle with honey to serve.

Savory Tomato Bell Peppers

INGREDIENTS for 4 servings

1 ½ lb yellow bell peppers	½ tbsp miso paste
½ cup stock	2 tbsp butter
¾ cup tomato sauce	1 garlic clove, minced
½ cup sweet onions	Salt and black pepper to taste

DIRECTIONS and total time: approx. 15 minutes

Melt butter on Sauté and cook onions, bell peppers, and garlic for 3 minutes until soft. Stir in the remaining ingredients. Seal the lid and cook for 3 minutes on Steam at High. When off, release the pressure quickly.

Portobello Mushroom & Leek Delight

INGREDIENTS for 4 servings

2 cups Portobello mushrooms	1 cup leeks, sliced
2 tbsp olive oil	2 tbsp red wine
2 tbsp basil, chopped	Salt and black pepper to taste
1 garlic clove, minced	1 cup vegetable broth

DIRECTIONS and total time: approx. 40 minutes

Chop the mushrooms and sprinkle with salt. Heat oil on Sauté. Cook mushrooms, garlic, and leeks for 5 minutes until soft and lightly browned. Pour in wine and vegetable broth. Seal the lid and cook for 7 minutes on Manual at High. When ready, release the pressure quickly. Serve topped with chopped basil.

Thyme & Frascati Cauliflower

INGREDIENTS for 6 servings

1 ½ lb cauliflower florets	3 tsp olive oil
1 large sweet onion, sliced	1 tsp garlic paste
1 cup Frascati, Italian wine	Salt and black pepper to taste
2 tsp thyme	½ cup vegetable broth

DIRECTIONS and total time: approx. 15 minutes

Heat olive oil on Sauté and cook onion and garlic paste for about 3 minutes. Stir in the remaining ingredients. Seal the lid and cook for 4 minutes on Manual at High. When ready, do a quick release. Serve warm or chilled.

Eggs Florentine Casserole

INGREDIENTS for 4 servings

½ lb ground turkey	6 eggs
½ tsp crushed red pepper flakes	3 oz ricotta cheese, crumbled
½ tsp fresh thyme, chopped	8 oz fresh baby spinach
½ tbsp rosemary, chopped	Salt and black pepper to taste
½ tbsp fresh sage, chopped	2 tbsp olive oil

DIRECTIONS and total time: approx. 35 minutes

Heat olive oil on Sauté in your IP and cook turkey with herbs for 5 minutes. Add in the spinach and cook until it wilts, about 4 minutes. Cover with ricotta cheese, and pour the mixture in a greased baking dish. In a bowl, whisk the eggs, season with salt and pepper, and pour them over the mixture. Pour 1 cup water in your IP and insert a trivet. Put the dish on the trivet. Seal the lid, select Manual at High, and cook for 10 minutes. When done, perform a natural pressure release for 10 minutes. Serve warm with crackers, bread or lettuce.

Thyme Potato & Cannellini Bean Pottage

INGREDIENTS for 4 servings

2 tbsp butter	1 tbsp thyme
1 cup cannellini beans, soaked	1 cup tomato sauce
1 cup scallions, chopped	2 cups vegetable broth
1 tbsp fresh ginger, minced	1 red bell pepper, chopped
½ lb potatoes, cubed	Salt and black pepper to taste
2 carrots, chopped	1 garlic clove, finely minced

DIRECTIONS and total time: approx. 30 minutes

Melt butter on Sauté. Cook scallions, garlic, ginger, carrots, and bell pepper for 3-4 minutes. Add the rest of the ingredients. Pour in 2 cups of water. Seal the lid, select Manual and cook for 15 minutes at High. Once done, perform a quick pressure release. Carefully open the lid, adjust the seasoning, and serve hot.

French Toast

INGREDIENTS for 4 servings

4 dozen eggs	2 tbsp brown sugar
½ tsp vanilla	2 tbsp walnuts, chopped
1 cup milk	Icing sugar, for dusting
½ loaf of bread, sliced	Maple syrup, for garnish
2 tsp cinnamon	

DIRECTIONS and total time: approx. 40 minutes

Lay the bread slices on a greased baking dish. In a bowl, whisk eggs, brown sugar, milk, salt, cinnamon, and vanilla. Pour the mixture on top of bread. Add 1 cup of water in the IP and insert a trivet. Place the baking dish on top. Seal the lid, select Manual at High, and cook for 25 minutes. When ready, release the pressure quickly. Transfer to a serving plate. Dust with icing sugar, drizzle with maple syrup, and serve.

Creamy Potatoes with Pancetta Crisps

INGREDIENTS for 4 servings

4 pancetta slices, chopped	1 tbsp orange juice
2 carrots, chopped	1 tbsp olive oil
½ onion, chopped	1 cup sour cream
1 garlic clove, minced	1 ½ cups chicken stock
2 potatoes, chopped	Salt and black pepper to taste

DIRECTIONS and total time: approx. 20 minutes

Set your Instant Pot to Sauté and cook the pancetta until crispy, 5 minutes. Remove to a plate. Add onion, garlic, potatoes, and carrots and cook for 5 minutes until soft. Pour in the stock and seal the lid. Cook for 5 minutes on Manual at High. Do a quick release. Stir in sour cream and orange juice. Adjust the seasoning. Serve topped with crispy pancetta slices.

Mustard & Sweet Zucchini

INGREDIENTS for 4 servings

1 lb zucchini, sliced	2 tsp garlic, minced
2 tbsp mustard	1 tsp paprika
2 tbsp butter, melted	Salt and black pepper to taste
2 tbsp honey	1 cup water

DIRECTIONS and total time: approx. 20 minutes

Arrange zucchinis on a greased baking dish and brush with some butter. Pour water in your Instant Pot and insert a trivet. Put the baking dish on the trivet. Seal the lid, and cook on Manual for 10 minutes at High. When ready, release the pressure quickly. Whisk together the remaining ingredients in a bowl. Pour over the zucchini and serve in a platter.

Homemade Asian-Style Tomato Chutney

INGREDIENTS for 8 servings

½ tbsp curry paste	3 lb cherry tomatoes, pureed
½ tsp turmeric	1 tbsp paprika
1 clove garlic, minced	Salt and black pepper to taste
2 cups brown sugar	2 tbsp raisins
1 cup onions, diced	½ cup pomegranate seeds

DIRECTIONS and total time: approx. 20 minutes

Add all ingredients in your IP. Pour in ½ cup water. Stir and select Manual. Seal the lid and cook for 15 minutes at High. When done, do a quick pressure release.

Cucumber, Pepper & Quinoa Salad

INGREDIENTS for 4 servings

2 tbsp olive oil	1 cup quinoa, rinsed
2 tbsp fresh basil, minced	½ cup bell pepper, chopped
1 tsp cayenne pepper	1 cup red onions, minced
2 tsp olive oil	1 cucumber, sliced
¼ cup fresh lemon juice	Salt and black pepper to taste

DIRECTIONS and total time: approx. 30 minutes

Add 2 cups water, quinoa, and salt in your IP. Seal the lid, select Manual, and cook for 8 minutes at High. Once done, allow for a natural pressure release, about 10 minutes. Transfer to a plate to cool slightly. In a bowl, add olive oil, cayenne pepper, lemon juice, bell peppers, cucumber, salt, and pepper and mix to combine. Stir the mixture in the quinoa and serve.

Savory Mushroom & Squash Platter

INGREDIENTS for 4 servings

1 cup mushrooms, sliced	1 garlic clove, minced
1 lb summer squash, sliced	1 tbsp chopped parsley
15 oz canned tomatoes	¼ tsp red pepper flakes
1 cup chopped leeks	2 tbsp butter

DIRECTIONS and total time: approx. 20 minutes

Melt butter on Sauté. Add leeks, mushrooms, and garlic and cook for 5 minutes until soft. Add squash and top with tomatoes. Seal the lid and cook for 2 minutes on Manual at High. When done, do a quick release. Stir in parsley and red flakes and season to taste.

Red Cabbage & Bell Pepper Side

INGREDIENTS for 6 servings

1 lb red cabbage, shredded	¼ cup parsley, chopped
1 cup bell peppers, sliced	3 tbsp olive oil
¼ cup white wine	1 tsp paprika
½ cup vegetable stock	1 cup canned tomatoes
1 cup onions, chopped	Salt and black pepper to taste

DIRECTIONS and total time: approx. 20 minutes

Heat oil on Sauté. Add in onions, bell peppers, paprika, salt, and pepper and cook until soft, about 5 minutes. Stir in cabbage, and cook for another 5-6 minutes. Pour in white wine, tomatoes, and vegetable stock. Seal the lid and cook for 10 minutes on Manual at High. When done, release the pressure quickly. Serve with parsley.

Sweet Potatoes with Brussel Sprouts

INGREDIENTS for 6 servings

1 ½ lb sweet potatoes, chopped	1 garlic clove, minced
½ lb Brussel sprouts, halved	1 ½ cups chicken stock
1 tsp Cajun seasoning	1 tbsp oil
1 onion, chopped	Salt and black pepper to taste

DIRECTIONS and total time: approx. 25 minutes

Heat oil on Sauté and cook onion and garlic for 3 minutes until soft. Pour in stock and add potatoes. Seal the lid and cook for 6 minutes on Manual at High. When ready, do a quick pressure release and add Brussel sprouts; continue cooking for 4 minutes on Sauté. Season with Cajun seasoning, and serve.

Grandma's Cabbage with Apples

INGREDIENTS for 4 servings

½ tbsp cornstarch mixed in 6 tsp red wine	1 onion, diced
1 head cabbage, shredded	¼ tsp allspice
1 ½ cups vegetable stock	Salt and black pepper to taste
½ cup dry red wine	2 tbsp olive oil
	2 apples, diced

DIRECTIONS and total time: approx. 35 minutes

Warm the oil on Sauté. Stir in apples and onion and sauté until soft, about 5 minutes. Add in the remaining ingredients, except for cornstarch slurry. Select Manual and cook for 15 minutes at High. Do a quick pressure release. Stir in the prepared cornstarch slurry. Boil for another 5 minutes on Sauté until thickened. Serve.

Tasty Potato & Carrot Mash

INGREDIENTS for 6 servings

3 tbsp cold butter, cubed	1 sprig dried thyme, crushed
½ tsp miso paste	¾ tsp red pepper flakes, crushed
¾ cup milk	2 sprigs dried rosemary, crushed
2 carrots, chopped	Salt and black pepper to taste
2 lb potatoes, chopped	2 tbsp squash seeds, toasted

DIRECTIONS and total time: approx. 20 minutes

Place potatoes and carrots in the Instant Pot and fill with water to cover. Sprinkle with salt and seal the lid. Select Manual and cook for 10 minutes at High. Do a quick release. Drain them in a colander. Mash with a potato masher and season with pepper flakes, black pepper, rosemary, thyme, and miso paste. Add butter and milk, and stir softly. Spoon the mash into a serving bowl and top with toasted squash seeds to serve.

Bok Choy & Tomato Side

INGREDIENTS for 6 servings

12 oz bok choy, sliced	1 ¼ cups veggie broth
1 cup tomatoes, chopped	1 tbsp lemon juice
2 garlic cloves, minced	2 tbsp olive oil
1 onion, diced	Salt and black pepper to taste

DIRECTIONS and total time: approx. 20 minutes

Set your IP to Sauté and warm olive oil. Cook onion and garlic for 3 minutes until soft. Stir in the remaining ingredients and seal the lid. Cook for 3 minutes on Manual at High. When ready, do a quick release. Serve.

Ginger Mustard Greens with Bacon

INGREDIENTS for 4 servings

2 slices bacon, chopped	2 tsp parsley
10 oz mustard greens, chopped	½ tsp coriander seeds
2 shallots, chopped	½ tsp cumin
1 tsp ginger powder	Salt and black pepper to taste

DIRECTIONS and total time: approx. 20 minutes

Pour 1 cup of water and insert a steamer basket. Place mustard greens inside the basket, seal the lid and cook on Manual for 3 minutes at High. When ready, do a quick pressure release. Transfer to a plate. Discard the water and press Sauté. Cook bacon for 3 minutes, add in spices and shallots to stir-fry for 4-5 minutes. Mix in the mustard greens. Top with parsley and serve.

Eggplant Caponata

INGREDIENTS for 4 servings

1 red onion, sliced	½ cup fresh basil, chopped
3 tbsp red wine	1 celery stick, diced
½ cup olive oil	3 Roma tomatoes, chopped
2 eggplants, cubed	2 tbsp capers, drained
Salt and black pepper to taste	½ cup toasted pine nuts
2 garlic cloves, minced	1 tbsp sugar

DIRECTIONS and total time: approx. 55 minutes

Heat oil on Sauté and stir-fry garlic, onion, celery, and eggplants for about 2-3 minutes. Pour in red wine, Roma tomatoes, and ½ cup water. Seal the lid and cook for 8 minutes on Manual at High. Once the cooking is over, do a quick pressure release. Sprinkle with fresh basil, capers, and pine nuts to serve.

Pumpkin Spice Oatmeal

INGREDIENTS for 4 servings

1 tbsp butter, softened	2 tbsp sugar
1 cup water	2 tbsp maple syrup
½ tbsp pumpkin pie spice	1 cup milk
½ tbsp cinnamon	7 oz canned pumpkin puree
½ tsp vanilla	1 cup steel-cut oats

DIRECTIONS and total time: approx. 25 minutes

Grease your Instant Pot with butter. Add in all the ingredients and stir to combine. Seal the lid, select Manual at High, and cook for 6 minutes. When ready, release the pressure naturally for 10 minutes. Serve.

Vanilla Sweet Potato Oatmeal

INGREDIENTS for 4 servings

6 ½ cups water	½ tsp cinnamon
1 ½ cups steel-cut oats	½ tsp nutmeg
¼ cup sugar	2 sweet potatoes, peeled
1 tbsp butter, melted	½ tsp vanilla extract

DIRECTIONS and total time: approx. 30 minutes

Pierce sweet potatoes with a fork all over and microwave for 5 minutes. Mash them with a fork in a bowl. Mix in the remaining ingredients and pour in your Instant Pot. Seal the lid, select Manual at High, and cook for 5 minutes. When ready, release the pressure naturally for 10 minutes. Stir well before serving.

Date & Coconut Granola

INGREDIENTS for 6 servings

3 tbsp brown sugar	1 cup coconut flakes
½ cup canola oil	1 ½ cups almonds, sliced
¼ tsp kosher salt	1 cup oats
1 tsp almond extract	2 cups brown rice cereal
3 tbsp honey	¼ tsp ground ginger
1 cup dates, chopped	½ tsp grated nutmeg
2 tbsp golden flax meal	3 cups water

DIRECTIONS and total time: approx. 35 minutes

Heat olive oil on Sauté. Add in honey, brown sugar, almond extract, salt, ginger, and nutmeg and whisk well. Mix in oats, rice cereal, coconut flakes, almonds, and flax meal one by one. Mix in the water. Seal the lid, select Manual at High, and cook for 15 minutes. When ready, release the pressure naturally for 10 minutes. Open the lid and stir in dates. Let cool and serve.

Chili Pancetta Hash

INGREDIENTS for 4 servings

1 tbsp olive oil	1 tsp dried oregano
½ lb pancetta	¼ tsp chili pepper
½ yellow onion, chopped	Salt black pepper to taste
1 red bell pepper, chopped	1 lb potatoes, chopped
1 green bell pepper, chopped	½ cup vegetable broth
½ tbsp garlic powder	1 tbsp chopped parsley

DIRECTIONS and total time: approx. 30 minutes

Heat olive oil on Sauté, and cook the pancetta for 5 minutes until crisp. Add in onion and bell peppers and cook for another 5 minutes until tender. Season with garlic powder, oregano, chili pepper, salt and black pepper; stir for 1 minute. Pour in potatoes and broth. Seal the lid, press Manual, and cook for 12 minutes at High. Once done, perform a quick pressure release. Remove lid and press Sauté. Cook for 2 minutes, stirring occasionally, until the remaining broth evaporates. Garnish with parsley and serve.

Cheese, Egg & Sausage Casserole

INGREDIENTS for 5 servings

5 large eggs	1 ½ cups cheddar, shredded
1 cup milk	¾ cup sausages, sliced
4 baby potatoes, cubed	Salt and black pepper to taste

DIRECTIONS and total time: approx. 25 minutes

In a bowl, beat eggs until smooth, add in milk, salt, and pepper; mix well. Arrange potatoes in a greased baking dish. Top with sausages and cheese. Spread the egg mixture over. Pour 1 cup of water in your Instant Pot and insert a trivet. Place the baking dish on the trivet. Seal the lid, select Manual at High, and cook for 12 minutes. When ready, do a quick release. Serve warm.

Apple Oatmeal

INGREDIENTS for 4 servings

1 tbsp butter	½ tsp vanilla
1 cup milk	1 tsp ground cinnamon
1 cup rolled oats	Pinch of salt
2 tbsp brown sugar	2 apples, cubed

DIRECTIONS and total time: approx. 25 minutes

Set your Instant Pot to Sauté and melt butter. Add in apples and cook for 3 minutes. Mix in the remaining ingredients. Pour in 2 cups water. Seal the lid, select Manual at High, and cook for 7 minutes. When ready, release the pressure naturally for 10 minutes. Serve.

Pumpkin Granola

INGREDIENTS for 12 servings

5 cups rolled oats	1 cup toasted pumpkin seeds
1 tsp ground cinnamon	½ cup honey
1 tbsp pumpkin pie spice	¾ cup canned pumpkin puree
1 cup dried cranberries	1 cup water

DIRECTIONS and total time: approx. 35 minutes

In your Instant Pot, stir all the ingredients, except for cranberries. Seal the lid, select Manual at High, and cook for 20 minutes. When done, release the pressure quickly. Stir in cranberries, let cool, and serve.

Easy Monkey Bread

INGREDIENTS for 4 servings

1 (7.5 oz) can of biscuits	4 tbsp melted butter
1 cup sugar	1/3 cup chopped walnuts
1 tsp cinnamon	1 tbsp ground cinnamon

DIRECTIONS and total time: approx. 40 minutes

Pour 1 cup of water in your IP and lower a trivet. In a bowl, mix butter with sugar and cinnamon. Spread the mixture on a greased baking dish. Top with biscuits. Place on the trivet. Seal the lid, press Manual, and cook for 25 minutes at High. Once the cooking is complete, do a quick pressure release. Invert the baking dish onto a serving plate and top with walnuts to serve.

Savory Faro Breakfast

INGREDIENTS for 4 servings

1 tbsp olive oil	2 cups vegetable broth
1 cup faro	Salt and black pepper to taste
1 shallot, chopped	2 hard-boiled eggs, quartered

DIRECTIONS and total time: approx. 30 minutes

In your Instant Pot, add shallot, millet, vegetable broth, salt, and pepper. Seal the lid, press Manual, and cook for 10 minutes at High. When ready, do a quick pressure release. Serve warm or cool, topped with eggs..

Beans & Grains

Pink Beans with Pancetta & Tomatoes

INGREDIENTS for 4 servings

1 cup pink beans, soaked	½ tsp rosemary
1 cups tomatoes, chopped	½ tsp thyme
4 pancetta slices, diced	Salt and black pepper to taste

DIRECTIONS and total time: approx. 40 minutes

Set the pot to Sauté and cook pancetta until crispy, about 5 minutes; set aside. Add tomatoes, thyme, and rosemary and cook for 2 minutes. Stir in the remaining ingredients, pour in 4 cups water, and seal the lid. Cook for 30 minutes on Manual at High. When ready, do a quick release. Stir in pancetta and serve.

Bean Soup with Pork & Vegetables

INGREDIENTS for 5 servings

1 lb lean pork loin, cubed	1 onion, chopped
3 tbsp olive oil	1 can (14-oz) diced tomatoes
5 cups chicken broth	Salt and black pepper to taste
1 can (15-oz) kidney beans	½ cup sour cream
1 cup red bell peppers, diced	1 tsp dried thyme
1 carrot, chopped	2 tsp caraway seeds
3 cups cabbage, sliced	2 garlic cloves, minced

DIRECTIONS and total time: approx. 50 minutes

Set your Instant Pot to Sauté and heat the olive oil. Add in onion, pork, bell peppers, carrots, garlic, thyme, caraway seeds, salt, and black pepper and cook for 5-6 minutes, stirring often. Pour in broth, tomatoes, cabbage, and kidney beans. Seal the lid, select Manual at High, and cook for 15 minutes. When ready, release the pressure naturally for 10 minutes. Serve warm in serving bowls with a dollop of sour cream on top.

Two-Bean & Chickpea Stew

INGREDIENTS for 6 servings

½ cup Anasazi beans, soaked	2 carrots, chopped
½ cup chickpeas	1 (14 oz) can tomatoes, diced
½ cup kidney beans, soaked	1 tbsp garlic paste
2 bell peppers, chopped	1 tbsp thyme
2 tbsp olive oil	Salt and black pepper to taste
2 onions, chopped	1 avocado, sliced to serve

DIRECTIONS and total time: approx. 40 minutes

Heat olive oil on Sauté and cook onions, garlic paste, bell peppers, and carrots for 5 minutes until tender. Pour in beans, tomatoes, chickpeas, and 4 cups of water. Season with salt, pepper, and thyme. Seal the lid, select Manual and cook for 30 minutes at High. Once ready, do a quick pressure release. Serve topped with avocado slices.

Lima Bean & Spinach Stew

INGREDIENTS for 6 servings

2 cups lima beans, soaked	2 shallots, chopped
2 cups spinach	1 (14-oz) can tomatoes, diced
2 cups vegetable stock	2 sprigs rosemary, chopped
2 cloves garlic, minced	Salt and black pepper to taste
2 tbsp olive oil	

DIRECTIONS and total time: approx. 40 minutes

Place lima beans in the pot and pour 4 cups water. Seal the lid, select Manual, and cook for 5 minutes at High. Do a quick pressure release. Drain and rinse the beans under cold water. Discard cooking liquid and set aside. Warm oil on Sauté and cook shallots and garlic for 3 minutes. Add in tomatoes, stock, and beans; season to taste. Seal the lid and set to High. Cook for 10 minutes. Quick-release the pressure. Stir in spinach and rosemary and cook until spinach wilts on Sauté, for 5 minutes. Serve.

Black Bean & Quinoa Stew

INGREDIENTS for 5 servings

2 red bell peppers, chopped	Salt and black pepper to taste
3 cups vegetable broth	1 onion, diced
1 cup kale, chopped	2 garlic cloves, minced
1 cup quinoa	1 cup canned black beans
½ cup celery, chopped	3 tbsp olive oil
½ tsp chili powder	Chopped chives for garnish

DIRECTIONS and total time: approx. 35 minutes

Set on Sauté and heat the olive oil. Add onions, bell peppers, celery, and garlic, and cook for 4 minutes. Add in quinoa, chili powder, black beans and stir well to combine. Seal the lid, select Manual at High, and cook for 7 minutes. When ready, release the pressure naturally for 10 minutes. Stir in kale and cook for 5 minutes on Sauté. Season with salt and pepper and ladle into bowls. Serve with freshly chopped chives.

Kidney Bean & Shiitake Spread

INGREDIENTS for 6 servings

2 cups kidney beans, soaked	1 tbsp butter
1 cup Shiitake mushrooms	1 tsp rosemary
1 cup red onions, chopped	½ tsp cumin
1 ½ tsp cayenne pepper	Salt and black pepper to taste

DIRECTIONS and total time: approx. 40 minutes

Melt butter on Sauté in your IP. Cook onions for 3 minutes until soft. Slice mushrooms, add to the pot, and cook for 3 more minutes until tender. Stir in the remaining ingredients and pour in 5 cups of water. Seal the lid and cook on Manual for 25 minutes at High. When ready, do a quick pressure release. Drain and transfer to a food processor. Pulse until smooth. Serve.

One-Pot Beef with Beans

INGREDIENTS for 4 servings

2 cups canned kidney beans	1 green onion, chopped
½ lb mixed ground beef	2 tbsp olive oil
¼ cup Colby cheese, shredded	Salt and black pepper to taste
1 tsp garlic, minced	3 cups chicken broth

DIRECTIONS and total time: approx. 25 minutes

Heat oil on Sauté, add green onion and garlic and cook for 2 minutes. Add beef and cook for 6 minutes, stirring often. Mix in beans and broth. Seal the lid, and cook for 10 minutes on Manual at High. Do a quick pressure release. Serve warm, topped with Colby cheese.

Mushroom & Cheese Buckwheat

INGREDIENTS for 4 servings

2 cups chicken broth	2 tbsp olive oil
1 cup buckwheat	2 tbsp sage
½ cup Pecorino Romano, grated	1 tsp garlic, minced
1 lb mushrooms, sliced	Salt and black pepper to taste
1 onion, chopped	2 tbsp parsley

DIRECTIONS and total time: approx. 40 minutes

Heat oil in on Sauté. Add in mushrooms, onion, and garlic and cook for 5 minutes. Stir in buckwheat and sage, for 1 more minute. Pour in chicken broth, salt, and pepper. Seal the lid, and cook for 8 minutes on Manual at High. Do a natural pressure release for 10 minutes. Stir in Pecorino cheese and parsley and serve.

Garbanzo Beans & Mixed Vegetable Stew

INGREDIENTS for 6 servings

4 carrots, peeled and chopped	2 cups vegetable broth
1 (16-oz) can garbanzo beans	1 (14-oz) can tomatoes, diced
1 zucchini, cubed	2 cloves garlic, minced
¼ tsp red pepper flakes	1 cup onions, diced
½ tsp cumin powder	2 turnips, cubed
Salt and black pepper to taste	2 tbsp parsley

DIRECTIONS and total time: approx. 26 minutes

In the Instant Pot, add tomatoes, garlic, onions, turnips, carrots, salt, pepper, red pepper flakes, and broth and stir to combine. Seal the lid, select Manual at High, and cook for 6 minutes. When done, do a quick release. Stir in garbanzo beans and zucchini, and cook the stew for 10 minutes on Sauté. Sprinkle with parsley to serve.

Grana Padano Grits with Ham & Eggs

INGREDIENTS for 6 servings

1 cup quick-cooking grits	3 tbsp butter
1 cup grated Grana Padano	1 shallot, chopped
10 oz cooked ham, diced	1 tsp paprika
2 eggs, whisked	Salt and black pepper to taste

DIRECTIONS and total time: approx. 30 minutes

Melt butter and sear the ham on Sauté. Stir in shallots and spices and cook for 2 minutes. Add in grits and pour 3 cups of water. Seal the lid and cook for 13 minutes on Manual at High. Do a quick pressure release. Stir in Grana Padano cheese and eggs for 4 minutes on Sauté.

Picante Red Bean & Corn Dip

INGREDIENTS for 6 servings

1 cup fresh corn kernels	Salt and black pepper to taste
1 cup red beans, soaked	½ tsp cumin
1 cup onions, finely chopped	1 cup mild picante sauce
½ tsp celery seeds	1 garlic clove, crushed
2 tbsp vegetable oil	2 tbsp parsley

DIRECTIONS and total time: approx. 35 minutes

Heat oil on Sauté, add onions, garlic, celery seeds, cumin, salt, and pepper and cook for 3 minutes. Pour in 3 cups water and corn kernels. Seal the lid, select Manual, and cook for 30 minutes at High. Once the cooking is over, do a quick pressure release. Transfer to a food processor and blitz until smooth. Stir in picante sauce and serve topped with parsley.

Curry Pinto Beans

INGREDIENTS for 4 servings

1 cup pinto beans, soaked	2 garlic cloves, minced
2 tomatoes, chopped	½ tsp cumin
1 onion, chopped	1 tsp paprika
1 tbsp curry powder	2 tbsp thyme, chopped
2 tbsp olive oil	Salt and black pepper to taste

DIRECTIONS and total time: approx. 45 minutes

Place pinto beans, salt, pepper, and 1 tbsp oil in your IP. Cover with water and seal the lid. Cook for 30 minutes on Manual at High. When ready, do a quick pressure release. Stir in the remaining ingredients. Cook for 5 more minutes on Sauté. Sprinkle with thyme to serve.

Homemade Bean Dip

INGREDIENTS for 6 servings

¼ cup serrano pepper, chopped	2 tbsp olive oil
1 cup kidney beans, soaked	1 tbsp lime juice
1 sweet onion, chopped	Salt and black pepper to taste
2 ripe tomatoes, chopped	Pita crackers to serve
1 tbsp cilantro, chopped	3 cups water

DIRECTIONS and total time: approx. 40 minutes

Add beans and water in your IP. Seal the lid and select Manual for 30 minutes at High. Once ready, do a quick pressure release. Transfer to a bowl and add the rest of the ingredients. Blend the mixture with an immersion blender until smooth, and serve with pita crackers.

Honey Quinoa with Walnuts

INGREDIENTS for 4 servings

1 cup quinoa	½ tsp cinnamon
2 tbsp walnuts, chopped	¼ tsp nutmeg
½ tsp cloves	¼ cup honey, reserve some

DIRECTIONS and total time: approx. 20 minutes

Place all ingredients in your Instant Pot; stir to combine well. Pour in 6 cups of water. Seal the lid and cook on Manual for 15 minutes at High. Once done, do a quick pressure release. Serve drizzled with a bit of honey.

Italian Sausage with Beans & Chickpeas

INGREDIENTS for 6 servings

3 Italian sausages, sliced	2 carrots, cut into sticks
1 cup black beans, soaked	1 tsp chili pepper, minced
1 cup chickpeas, soaked	Salt and black pepper to taste
1 red bell pepper, sliced	1 cup sweet onions, chopped
4 cups chicken broth	3 cloves garlic, minced
2 tomatoes, chopped	1 bay leaf
3 tsp vegetable oil	2 tbsp parsley, for garnishing

DIRECTIONS and total time: approx. 35 minutes

Heat oil on Sauté, add the sausages and brown for 3-5 minutes. Stir in onions and garlic, and stir-fry for 2-3 minutes. Add in the remaining ingredients, select Manual, and cook for 20 minutes at High. When ready, do a quick pressure release. Serve with parsley.

Best Black Bean Chili

INGREDIENTS for 4 servings

1 cup black beans, soaked	1 tsp chili powder
1 cup red onions, chopped	1 garlic clove, minced
1 carrot, chopped	Salt and black pepper to taste
2 tbsp cilantro, chopped	2 tbsp olive oil
½ tsp cumin	2 tomatoes, chopped

DIRECTIONS and total time: approx. 40 minutes

On Sauté, heat olive oil and cook onions, carrot, garlic, cumin, and chili for 3 minutes, stirring frequently. Pour in 4 ½ cups of water, and add tomatoes and beans. Seal the lid, and cook on Manual for 30 minutes at High. When done, do a quick release. Adjust the seasoning, ladle into bowls and serve topped with cilantro.

Tiger Prawns with Red Lentils

INGREDIENTS for 6 servings

2 cups red lentils	2 tbsp grapeseed oil
1 lb tiger prawns	2 plum tomatoes, chopped
1 cup green onions, chopped	1 tsp molasses
½ tbsp miso paste	Salt and black pepper to taste
2 bell peppers, chopped	½ tsp cumin
4 cups vegetable stock	2 tbsp parsley

DIRECTIONS and total time: approx. 30 minutes

Heat oil on Sauté, and stir-fry prawns for 8 minutes; set aside. Add green onions and bell peppers and cook for 3 minutes. Stir in miso paste, cumin, molasses, salt, and black pepper for 1 minute. Pour in the stock and red lentils, then seal the lid, and cook on Manual for 15 minutes at High. Once done, do a quick pressure release. Add in prawns and top with parsley to serve.

Rosemary Butter Beans

INGREDIENTS for 6 servings

2 tsp olive oil	Salt and black pepper to taste
2 cups butter beans, soaked	1 onion, chopped
2 cloves garlic, minced	2 tomatoes, chopped
1 bay leaf	2 tbsp rosemary, chopped

DIRECTIONS and total time: approx. 20 minutes

Heat olive oil on Sauté and cook onion, garlic, salt, and pepper for 3 minutes until soft. Pour in butter beans, tomatoes, and 4 cups of water. Seal the lid, select Manual and cook for 15 minutes at High. Once done, do a quick pressure release. Discard bay leaf and top with rosemary to serve. Enjoy with roasted bread.

Buckwheat with Vegetables & Ham

INGREDIENTS for 4 servings

½ cup buckwheat	2 green onions, chopped
½ lb cooked ham, chopped	2 cups veggie stock
1 cup mushrooms, sliced	1 tsp turmeric, minced
1 cup bell peppers, chopped	¼ cup fennel, chopped
2 tbsp butter	Salt and black pepper to taste

DIRECTIONS and total time: approx. 30 minutes

Melt butter on Sauté, add onions, and cook for 3 minutes. Stir in mushrooms, fennel, and bell peppers and cook for 3 more minutes. Add ham and turmeric and cook for 1 minute. Stir in the remaining ingredients. Seal the lid and cook on Manual for 18 minutes at High. When done, release the pressure quickly. Serve.

Fresh Fig & Banana Barley

INGREDIENTS for 4 servings

1 cup barley, rinsed	2 cups water
¼ cup fresh figs, chopped	½ tsp vanilla extract
2 bananas, sliced	½ tsp cinnamon
1 cup milk	½ cup sugar

DIRECTIONS and total time: approx. 20 minutes

In your IP, place barley, vanilla, sugar, milk, and water. Seal the lid, select Manual, and cook for 10 minutes at High. When ready, do a quick pressure release. Fluff the barley with a fork and stir in bananas and figs. Serve sprinkled with cinnamon.

Vegan White Bean & Avocado Salad

INGREDIENTS for 4 servings

2 avocados, diced
Salt and black pepper to taste
½ cup fresh cilantro, chopped
¼ tsp hot pepper sauce

2 tbsp olive oil
1 cup white beans, soaked
1 lime, juiced
1 cup red onions, chopped

DIRECTIONS and total time: approx. 35 minutes

Pour 2 cups of water and add the white beans to your IP. Select Manual and cook for 30 minutes at High. When done, do a quick pressure release. Drain the beans and transfer to a bowl to cool. Add in hot pepper sauce, avocados, olive oil, lime juice, salt, and pepper and toss to coat. Serve topped with cilantro.

Favorite "Ever" Cornbread

INGREDIENTS for 4 servings

1 ¼ cups cornmeal
1 cup heavy cream
2 tbsp butter, melted
2 eggs, beaten

½ cup sugar
½ tsp salt
1 tsp baking powder

DIRECTIONS and total time: approx. 40 minutes

Combine the dry ingredients in a bowl. Whisk the wet ones in another bowl. Gently stir the wet ingredients into the dry ingredients. Transfer the mixture to a greased baking dish. Pour 1 cup water in your IP and lower a trivet. Place the dish on the trivet and seal the lid. Cook on Manual for 30 minutes at High. When ready, do a quick release. Serve chilled.

Pearl Barley & Black Olive Salad

INGREDIENTS for 4 servings

¼ cup pearl barley, rinsed
½ cup onion, thinly sliced
½ cup black olives, sliced
2 tbsp olive oil
2 bell peppers, thinly sliced

1 cup grape tomatoes, diced
1 tbsp vinegar
½ cup blue cheese, crumbled
Salt and black pepper to taste
1 tsp dried basil

DIRECTIONS and total time: approx. 20 minutes

To the Instant Pot, add barley, 4 cups water, and salt. Seal the lid and cook for 10 minutes on Manual at High. When ready, do a quick release and open the lid. Drain and transfer the barley to a bowl to cool. Add in onion, bell peppers, tomatoes, and black olives and mix to combine. Transfer to a salad platter. In a bowl, whisk olive oil, vinegar, salt, pepper, and basil and pour over the salad. Top with blue cheese to serve.

Easy Barley Pilaf with Cashews

INGREDIENTS for 6 servings

1 ½ cups barley
2 tsp butter

3 cups chicken stock
2 white onions, chopped

2 carrots, chopped
Salt and black pepper to taste

4 tbsp cashews, toasted
1 garlic clove, minced

DIRECTIONS and total time: approx. 15 minutes

Select Sauté and melt the butter. Cook onions and garlic for 3 minutes until tender. Add in the carrots and cook for another 4 minutes. Stir in the remaining ingredients, except for the cashews. Seal the lid, select Manual and cook for 8 minutes at High. After, do a quick pressure release. Fluff the barley with a fork and transfer to a plate. Serve scattered with cashews.

Split Pea Beef Stew

INGREDIENTS for 4 servings

1 ½ cups green split peas
½ lb beef stew meat, cubed
1 cup scallions, chopped
2 garlic cloves, minced
4 potatoes, peeled and diced
1 cup carrots, chopped

2 tsp vegetable oil
1 cup fennel, chopped
2 cups chicken stock
Salt and black pepper to taste
1 bay leaf
1 (14-oz) can diced tomatoes

DIRECTIONS and total time: approx. 40 minutes

Heat oil on Sauté and cook scallions, garlic, carrots, fennel, salt, and pepper for 4 minutes. Add in beef and cook for 5 minutes until slightly browned. Add in tomatoes, potatoes, bay leaf, and stock. Seal the lid, and cook on Manual for 20 minutes at High. When ready, do a quick pressure release. Discard the bay leaf.

Fennel White Bean Stew

INGREDIENTS for 4 servings

2 cups white beans, soaked
½ fennel bulb, chopped
½ cup Grana Padano, grated
½ cup spring onions, chopped
2 tsp olive oil

3 cloves garlic, minced
Salt and black pepper to taste
2 tbsp parsley, chopped
1 tsp paprika
1 (14-oz) can diced tomatoes

DIRECTIONS and total time: approx. 40 minutes

Select Sauté and heat the olive oil. Add in garlic, fennel, and spring onions, and cook until tender. Add in the remaining ingredients, except for the cheese. Pour in 4 cups of water. Seal the lid, press Manual, and cook for 30 minutes at High. Once the cooking is done, do a quick pressure release. Serve topped with grated Grana Padano cheese and sprinkle with parsley.

Barley & Potato Soup

INGREDIENTS for 4 servings

½ cup pearl barley
4 potatoes, peeled and diced
1 carrot, diced
1 tsp garlic paste
1 celery stalk, chopped
1 cup red onions, chopped

3 tsp olive oil
4 cups chicken stock
½ tsp dried sage
1 tsp red pepper flakes
Salt and black pepper to taste
2 tbsp parsley

DIRECTIONS and total time: approx. 45 minutes

Heat oil on Sauté and stir-fry carrot, garlic paste, celery, red onions, sage, salt, and pepper for 5 minutes. Add in barley and stock. Seal the lid, select Manual and cook for 30 minutes at High. Once ready, do a natural release for 10 minutes. Serve topped with parsley.

Spelt & Red Beans with Mushrooms

INGREDIENTS for 4 servings

1 cup red beans	2 tsp olive oil
½ cup grain spelt	½ serrano pepper, minced
2 cups mushrooms, sliced	1 cup tomatoes, diced
4 green onions, chopped	3 cups chicken broth
1 garlic clove, minced	Salt and black pepper to taste

DIRECTIONS and total time: approx. 30 minutes

Heat olive oil on Sauté and cook green onions, garlic, mushrooms, and serrano pepper for 5 minutes until tender. Add in the remaining ingredients. Seal the lid and cook on Manual for 25 minutes at High. When ready, do a quick pressure release. Serve warm.

Paprika Lima Bean Dip with Pancetta

INGREDIENTS for 6 servings

4 pancetta slices, chopped	½ tsp paprika
20 oz frozen lima beans	Salt and black pepper to taste
3 tsp butter, melted	

DIRECTIONS and total time: approx. 30 minutes

Set on Sauté and cook pancetta for 5 minutes; set aside. Add the beans to the pot and cover with water. Seal the lid and cook on Manual for 10 minutes at High. When ready, do a quick pressure release. Drain and transfer to a food processor along with butter, paprika, salt, and pepper. Process until smooth, and serve with pancetta.

Peach & Golden Raisin Porridge

INGREDIENTS for 4 servings

1 ½ cups steel cut oats	8 peaches, chopped
1 ½ cups milk	1 tsp vanilla paste
A handful of golden raisins	¾ cup brown sugar

DIRECTIONS and total time: approx. 15 minutes

Combine all ingredients in your IP. Pour in 2 ¼ cups of water. Seal the lid, select Manual, and cook for 8 minutes at High. After, do a quick pressure release.

Spicy Mashed Pinto Beans

INGREDIENTS for 6 servings

1 ½ tsp garlic powder	1 tsp chili powder
1 cup sweet onions, chopped	¼ tsp red pepper
2 cups pinto beans, soaked	Salt and black pepper to taste
3 tsp vegetable oil	½ cup fresh cilantro, chopped

DIRECTIONS and total time: approx. 40 minutes

Heat oil on Sauté, and cook onions for 3 minutes. Add in beans and 4 cups of water. Season with salt, black and red peppers. Seal the lid, select Manual, and cook for 30 minutes at High. When ready, do a quick release. Drain the beans and mash them with a potato masher. Stir in garlic and chili powders, red pepper, salt, and pepper. Sprinkled with cilantro to serve.

Cheesy Bulgur with Spring Onions

INGREDIENTS for 6 servings

2 cups bulgur	½ cup goat cheese
4 cups vegetable stock	Salt and black pepper to taste
3 tbsp butter	1 tsp rosemary
1 cup spring onions, chopped	1 garlic clove, minced

DIRECTIONS and total time: approx. 25 minutes

Melt butter on Sauté. Add spring onions and garlic and cook until soft, about 3 minutes. Stir in the remaining ingredients, except for the cheese. Seal the lid and cook for 15 minutes on Manual at High. When ready, do a quick pressure release. Stir in goat cheese and serve.

Yellow Lentil Dip

INGREDIENTS for 6 servings

1 cup yellow lentils, rinsed	2 tbsp vegetable oil
¼ tsp dukkah	½ tsp maple syrup
1 garlic clove, minced	Salt and black pepper to taste
1 tbsp tomato paste	½ tsp dry sage, minced
1 tbsp tahini	¼ tsp cardamom

DIRECTIONS and total time: approx. 20 minutes

Pour 2 cups of water and add lentils to the pot. Seal the lid and cook on Manual for 5 minutes at High. Allow for a natural pressure release, around 10 minutes. Drain and transfer to a food processor. Add in the remaining ingredients and pulse until smooth. Serve warm.

Black Bean & Green Chili con Queso

INGREDIENTS for 4 servings

4 oz Pepper Jack cheese, cubed	2 oz diced green chilies
4 oz cream cheese	1 cup black beans, soaked
½ tsp red pepper sauce	¼ cup Parmesan, grated
1 tsp crushed red pepper	½ cup mayonnaise
1 clove garlic, minced	

DIRECTIONS and total time: approx. 15 minutes

Place the black beans in your Instant Pot and cover with water. Seal the lid, press Manual and cook for 30 minutes at High. After cooking, do a quick pressure release. Drain the beans and transfer to a bowl. Whisk the cheeses with the remaining ingredients in another bowl. Add the mixture to the beans and toss to combine.

White Beans with Tuna

INGREDIENTS for 4 servings

20 oz canned white tuna in water, drained and flaked
1 lb white beans, soaked
2 cups tomatoes, chopped
1 clove garlic, crushed
Salt and black pepper to taste
4 tbsp olive oil
2 tbsp basil, chopped

DIRECTIONS and total time: approx. 50 minutes

Heat olive oil on Sauté. Fry garlic for 1 minute. Add in beans and cover with water. Seal the lid, select Manual, and cook for 30 minutes at High. When ready, do a quick release. Stir in tuna, tomatoes, salt, and pepper, and cook for 3 minutes on Sauté. Sprinkle with basil.

Hazelnut Banana & Date Millet

INGREDIENTS for 6 servings

2 cups millet
1 cup milk
2 bananas, sliced
½ cup hazelnuts, chopped
¼ cup dates, chopped
½ tsp vanilla
½ tsp cinnamon
2 tbsp olive oil
A pinch of salt

DIRECTIONS and total time: approx. 25 minutes

Combine all ingredients, except for bananas and hazelnuts, in your Instant Pot. Pour in 2 cups of water, seal the lid and cook for 10 minutes on Manual at High. When ready, do a quick release. Serve topped with sliced bananas and chopped hazelnuts.

Apple & Brazil Nut Porridge

INGREDIENTS for 4 servings

½ cup Brazil nuts, chopped
1 ½ cups oats
½ cup milk
2 apples, sliced
1 tbsp maple syrup
2 tsp butter
½ tsp honey
2 ½ cups water

DIRECTIONS and total time: approx. 15 minutes

Place all ingredients, except apples and Brazil nuts, in your IP. Pour in water. Seal the lid and cook for 8 minutes on Manual at High. When ready, do a quick pressure release. Top with apples and nuts to serve.

Papaya & Honey Quinoa

INGREDIENTS for 6 servings

1 ½ cups white quinoa
½ cup honey
1 cup papaya, crushed
2 tbsp butter
½ tsp vanilla
A pinch of salt

DIRECTIONS and total time: approx. 15 minutes

Place quinoa, 3 cups of water, butter, vanilla, and salt in your Instant Pot. Seal lid and cook for 8 minutes on Manual at High. When done, release the pressure quickly. Stir in papaya and drizzle with honey to serve.

Couscous with Cherries & Macadamia

INGREDIENTS for 4 servings

1 ½ cups couscous
½ cup macadamia, chopped
¼ cup cherries, chopped
½ fennel bulb, chopped
Salt and black pepper to taste
½ onion, chopped
14 oz chicken broth
1 tbsp butter

DIRECTIONS and total time: approx. 15 minutes

Melt butter on Sauté and cook onion and fennel for 4 minutes. Stir in remaining ingredients. Pour in ¼ cup water. Seal the lid and cook for 3 minutes on Manual at High. When done, release the pressure quickly. Serve.

Creamy Chicken with Quinoa

INGREDIENTS for 4 servings

2 tsp olive oil
1 ½ cups quinoa
3 cups chicken broth
½ cup Colby cheese, shredded
1 cup chicken breasts, chopped
1 cup half-and-half
¼ cup Parmesan cheese, grated
Salt and black pepper to taste

DIRECTIONS and total time: approx. 15 minutes

Heat olive oil on Sauté and sear chicken for 5 minutes. Add in quinoa and broth. Seal the lid and cook on Manual for 12 minutes at High. Do a quick pressure release. Stir in half-and-half, Colby and Parmesan cheeses and cook for 3 minutes on Sauté. Serve hot.

Serrano Pepper Bulgur

INGREDIENTS for 4 servings

2 tbsp parsley
1 tsp serrano pepper, minced
1 garlic clove, minced
1 cup bulgur
2 tbsp olive oil
4 green onions, chopped
1 cup tomatoes, diced
Salt and black pepper to taste

DIRECTIONS and total time: approx. 30 minutes

Heat olive oil on Sauté and cook green onions, garlic, mushrooms, and serrano pepper for 5 minutes. Add in bulgur, tomatoes, and 2 cups of water. Seal the lid, select Manual and cook for 15 minutes at High. When ready, do a quick pressure release. Serve warm.

Bulgur with Vegetables

INGREDIENTS for 4 servings

1 cup bulgur
1 onion, chopped
1 cup cauliflower florets
1 carrot, sliced
1 cup peas
1 tbsp olive oil
2 tsp lemon zest
¼ cup lemon juice
2 cups veggie stock
Salt and black pepper to taste

DIRECTIONS and total time: approx. 20 minutes

Heat oil on Sauté; cook onion for 2 minutes. Stir in the remaining ingredients, seal the lid, and cook for 10 minutes on Manual. Do a quick pressure release. Serve.

Pasta & Rice

Cheesy Sausage & Pepperoni Linguine

INGREDIENTS for 4 servings

4 oz provolone cheese, shredded	4 oz pepperoni, sliced
1 lb linguine	4 oz mozzarella, shredded
14 oz pasta sauce	2 tbsp olive oil
½ lb Italian sausages, sliced	1 tsp garlic, minced
	Salt and black pepper to taste

DIRECTIONS and total time: approx. 20 minutes

Heat olive oil on Sauté. Cook sausages and garlic for 4-5 minutes. Stir in the remaining ingredients, except for the cheeses and pepperoni. Pour in 2 cups of water. Seal the lid and cook for 8 minutes on Manual at High. When it goes off, do a quick pressure release. Stir in the cheeses and top with pepperoni. Serve immediately.

Creamy Turkey & Cauliflower Tortellini

INGREDIENTS for 4 servings

2 tbsp olive oil	¼ cup heavy cream
2 tbsp basil, chopped	2 cups chicken stock
½ lb turkey breast, diced	1 onion, chopped
2 cups cauliflower florets	1 tbsp chopped parsley
8 oz cheese tortellini	Salt and black pepper to taste

DIRECTIONS and total time: approx. 20 minutes

Heat olive oil on Sauté and sweat onion for 3 minutes. Add turkey and cook until no longer pink, 5 minutes. Stir in the remaining ingredients, except for heavy cream and basil. Seal the lid and cook for 8 minutes on Manual at High. When done, do a quick release. Stir in heavy cream and top with basil to serve.

Vegetable Lasagna with Mushrooms

INGREDIENTS for 4 servings

1 ¼ cups mushrooms, sliced	1 tsp red pepper flakes
3 cups pasta sauce	½ tsp dried oregano
1 tsp paprika	Salt and black pepper to taste
2 tsp dried basil	1 ½ cups half-and-half
1 cup grated mozzarella	6 lasagna sheets

DIRECTIONS and total time: approx. 40 minutes

Spread a layer of pasta sauce on the bottom of a greased baking dish. Cover with a layer of lasagna sheets. Spread some pasta sauce. Top with one layer each of half-and-half, cheese, mushrooms, and pasta sauce. Sprinkle with spices and herbs. Repeat the layering until you have used all ingredients finishing with cheese. Fit a trivet in your IP and pour in 1 cup water. Lower the baking dish onto trivet, seal the lid and cook for 25 minutes at High. Do a quick pressure release. Let lasagna rest for 10 minutes before serving.

Rotini with Beef & Monterey Jack Cheese

INGREDIENTS for 4 servings

1 lb ground beef	1 garlic clove, minced
2 spring onions, chopped	2 cups mild salsa
16 oz rotini pasta	1 tbsp tomato paste
2 tbsp butter	1 tbsp oregano
½ cup Monterey Jack, grated	Salt and black pepper to taste

DIRECTIONS and total time: approx. 20 minutes

Place the paste in the inner pot and cover with salted water. Seal the lid, and cook for 4 minutes on Manual at High. Release the pressure quickly. Drain and set aside. Clean the pot and melt butter on Sauté; cook spring onions and garlic for 3 minutes until soft. Add in beef and cook until browned for 5-6 minutes. Stir in salsa, tomato paste, oregano, salt, and pepper and cook for 15 minutes. Stir in pasta and remove to a serving plate. Sprinkle with Monterey Jack cheese and serve.

Penne with Sage & Pancetta

INGREDIENTS for 4 servings

16 oz penne pasta	1 tbsp olive oil
1 cup chopped onions	½ cup mozzarella, grated
1 cup diced pancetta	Salt to taste
1 cup dry white wine	2 tbsp chopped fresh sage

DIRECTIONS and total time: approx. 20 minutes

Fry pancetta on Sauté until brown and crispy, about 3 minutes; set aside. Add onions to the pot and sweat them for 3 minutes until soft. Stir in pasta, wine, and salt and cover with enough water. Seal the lid and cook for 6 minutes on Manual at High. When done, release the pressure quickly. Drain the pasta and transfer to a serving bowl. Stir in mozzarella cheese and pancetta. Drizzle with olive oil and serve topped with fresh sage.

Chicken with Farfalle & Enchilada Sauce

INGREDIENTS for 4 servings

2 chicken breasts, diced	1 garlic clove, minced
16 oz farfalle pasta	1 tsp taco seasoning
10 oz tomatoes, chopped	1 tbsp olive oil
20 oz canned enchilada sauce	2 cups Colby cheese, shredded
1 cup diced onions	Salt and black pepper to taste

DIRECTIONS and total time: approx. 20 minutes

Place farfalle in your IP and cover with salted water. Seal the lid, and cook for 4 minutes on Manual at High. Release the pressure quickly. Drain and set aside. Clean the pot and heat oil on Sauté. Cook chicken, onions and garlic for 5 minutes. Stir in tomatoes, enchilada sauce, 1 cup water, taco seasoning, salt, and pepper. Seal the lid and cook for 8 minutes on Manual at High. When ready, do a quick release. Mix in cheese and pasta and cook on Sauté for 2 minutes until the cheese melts. Serve.

Ziti Pasta with Pork Balls & Vegetables

INGREDIENTS for 4 servings

1 lb ground pork	2 cups broccoli florets
16 oz ziti pasta	2 bell peppers, chopped
2 tomatoes, chopped	1 red onion, chopped
1 cup chicken stock	½ tbsp basil
3 tsp olive oil	Salt and black pepper to taste

DIRECTIONS and total time: approx. 35 minutes

In your Instant Pot, cook ziti pasta in salted water for 4 minutes on Manual at High. Release the pressure quickly. Drain and set aside. Mix pork, salt, pepper, and basil, and shape the mixture into 4 meatballs. Wipe the pot clean and heat olive oil on Sauté. Cook the meatballs for 7-8 minutes on both sides until browned; reserve. Add onion, broccoli, and bell peppers to the pot and cook for 5 minutes until soft. Stir in tomatoes, stock, and the reserved meatballs. Seal the lid and cook for 6 minutes on Manual at High. When ready, do a quick pressure release. Mix in pasta and serve hot.

White Wine Pasta Bolognese

INGREDIENTS for 4 servings

2 tsp butter	2 tsp garlic, minced
16 oz tagliatelle	4 oz bacon, diced
1 lb mixed ground meat	½ cup white wine
1 lb tomato pasta sauce	1 cup half-and-half
1 tsp oregano	1 cup Parmesan, grated
1 cup onions, chopped	Salt and black pepper to taste

DIRECTIONS and total time: approx. 20 minutes

Melt the butter on Sauté and cook onions and garlic for 3 minutes, until soft and fragrant. Add meat and bacon and cook for 5-6 minutes. Stir in the remaining ingredients, except for the half-and-half and Parmesan cheese. Pour enough water to cover entirely. Seal the lid and cook for 10 minutes on Manual at High. When ready, do a quick release. Stir in heavy cream and serve with grated Parmesan cheese.

Tuna & Artichoke Egg Noodles

INGREDIENTS for 2 servings

8 oz egg noodles	1 tbsp olive oil
1 can diced tomatoes	1 tsp parsley
1 can tuna flakes, drained	1 tbsp sage
½ cup red onions, chopped	½ cup goat cheese, crumbled
7 ½ oz canned artichoke hearts	Salt and black pepper to taste

DIRECTIONS and total time: approx. 15 minutes

Heat olive oil on Sauté and sweat onions for 3 minutes until translucent. Stir in the remaining ingredients, except for goat cheese. Pour in 2 cups water, seal the lid and cook for 5 minutes at High. When done, release the pressure quickly. Stir in the goat cheese and serve.

Zucchini & Beef Lasagna

INGREDIENTS for 4 servings

12 lasagna sheets	2 large zucchini, chopped
1 (14 oz) tomato sauce	2 tbsp vegetable oil
1 red onion, sliced	¼ cup fresh basil leaves
1 lb ground beef, cooked	Salt and black pepper to taste
1 bell pepper, sliced	1 cup grated Parmesan

DIRECTIONS and total time: approx. 45 minutes

Set on Sauté and heat vegetable oil. Add beef, bell pepper, zucchini, and onion and cook for 5 minutes. Season with salt and pepper. Cover the bottom of a greased baking dish with half of the lasagna sheets. Spread half of tomato sauce on top and make a layer with half of the beef mixture and half of basil leaves. Sprinkle with some Parmesan cheese. Make a second layer in the same order. Pour 1 cup of water in the pot and fit in a trivet. Put the dish on top, seal the lid, select Manual at High, and cook for 25 minutes. When off, do a natural pressure release for 10 minutes. Serve warm.

Kale Pesto Tagliatelle with Green Beans

INGREDIENTS for 4 servings

16 oz tagliatelle	½ tbsp lemon juice
6 oz green beans, chopped	¼ cup grated Parmesan
Salt to taste	½ cup olive oil
½ lb baby kale	1 onion, chopped
2 tbsp basil leaves, chopped	¼ cup pine nuts, toasted

DIRECTIONS and total time: approx. 10 minutes

In your Instant Pot, place tagliatelle and green beans and cover with salted water. Seal the lid, select Manual, and cook for 4 minutes at High. When ready, do a quick pressure release. Drain and remove to a bowl. Blend kale, basil, pine nuts, Parmesan cheese, and lemon juice in a food processor until finely chopped. While the blender is running, gradually add olive oil until well mixed; season with salt. Pour pesto over the pasta and beans; toss to coat. Serve immediately.

Traditional Italian Peperonata

INGREDIENTS for 4 servings

1 green bell pepper, sliced	2 garlic cloves, minced
2 yellow bell peppers, sliced	2 cups veggie stock
2 red bell peppers, sliced	2 tbsp olive oil
3 tomatoes, chopped	Salt and black pepper to taste
1 red onion, chopped	4 cup egg noodles, cooked

DIRECTIONS and total time: approx. 20 minutes

Heat olive oil on Sauté and cook onion, garlic, and bell peppers for 4 minutes until tender. Stir in tomatoes, pour in stock, seal the lid, and cook for 4 minutes on Manual at High. When done, do a quick pressure release. Serve over egg noodles and enjoy!

Sausage with Fusilli Pasta & Cheese

INGREDIENTS for 6 servings

18 oz fusilli pasta	2 tsp garlic, minced
16 oz sausages	1 tsp parsley, chopped
2 cups tomato sauce	¼ cup Pecorino Romano, grated
3 tbsp olive oil	

DIRECTIONS and total time: approx. 20 minutes

Heat olive oil on Sauté, and cook the sausages until browned, while crumbling, for 5 minutes. Add garlic and cook for 1 minute. Stir in the remaining ingredients, except for Pecorino cheese and parsley. Cover with water, seal the lid and cook for 4 minutes on Manual at High. When done, release the pressure quickly. Top with Pecorino cheese and sprinkle with parsley.

Dill Mackerel & Pasta Stew

INGREDIENTS for 4 servings

2 green onions, diced	14 oz marinara sauce
2 tbsp olive oil	1 lb mackerel, chopped
½ cup chicken broth	1 garlic clove, minced
1 cup clam juice	2 tbsp chopped dill
1 lb macaroni	Salt and black pepper to taste

DIRECTIONS and total time: approx. 30 minutes

Heat half of the olive oil on Sauté. Add mackerel, green onions, and garlic, and cook for 3-4 minutes. Pour in chicken broth to deglaze the bottom of the pot. Stir in marinara sauce, macaroni, 2 cups of water, and clam juice. Seal the lid, select Manual, and set the cooking time to 5 minutes at High. When ready, do a quick pressure release. Top with dill and serve in bowls.

Ramen Noodles with Beef Meatballs

INGREDIENTS for 6 servings

10 oz ramen noodles	1 yellow onion, grated
Salt and black pepper to taste	1 egg
1 lb ground beef	½ cup soy sauce
¼ cup breadcrumbs	1 garlic clove, minced

DIRECTIONS and total time: approx. 35 minutes

Combine beef, breadcrumbs, garlic, onion, and egg in a bowl. Mix and shape the mixture into 6 meatballs. Add soy sauce and meatballs to the inner pot. Pour enough water to cover. Seal the lid and cook on Manual at High for 15 minutes. When ready, do a quick pressure release. Stir in noodles and press Sauté. Cook for 4 minutes until tender. Divide between bowls and serve.

Penne with Mixed Peppers & Beans

INGREDIENTS for 4 servings

16 oz dried penne	2 tbsp olive oil
Salt and black pepper to taste	1 onion, chopped
2 garlic cloves, minced	1 tsp cumin powder
2 mixed bell peppers, chopped	1 tsp coriander powder
1 habanero pepper, chopped	1 (14 oz) canned white beans
1 (14 oz) can tomatoes	2 tbsp chopped parsley

DIRECTIONS and total time: approx. 25 minutes

In your Instant Pot, add penne and cover with salted water. Seal the lid, and cook on Manual for 4 minutes at High. When ready, do a quick pressure release and drain pasta; set aside. Press Sauté and heat olive oil. Cook onion and garlic for 3 minutes. Add bell peppers, habanero, tomatoes, cumin, beans, coriander, salt, and pepper. Seal the lid, select Manual, and cook for 8 minutes at High. When ready, do a natural release for 10 minutes. Stir in pasta. Serve topped with parsley.

Pork with Brown Rice

INGREDIENTS for 4 servings

1 lb pork loin, cubed	1 cup brown rice, cooked
2 tbsp olive oil	1 onion, chopped
Salt and black pepper to taste	1 tsp Italian seasoning
2 cups chicken broth	2 tbsp parsley, chopped

DIRECTIONS and total time: approx. 45 minutes

On Sauté, heat the olive oil. Cook onion and pork for 5 minutes. Stir in rice, Italian seasoning, parsley, salt and pepper, and cook for 2 minutes. Pour in broth, seal the lid, select Manual at High, and cook for 20 minutes. When done, release the pressure quickly.

Meatless Mexican Rice

INGREDIENTS for 2 servings

1 tbsp olive oil	½ cup tomato puree
2 green onions, chopped	2 garlic cloves, minced
½ cup rice	2 tbsp ground coriander
1 cup vegetable broth	Salt and pepper, to taste

DIRECTIONS and total time: approx. 10 minutes

Heat oil on Sauté and sweat onions for 3 minutes. Stir in the remaining ingredients. Seal the lid and press Manual for 3 minutes at High. After, do a quick release.

Apricot Wild Rice Pudding

INGREDIENTS for 4 servings

1 cup wild rice	½ tsp vanilla extract
2 tbsp maple syrup	¼ tsp grated nutmeg
¼ cup dried apricots, chopped	½ tsp cinnamon
1 ½ cups milk	Fresh raspberries to serve

DIRECTIONS and total time: approx. 25 minutes

Combine all ingredients in your Instant Pot. Pour in 2 cups of water. Seal the lid and cook on Manual for 15 minutes at High. Do a quick pressure release. Let chill for a few minutes and serve decorated with raspberries.

Burgundy Beef Rice Stew

INGREDIENTS for 4 servings

1 cup beef broth	3 tbsp tomato paste
2 tbsp olive oil	Salt and black pepper to taste
2 lb beef round steak, cubed	1 cup basmati rice
1 cup onion, chopped	½ cup sour cream
1 tsp horseradish sauce	½ tsp dried thyme leaves
1 cup mushrooms, sliced	1 bay leaf
1 cup Burgundy red wine	2 cloves garlic, minced

DIRECTIONS and total time: approx. 33 minutes

Add rice and 2 cups water in the inner pot and season with salt and pepper. Seal the lid and set on Manual for 6 minutes at High. When done, release the pressure quickly. Remove the rice to a bowl. Clean the pot and heat oil on Sauté. Add beef, onion, mushrooms, tomato paste, garlic, thyme, salt, and pepper; cook for 5 minutes. Pour in broth, wine and bay leaf. Seal the lid, set to Manual at High, and cook for 15 minutes. When done, do a quick release. Discard bay leaf and stir in sour cream and horseradish sauce. Serve over a bed of rice.

Risotto with Green Peas & Mushrooms

INGREDIENTS for 4 servings

2 tbsp butter	¾ cup white wine
2 cups Bella mushrooms, sliced	2 cups vegetable broth
1 cup onion, chopped	Salt and black pepper to taste
2 garlic cloves, minced	½ cup grated Parmesan
1 sprig rosemary, chopped	½ cup green peas
1 ½ cups Arborio rice	1 tbsp chopped parsley

DIRECTIONS and total time: approx. 15 minutes

On Sauté, melt the butter. Stir-fry mushrooms, onion, garlic, and rosemary for 5 minutes. Stir in rice, wine, and broth, and season with salt and pepper. Seal the lid, select Manual at High, and cook for 8 minutes. Once off, do a quick release. Stir in green peas and Parmesan until the cheese melts. Sprinkle with parsley to serve.

Chili Rice with Vegetables

INGREDIENTS for 4 servings

2 tbsp butter	2 cups water
2 white onions, thinly sliced	1 orange, zested and juiced
½ tsp cumin powder	¾ cup raisins
½ tsp cinnamon powder	1 cup basmati rice
1 tsp chili powder	¾ cup hazelnuts

DIRECTIONS and total time: approx. 25 minutes

On Sauté mode, melt the butter and cook onions until softened, 3 minutes. Stir in cumin, cinnamon, chili, salt, and pepper for 30 seconds and pour in water, orange zest, juice, raisins, and rice. Seal the lid, select Rice, and cook for 12 minutes. When ready, do a quick pressure release. Stir in hazelnuts and serve.

Beef & Rice Stuffed Cabbage Leaves

INGREDIENTS for 4 servings

1 lb lean ground beef	8 cabbage leaves, blanched
1 (14-oz) can tomatoes, diced	Salt and black pepper to taste
1 cup tomato sauce	½ cup green bell peppers, diced
1 cup rice	1 onion, chopped

DIRECTIONS and total time: approx. 40 minutes

Mix ground beef with bell peppers, rice, onion, salt, and pepper. Shape the mixture into 8 equal parts. Wrap each part in a cabbage leaf, folding the ends and sides. In a bowl, mix 1 cup water, tomato sauce, and tomatoes. Lay the cabbage rolls on the bottom of your Instant Pot's inner pot. Pour the tomato mixture over and seal the lid. Select Manual and cook for 20 minutes at High. When ready, do a pressure release, and serve.

Saucy Basmati Rice

INGREDIENTS for 4 servings

1 cup basmati rice	2 tsp olive oil
1 celery stalk, chopped	2 tbsp parsley, chopped
2 spring onions, sliced	Salt and black pepper to taste
1 carrot, chopped	2 cups stock

DIRECTIONS and total time: approx. 20 minutes

On Sauté, heat the olive oil. Cook spring onions, celery, and carrot for 2-3 minutes. Add in the remaining ingredients, except for parsley. Press Manual and cook for 10 minutes at High. When ready, do a quick release. Fluff the rice with a fork and serve topped with parsley.

Chicken with Carrot & Brown Rice

INGREDIENTS for 4 servings

1 cup brown rice	1 bell pepper, chopped
2 chicken breasts, diced	2 tbsp olive oil
1 carrot, chopped	2 cups chicken broth
2 garlic cloves, minced	1 tsp rosemary
1 onion, chopped	Salt and black pepper to taste

DIRECTIONS and total time: approx. 45 minutes

Heat olive oil on Sauté and stir-fry onion, garlic, and bell pepper for 3-4 minutes until tender. Stir in the remaining ingredients, seal the lid and cook for 20 minutes on Manual at High. When ready, do a quick pressure release. Serve warm or slightly chilled.

Swiss Chard, Zucchini & Mushroom Rice

INGREDIENTS for 4 servings

1 cup mushrooms, sliced	1 shallot, chopped
1 cup Swiss chard, chopped	2 garlic cloves, minced
1 cup rice	2 tbsp olive oil
1 zucchini, sliced	2 cups chicken stock
½ cup Grana Padano, shredded	Salt and black pepper to taste

DIRECTIONS and total time: approx. 20 minutes

Heat olive oil on Sauté, and cook shallot and garlic for 3 minutes. Add mushrooms and zucchini; cook for 3 more minutes until soft. Pour in chicken broth and rice. Seal lid, and cook for 8 minutes on Manual at High. When ready, do a quick release. Stir in Swiss chard for 3 minutes. Serve topped with Grana Padano cheese.

Rosemary Salmon Soup with Rice

INGREDIENTS for 6 servings

6 cups fish stock	Salt and cayenne pepper to taste
1 tbsp olive oil	½ lb salmon steaks, cubed
2 garlic cloves, minced	½ cup brown rice
½ tsp mustard powder	1 cup mushrooms, sliced
½ tsp dry rosemary	½ celery stalk, sliced
2 slices bacon, chopped	1 onion, chopped

DIRECTIONS and total time: approx. 50 minutes

On Sauté, cook the bacon for 5 minutes; reserve. Add olive oil to the pot and sauté garlic, onion, celery, and mushrooms for 4 minutes. Stir in stock, mustard powder, rosemary, salmon, rice, salt and cayenne pepper. Seal the lid, select Manual at High, and cook for 20 minutes. When ready, do a natural pressure release for 10 minutes. Serve warm, topped with bacon.

Cheesy Shrimp Risotto

INGREDIENTS for 4 servings

1 lb shrimp, deveined	2 garlic cloves, minced
1 cup arborio rice	2 shallots, chopped
2 tbsp olive oil	¼ cup white wine
2 tbsp butter	Salt and black pepper to taste
3 cups fish stock	1 cup Parmesan, shredded

DIRECTIONS and total time: approx. 20 minutes

Heat oil on Sauté and cook shallots and garlic for 3 minutes. Add shrimp and cook for 3 minutes. Stir in the remaining ingredients and seal the lid. Cook for 8 minutes on Manual at High. When ready, do a quick pressure release. Serve topped with Parmesan cheese.

Basmati Rice with Pumpkin

INGREDIENTS for 4 servings

1 tbsp olive oil	1 tsp turmeric powder
1 yellow onion, chopped	Salt and black pepper to taste
½ lb pumpkin, chopped	½ cup cashews, toasted
1 cup basmati rice	Chopped cilantro to garnish

DIRECTIONS and total time: approx. 20 minutes

Press Sauté and heat olive oil. Cook onion and pumpkin for 6 minutes. Stir in rice, turmeric, salt, pepper, and 2 cups of water. Seal the lid, select Manual, and cook for 6 minutes. When ready, do a quick pressure release, fluff the rice. Top with cilantro and cashews to serve.

Chicken & Veggie Gumbo

INGREDIENTS for 4 servings

2 tbsp olive oil	1 cup rice
1 carrot, diced	2 red chilies, chopped
1 yellow onion, chopped	2 cups vegetable stock
2 garlic cloves, minced	½ cup baby okras
1 celery stick, chopped	Salt and black pepper to taste
1 green bell pepper, chopped	3 tbsp chopped cilantro
2 tbsp tomato puree	½ chicken breast, chopped

DIRECTIONS and total time: approx. 15 minutes

Select Sauté and heat olive oil. Cook chicken, carrot, onion, garlic, celery, and bell pepper for 5 minutes. Stir in tomato puree. Add rice, red chilies, stock, and baby okras; season with salt and black pepper. Seal the lid, select Manual, and cook for 8 minutes at High. Once done, do a natural pressure release for 10 minutes. Fluff Gumbo with a fork and stir in cilantro. Serve warm.

Wild Rice with Three-Color Bell Peppers

INGREDIENTS for 6 servings

2 cups wild rice	2 tomatoes, chopped
4 cups veggie broth	1 red onion, chopped
½ cup carrots, chopped	3 tsp olive oil
1 red bell pepper, chopped	1 tbsp rosemary, chopped
1 yellow bell pepper, chopped	1 cup green peas
1 green bell pepper, chopped	Salt and black pepper to taste

DIRECTIONS and total time: approx. 30 minutes

Heat oil on Sauté and cook onion for 3 minutes. Add carrots and bell peppers and cook for 2 more minutes. Stir in the remaining ingredients, except for green peas and rosemary. Seal the lid and cook for 8 minutes Manual at High. When ready, do a quick pressure release. Stir in green peas and cook on Sauté for 5 minutes. Serve hot topped with rosemary.

Cheesy Porcini Mushroom Risotto

INGREDIENTS for 4 servings

½ cup grated Pecorino Romano cheese, reserve some	
1 cup Arborio rice	2 cups chicken stock
½ cup porcini mushrooms	2 tbsp butter
1 carrot, chopped	Salt and black pepper to taste
1 onion, chopped	2 tbsp heavy cream
2 garlic cloves, minced	2 tbsp parsley, chopped

DIRECTIONS and total time: approx. 20 minutes

Melt butter on Sauté and cook onion, garlic, carrot, salt, and pepper for 3 minutes until soft and fragrant. Slice mushrooms and add them along with rice and chicken stock to the pot. Seal the lid and cook for 8 minutes on Manual at High. When ready, do a quick pressure release. Stir in heavy cream. Serve sprinkled with reserved Pecorino Romano cheese and parsley.

Simple Celery Jasmine Rice

INGREDIENTS for 4 servings

1 cup jasmine rice	2 cups chicken stock
1 celery stalk, chopped	1 tsp sage
2 spring onions, chopped	1 tbsp rosemary
1 parsnip, chopped	2 tbsp olive oil
1 carrot, chopped	Salt and black pepper to taste

DIRECTIONS and total time: approx. 25 minutes

Heat olive oil on Sauté and cook spring onions until soft, 3 minutes. Add parsnip, carrot, and celery and cook for 2 minutes. Stir in the remaining ingredients. Seal the lid and cook for 10 minutes on Manual at High. When ready, do a quick pressure release. Serve.

Arroz con Leche with Prunes

INGREDIENTS for 6 servings

2 cups white rice	3 tsp olive oil
½ cup prunes, chopped	¼ tsp ground cinnamon
2 eggs + 1 egg yolk	½ tbsp vanilla extract
8 oz milk	¼ tsp kosher salt
¼ cup sugar	¼ tsp ground cardamom

DIRECTIONS and total time: approx. 20 minutes

Add olive oil, 1 cup water, milk, rice, sugar, cinnamon, vanilla, salt, and cardamom in the inner pot. Seal the lid, press Manual and cook for 8 minutes at High. Once ready, do a quick pressure release. Add the whisked eggs and prunes, stirring constantly. Select Sauté and cook until the mixture boils. Let cool before serving.

Date & Almond Rice Pudding

INGREDIENTS for 3 servings

1 cup rice	½ tsp anise seed
4 tbsp almonds, chopped	1 cup milk
1 tsp vanilla paste	¼ cup sugar
1 egg plus 1 yolk	½ tsp almond extract
½ cup dates	

DIRECTIONS and total time: approx. 35 minutes

Pour 1½ cups of water in your IP and lower a trivet. Mix together all ingredients in a baking dish. Place the dish on top of trivet and cover with foil. Seal the lid and cook on Manual for 25 minutes at High. When done, release the pressure quickly. Serve chilled.

Chorizo & Cheese Rice

INGREDIENTS for 4 servings

1 tbsp vegetable oil	2 cups vegetable stock
4 chorizo sausages, sliced	2 bell peppers, sliced
2 garlic cloves, crushed	1 cup rice
½ cup tamari sauce	1 cup Monterey Jack, grated
2 shallots, chopped	Salt and black pepper to taste

DIRECTIONS and total time: approx. 30 minutes

Heat oil on Sauté and cook garlic and shallots for 3 minutes. Stir in chorizo and cook for 5 minutes. Add in the remaining ingredients, except for the cheese. Seal the lid, select Manual, and cook for 15 minutes at High. Once ready, do a quick release. Serve topped with Monterey Jack cheese.

Sweet Rice Pudding with Hazelnuts

INGREDIENTS for 4 servings

1 cup jasmine rice, rinsed	¼ cup honey
4 cups milk	½ cup raisins
½ tsp nutmeg powder	¼ cup hazelnuts, chopped
1 tsp vanilla extract	

DIRECTIONS and total time: approx. 15 minutes

In your Instant Pot, pour rice, milk, nutmeg, vanilla extract, and honey. Seal the lid, select Manual, and cook for 5 minutes at High. When done, do a quick pressure release. Stir in the raisins for a few minutes. Plate the pudding in cups topped with hazelnuts.

Sausage Pilaf with Sun-Dried Tomatoes

INGREDIENTS for 4 servings

2 tbsp butter	½ cup white wine
3 garlic cloves, minced	Salt and black pepper to taste
1 white onion, chopped	½ cup grated cheddar cheese
1 cup rice	¼ cup heavy cream
6 sun-dried tomatoes, minced	1 cup chopped sausages
1 ½ cups vegetable broth	2 tbsp dried basil

DIRECTIONS and total time: approx. 15 minutes

On Sauté, melt butter and cook sausages, garlic, and onion for 3 minutes. Stir in rice and tomatoes; cook for 3 minutes. Pour in broth, wine, salt, and pepper. Seal the lid, select Manual, and cook for 8 minutes at High. When done, do a quick pressure release. Stir in heavy cream. Top with cheddar cheese and basil to serve.

Spanish Rice with Chicken Legs

INGREDIENTS for 4 servings

2 tbsp olive oil	1 cup yellow Spanish rice
1 lb chicken legs	2 tomatoes, chopped
½ red bell pepper, diced	¼ cup dry white wine
1 onion, chopped	3 garlic cloves, minced
1 tsp paprika	Salt and black pepper to taste
1 cup green peas	2 cups chicken broth

DIRECTIONS and total time: approx. 15 minutes

Heat olive oil on Sauté and cook chicken, garlic, bell pepper, and onion for 3 minutes. Stir in paprika, rice, tomatoes, peas, salt, and pepper, and pour in wine and broth. Seal the lid, select Manual, and cook for 8 minutes at High. When ready, do a quick release. Serve.

Fish & Seafood

Creamy Shrimp Risotto

INGREDIENTS for 4 servings

2 garlic cloves, minced	1 cup brown Arborio rice
1 egg, beaten	¼ cup white wine
½ tsp ginger, grated	1 chopped onion
2 tbsp canola oil	12 oz peeled shrimp
1 tbsp butter	3 tbsp whipping cream
¼ tsp chili powder	2 tbs Pecorino Romano, grated
1 cup frozen peas	Salt and black pepper to taste

DIRECTIONS and total time: approx. 30 minutes

Warm oil and scramble the egg, stirring constantly, about 4-5 minutes on Sauté. Transfer to a plate. Melt butter and cook onion and garlic for 4 minutes until translucent. Stir in rice, ginger, chili powder, wine, 2 cups of water, salt and pepper. Seal the lid, cook on Manual for 10 minutes at High. Once ready, do a quick release. Stir in shrimp and peas for 4-5 minutes then mix in Pecorino Romano cheese, whipping cream, and egg and let them heat for 30 seconds on Sauté. Serve.

Healthy Salmon with Broccoli

INGREDIENTS for 2 servings

2 salmon fillets	2 tsp sesame oil
4 new potatoes	½ tsp dill
1 cup broccoli florets	Salt and black pepper to taste

DIRECTIONS and total time: approx. 15 minutes

Pour 1 cup of water and lower a steamer basket in your Instant Pot. Season potatoes with salt and pepper, and place them in the basket. Drizzle with half of the sesame oil. Seal the lid, select Manual, and cook for 2 minutes at High. When done, release the pressure quickly. Add broccoli to the basket. Sprinkle salmon with dill, salt, and pepper and arrange on top of the veggies. Drizzle with the remaining oil. Seal the lid and cook on Steam for 3 minutes at High. Serve hot.

Carrot & Onion Crabmeat

INGREDIENTS for 4 servings

¼ cup butter	½ cup half-and-half
1 small red onion, chopped	1 cup chicken broth
1 lb lump crabmeat	Salt and black pepper to taste
½ carrot, chopped	2 tbsp parsley

DIRECTIONS and total time: approx. 20 minutes

Melt butter on Sauté and cook onion and carrot for 3 minutes. Place in crabmeat and stir in broth and half-and-half. Seal the lid, set to Manual for 10 minutes at High. Once ready, do a quick pressure release. Season with salt and pepper, and serve topped with parsley.

Prawn & Tuna Skewers with Soy Sauce

INGREDIENTS for 4 servings

1 packet dry ranch dressing mix	1 lb king prawns, deveined
	Salt and black pepper to taste
1 red bell pepper, cut into 2-inch pieces	1 onion, cut into wedges
	1 chili pepper, chopped
1 lb tuna fillets, cubed	1 tsp soy sauce

DIRECTIONS and total time: approx. 20 minutes

In a large bowl, mix fish and prawns, and season with salt and pepper. Use wooden skewers to prick the fish and prawns by separating them with bell pepper and onion pieces. In your IP, mix 1 cup of water with ranch dressing mix, chili pepper, and soy sauce and stir until the dressing mix dissolves. Fit a trivet in the IP. Lay the skewers over the trivet crosswise. Seal the lid, set to Manual for 4 minutes at High. When done, do a quick release. Serve skewers drizzled with cooking juices.

Traditional Catfish Chowder

INGREDIENTS for 4 servings

1 tbsp cornstarch	1 diced onion
2 tbsp olive oil	Salt and black pepper to taste
1 cup milk	½ tsp hot sauce
2 potatoes, chopped	½ celery stalk, chopped
½ lb catfish, chopped	½ tsp dried oregano
3 cups chicken stock	¼ cup fresh parsley, chopped

DIRECTIONS and total time: approx. 25 minutes

Heat olive oil on Sauté and cook onion and celery for 3 minutes. Add in catfish, potatoes, hot sauce, oregano, stock, milk, salt, and pepper. Seal the lid, select Manual, and set the timer to 10 minutes at High. When the timer goes off, do a quick pressure release. In a bowl, stir cornstarch with ½ cup of the cooking liquid until well combined, and pour in the pot. Select Sauté and cook for about 5 minutes until the soup thickens. Serve hot.

Herby Clams in White Wine

INGREDIENTS for 4 servings

¼ cup white wine	2 tbsp olive oil
2 cups veggie broth	2 lb clams
1 tbsp tarragon, chopped	2 tbsp lemon juice
2 tbsp parsley, chopped	2 garlic cloves, minced

DIRECTIONS and total time: approx. 20 minutes

Heat olive oil on Sauté and cook garlic for 1 minute until fragrant. Pour in wine, broth, tarragon, and lemon juice. Bring to a boil and cook for 1 minute. Fit in a steamer basket and place the clams inside. Seal the lid, set to Steam, and cook for 6 minutes at High. When done, release the pressure quickly. Remove the clams to a bowl, discard the closed ones. Drizzle with the cooking juices and sprinkle with fresh parsley to serve.

Mediterranean Cod

INGREDIENTS for 4 servings

4 cod fillets
4 tomatoes
1 tbsp olive oil
Salt and black pepper to taste
10 olives stuffed with anchovies
¼ cup capers

DIRECTIONS and total time: approx. 20 minutes

Place the tomatoes in a baking dish and crush them with a fork. Sprinkle with salt and pepper. Season the cod fillets with salt and pepper and place them over the tomatoes, and drizzle with olive oil. Pour 1 cup water in the pot and insert a trivet. Place the dish on the trivet. Seal the lid and cook on Manual for 5 minutes at High. When ready, release the pressure naturally for 10 minutes. Serve topped with olives and capers.

Sunday Crab Legs with White Wine

INGREDIENTS for 4 servings

1 ½ lb crab legs
2 tbsp butter, melted
1 cup veggie broth
½ cup white wine
1 tsp chopped parsley
½ tsp lemon juice
Salt and black pepper to taste

DIRECTIONS and total time: approx. 15 minutes

Pour broth and wine in the pot. Fit a steamer basket, and add in the crab. Seal the lid and cook for 5 minutes on Manual at High. When done, do a quick release. Serve drizzled with butter, parsley and lemon juice.

Gruyère Cheese & Lobster Pasta

INGREDIENTS for 4 servings

8 oz dried ziti pasta
1 cup whipping cream
1 tbsp tarragon, chopped
¾ cup Gruyère cheese, grated
4 lobster tails, 6 oz each
½ cup white wine
Salt and black pepper to taste
1 tbsp Worcestershire sauce

DIRECTIONS and total time: approx. 20 minutes

Pour 6 cups water in the pot, and add lobster and ziti. Seal the lid, cook on Manual for 4 minutes at High. Once ready, do a quick release. Drain and separate the pasta in a bowl. Remove the meat from the tails, chop it, and stir in the pasta bowl. In the pot, mix the rest of the ingredients, press Sauté, and cook until the sauce thickens, about 3 minutes. Stir in pasta and lobster.

Best Crab Patties

INGREDIENTS for 2 servings

1 cup crab meat
¼ cup black olives, chopped
½ carrot, shredded
½ cup potato mash
¼ cup flour
¼ cup onions, grated
1 cup tomato sauce
½ lime, juiced
1 tsp cayenne pepper
2 tbsp olive oil
½ cup chicken broth
Salt and black pepper to taste

DIRECTIONS and total time: approx. 15 minutes

Place crab meat, carrot, olives, flour, mash, lime juice, cayenne, onions, salt, and pepper in a bowl. Mix until incorporated, and shape into 2 patties. Heat olive oil on Sauté. Add the crab cakes and cook for 2-3 minutes, in total. Pour in broth and tomatoes, and seal the lid. Select Manual and set to 2 minutes at High. When the timer goes off, do a quick pressure release. Serve hot.

Egg Noodles with Tuna & Peas

INGREDIENTS for 4 servings

1 can tuna, drained
4 oz Monterey cheese, grated
16 oz egg noodles
¼ cup breadcrumbs
1 cup frozen peas
10 oz canned mushroom soup
Salt and black pepper to taste
¼ cup milk

DIRECTIONS and total time: approx. 15 minutes

Place noodles in your IP and cover with water. Seal the lid and cook for 4 minutes on Manual at High. When ready, do a quick pressure release. Transfer to a baking dish and mix in tuna, cheese, peas, soup, milk, salt, and pepper. Sprinkle with breadcrumbs. Insert a trivet and pour 1 cup of water in the pot. Put the dish on top, seal the lid, and cook 3 minutes on Steam at High. Serve.

Parsley Haddock with Potatoes

INGREDIENTS for 4 servings

4 haddock fillets
4 sage sprigs, chopped
2 potatoes, sliced
1 lemon, sliced
1 onion, sliced
A handful of fresh parsley
Salt and black pepper to taste
2 tbsp olive oil

DIRECTIONS and total time: approx. 15 minutes

Divide haddock fillets, potatoes, sage, parsley, onion, and lemon between 4 parchment papers. Drizzle each one with ½ tbsp of olive oil and mix to coat. Wrap the fish with the paper. Wrap each of the 'packets' in foil. Pour 1 cup of water in your IP and insert a trivet. Place the packets on top. Seal the lid and cook for 5 minutes on Manual at High. When ready, do a quick release.

Ginger Lime Salmon

INGREDIENTS for 4 servings

1 ½ lb salmon side
1 lime, sliced into rounds
1 tbsp olive oil
1 tsp ginger, minced
Salt and black pepper to taste
2 tbsp dill, chopped

DIRECTIONS and total time: approx. 15 minutes

Pour 1 cup water in your IP and fit in a trivet. Place salmon, skin side down on the trivet. Rub with ginger, salt, pepper, and olive oil. Top with lime slices. Seal the lid and cook on Manual for 4 minutes at High. Release the pressure quickly. Scatter with dill to serve.

Tasty Trout with Spiralized Vegetables

INGREDIENTS for 4 servings

4 trout fillets
2 tbsp olive oil
1 large carrot, spiralized
2 potatoes, spiralized
1 zucchini, spiralized

1 thyme sprig
2 garlic cloves, minced
2 tbsp fresh parsley, chopped
Salt and black pepper to taste
1 lemon, cut into wedges

DIRECTIONS and total time: approx. 15 minutes

Pour 1 cup of water and add thyme sprig to your IP. Insert a steamer basket. Place the spiralized veggies in the basket and top with the trout fillets. Season with garlic, salt, and pepper, and drizzle with olive oil. Seal the lid, press Manual, and cook for 7 minutes at High. When the timer goes off, do a quick pressure release. Sprinkle with parsley and serve with lemon wedges.

Drunken Mussels

INGREDIENTS for 4 servings

1 onion, chopped
2 lb mussels, cleaned
1 cup white wine
1 garlic clove, crushed

Juice of 1 lemon
1 tsp oregano
Salt and black pepper to taste
2 tbsp butter

DIRECTIONS and total time: approx. 30 minutes

Melt butter on Sauté and stir-fry onion and garlic for 3 minutes, until soft. Add oregano, lemon juice, white wine, salt, and pepper; cook for 1 minute. Pour in 1 cup water and mussels, and seal the lid. Cook for 3 minutes on Manual at High. When ready, let the pressure drop naturally for 10 minutes. Arrange mussels on a serving platter, spoon cooking juices over and serve warm.

Nut Crusted Tilapia

INGREDIENTS for 4 servings

4 tilapia fillets
⅔ cup cashews, crushed
2 tbsp Dijon mustard

1 tsp olive oil
Salt and black pepper to taste
1 tbsp basil

DIRECTIONS and total time: approx. 15 minutes

Pour 1 cup of water in your IP and fit in a trivet. Mix olive oil, salt, pepper, basil, and mustard in a bowl. Brush the fillets with the mustard mixture on all sides. Coat the fish in cashews. Arrange the fillets on top of the trivet, seal the lid, select Manual, and cook for 10 minutes at High. When ready, do a quick release.

Smoked Paprika Squid with Green Beans

INGREDIENTS for 4 servings

2 tbsp olive oil
1 lb squid, chopped
1 lb green beans
2 green onions, chopped

2 cups canned tomatoes
½ cup white wine
Salt and black pepper to taste
2 tsp smoked paprika

DIRECTIONS and total time: approx. 45 minutes

Heat olive oil on Sauté, and cook green onions for 3 minutes until soft. Add squid and cook for another 3 minutes, stirring occasionally. Stir in smoked paprika for a minute. Add in white wine to scrape off any browned bits from the bottom of the pot. Let simmer until the wine reduces by half, then add the remaining ingredients. Cover with water and seal the lid. Cook on Manual at High for 20 minutes. Once ready, do a natural pressure release for 10 minutes. Serve hot.

Rosemary Salmon with Spinach

INGREDIENTS for 4 servings

4 salmon fillets
2 tbsp olive oil
2 tbsp rosemary

1 cup cherry tomatoes, halved
15 oz spinach
Salt and black pepper to taste

DIRECTIONS and total time: approx. 15 minutes

Pour 1 cup of water and insert a trivet in your IP. Place salmon on top, sprinkle with rosemary, and arrange the spinach over the fillets. Seal the lid and cook on Steam for 3 minutes at High. Do a quick release. Remove to a platter and cover with cherry tomatoes. Season with salt and pepper, and drizzle with olive oil. Serve warm.

Simple Basil & Haddock with Capers

INGREDIENTS for 4 servings

1 lb haddock fillets
2 tbsp olive oil
1 lemon, juiced

2 tbsp capers
2 tbsp basil, chopped
Salt and black pepper to taste

DIRECTIONS and total time: approx. 25 minutes

Pour 1 cup of water in your IP and insert a trivet. Place fillets on the trivet. Season with salt and pepper, and drizzle with olive oil. Seal the lid, select Manual, and cook for 4 minutes at High. When done, release the pressure naturally for 10 minutes. In a bowl, mix capers with lemon juice. Pour over the fish and top with basil.

Clams a la Marinera

INGREDIENTS for 4 servings

28 scrubbed clams
1 ½ cups fish broth
2 tbsp olive oil
1 onion, chopped
1 cup basmati rice, rinsed

2 garlic cloves, minced
½ cup sherry white wine
3 tbsp lemon juice
1 tsp fresh parsley, chopped
Salt and black pepper to taste

DIRECTIONS and total time: approx. 10 minutes

Heat olive oil on Sauté and stir-fry garlic and onion for 3 minutes. Stir in rice for 1 minute. Add in wine, broth, and lemon juice; season. Seal the lid, set to Manual for 6 minutes at High. Release the pressure quickly; discard closed clams. Sprinkle with parsley to serve.

Salmon with Parsley-Lemon Sauce

INGREDIENTS for 4 servings

4 salmon fillets	1 tsp chipotle powder
1 tbsp honey	1 tbsp chopped fresh parsley
½ tsp cumin	¼ cup lemon juice
1 tbsp olive oil	Salt and black pepper to taste
1 small shallot, chopped	

DIRECTIONS and total time: approx. 15 minutes

Pour 1 cup water in your IP and fit in a trivet. Arrange the salmon fillets, skin side down on a greased baking dish and season with salt and pepper. Place the dish on the trivet. Seal the lid and cook for 3 minutes on Manual at High. Whisk together the remaining ingredients, except for parsley, with 1 tbsp hot water to form a sauce. Once cooking is over, release the pressure quickly, and drizzle the sauce over the salmon. Seal the lid again, and cook for 3 more minutes on Manual at High. Do a quick release and serve with parsley.

Salmon Loaf with Cucumber Sauce

INGREDIENTS for 4 servings

1 can (15-oz) salmon, drained	Salt and black pepper to taste
1 egg, whisked	1 cup breadcrumbs
1 tsp dried dill weed	¼ cup milk
2 tbsp capers	½ cup plain yogurt
2 tbsp lemon juice	½ cup cucumber, chopped
¼ cup green onions, chopped	½ tsp dill weeds

DIRECTIONS and total time: approx. 17 minutes

In a bowl, add salmon, egg, capers, lemon juice, green onions, milk, breadcrumbs, salt, and pepper. Shape into a loaf. Place the loaf into a greased baking dish. Add 1 cup of water and fit a trivet in the pot. Lower the dish onto the trivet. Seal the lid, select Manual, and cook for 7 minutes at High. When ready, do a quick release. Remove the salmon loaf from the pot. Mix yogurt, cucumber, dill, salt, and pepper in a bowl. Slice the loaf and drizzle with the cucumber sauce to serve.

Canned Tuna Casserole

INGREDIENTS for 4 servings

2 cans (5-oz) tuna, flaked	Salt and black pepper to taste
1 cup celery, diced	1 cup green peas
½ cup mayonnaise	2 cups potato chips, crushed
4 chopped hard-boiled eggs	1 cup water

DIRECTIONS and total time: approx. 29 minutes

Pour 1 cup water in your IP and insert a trivet. In a bowl, whisk tuna, celery, mayonnaise, eggs, salt, peas, and pepper until combined. Pour mixture into a greased baking dish. Top with potato chips. Place the dish on the trivet. Seal the lid, select Manual, and cook for 4 minutes at High. Do a quick pressure release. Serve.

Poached Trout with Pomegranate

INGREDIENTS for 4 servings

1 pound trout fillets	1 cup pomegranate juice
4 lemon slices	1 fennel bulb, sliced
¼ cup pomegranate seeds	2 tbsp olive oil
1 tbsp white wine vinegar	1 purple onion, sliced
1 tbsp honey	1 tbsp allspice
2 tbsp fresh mint, chopped	Salt and black pepper to taste

DIRECTIONS and total time: approx. 25 minutes

Heat olive oil on Sauté and cook onion and fennel for 3 minutes. Place in trout and pour in vinegar, pomegranate juice, allspice, salt, and pepper. Mix honey and 1 cup water in a bowl, and add to the pot. Seal the lid, select Manual and cook for 4 minutes at High. When ready, do a quick release. Remove the fish to a platter, drizzle with the cooking sauce and serve topped with mint, pomegranate seeds, and lemon slices.

Delicious Cod with Cherry Tomatoes

INGREDIENTS for 4 servings

1 lb black cod fillets	2 cups cherry tomatoes, halved
1 tbsp tomato paste	¼ tsp allspice
1 tsp honey	2 garlic cloves, minced
1 Fresno chili pepper, minced	1 tbsp red wine vinegar
2 tbsp cilantro, chopped	1 tsp paprika
2 tbsp olive oil	½ tsp red pepper flakes

DIRECTIONS and total time: approx. 30 minutes

Add tomato paste, chili, honey, olive oil, allspice, garlic, paprika, and flakes in a bowl and mix well. Place the fish into the inner pot and pour mixture over the fish. Put cherry tomatoes on top. Pour in 1 cup of water. Seal the lid, select Manual, and cook for 5 minutes at High. When ready, do a natural pressure release for 10 minutes. Serve sprinkled with fresh cilantro.

Greek Kakavia Fish Soup

INGREDIENTS for 6 servings

12 oz shrimp, deveined	2 tbsp parsley, chopped
2 cod fillets, skinless, cubed	1 bay leaf
1 can (14.5-oz) tomatoes	1 carrot, chopped
1 leek, sliced	2 garlic cloves, minced
Salt and black pepper to taste	1 celery stalk, chopped
12 mussels	½ cup dry white wine
12 clams	4 tbsp lemon juice

DIRECTIONS and total time: approx. 25 minutes

Heat oil on Sauté. Cook leek, garlic, carrot, and celery for 5 minutes. Add the remaining ingredients, except parsley and 6 cups water. Seal the lid, select Manual, and cook for 5 minutes at High. Do a quick release. Season with salt and pepper. Remove any unopened clams and mussels; discard bay leaf. Top with parsley.

Tomato Beans with Tuna

INGREDIENTS for 4 servings

20 oz canned white tuna in water, drained and flaked	Salt and black pepper to taste
1 lb white beans, soaked	2 tbsp olive oil
2 cups tomatoes, chopped	1 onion, chopped
2 garlic cloves, minced	1 tsp paprika
	2 tbsp basil, chopped

DIRECTIONS and total time: approx. 50 minutes

Heat olive oil on Sauté and cook onion and garlic for 3 minutes. Stir in paprika for a minute, and add in beans and 6 cups of water. Seal the lid, select Manual, and cook for 30 minutes at High. When ready, do a quick release. Stir in tuna, tomatoes, salt, and pepper, and cook for 3 minutes on Sauté. Serve topped with basil.

Easy Citrus Fish

INGREDIENTS for 4 servings

Orange and lemon slices for garnishing	Salt and black pepper to taste
1 lb tilapia fillets	2 tsp grated lemon rind
2 tbsp olive oil	1 onion, chopped
2 tsp grated orange rind	2 tbsp chopped parsley
	1 cup fish broth

DIRECTIONS and total time: approx. 25 minutes

Heat olive oil on Sauté and cook onion for 3 minutes. Add in lemon and orange rinds, and stir for 2 minutes. Season tilapia with salt and pepper and place in the pot. Pour in broth. Seal the lid, select Manual, and cook for 5 minutes at High. When ready, do a quick release. Top with orange and lemon slices and parsley, and serve.

Seafood Paella with Broccoli

INGREDIENTS for 4 servings

A pinch of saffron, soaked in 2 tsp hot water	1 onion, diced
1 red bell pepper, diced	1 cup rice, rinsed
2 tbsp olive oil	2 cups broccoli florets
1 cup scallops	2 cups fish stock
2 cups mussels	Salt and black pepper to taste
	2 tbsp chopped parsley

DIRECTIONS and total time: approx. 25 minutes

Warm olive oil on Sauté, add onions and bell peppers and cook for 4 minutes. Stir in scallops and cook for another 2 minutes. Add in the remaining ingredients, except for parsley. Seal the lid and cook on Manual for 8 minutes at High. When ready, do a quick release. Serve warm, sprinkled with parsley.

Buttered Trout

INGREDIENTS for 2 servings

1 cup fish stock	1 lb trout fillets, skinned
½ cup butter + some more	4 lemon slices

DIRECTIONS and total time: approx. 18 minutes

Melt butter on Sauté in the Instant Pot. Add in the trout and stock. Seal the lid, select Manual, and cook for 5 minutes at High. When done, do a quick release. Serve topped with lemon slices and some extra butter.

Steamed Salmon with Caper Sauce

INGREDIENTS for 4 servings

4 salmon fillets	Salt and white pepper to taste
½ cup dry white wine	1 yellow onion, sliced thin
1 bay leaf	¼ cup capers

DIRECTIONS and total time: approx. 25 minutes

Add ½ cup water, onion, wine, and bay leaf in your IP. Insert a trivet. Season the fillets with salt and white pepper, and place them on the trivet. Seal the lid, select Steam at High, and cook for 3 minutes. When done, do a natural pressure release for 10 minutes. Remove the fish to a plate. Discard bay leaf and press Sauté; cook until the sauce reduces by half. Then, blend the sauce in a food processor until smooth. Stir in capers and pour the sauce over the fish.

Bell Pepper & Salmon One-Pot

INGREDIENTS for 4 servings

1 green bell pepper, sliced into rings	1 can (10.5-oz) celery soup
1 lb salmon, sliced	1 tbsp lemon juice
2 tbsp olive oil	Salt and black pepper to taste
6 eggs	½ cup milk
	1 cup cheddar, shredded

DIRECTIONS and total time: approx. 33 minutes

On Sauté, heat olive oil and cook salmon for 2 minutes per side. Lay bell pepper rings over the salmon. In a medium bowl, whisk together eggs, milk, celery soup, salt, and pepper until well combined. Pour the mixture over the salmon and sprinkle with cheddar cheese. Seal the lid, select Manual at High, and cook for 6 minutes. When ready, do a quick pressure release. Serve hot.

Halibut with Mango Sauce

INGREDIENTS for 2 servings

2 halibut steaks	1 mango, chopped
½ tsp chili powder	1 jalapeño pepper, minced
Salt and black pepper to taste	1 tbsp cilantro, chopped
1 tbsp olive oil	1 garlic clove, minced
3 tbsp fresh lime juice	1 cup water

DIRECTIONS and total time: approx. 35 minutes

Place halibut in the pot. Blend the remaining ingredients in a food processor and pour over the fish. Seal the lid, press Manual and cook for 15 minutes at High. After cooking, do a quick pressure release. Serve warm.

Paprika & Garlic Shrimp

INGREDIENTS for 6 servings

2 lb jumbo shrimp, deveined
3 tbsp olive oil
¼ tsp red pepper flakes
Salt and black pepper to taste

2 tbsp parsley, chopped
3 garlic cloves, minced
1 tsp paprika
1 cup fish broth

DIRECTIONS and total time: approx. 30 minutes

Add olive oil, red flakes, salt, black pepper, garlic, and paprika to the pot. Press Sauté and stir-fry for 5 minutes. Stir in shrimp for 2 minutes and pour in fish broth. Seal the lid, select Manual, and cook for 2 minutes at High. After cooking, do a natural pressure release for 10 minutes. Serve topped with parsley.

Eggplant & Tilapia Curry

INGREDIENTS for 6 servings

1 eggplant, chopped
2 tbsp ginger, minced
4 tbsp olive oil
3 garlic cloves, minced
1 onion, chopped
2 tomatoes, chopped
1 tsp ground cumin

1 tsp ground turmeric
2 chili peppers, minced
5 cups fish stock
1 cup milk
1 tbsp curry powder
6 tilapia fillets, chopped
1 tsp ground coriander

DIRECTIONS and total time: approx. 30 minutes

On Sauté, heat olive oil and stir-fry onion, garlic, and eggplant for 3 minutes. Add the fish and cook for 2 more minutes, stirring occasionally. Add in the remaining ingredients. Seal the lid, select Manual at High, and cook for 5 minutes. When ready, perform natural pressure release for 10 minutes. Serve warm.

Dilled Salmon with Fennel & Lemon

INGREDIENTS for 4 servings

4 salmon fillets
1 fresno chili pepper, minced
Salt and black pepper to taste
4 tbsp dill, chopped

2 tbsp olive oil
1 fennel bulb, sliced
1 lemon, cut into wedges
1 cup water

DIRECTIONS and total servings: 20 minutes

Add the water to your Instant Pot and insert a trivet. Arrange salmon fillets on a baking dish. Season with salt and pepper, drizzle with olive oil and top with chili pepper and fennel slices. Place the dish on the trivet. Seal the lid, select Manual, and cook for 3 minutes at High. When ready, do a quick pressure release. Serve warm sprinkled with dill and lemon wedges.

Steamed Pollock

INGREDIENTS for 4 servings

4 Alaskan pollock fillets
1 tsp sea salt

1 lemon, sliced
2 tbsp parsley, chopped

DIRECTIONS and total time: approx. 25 minutes

Add 1 cup of water to your Instant Pot and insert a trivet. Place the fillets on the trivet. Seal the lid, select Manual, and cook for 6 minutes at High. When done, release the pressure naturally for 10 minutes. Serve topped with parsley, sea salt, and lemon slices.

Homemade Grits with Shrimp

INGREDIENTS for 4 servings

1 cup grits
1 tbsp chopped chives
1 cup cheddar, shredded
¼ cup heavy cream

1 lb cooked deveined shrimp
2 tsp hot sauce
Salt and black pepper to taste
2 tbsp butter

DIRECTIONS and total time: approx. 25 minutes

Add 4 cups of water, grits, salt, and pepper into your IP and toss to combine. Seal the lid, select Manual, and cook for 5 minutes at High. When done, do a quick pressure release. Remove to a bowl. Set the pot to Sauté and combine heavy cream, hot sauce, shrimp, cheese, and butter. Stir until the cheese melts. Serve the grits topped with shrimp, cheese sauce, and chives.

Basil Infused Salmon with Chickpeas

INGREDIENTS for 4 servings

2 tsp butter, melted
4 salmon fillets
A bunch of basil leaves
2 tsp Italian seasoning

15 oz canned chickpeas
½ tsp lime juice
1 green onion, chopped
Salt and black pepper to taste

DIRECTIONS and total time: approx. 20 minutes

Rub the seasoning all over the fish. Lay the basil leaves on the bottom of your Instant Pot and put the salmon on top. Drizzle with butter and pour in 1 cup of water. Seal the lid, and set on Manual at High for 3 minutes. When ready, do a natural pressure release for 10 minutes. In a bowl, mix chickpeas with lime juice, green onion, salt, and black pepper. Plate the salmon and garnish with chickpea mixture.

Dill & Potato Salmon Chowder

INGREDIENTS for 4 servings

½ cup half-and-half
2 tbsp olive oil
3 potatoes, cubed
½ tsp garlic powder
½ tsp chili powder

1 onion, chopped
4 cups fish stock
½ lb salmon, cubed
Salt and white pepper to taste
2 tbsp dill, chopped

DIRECTIONS and total time: approx. 30 minutes

Heat olive oil on Sauté and cook onion for 3 minutes until fragrant. Stir in potatoes, garlic and chili powders, stock, salt, and black pepper. Seal the lid, select Manual, and cook for 6 minutes at High.

When ready, do a quick release. Add the mixture to a food processor and blend until uniform. Bring the mixture back to the pot and add salmon. Seal the lid, select Manual, and cook for 3 minutes at High. When ready, do a quick pressure release. Stir in half-and-half and adjust the seasoning. Serve topped with dill.

Spicy Coconut Salmon Curry

INGREDIENTS for 4 servings

2 tbsp sesame oil	1 tsp chili powder
½ cup vegetable stock	2 tsp minced ginger
2 tsp chopped cilantro	2 garlic cloves, minced
Salt and black pepper to taste	1 celery stalk, chopped
1 lb salmon, cubed	1 can (14.5-oz) coconut milk
1 tsp smoked paprika	1 can (14.5-oz) tomato sauce

DIRECTIONS and total time: approx. 22 minutes

Heat sesame oil on Sauté and cook celery, garlic, ginger, chili, and smoked paprika for 3 minutes. Stir in salmon for a minute and pour in coconut milk, tomato sauce, and stock. Seal the lid, select Manual, and cook for 5 minutes at High. When done, do a natural release for 8 minutes. Sprinkle with cilantro and serve.

Fennel-Scented Fish Stew

INGREDIENTS for 6 servings

2 lb halibut fillets, cubed	1 tsp fennel seeds
3 tbsp olive oil	1 cup carrots, chopped
2 cups fish stock	1 cup onions, diced
½ cup dry white wine	2 tbsp parsley, chopped
Salt and white pepper to taste	3 garlic cloves, minced
1 tbsp orange zest	3 large tomatoes, chopped

DIRECTIONS and total time: approx. 30 minutes

On Sauté, heat olive oil, and stir-fry fish cubes, carrots, onions, fennel, and garlic for 2-3 minutes. Pour in fish stock, wine, orange zest, tomatoes, salt, and white pepper. Seal the lid, select Manual, and cook for 6 minutes at High. When ready, do a natural pressure release for 10 minutes. Serve sprinkled with parsley.

Wild Rice & Salmon Soup

INGREDIENTS for 4 servings

4 cups fish stock	½ lb salmon, cubed
2 tbsp olive oil	½ cup milk
2 garlic cloves, minced	½ cup wild rice
½ tsp mustard powder	1 cup mushrooms, sliced
½ tsp dry rosemary	½ celery stalk, sliced
Cayenne pepper to taste	1 onion, chopped

DIRECTIONS and total time: approx. 40 minutes

Heat olive oil on Sauté and stir-fry garlic, onion, celery, and mushrooms for 4 minutes. Stir in mustard powder, fish, rice, rosemary, and cayenne pepper for 2 minutes.

Pour in stock and milk. Seal the lid, select Manual, and cook for 10 minutes at High. When ready, do a natural pressure release for 10 minutes. Serve hot.

Bell Pepper & Zucchini Salmon

INGREDIENTS for 4 servings

1 tbsp Italian seasoning	Salt and black pepper to taste
1 red bell pepper, chopped	1 small zucchini, sliced
2 tbsp olive oil	1 tsp garlic powder
1 tomato, sliced	4 salmon fillets
1 tsp onion powder	1 cup fish broth

DIRECTIONS and total time: approx. 20 minutes

Heat olive oil on Sauté and cook zucchini, Italian seasoning, bell pepper, onion and garlic powders, tomato, and black pepper for 3 minutes. Add in salmon fillets and fish broth. Seal the lid, select Manual at High, and cook for 3 minutes. When done, release the pressure naturally for 10 minutes. Serve warm.

Jalapeño Seafood Jambalaya

INGREDIENTS for 4 servings

½ lb white fish fillets, cubed	2 tbsp parsley, chopped
½ lb shrimp, shell-on	A pinch of cumin
½ cup carrots, sliced	Salt and black pepper to taste
1 onion, sliced	1 cup jalapeño, minced
2 red bell peppers, sliced	2 tbsp olive oil
1 celery stalk, diced	1 cup basmati rice, rinsed

DIRECTIONS and total time: approx. 30 minutes

Heat olive oil on Sauté and stir-fry celery, jalapeño, carrots, onion, bell peppers, cumin, salt, and pepper for 5 minutes. Stir in fish, shrimp, and basmati rice for 2 minutes. Pour in 2 cups of water. Seal the lid, select Manual, and cook for 4 minutes at High. When ready, do a quick release. Serve hot topped with parsley.

Garlic & Chili Prawns

INGREDIENTS for 4 servings

1 lb prawns with tails intact	2 tbsp chopped cilantro
2 tbsp butter	1 tsp onion powder
1 tbsp olive oil	2 cloves garlic, crushed
1 lemon, cut into wedges	2 ½ tbsp ginger paste
Salt and black pepper to taste	1 cup chicken stock
½ red chili pepper, minced	1 stick lemongrass, chopped

DIRECTIONS and total time: approx. 30 minutes

Warm olive oil and butter on Sauté and cook ginger, garlic, lemongrass, red chili pepper, onion powder, salt, and pepper for 3 minutes, stirring often. Stir in prawns for 2 minutes and pour in chicken stock. Seal the lid, press Manual, and cook for 10 minutes at High. After cooking, do a natural pressure release for 10 minutes. Sprinkle with cilantro and serve with lemon wedges.

Manhattan-Style Clam Chowder

INGREDIENTS for 4 servings

4 bacon slices, diced
1 celery stalk, thinly sliced
1 carrot, thinly sliced
1 onion, chopped
8 oz clam juice
20 oz minced clams
2 potatoes, diced
1 tsp dried thyme
1 bay leaf
Salt and black pepper to taste
30 oz canned tomatoes
2 tbsp parsley, chopped

DIRECTIONS and total time: approx. 35 minutes

Fry bacon in your IP for 5 minutes on Sauté; set aside. Add celery, carrot, onion, salt, and pepper, to the pot and cook for 5 minutes. Stir in the remaining ingredients, except for parsley. Seal the lid, select Manual, and cook for 6 minutes at High. When ready, do a quick release. Discard bay leaf and serve topped with parsley and cooked bacon.

Sweet & Sour Shrimp

INGREDIENTS for 4 servings

1 cup Chinese pea pods, chopped
1 lb shrimp, deveined
2 tbsp sesame oil
1 cup chicken broth
1 tbsp sugar
½ tsp ground ginger
15 oz pineapple tidbits
2 tbsp cider vinegar
1 tbsp soy sauce
2 tbsp cornstarch
1 tbsp white sesame seeds

DIRECTIONS and total time: approx. 30 minutes

On Sauté, heat the oil, and cook shrimp for 3 minutes, until opaque. Stir in the remaining ingredients, except for cornstarch and seeds. Seal the lid, press Manual, and cook for 4 minutes at High. When done, allow for a natural release for 10 minutes. Whisk cornstarch with 2 tbsp of water and pour in the pot. Cook for 2 minutes on Sauté. Sprinkled with sesame seeds to serve.

Creole Seafood Gumbo

INGREDIENTS for 4-6 servings

1 lb white fish, cubed
2 tbsp olive oil
2 garlic cloves, minced
1 tbsp Creole seasoning
1 yellow onion, diced
1 green bell pepper, diced
1 celery rib, diced
1 (14-oz) can diced tomatoes
1 bay leaf
2 cups vegetable broth
1 lb shrimp, deveined
Salt and black pepper to taste

DIRECTIONS and total time: approx. 30 minutes

Heat olive oil on Sauté and cook fish for 4 minutes, stirring occasionally; set aside. Add onion, garlic, celery, green pepper, and Creole seasoning to the pot and cook for 3 minutes. Pour in tomatoes, vegetable broth, shrimp, and bay leaf and return the fish; stir. Seal the lid, select Manual, and cook for 4 minutes at High. When done, release the pressure naturally for 10 minutes. Adjust the seasoning and serve hot.

Garlic & Chili Crab Legs

INGREDIENTS for 4 servings

2 lb king crab legs
1 tsp dried chili flakes
2 tbsp butter, melted
2 garlic cloves, minced
4 lemon wedges
2 tbsp parsley, chopped

DIRECTIONS and total time: approx. 20 minutes

Pour 1 cup of water in your IP and insert a trivet. Break the crab legs in half and place on the trivet. Seal the lid, select Manual, and cook for 4 minutes at High. When done, release the pressure naturally for 10 minutes. Remove crab legs to a serving platter.

In a bowl, combine butter, chili flakes, and garlic and pour the mixture over the crab legs. Sprinkle with parsley and serve with lemon wedges.

Steamed Tilapia with Radicchio Salad

INGREDIENTS for 4 servings

1 lemon, juiced
4 tilapia fillets
2 tbsp butter, melted
Salt and black pepper to taste
½ tsp chili pepper
1 head radicchio, chopped
2 tbsp olive oil
5 oz arugula

DIRECTIONS and total time: approx. 25 minutes

Add 1 cup of water to your IP and insert a trivet. Brush the fish with butter. Season with salt, black and chili peppers. Place fillets on the trivet.

Seal the lid, select Manual, and cook for 5 minutes at High. Once cooking is over, do a quick release. Mix radicchio and arugula in a serving plate and toss to coat with lemon juice, olive oil, and salt. Top the salad with the cooked tilapia and serve.

Salmon & Asparagus Frittata

INGREDIENTS for 4 servings

6 eggs
½ cup crème fraiche
Salt and black pepper to taste
1 tsp Italian seasoning
1 cup grated Parmesan
1 cup chopped asparaus
½ lb chopped salmon
2 tbsp dill, chopped

DIRECTIONS and total time: approx. 40 minutes

Whisk together eggs with crème fraiche in a bowl. Add in asparagus, salmon, and Parmesan cheese and stir well to combine. Season with Italian seasoning, salt, and pepper. Pour the mixture in a greased baking dish. Add 1 cup of water in your IP and fit in a trivet. Place the baking dish on the trivet.

Seal the lid, select Manual, and cook for 20 minutes at High. When done, release the pressure naturally for 10 minutes. Remove the frittata and let sit for a few minutes before slicing. Serve scattered with dill.

Poultry

Chicken in Roasted Red Pepper Sauce

INGREDIENTS for 4 servings

1 lb chicken breasts, cubed	½ cup chicken broth
1 cup shallots, chopped	Juice of ½ Lemon
2 garlic cloves	2 tbsp chopped parsley
8 oz roasted red peppers	2 tbsp olive oil
1 tsp adobo sauce	Salt and black pepper to taste

DIRECTIONS and total time: approx. 40 minutes

Place garlic, red peppers, adobo sauce, lemon juice, salt, and pepper in a food processor and process until smooth. Set your Instant Pot to Sauté, heat olive oil and cook shallots for 2 minutes. Add the chicken and sear for 5 minutes, stirring occasionally. Mix in the prepared sauce and broth. Seal the lid, press Manual, and set timer to 15 minutes at High. When ready, do a quick pressure release. Serve with fresh parsley.

Caraway Chicken with Vegetables

INGREDIENTS for 4 servings

2 tbsp olive oil	1 tbsp caraway seeds
1 onion, chopped	2 cups mushrooms, sliced
2 garlic cloves, minced	¼ cup all-purpose flour
2 tbsp parsley, chopped	1 carrot, chopped
1 lb chicken breasts, sliced	2 ¼ cups chicken stock
1 cup celery, chopped	Salt and black pepper to taste

DIRECTIONS and total time: approx. 35 minutes

Heat olive oil on Sauté and cook chicken for 6 minutes; set aside. Add onion, garlic, celery, caraway seeds, carrot, and mushrooms; stir-fry for 5 minutes. Pour in stock and return the chicken; season with salt and pepper. Seal the lid and cook on Manual for 15 minutes at High. When ready, release the pressure naturally for 10 minutes. Serve topped with parsley.

Hot Chicken & Leek Cassoulet

INGREDIENTS for 4 servings

1 garlic clove, minced	1 tsp paprika
1 lb chicken sausages, sliced	Salt and black pepper to taste
2 tbsp olive oil	2 jalapenos, chopped
2 cups chicken stock	14 oz canned tomatoes, diced
2 leeks, chopped	2 cups canned kidney beans

DIRECTIONS and total time: approx. 35 minutes

Heat olive oil on Sauté and brown the sausages for 5 minutes on all sides; reserve. Add leeks, garlic, paprika, and jalapeños and cook for 3 minutes. Stir in tomatoes, beans, stock, salt, pepper, and the reserved sausages. Seal the lid and cook for 10 minutes on Manual at High. When ready, do a quick release and serve.

Chicken with Green Beans & Potatoes

INGREDIENTS for 4 servings

1 ½ lb chicken thighs	½ cup vegetable broth
1 tbsp butter	2 tbsp olive oil
1 onion, chopped	2 garlic cloves, minced
¼ tsp dried oregano	½ lb green beans
½ tsp dried sage	1 lb potatoes, sliced
Juice of 1 lemon	Salt and black pepper to taste

DIRECTIONS and total time: approx. 40 minutes

Heat oil and butter on Sauté and cook garlic and onion for 3 minutes until soft. Place in chicken thighs and sear them for 5-6 minutes on both sides until golden. Stir in herbs and lemon juice for an additional minute. Mix in all the remaining ingredients and stir to combine. Seal the lid and cook on Manual for 15 minutes at High. When done, release the pressure quickly. Serve warm.

Thyme Chicken with Red Currant Sauce

INGREDIENTS for 6 servings

1 ½ lb chicken breasts	2 tbsp cornstarch
1 tbsp red currant jelly	2 tbsp sesame oil
2 garlic cloves, minced	1 tsp coriander seeds
2 ¼ cups chicken broth	2 tbsp fresh thyme, chopped
1 cup green onions	Salt and black pepper to taste

DIRECTIONS and total time: approx. 35 minutes

Heat sesame oil on Sauté and cook green onions, coriander, and garlic for 3 minutes. Season the chicken with salt and pepper and add it to the pot; cook for 6 minutes on both sides. Pour in the broth and seal the lid. Cook on Poultry for 15 minutes at High. When done, release the pressure quickly. Remove the chicken to a cutting board to cool slightly before slicing. Puree the remaining cooked ingredients with an immersion blender until smooth. In a bowl, whisk 1 cup of the cooking juices with cornstarch and red jelly, and pour the mixture into the pot. Select Sauté and cook for 4 minutes until thickened. Pour over the chicken, sprinkle with thyme and serve warm.

Colby Cheese Chicken Drumsticks

INGREDIENTS for 4 servings

4 chicken drumsticks	2 tbsp butter
1 cup sour cream	1 tsp chipotle powder
1 cup marinara sauce	½ tsp thyme
1 cup grated Colby cheese	Salt and black pepper to taste

DIRECTIONS and total time: approx. 35 minutes

Melt butter on Sauté. Add marinara sauce, chipotle, thyme, and chicken; season with salt and pepper. Pour in ¾ cup of water. Seal the lid and cook for 15 minutes on Poultry at High. When ready, release the pressure quickly. Stir in cheese and sour cream and serve.

Garlicky Chicken with Mushrooms

INGREDIENTS for 4 servings

1 lb chicken breasts, cubed	1 carrot, chopped
1 tbsp butter	½ cup milk
1 lb mushrooms, sliced	Salt and black pepper to taste
½ cup chicken broth	2 scallions, sliced
2 tbsp cornstarch	¼ tsp garlic powder

DIRECTIONS and total time: approx. 40 minutes

Melt butter on Sauté and sear chicken until no longer pink and slightly golden, 5 minutes. Transfer to a plate. Add scallions, carrot, and mushrooms to the pot and stir-fry for 3 minutes. Return the chicken, season with salt, pepper and garlic powder, and pour in broth. Stir and seal the lid. Cook on Manual for 15 minutes at High. When done, release the pressure quickly. In a bowl, whisk together milk and cornstarch. Pour the mixture over the chicken and set to Sauté. Cook until the sauce thickens, 2-3 minutes. Serve warm.

Creamy Chicken with Tomato Sauce

INGREDIENTS for 2 servings

2 chicken drumsticks	1 tsp garlic paste
1 cup tomato sauce	1 tbsp basil, chopped
½ cup heavy cream	Salt and black pepper to taste
¼ cup Pecorino Romano, grated	½ tsp rosemary, chopped
2 tbsp butter	½ cup chicken broth

DIRECTIONS and total time: approx. 40 minutes

Melt butter on Sauté and cook garlic paste, tomato sauce, rosemary, and basil for 3 minutes. Sprinkle the chicken drumsticks with salt and black pepper. Place drumsticks on top of the sauce, to resemble a nestle. Pour in chicken broth, seal the lid, select Poultry mode, and cook for 15 minutes at High. Once done, release the pressure naturally for 10 minutes. Stir in cheese and heavy cream and serve right away.

Parsley & Carrot Chicken Stew

INGREDIENTS for 4 servings

1 cup chicken stock	1 tsp chili pepper
2 tsp vegetable oil	Salt and black pepper to taste
3 carrots, sliced	1 lb chicken thighs, bone-in
2 tomatoes, chopped	2 garlic cloves, minced
1 sweet onion, thinly sliced	2 tbsp chopped parsley

DIRECTIONS and total time: approx. 35 minutes

Sprinkle the chicken with salt, chili and black peppers. Heat vegetable oil on Sauté and lightly brown the thighs on both sides; set aside. Add carrots tomatoes, garlic, and onion and sauté for 3 minutes. Pour in stock and browned chicken. Seal the lid and cook for 15 minutes on Poultry at Hgh. When ready, release the pressure quickly. Top with parsley to serve.

Lemony Chicken with Thyme & Garlic

INGREDIENTS for 4-6 servings

2 tbsp olive oil	1 tsp dried thyme
1 (3.5-lb) whole chicken	Salt and black pepper to taste
1 tbsp paprika	1 ½ cups chicken broth
2 bay leaves	¼ cup lemon juice
2 garlic cloves, crushed	1 lemon, quartered
1 onion, sliced	2 tbsp parsley, chopped

DIRECTIONS and total time: approx. 60 minutes

In a bowl, mix salt, pepper, thyme, and paprika. Rub the chicken with the mixture. Put onion, garlic, lemon, and bay leaves into the cavity. Place the chicken in your IP, pour in broth and lemon juice around, and drizzle with olive oil. Seal the lid and cook for 30 minutes on Manual at High. When done, release the pressure naturally for 10 minutes. Remove the chicken and let rest for 5 minutes before carving. Serve drizzled with the cooking juices and topped with fresh parsley.

Coq Au Vin

INGREDIENTS for 6 servings

2 lb chicken thighs	1 cup mushrooms, sliced
4 oz pancetta, chopped	1 tsp garlic paste
1 cup red wine	1 tbsp flour
1 cup parsley, chopped	3 tbsp olive oil
1 onion, chopped	2 cups chicken broth
1 lb small potatoes, halved	Salt and black pepper to taste

DIRECTIONS and total time: approx. 35 minutes

Heat olive oil on Sauté and brown chicken on all sides; set aside. Add onion, garlic, mushrooms, and pancetta to the pot and cook for 5 minutes. Whisk in flour and red wine. Pour in potatoes and chicken broth and season with salt and pepper. Seal the lid, press Manual, and cook for 15 minutes at High. When done, release the pressure quickly. Serve warm, topped with parsley.

Ginger & Scallion Chicken

INGREDIENTS for 4 servings

1 lb chicken breasts, sliced	¼ cup white wine
4 scallions, chopped	1 cup chicken broth
2 tbsp chives, chopped	2 tbsp olive oil
1 tbsp ginger, grated	1 celery stalk, chopped
2 tsp soy sauce	Salt and black pepper to taste

DIRECTIONS and total time: approx. 35 minutes

Heat olive oil on Sauté and brown chicken on all sides for 5-6 minutes; set aside. Add celery, ginger, and scallions to the pot and sauté for 3 minutes. Stir in wine to deglaze and pour in broth, soy sauce, and chicken; season with salt and pepper. Seal the lid and cook for 15 minutes on Manual at High. When ready, release the pressure quickly. Serve sprinkled with chives.

Chicken with Baby Carrots & Mushrooms

INGREDIENTS for 4 servings

8 oz Shiitake mushrooms, sliced
1 (10.75 oz) can mushroom soup
4 chicken breasts, halved
1 onion, diced
½ lb baby carrots
1 tbsp butter
1 tbsp olive oil
2 tbsp buttermilk
Salt and black pepper to taste
2 tbsp parsley, chopped

DIRECTIONS and total time: approx. 20 minutes

Heat olive oil and butter on Sauté and cook onion, carrots, and mushrooms for 5 minutes. Add chicken and cook for 5-6 minutes on both sides. Pour in mushroom soup and 1 cup of water. Seal the lid and cook for 12 minutes on Manual at High. When ready, do a quick pressure release and remove the mushrooms, chicken, and carrots to a plate. In the pot, stir in buttermilk and parsley cook until the sauce thickens on Sauté, for 3 minutes. Plate the dish and serve drizzled with sauce.

Chicken in Honey & Habanero Sauce

INGREDIENTS for 4 servings

1 lb chicken breasts
4 tbsp habanero sauce
¼ cup tomato puree
1 tbsp honey
½ tsp cumin
1 tsp smoked paprika
Salt and black pepper to taste
1 cup water

DIRECTIONS and total time: approx. 30 minutes

Pour water in your IP and place the chicken inside. Season with salt and black pepper. Seal the lid, press Poultry and cook for 15 minutes at High. When ready, release the pressure quickly. Remove and shred the chicken. Add the remaining ingredients to the pot, press Sauté, and cook for 5-6 minutes until thickened. Pour the sauce over the chicken and serve hot.

Tuscan Turkey Breast with Beans

INGREDIENTS for 4 servings

1 lb turkey breast, sliced
4 oz pancetta, chopped
1 tsp paprika
10 oz baby spinach
1 (16 oz) can diced tomatoes
1 (16 oz) can kidney beans
1 cup chicken stock
1 tsp oregano
Salt and black pepper to taste
2 tbsp basil, chopped
1 onion, chopped
2 tbsp grated Parmesan

DIRECTIONS and total time: approx. 25 minutes

Set your IP to Sauté and cook pancetta for 5 minutes; set aside. In the pot, add onion and turkey and cook for 4-5 minutes, stirring occasionally. Mix in paprika, oregano, beans, tomatoes, pancetta, and chicken stock; season to taste. Seal the lid and cook on Manual for 15 minutes at High. When done, release the pressure quickly. Stir in spinach until it wilts, for 3 minutes. Sprinkle with basil and Parmesan cheese, and serve.

Oregano Chicken with Garlic & Tomatoes

INGREDIENTS for 4 servings

4 chicken legs
1 red onion, sliced
2 tomatoes, chopped
2 garlic cloves, minced
2 tbsp cornflour
1 ½ cups chicken broth
2 tsp olive oil
1 tsp ground cumin
2 tsp dried oregano
Salt and black pepper to taste
½ cup feta cheese, cubed
10 kalamata olives

DIRECTIONS and total time: approx. 35 minutes

Season the chicken with salt, pepper, oregano, and cumin. Heat olive oil on Sauté and brown the legs for 3 minutes per side. Stir in onion and garlic and cook for 4 minutes. Whisk cornflour with chicken stock to make a slurry. Pour in the pot along with tomatoes and stir. Seal the lid, press Manual and cook for 15 minutes at High. Once it goes off, release the pressure quickly. Serve with a side of feta cheese and kalamata olives.

Chicken with Green Chilies

INGREDIENTS for 4 servings

1 lb chicken breasts
2 cups diced tomatoes
½ tsp thyme
2 green chilies, chopped
½ tsp smoked paprika
1 tbsp sugar
2 tbsp cilantro, chopped
2 tbsp olive oil
Salt and black pepper to taste
1 cup water

DIRECTIONS and total time: approx. 45 minutes

In a mixing dish, combine olive oil with all the spices and sugar. Rub the chicken breasts with the mixture and place them in the inner pot. Cover with tomatoes, chilies and water, and seal the lid. Cook for 15 minutes on Manual at High. Once ready, do a quick pressure release. Remove chicken to a cutting board, and shred it. Return the shredded chicken to the pot. Set to Sauté and let simmer for about 2-3 minutes. Serve warm.

Serrano Chili Chicken

INGREDIENTS for 6 servings

1 ½ lb chicken legs, cut up, bone-in
Salt and black pepper to taste
1 tsp dry basil
2 serrano chili peppers, diced
½ cup parsley, chopped
1 tsp sugar
2 garlic cloves, chopped
2 tbsp lime juice
¼ cup olive oil

DIRECTIONS and total time: approx. 30 minutes

Pour 1 cup of water in your Instant Pot and fit in a trivet. Season the chicken with salt, pepper and basil, and place on the trivet. Seal the lid and cook for 15 minutes at High on Manual mode. When done, release the pressure quickly. Blend chili peppers, parsley, sugar, garlic, lime juice, and olive oil in a food processor until well combined. Plate the chicken legs and top with the sauce to serve.

Adobo Chicken in Roasted Pepper Sauce

INGREDIENTS for 4 servings

1 lb chicken breasts, cubed	½ cup vegetable broth
1 onion, diced	½ tsp cumin
2 garlic cloves	2 tbsp chopped cilantro
12 oz roasted bell peppers	1 tbsp olive oil
2 tsp adobo sauce	Salt and black pepper to taste

DIRECTIONS and total time: approx. 20 minutes

Blend the garlic, peppers, adobo sauce, cumin, broth, salt, and pepper in a food processor until the mixture becomes smooth. On Sauté, heat the olive oil, and cook onion and chicken for 5 minutes, stirring occasionally. Pour the prepared sauce and broth over. Seal the lid, press Manual, and cook for 15 minutes at High. Do a quick pressure release. Sprinkle with cilantro to serve.

Creamy Chicken Legs

INGREDIENTS for 4 servings

4 chicken legs	1 tbsp olive oil
1 onion, chopped	2 tsp chipotle powder
1 tomato, chopped	½ tsp garlic powder
½ cup buttermilk	1 tsp thyme
1 cup chicken broth	Salt and black pepper to taste

DIRECTIONS and total time: approx. 35 minutes

Rub the chicken with salt, black pepper, garlic and chipotle powders in a bowl. Heat olive oil on Sauté and add the seasoned legs. Cook until browned on all sides, 5 minutes; reserve. Add onion, tomato, and thyme and sauté for 3 minutes. Pour in buttermilk and broth and seal the lid. Cook for 15 minutes on Manual at High. When done, release pressure naturally for 10 minutes.

Juicy Chili Orange Wings

INGREDIENTS for 4 servings

1 lb chicken wings	2 onions, sliced
¼ cup orange juice	1 cup chicken stock
4 tbsp butter, softened	½ tsp chili pepper
2 cups cherries, deseeded	Salt and black pepper to taste

DIRECTIONS and total time: approx. 30 minutes

Melt butter on Sauté. Add in chicken wings, season with salt, black and chili peppers, and cook until browned for 6-7 minutes. Stir in the remaining ingredients. Seal the lid. Cook for 10 minutes on Manual at High. When ready, release the pressure quickly and serve.

Cajun Chicken with Snow Beans

INGREDIENTS for 4 servings

4 chicken breasts, sliced	1 tsp Cajun seasoning
2 cups snow beans	1 cup chicken broth
14 oz cornbread stuffing mix	Salt and black pepper to taste

DIRECTIONS and total time: approx. 35 minutes

Add chicken and broth to your Instant Pot. Season with salt and pepper, seal the lid, and cook on Manual for 15 minutes at High. When ready, do a quick pressure release. Stir in beans, cornbread mix, and Cajun seasoning and cook for 5 minutes on Sauté. Serve hot.

Italian Chicken Breasts

INGREDIENTS for 4 servings

1 cup spinach, chopped	¾ cup whipping cream
4 chicken breasts, halved	½ cup sun-dried tomatoes
¾ cup chicken broth	2 tsp Italian seasoning
2 garlic cloves, minced	½ cup Pecorino Romano, grated
3 tbsp olive oil	Salt and black pepper to taste

DIRECTIONS and total time: approx. 40 minutes

In a small bowl, combine half of oil with garlic, salt, and Italian seasoning. Rub the chicken on all sides with this mixture. Heat the remaining oil on Sauté and brown the chicken on all sides, about 4-5 minutes. Pour in broth in and seal the lid. Press Manual and cook for 15 minutes at High. When ready, do a quick pressure release. Open the lid and add in tomatoes and spinach. Cook for 3-4 minutes just until the spinach wilts on Sauté. Stir in cream. Top with grated cheese to serve.

Sweet Chicken Drumsticks

INGREDIENTS for 4 servings

4 chicken drumsticks	1 tbsp brown sugar
1 cup mango, chopped	2 tbsp lime juice
½ cup milk	Salt and black pepper to taste
¼ cup tomato puree	1 cup chicken broth

DIRECTIONS and total time: approx. 25 minutes

In a bowl, whisk together all ingredients, except for the chicken and mango. Place chicken drumsticks and mango in the inner pot, and pour the sauce over. Seal the lid, and cook on Manual for 15 minutes at High. Once ready, do a quick pressure release. Serve hot.

Saucy Chicken Teriyaki

INGREDIENTS for 4 servings

1 cup chicken broth	½ cup soy sauce
1 tbsp brown sugar	1 cup chopped pineapple
1 tbsp ground ginger	1 tsp garlic powder
Salt and black pepper to taste	½ tsp oregano
1 lb chicken thighs	2 tbsp sesame oil

DIRECTIONS and total time: approx. 25 minutes

Heat sesame oil on Sauté and cook chicken, ginger, garlic powder, salt, and pepper for 5 minutes. Place in all the remaining ingredients and mix to combine. Seal the lid, press Poultry, and cook for 15 minutes at High. When ready, do a quick pressure release. Serve warm.

Chicken Jambalaya

INGREDIENTS for 4 servings

1 lb chicken breasts, cut into pieces	1 ½ cups green onions, chopped
3 cups chicken stock	1 cup white rice
2 garlic cloves, minced	2 tbsp tomato puree
1 tsp Cajun seasoning	Salt and black pepper to taste
1 celery stalk, diced	3 tbsp olive oil
	2 tbsp cilantro, chopped

DIRECTIONS and total time: approx. 30 minutes

Heat olive oil on Sauté and brown the chicken for 5 minutes. Add garlic and celery and sauté for 2 minutes. Deglaze with broth. Add the remaining ingredients and seal the lid. Select Poultry and cook for 15 minutes at High. When ready, do a quick pressure release. Serve warm in bowls, topped with cilantro.

Simple Sage Whole Chicken

INGREDIENTS for 4-6 servings

1 (3-lb) whole chicken	Salt and black pepper to taste
2 tbsp olive oil	2 fresh sage, chopped

DIRECTIONS and total time: approx. 35 minutes

Season the chicken with salt and black pepper, and brush with olive oil. Insert a trivet in your IP and pour in 1 cup of water. Lower the chicken onto the trivet. Seal the lid, press Manual and cook for 25 minutes at High. Once ready, do a quick pressure release. Let cool for a few minutes, carve, and sprinkle with sage.

Herb Chicken with Potatoes & Green Beans

INGREDIENTS for 6 servings

2 lb chicken thighs	3 tbsp olive oil
¼ tsp dried parsley	2 garlic cloves, minced
¼ tsp dried sage	1 lb green beans
Juice of 1 lemon	1 lb red potatoes, halved
2 cups chicken broth	Salt and black pepper to taste

DIRECTIONS and total time: approx. 25 minutes

Heat olive oil on Sauté and sauté the garlic for a minute. Place the thighs and cook them on both sides until golden. Stir in the herbs and the lemon juice, and cook for an additional minute. Add all the remaining ingredients and stir to combine. Seal the lid and cook on Manual at High for 15 minutes. When done, release the pressure quickly. Serve immediately.

Sweet & Spicy Chicken Thighs

INGREDIENTS for 4 servings

4 chicken thighs	2 tsp butter
1 sweet onion, chopped	1 cup chicken broth
1 apple, sliced	1 tsp chili powder
2 tbsp balsamic vinegar	Salt and black pepper to taste

DIRECTIONS and total time: approx. 40 minutes

Melt butter on Sauté. Add chicken and sprinkle with the spices. Brown on all sides for 5-6 minutes. Stir in the remaining ingredients. Seal the lid and cook for 15 minutes on Poultry at High. When ready, release pressure naturally for 10 minutes. Serve immediately.

Sage Drumsticks with Red Sauce

INGREDIENTS for 4 servings

4 chicken drumsticks	½ lemon, zested and juiced
1 onion, sliced	2 tbsp olive oil
¼ cup tomato puree	Salt and black pepper to taste
2 tbsp sage, chopped	1 cup vegetable stock

DIRECTIONS and total time: approx. 30 minutes

Heat olive oil on Sauté and sear the drumsticks for 5-6 minutes until lightly browned. Stir in onion and sage, and sauté for 3 minutes. Mix in the remaining ingredients along with 1 cup of water and seal the lid. Cook for 15 minutes on Manual at High. Once ready, release the pressure naturally for 10 minutes. Serve.

Thyme Chicken Soup

INGREDIENTS for 6 servings

1 lb chicken thighs, diced	1 cup green onions, chopped
1 cup carrots, diced	2 cloves garlic, minced
1 (8 oz) cans white beans	1 tsp thyme
2 tomatoes, chopped	6 cups vegetable stock
1 potato, chopped	Salt and black pepper to taste

DIRECTIONS and total time: approx. 35 minutes

Place all ingredients, except for the beans, in your Instant Pot and seal the lid. Cook for 20 minutes on Manual at High. When done, release the pressure quickly. Stir in the beans, and let them heat through for 10 minutes on Sauté mode. Serve warm.

Chicken Garam Masala

INGREDIENTS for 4 servings

1 ½ lb chicken thighs	1 tsp paprika
2 cups chopped tomatoes	1 tsp Garam masala
1 onion, chopped	2 tbs cilantro
2 tbsp butter	1 tsp cayenne powder
1 cup milk	1 tsp garlic powder
½ cup chopped hazelnuts	Salt and black pepper to taste

DIRECTIONS and total time: approx. 25 minutes

Melt butter on Sauté and cook onion until translucent, about 3 minutes. Stir in the spices for an additional minute. Pour in tomatoes, milk, and 1 cup water. Place in chicken thighs and seal the lid. Cook on Manual at High for 13 minutes. When ready, do a quick pressure release. Serve sprinkled with hazelnuts and sage.

Paprika Chicken in White Wine Sauce

INGREDIENTS for 4 servings

1 chicken breasts, sliced	¾ tsp rosemary
½ cup white wine	¾ tsp garlic powder
2 tbsp olive oil	¼ tsp onion powder
1 tsp paprika	Salt and black pepper to taste

DIRECTIONS and total time: approx. 40 minutes

In a bowl, combine olive oil and spices. Rub the chicken with the mixture. On Sauté, sear the chicken on all sides until golden. Pour white wine and 1 cup of water around the chicken and seal the lid. Cook on Manual for 15 minutes at High. When ready, do a quick pressure release. Serve with steamed vegetables.

Lime Chicken with Pesto Sauce

INGREDIENTS for 4 servings

1 lb chicken thighs	¼ cup pesto sauce
4 potatoes, cut into wedges	1 onion, sliced
1 tsp lime juice	1 cup chicken broth
1 carrot, chopped	Salt and black pepper to taste

DIRECTIONS and total time: approx. 30 minutes

In a bowl, mix pesto sauce with lime juice. Add the chicken and coat well. Transfer to the pot and add in the remaining ingredients. Add in the coated chicken. Seal the lid and cook on Manual for 15 minutes at High. When ready, do a natural release for 10 minutes.

BBQ Chicken Wings with Shallots

INGREDIENTS for 4 servings

2 lb chicken wings	1 cup barbeque sauce
2 tbsp butter	2 shallots, sliced
1 tbsp rosemary	Salt and black pepper to taste

DIRECTIONS and total time: approx. 20 minutes

Add butter, bbq sauce, rosemary, chicken, and 1 cup water in your Instant Pot. Select Manual, seal the lid, and cook for 15 minutes at High. When ready, do a quick pressure release. Garnish with shallots and serve.

Hot Chicken Wings with Sage

INGREDIENTS for 4 servings

16 chicken wings	2 tbsp butter
1 cup hot sauce	2 tbsp sage, chopped
1 cup chicken broth	Salt and black pepper to taste

DIRECTIONS and total time: approx. 30 minutes

Heat olive oil on Sauté and sear the chicken wings for 5 minutes. Add in hot sauce, chicken broth, salt, and pepper, and seal the lid. Cook on Manual for 15 minutes at High. When ready, release pressure naturally for 10 minutes. Sprinkle with sage and serve hot.

Chicken with Vegetables & Salad

INGREDIENTS for 4 servings

2 cups cauliflower florets	3 cucumbers, chopped
1 carrot, julienned	10 cherry tomatoes, halved
1 green bell pepper, chopped	¼ cup red onion, chopped
1 onion, chopped	4 chicken breasts
4 tbsp olive oil	Zest and juice from 2 lemons
¼ cup Greek dressing	Salt and black pepper to taste
¼ cup black olives	½ tsp oregano

DIRECTIONS and total time: approx. 35 minutes

On Sauté, heat 2 tbsp olive oil and brown the chicken for 3 minutes per side. Add in zest and lemon juice, oregano, salt, pepper, and 1 cup of water. Seal the lid, select Manual, and cook for 15 minutes at High. When ready, release the pressure quickly. Remove and slice the chicken; set aside. Press Sauté and heat the remaining olive oil. Add in cauliflower, bell pepper, carrot, and onion and sauté for 5-8 minutes until soft; season to taste and remove to a platter. Top with chicken. In a bowl, mix together cucumbers, cherry tomatoes, red onion, black olives, and Greek dressing; toss to coat. Serve with chicken and veggies.

Asian-Style Chicken Thighs

INGREDIENTS for 4 servings

1 tbsp honey	2 slices fresh ginger root
2 cloves garlic, minced	¼ cup soy sauce
1 lb chicken thighs	2 tbsp sesame seeds for garnish

DIRECTIONS and total time: approx. 30 minutes

Place the thighs in your Instant Pot. In a blender, mix together the remaining ingredients, except for the sesame seeds, with 1 cup of water until well blended. Spread the mixture over the chicken thighs. Seal the lid, select Manual, and cook for 15 minutes at High. When ready, allow for a natural release for 10 minutes. Sprinkle with sesame seeds and serve hot.

Garlic Basil Chicken with Carrots

INGREDIENTS for 6 servings

1 (3.5-oz) whole chicken	2 tbsp garlic powder
4 baby carrots	1 yellow onion, chopped
3 garlic cloves, smashed	A handful of basil
4 tbsp butter, melted	Salt and black pepper to taste

DIRECTIONS and total time: approx. 45 minutes

Rub garlic powder, butter, salt, and pepper all over the chicken. Add basil and smashed garlic cloves in the chicken's cavity. Arrange onion and carrots at the bottom of the inner pot, then place the chicken on top. Pour in 2 cups of water. Seal the lid, select Manual, and cook for 30 minutes at High. When ready, release the pressure naturally for 10 minutes. Serve immediately.

Mushroom & Green Onion Chicken

INGREDIENTS for 4 servings

1 lb chicken breasts, cubed	¼ cup milk
2 tbsp canola oil	Salt and black pepper to taste
1 lb mushrooms, sliced	2 green onions, sliced
1 cup chicken broth	¼ tsp garlic powder
1 tbsp cornstarch	2 tbsp dill, chopped

DIRECTIONS and total time: approx. 20 minutes

Heat canola oil on Sauté and cook the chicken until no longer pink and slightly golden, 4-5 minutes; reserve. To the cooker, add green onions and mushrooms and sauté for 5 minutes. Return the chicken, season with salt, pepper, and garlic powder, and pour in broth. Give it a good stir to combine well. Seal the lid and cook on Manual for 15 minutes at High. When done, release the pressure quickly. In a bowl, whisk together the milk and cornstarch. Pour in the pot and set to Sauté. Cook until the sauce thickens. Top with dill to serve.

Chili Chicken Breasts with Bell Peppers

INGREDIENTS for 4 servings

2 bell peppers, diced	¾ tsp sweet chili powder
1 serrano pepper, diced	Salt and black pepper to taste
1 lb chicken breasts	Juice of ½ lemon
14 oz tomato sauce	½ cup chicken broth
1 red onion, diced	2 tbsp olive oil
½ tsp cumin	2 tbsp rosemary, chopped

DIRECTIONS and total time: approx. 25 minutes

Heat olive oil on Sauté and cook onion and peppers for 3 minutes until soft. Add in chicken, chili powder, cumin, salt, and pepper and sauté for 4-5 minutes. Stir in tomato sauce, lemon juice, and chicken broth. Seal the lid, press Manual, and cook for 15 minutes at High. After it beeps, release the pressure quickly. Shred the chicken inside the pot with two forks, then stir to combine with the juices. Serve topped with rosemary.

Herby Chicken Thighs

INGREDIENTS for 4 servings

1 lb chicken thighs	½ tsp thyme
1 tbsp honey	½ tsp sage
3 tsp grated ginger	½ cup hoisin sauce
2 garlic clove, minced	4 tbsp sriracha sauce
2 cups vegetable broth	2 tbsp sesame oil
½ cup soy sauce	Salt and black pepper to taste

DIRECTIONS and total time: approx. 25 minutes

Lay the chicken at the bottom of your IP. Mix the remaining ingredients with ½ cup of water in a bowl. Pour the mixture over the chicken. Seal the lid, select Manual, and set the time to 15 minutes at High. When ready, do a quick pressure release. Serve immediately.

Dijon Chicken with Mushrooms & Kale

INGREDIENTS for 4 servings

1 lb button mushrooms, halved	1 tsp cornstarch
4 chicken breasts, cubed	1 carrot, chopped
2 tbsp olive oil	1 cup kale, chopped
1 large onion, sliced	1 ½ cups chicken stock
5 cloves garlic, minced	1 tsp Dijon mustard
Salt and black pepper to taste	1 cup buttermilk

DIRECTIONS and total time: approx. 40 minutes

Heat olive oil on Sauté and cook onion for 3 minutes. Stir in mushrooms, carrot, chicken, garlic, salt, pepper, mustard and sauté for 5 minutes. Pour in stock, seal the lid, select Manual and cook for 15 minutes at High. Once ready, do a quick release. Mix cornstarch with 1 cup of cooking liquid. Pour into the pot and stir in buttermilk. Press Sauté and let the sauce thicken a bit. Add in kale and cook for 4 minutes until it wilts. Serve.

Curry Chicken with Edamame

INGREDIENTS for 4 servings

1 lb chicken breast, cubed	1 tsp cumin
2 cups cubed sweet potatoes	2 tbsp cilantro, chopped
2 cups edamame	½ cup milk
1 onion, chopped	2 tsp coconut oil
1 yellow bell pepper, sliced	1 tbsp curry powder
1 tsp freshly grated ginger	1 cup chicken broth
2 garlic cloves, minced	Salt and black pepper to taste

DIRECTIONS and total time: approx. 25 minutes

Warm coconut oil on Sauté. Add in onion, garlic, bell pepper, and ginger and cook for 3 minutes until soft. Add the remaining ingredients, except for milk and cilantro, and stir to combine. Seal the lid, press Manual, and cook 12 minutes at High. When ready, do a quick pressure release. Stir in milk and hit Sauté. Cook for 3 minutes. Serve topped with cilantro.

Cheesy Potatoes with Chicken Sausage

INGREDIENTS for 4 servings

1 (10.75-oz) can condensed chicken soup	Salt and black pepper to taste
½ lb russet potatoes, diced	¼ tsp oregano, dried
1 green bell pepper, diced	½ cup sour cream
1 red bell pepper, diced	1 cup cheddar, shredded
2 tbsp parsley, chopped	1 onion, diced
	1 lb chicken sausages, sliced

DIRECTIONS and total time: approx. 25 minutes

Combine the potatoes, sausages, peppers, sour cream, onion, and oregano in your Instant Pot. Gently pour in the chicken soup along with 1 cup of water, salt, and black pepper. Seal the lid, select Manual, and cook for 10 minutes at High. When ready, do a quick release. Stir in cheddar cheese and serve garnished with parsley.

Chicken Tikka Masala

INGREDIENTS for 4 servings

4 chicken thighs, bone-in	2 tbsp olive oil
2 tbsp tomato paste	1 tsp curry powder
2 tbsp fresh cilantro, chopped	Salt and black pepper to taste
2 tbsp flour	¼ cup Greek yogurt
1 cup coconut milk	1 (14.5-oz) cans tomatoes, diced
1 onion, chopped	2 garlic cloves, minced
1 tbsp garam masala	1 tsp paprika

DIRECTIONS and total time: approx. 48 minutes

Heat olive oil on Sauté, and cook garlic, ginger, chicken thighs, and onion for about 5 minutes, stirring occasionally. Add in tomatoes and tomato paste and cook for about 3 minutes. Whisk 1/3 cup water with flour in a bowl until smooth. Pour into the pot. Stir in garam masala, paprika, curry powder, coconut milk, salt, and pepper. Pour in 1 cup of water. Seal the lid, select Manual, and cook for 15 minutes at High. When ready, do a quick release. Serve in bowls topped each one with a dollop of yogurt and cilantro.

Garlicky Chicken Wings with Herbs

INGREDIENTS for 4 servings

12 chicken wings	½ tsp sage
½ cup chicken broth	1 tbsp garlic, minced
1 tsp basil	2 tbsp olive oil
1 tsp thyme	Salt and black pepper to taste

DIRECTIONS and total time: approx. 20 minutes

Pour 1 cup of water in your Instant Pot and fit a trivet. Place chicken in a bowl and mix well the remaining ingredients. Cover the bowl and let the wings sit for 15 minutes. Arrange them on the trivet and seal the lid. Select Manual and cook for 10 minutes at High. When ready, do a quick pressure release. Serve warm.

Cumin Chicken with Salsa Verde

INGREDIENTS for 4 servings

1 lb chicken thighs	Salt and black pepper to taste
2 tbsp olive oil	2 garlic cloves, minced
1 cup salsa verde	1 yellow onion, chopped
½ tsp thyme, dried	2 tbsp lime juice
1 tsp cumin	Cilantro, chopped for garnish

DIRECTIONS and total time: approx. 43 minutes

Heat oil on Sauté and cook chicken thighs for 5 minutes in total. Add salsa verde, thyme, garlic, onion, salt and pepper, and cook for 3 minutes. Pour in 2 cups of water. Seal the lid, select Manual, and cook for 20 minutes at High. When ready, do a quick release and remove the thighs to a plate. Discard the bones and shred the meat, then return it to the pot to warm up. Garnish with cilantro and lime juice and serve.

Cheesy Chicken Piccata with Olives

INGREDIENTS for 4 servings

4 chicken breasts, halved	1 tsp dried basil
3 tbsp olive oil	Salt and black pepper to taste
2 tbsp lemon juice	¼ cup Pecorino Romano, grated
1 tbsp sherry wine	½ cup flour
2 shallots, chopped	¼ cup sour cream
2 garlic cloves, crushed	1 cup black olives, chopped
1 cup chicken broth	2 tbsp parsley, chopped

DIRECTIONS and total time: approx. 35 minutes

In a bowl, combine flour, salt, and pepper. Dip chicken into flour and shake off the excess. Warm olive oil on Sauté and brown the chicken on both sides for 3-4 minutes; reserve. Add shallots and garlic to the pot and sauté for 2 minutes. Stir in sherry, broth, lemon juice, olives, basil, salt, and pepper. Bring back the chicken. Seal the lid, set to Manual, and cook for 15 minutes at High. Do a quick pressure release. Stir in sour cream and Pecorino cheese. Sprinkle with parsley and serve.

Mediterranean Chicken

INGREDIENTS for 4 servings

2 tbsp olive oil	2 tbsp tomato paste
2 carrots, sliced	Salt and black pepper to taste
1 lb chicken breasts, sliced	½ cup raisins
2 tbsp lemon juice	½ cup dried apricots, chopped
2 onions, sliced	2 cups chicken broth
2 garlic cloves, minced	2 tbsp flour
1 tsp ground cumin	Chopped parsley for garnish

DIRECTIONS and total time: approx. 35 minutes

Heat olive oil on Sauté and cook carrots, garlic, and onions for 3 minutes. Rub the chicken with salt and pepper and add it to the pot. Cook for another 5 minutes, stirring occasionally. In a mixing bowl, whisk tomato paste, lemon juice, flour, broth, and cumin until well combined; stir in apricots and raisins. Pour the mixture over the chicken. Seal the lid, select Manual, and cook for 15 minutes at High. When ready, do a quick release. Serve hot sprinkled with parsley.

Teriyaki-Style Chicken Thighs

INGREDIENTS for 4 servings

1 tbsp honey	1 tsp grated ginger
Salt and black pepper to taste	½ cup coconut aminos
1 lb chicken thighs	Chopped scallions for garnish

DIRECTIONS and total time: approx. 18 minutes

Place chicken in your IP. In a bowl, mix the remaining ingredients with 1 cup of water until well combined. Pour the mixture over the chicken. Seal the lid, press Manual, and cook for 15 minutes at High. When ready, release the pressure quickly. Sprinkle with scallions.

Chicken with Brown Rice

INGREDIENTS for 4 servings

2 tbsp lime juice	1 cup brown rice
2 tbsp olive oil	Salt and black pepper to taste
½ cup chunky salsa	½ cup Mexican cheese blend
2 chicken breasts	2 tbsp tomato puree
½ tsp garlic powder	2 tbsp cilantro, chopped

DIRECTIONS and total time: approx. 45 minutes

Lay the chicken breasts inside your IP. Pour in lime juice, salt, garlic powder, olive oil, tomato puree, black pepper, and 1 cup of water. Seal the lid and cook for 15 minutes on Manual at High. When ready, do a quick release. Remove the chicken to a plate. To the pot, add brown rice and 1 cup of water. Seal the lid again and cook for 20 minutes on Manual at High. Do a quick pressure release. Fluff with a fork and transfer to the chicken plate. Serve topped with cheese and cilantro.

Picante Chicken Thighs

INGREDIENTS for 4 servings

1 lb boneless chicken thighs	½ tsp onion powder
2 bell peppers, sliced	1 tsp oregano
1 ½ cups vegetable broth	½ tsp cayenne pepper
1 tbsp green chili powder	2 tbsp olive oil
1 tsp cumin	1 tbsp cornstarch
½ tsp garlic powder	Salt and black pepper to taste

DIRECTIONS and total time: approx. 30 minutes

Warm olive oil on Sauté. Combine all spices in a bowl and rub the mixture all over the chicken. Put the chicken in the pot and cook until golden on all sides, 5 minutes. Stir in bell peppers for 3 minutes and pour broth over. Seal the lid, set the timer to 15 minutes on Manual at High. When ready, do a quick release. In a small bowl, stir cornstarch with 1 cup of cooking liquid. Pour in the pot, press Sauté and cook until the sauce thickens, about 3 minutes. Serve immediately.

Spicy Chicken Soup

INGREDIENTS for 6 servings

1 lb chicken breasts	1 tsp oregano
1 tbsp chili powder	3 tbsp olive oil
2 garlic cloves, minced	1 bell pepper, sliced
6 cups chicken broth	1 onion, sliced
1 carrot, chopped	Salt and black pepper to taste

DIRECTIONS and total time: approx. 40 minutes

Heat olive oil on Sauté and cook onion, garlic, carrot, and bell pepper for 5 minutes until tender. Stir in chili powder and oregano for 1 minute. Pour in broth and seal the lid. Select Manual and cook for 15 minutes at High. When ready, do a natural release for 10 minutes. Adjust the seasoning with salt and pepper to serve.

Chicken Alfredo

INGREDIENTS for 4 servings

2 tbsp olive oil	4 oz cream cheese, softened
1 lb chicken breasts, halved	1 onion, chopped
2 tbsp parsley, chopped	2 garlic cloves, minced
16 oz fettuccine pasta	½ cup dry white wine
1 cup mushrooms, chopped	½ cup grated Parmesan

DIRECTIONS and total time: approx. 35 minutes

Cover pasta with salted water in your IP and seal the lid. Cook on Manual for 4 minutes at High. Do a quick release. Drain pasta and set aside, reserving 1 cup of the cooking water. Season the chicken with salt and pepper. Heat oil on Sauté and cook the chicken for 5-6 minutes on both sides; reserve. Add onion, mushrooms, and garlic to the pot and sauté for 3 minutes. Pour in wine to deglaze. Return chicken, add in the reserved pasta water and season with salt and pepper. Seal the lid, select Manual, and cook for 15 minutes at High. When ready, release the pressure quickly. Remove the chicken to a cutting board and slice. Whisk the cream cheese with cooking liquid and pour in the pot. Stir for 3 minutes just to heat. Mix in pasta and Parmesan cheese. Serve topped with sliced chicken and parsley.

Spicy Roasted Whole Chicken

INGREDIENTS for 4-6 servings

1 (3.5-oz) whole chicken	1 tbsp Garam masala
1 tbsp garlic powder	1 tbsp chili powder
1 tbsp onion powder	Salt and black pepper to taste
2 tbsp olive oil	Chopped green onions

DIRECTIONS and total time: approx. 35 minutes

Put all ingredients, except for the chicken and green onions, in a bowl and mix well. Rub the mixture onto chicken. Pour 1 cup of water in the cooker and fit in a trivet. Place the chicken on the trivet. Seal the lid, select Manual, and cook for 25 minutes at High. Do a quick release. Scatter some green onions and serve.

Slow-Cooked Honey-Mustard Chicken

INGREDIENTS for 4 servings

1 lb chicken breasts	1 tbsp honey
2 tsp chipotle powder	2 garlic cloves, minced
1 tbsp rosemary	4 tbsp olive oil
1 tsp liquid smoke	1 cup chicken broth
1 tbsp yellow mustard	Salt and black pepper to taste

DIRECTIONS and total time: approx. 4 hrs and 10 minutes

Brush the chicken with olive oil and brown it on all sides for 3-4 minutes on Sauté. Pour broth and all the remaining ingredients in a bowl. Stir to combine. Pour the mixture over the chicken. Seal the lid, set to Slow Cook mode at Low for 4 hours. When ready, serve hot.

Basil Chicken Casserole

INGREDIENTS for 4 servings

1 lb chicken thighs	2 garlic cloves, minced
½ cup pimento olives	1 tsp dried oregano
1 lb cherry tomatoes	2 tbsp butter
A handful of basil leaves	Salt and black pepper to taste

DIRECTIONS and total time: approx. 25 minutes

Season the thighs with salt and pepper. Melt butter on Sauté and brown chicken for about 4 minutes, flipping once; set aside. Place the tomatoes in a plastic bag and smash with a meat pounder. Combine tomatoes, garlic, 1 cup of water, and oregano in the pot. Seal the lid and cook on Poultry for 15 minutes at High. When ready, do a quick release. Stir in basil and olives, and serve.

Thai Chicken

INGREDIENTS for 6 servings

1 red bell pepper, cut into strips	
½ cup roasted peanuts, chopped	
6 chicken breasts, sliced	3 cloves garlic, minced
3 green onions, chopped	1 tbsp ground cumin
¼ cup lime juice	1 cup chicken broth
½ cup peanut butter	1 onion, chopped
2 tbsp cornstarch	¼ cup cilantro, chopped
½ tsp red pepper flakes	3 cups cooked rice

DIRECTIONS and total time: approx. 35 minutes

Heat peanut butter on Sauté and cook the chicken for 5 minutes, stirring occasionally; reserve. Add onion, garlic, and bell pepper to the pot and sauté for 3 minutes until tender. Stir in cumin and pepper flakes for 1 minute and pour in broth and lime juice. Seal the lid, select Manual, and cook for 15 minutes at High. When ready, quick-release the pressure. In a bowl, whisk cornstarch with 1 cup of the cooking liquid. Stir in the pot and mix well. Select Sauté and cook for 3 minutes until thickened. Garnished with cilantro, peanuts and green onions and serve.

Chicken Cordon Bleu

INGREDIENTS for 6 servings

1 (10.75 oz) can chicken soup	4 oz sliced Gruyere cheese
6 chicken breasts	4 oz sliced ham
3 tbsp butter, melted	½ cup milk
1 cup panko breadcrumbs	Chopped parsley for garnish

DIRECTIONS and total time: approx. 30 minutes

In a bowl, combine milk, soup, and 1 cup water. Pour the mixture in your IP. Add in chicken and cover with ham and cheese. Top with breadcrumbs and pour over butter. Seal the lid, select Manual, and cook for 15 minutes at High. When ready, release the pressure naturally for 10 minutes. Serve topped with parsley.

Maple Barbecued Chicken

INGREDIENTS for 4 servings

4 chicken breasts, halved	¼ tsp garlic powder
2 tbsp BBQ sauce	2 tsp lemon juice
1/8 tsp cayenne pepper	2 tbsp yellow mustard
½ tsp chili powder	1 cup ketchup
2 tbsp Worcestershire sauce	2 cups basmati rice cooked
1 tbsp maple syrup	Chopped chives for garnish

DIRECTIONS and total time: approx. 40 minutes

Lay chicken breasts in your IP. Combine the remaining ingredients in a bowl and mix to combine. Pour the mixture over the chicken. Pour in 1 cup of water. Seal the lid, select Manual, and cook for 15 minutes at High. When ready, release the pressure naturally for 10 minutes. Shred the chicken with two forks. Return to the pot and stir well. Serve on top of cooked basmati rice, garnished with freshly chopped chives.

Chicken Marrakesh

INGREDIENTS for 4 servings

1 onion, sliced	1 carrot, diced
2 tbsp butter	2 cloves garlic, minced
1 lb chicken breasts, cubed	1 tsp parsley
½ tsp turmeric	Salt and black pepper to taste
½ tsp cumin	1 (14.5-oz) can tomatoes
1 (14-oz) can garbanzo beans	2 cups chicken broth
2 sweet potatoes, diced	Chopped chives for garnish

DIRECTIONS and total time: approx. 40 minutes

Mix cumin, black pepper, parsley, turmeric, and salt in a mixing bowl; stir well to combine. Rub the chicken with this mixture. Melt butter on Sauté and cook the chicken for 5 minutes, stirring occasionally. Add in the remaining ingredients and mix well. Seal the lid, select Manual, and cook for 20 minutes at High. When ready, do a quick release. Serve topped with chopped chives.

Thyme & Bell Pepper Chicken

INGREDIENTS for 4 servings

2 tbsp olive oil	1 tbsp tomato puree
1 lb chicken drumsticks	1 tsp paprika
2 garlic cloves, minced	½ tbs rosemary
½ bell pepper, diced	1 tbsp thyme, chopped
½ onion, diced	Salt and black pepper to taste

DIRECTIONS and total time: approx. 30 minutes

Warm oil on Sauté and sear chicken on all sides for 5 minutes; set aside. Add onion, garlic, and bell pepper and sauté for 4 minutes. Stir in rosemary and paprika, and add in tomato puree. Return chicken and pour in 2 cups of water. Seal the lid, set to Poultry, and cook for 15 minutes at High. When ready, do a quick pressure release. Season to taste and sprinkle with thyme.

Marsala Wine Chicken with Mushrooms

INGREDIENTS for 4 servings

1 cup white mushrooms	1 cup chicken broth
2 tbsp olive oil	2 garlic cloves, minced
1 tbsp balsamic vinegar	2 tbsp arrowroot starch
2 tbsp milk	1 tsp parsley
½ cup Marsala wine	4 chicken breasts, halved
Salt and black pepper to taste	2 tbsp cilantro, chopped

DIRECTIONS and total time: approx. 40 minutes

Heat olive oil on Sauté and cook garlic, chicken, and mushrooms for 5 minutes. Pour in broth, vinegar, milk, and wine. Season with salt, pepper, and parsley. Seal the lid, select Manual, and cook for 18 minutes at High. When done, release the pressure naturally for 10 minutes. Mix arrowroot and 4 tbsp water and stir in the pot; cook for 2 minutes on Sauté. Top with cilantro.

Chicken & Mushrooms in Wine Sauce

INGREDIENTS for 4 servings

1 (10.75-oz) can mushroom soup	
4 chicken breasts, halved	¼ tsp garlic powder
2 tbsp butter	¼ cup white wine
Salt and black pepper to taste	1 tsp parsley
1 cup mushrooms, sliced	1 onion, chopped
2 tbsp milk	Chopped chives for garnish

DIRECTIONS and total time: approx. 40 minutes

Melt butter on Sauté and cook the chicken on both sides for 5 minutes; set aside. Add onion and mushrooms and sauté for 3 minutes until tender. Deglaze the pot pouring in the white wine and add in mushroom soup, milk, and 1 cup of water. Season with parsley, garlic powder, salt, and pepper. Seal the lid, select Manual, and cook for 15 minutes at High. When ready, do a quick pressure release. Serve topped with chives.

Honey Garlic Chicken

INGREDIENTS for 5 servings

5 chicken thighs	1 onion, chopped
3 tbsp vegetable oil	2 cloves garlic, minced
Salt and black pepper to taste	3 tbsp ketchup
1 tbsp cornstarch	1 tbsp honey
¼ cup soy sauce	2 green onions, chopped

DIRECTIONS and total time: approx. 38 minutes

On Sauté, heat vegetable oil and cook the chicken for 5 minutes until no longer pink. Mix soy sauce, honey, onion, ketchup, garlic, and 1 cup of water in a bowl. Pour over the chicken. Seal the lid, select Manual, and cook for 15 minutes at High. Do a quick release. In a bowl, mix the cornstarch and ¼ cup of the cooking liquid. Stir this mixture in the cooker to thicken the sauce for 2-3 minutes on Sauté. Top with green onions.

Sweet & Spicy Chicken Mole

INGREDIENTS for 4 servings

¼ cup milk	2 chili peppers, sliced
1 oz dark chocolate, melted	4 garlic cloves, minced
1 tsp ground cinnamon	1 yellow onion, chopped
½ tsp cumin	1 lb chicken thighs
Salt and black pepper to taste	2 tbsp olive oil
3 tomatoes, diced	Chopped green onions

DIRECTIONS and total time: approx. 24 minutes

Season the chicken thighs with salt and black pepper. On Sauté, heat olive oil and brown the chicken for 3 minutes per side; set aside. Add onion to the pot and sweat for 2-3 minutes. Bring back the chicken. Combine the rest of the ingredients in a bowl, except for green onions. Add the mixture to the pot and pour in 2 cups of water. Seal the lid, select Manual, and cook for 15 minutes at High. When done, do a natural pressure release for 5 minutes. Top with green onions.

Chipotle Chicken with Chives & Avocado

INGREDIENTS for 4 servings

3 chipotle peppers in adobo sauce, minced	2 cloves garlic, minced
	2 tbsp melted butter
4 chicken breasts, halved	Salt and black pepper to taste
1 tbsp adobo sauce	Shredded chives for garnish
8 oz cream cheese, cubed	1 (10.75-oz) can chicken soup
1 cup chicken broth	1 avocado, sliced

DIRECTIONS and total time: approx. 35 minutes

In a bowl, mix garlic, butter, salt, and black pepper. Rub the chicken with the mixture and place it in your IP. Add in the remaining ingredients and toss to combine. Seal the lid, select Manual, and cook for 15 minutes at High. When ready, release the pressure naturally for 10 minutes. Serve warm garnished with chives.

Jamaican-Style Jerk Chicken

INGREDIENTS for 4 servings

2 bunches scallions, chopped	Salt and black pepper to taste
2 tsp allspice	2 tbsp olive oil
1 jalapeno pepper, chopped	½ tsp ground cardamom
4 chicken breasts, sliced	2 garlic cloves, minced
½ cup molasses	Chopped chives for garnish

DIRECTIONS and total time: approx. 60 minutes

In a bowl, add all the ingredients, except for the chicken and chives, and mix well. Coat the chicken with the mixture and let sit covered in the fridge for 10 minutes. On Sauté, cook the chicken mixture for 5-6 minutes, stirring often. Pour in 1 cup of water and seal the lid. Select Manual and cook for 18 minutes at High. When ready, release the pressure naturally for 10 minutes. Serve topped with freshly chopped chives.

Herby Chicken with Tomatoes

INGREDIENTS for 4 servings

4 chicken breasts, sliced	2 tbsp olive oil
1 (14.5-oz) can tomatoes	½ cup balsamic vinegar
1 tsp rosemary, dried	2 garlic cloves
1 tsp oregano, dried	1 onion, sliced
½ tsp thyme	Salt and black pepper to taste
1 tsp basil, dried	Chopped green onions

DIRECTIONS and total time: approx. 30 minutes

Mix all the herbs with olive oil, salt, and pepper in a bowl. Add in chicken and toss to coat; let marinate for 10 minutes. Preheat your Instant Pot on Sauté. Pour in the chicken and cook for 3-4 minutes, stirring occasionally. Stir in onion and garlic for another 2 minutes, then pour in tomatoes and 1 cup of water. Seal the lid, select Manual, and cook for 12 minutes at High. When ready, do a quick pressure release. Top with green onions and serve warm.

Winter Chicken Hotpot

INGREDIENTS for 4 servings

½ lb chicken tenders, sliced	½ cup red cider vinegar
½ lb chicken sausages, sliced	1 (14.5-oz) can tomatoes, diced
½ tsp thyme	1 green bell pepper, sliced
½ tsp rosemary	2 tbsp olive oil
½ tsp basil	1 leek, chopped
1 tsp onion powder	1 carrot, peeled, chopped
Salt and black pepper to taste	2 garlic cloves, minced
1 cup chicken broth	Chopped cilantro for garnish

DIRECTIONS and total time: approx. 40 minutes

In a bowl, combine thyme, rosemary, basil, onion powder, salt, and pepper; mix well. Rub the chicken tenders with the mixture. Heat olive oil and add in chicken tenders and sausage links to cook for 3-4 minutes, stirring occasionally. Add in garlic, leek, and bell pepper; sauté for another 3 minutes. Pour in tomatoes, broth, and vinegar; season. Seal the lid, select Manual, and cook for 15 minutes at High. When ready, do a quick release. Top with cilantro to serve.

Parmesan Chicken with Rice

INGREDIENTS for 4 servings

1 (10.5-oz) can celery soup	¼ cup Parmesan, grated
2 tbsp butter	1 cup rice
4 chicken breasts, halved	1 oz dry onion soup mix
Salt and black pepper to taste	Chopped parsley for garnish

DIRECTIONS and total time: approx. 41 minutes

Melt butter on Sauté and cook chicken for 5-6 minutes on both sides. In a bowl, combine celery soup, onion soup mix, and rice and stir well. Pour the mixture over the chicken, season to taste, and add in 1 cup of water. Seal the lid, select Manual, and cook for 15 minutes at High. When ready, release the pressure naturally for 10 minutes. Fluff the rice with a fork and serve topped with Parmesan cheese and parsley.

Cashew Flavored Chicken

INGREDIENTS for 4 servings

1 lb chicken breasts, sliced	1 tbsp honey
1 red bell pepper, chopped	2 tbsp apple cider vinegar
2 cups chicken broth	¾ cup cashew nuts, chopped
¼ cup coconut aminos	2 tbsp olive oil
1 tbsp garlic-chili sauce	½ cup flour
3 tbsp ketchup	Chopped cilantro for garnish

DIRECTIONS and total time: approx. 40 minutes

Coat the chicken in the flour. Heat the olive oil on Sauté and cook the chicken until brown, about 5 minutes. Add in the remaining ingredients, except for cashews. Seal the lid, select Manual, and cook for 15 minutes at High. When ready, release the pressure naturally for 10 minutes. Top with nut and cilantro.

Chicken with Spicy Honey-Orange Sauce

INGREDIENTS for 4 servings

2 tsp red pepper flakes	1 cup chicken broth
2 tbsp olive oil	1 tsp honey
½ cup orange juice	Salt and black pepper to taste
1 lb chicken tenderloins	Chopped cilantro for garnish

DIRECTIONS and total time: approx. 30 minutes

Season tenderloins with salt and pepper. Heat olive oil on Sauté and sear chicken for 5-6 minutes on both sides. In a bowl, mix together the remaining ingredients until well combined. Pour the mixture over the chicken. Seal the lid, select Manual, and cook for 12 minutes at High. When done, release the pressure naturally for 10 minutes. Serve sprinkled with cilantro and enjoy.

Garlic & Paprika Chicken

INGREDIENTS for 4 servings

1 lb chicken breasts	2 tbsp olive oil
2 cloves garlic, minced	1 tsp paprika
Salt and black pepper to taste	1 cup water
1 yellow onion, chopped	Chopped parsley for garnish

DIRECTIONS and total time: approx. 35 minutes

Mix black pepper, salt, paprika, and some olive oil to make a paste. Cut the chicken into strips. Rub the paste all over the chicken strips. Coat the inside of your Instant Pot with cooking spray. Mix onion, garlic, and remaining olive oil in a bowl. Add the chicken to the pot and cover with the onion mixture. Pour in water. Seal the lid, select Manual, and cook for 18 minutes at High. Do a quick release. Granish with fresh parsley.

Jalapeño Chicken with Herbs

INGREDIENTS for 4 servings

1 cup chicken broth	2 tbsp dried dill
2 tbsp butter	2 tbsp garlic powder
1 tbsp cornstarch	2 tbsp onion powder
1 lb chicken breasts	1 tsp dried chives
2 jalapeño peppers, diced	Salt and black pepper to taste
2 tbsp dried parsley	2 tbsp cilantro, chopped

DIRECTIONS and total time: approx. 25 minutes

In a bowl, mix parsley, dill, garlic and onion powders, chives, salt, and pepper and rub the chicken breasts all over. Melt butter on Sauté and cook chicken breasts until golden, 5 minutes; set aside. Add jalapeño peppers and sauté for 2 minutes. Stir in chicken broth and return the chicken. Seal the lid, select Manual, and set the timer to 18 minutes at High. When ready, do a quick release. Remove the chicken to a plate and shred it with two forks. In a small bowl, mix cornstarch with some cooking liquid and pour in the pot. Press Sauté and cook until thickened, about 3 minutes. Stir in the shredded chicken. Serve sprinkled with cilantro.

Orange Glazed Chicken

INGREDIENTS for 4 servings

2 tbsp olive oil	1 tbsp chili powder
1 lb chicken thighs	1 tbsp coriander powder
1 cup orange marmalade	Salt and black pepper to taste
1 cup chicken broth	

DIRECTIONS and total time: approx. 30 minutes

Heat olive oil on Sauté. Season the chicken with chili and coriander powders, salt, and pepper and add it to the pot; cook for 5 minutes on all sides. In a bowl, mix orange marmalade and chicken broth. Pour over the chicken. Seal the lid, select Manual, and cook for 20 minutes at High. When ready, do a quick release.

Spinach & Gnocchi Chicken Sausage Pot

INGREDIENTS for 4 servings

2 tbsp olive oil	1 yellow onion, chopped
1 lb chicken sausages, sliced	Salt and black pepper to taste
2 garlic cloves, minced	2 cups chicken broth
2 cups baby spinach, chopped	16 oz fresh potato gnocchi
1 cup canned diced tomatoes	Chopped chives for garnish

DIRECTIONS and total time: approx. 35 minutes

Heat olive oil on Sauté and add sausages, garlic, and onion; cook for 4-5 minutes, stirring periodically. Pour in tomatoes, and chicken broth; season to taste. Seal the lid, select Manual for 15 minutes at High. When done, release the pressure quickly. Stir in baby spinach and potato gnocchi for 3-4 minutes until gnocchi floats to the top. Sprinkle with chives and serve.

Chicken Stew with Potatoes & Barley

INGREDIENTS for 4 servings

2 cups chicken broth	1 cup canned diced tomatoes
2 garlic cloves, minced	1 bay leaf
1 lb chicken breasts, cubed	1 tsp smoked paprika
3 potatoes, cubed	2 tbsp olive oil
2 carrots, sliced	½ tsp thyme
1 sweet onion, chopped	Salt and black pepper to taste
½ cup barley	Cilantro, chopped for garnish

DIRECTIONS and total time: approx. 40 minutes

Heat olive oil on Sauté and cook garlic, carrots, onion, and chicken for 5-6 minutes, stirring often. Stir in smoked paprika, barley, thyme, salt, and pepper for 1 minute. Pour in tomatoes, chicken broth, potatoes, and bay leaf. Seal the lid, select Manual, and cook for 15 minutes at High. Do a quick release. Remove and discard the bay leaf. Scatter with cilantro and serve hot.

Apple & Honey Chicken Drumsticks

INGREDIENTS for 4 servings

2 tbsp butter	Zest and juice from 1 lemon
1 tsp honey	1 apple, chopped
4 tbsp soy sauce	1 lb chicken drumsticks
Salt and black pepper to taste	Chopped parsley for garnish

DIRECTIONS and total time: approx. 35 minutes

Season the chicken drumsticks with salt and pepper. Melt butter on Sauté and cook drumsticks for 5 minutes on all sides. In a bowl, mix the remaining ingredients with 1 cup of water; combine well. Pour the mixture over the drumsticks. Seal the lid, select Manual, and cook for 20 minutes at High. When done, quick release the pressure. Serve drumsticks sprinkled with parsley.

Shallot Turkey with Apricot Gravy

INGREDIENTS for 4 servings

2 tbsp olive oil	12 dried apricots, soaked
1 lb turkey breast	2 cups chicken broth
1 carrot, sliced	1 celery stalk, diced
2 shallots, chopped	Salt and black pepper to taste
2 tsp balsamic vinegar	2 tbsp rosemary, chopped

DIRECTIONS and total time: approx. 35 minutes

Heat olive oil on Sauté and cook carrot, shallots, and celery for 5 minutes, stirring often. Add in turkey and chicken broth; season to taste. Seal the lid and cook for 15 minutes on Manual at High. When ready, do a quick release. Remove turkey and shred it with two forks.

Strain the cooking liquid and return it to the pot. Chop apricots and pour in the sauce with balsamic vinegar. Press Sauté and cook until thickened, 3-4 minutes. Pour sauce over the turkey and serve topped with rosemary.

Juicy Turkey with Mushrooms

INGREDIENTS for 4 servings

1 cup white button mushrooms, sliced

1 lb turkey breast	2 garlic cloves, minced
1 cup leeks, chopped	2 tbsp olive oil
½ tsp dried sage	3 tbsp whipping cream
¼ cup dry white wine	2 tbsp parsley, chopped
1 cup chicken stock	Salt and black pepper to taste

DIRECTIONS and total time: approx. 35 minutes

Warm olive oil on Sauté. Season turkey with salt and pepper and sear for 3 minutes on each side. Transfer to a plate. Add leeks, garlic, sage, and mushrooms to the pot and stir-fry for 3-4 minutes. Add in white wine to scrape off any brown bits at the bottom. When the alcohol evaporates, return the turkey and pour in chicken stock. Seal the lid and cook on Manual for 15 minutes at High. Do a quick pressure release. Remove turkey and stir whipping cream in the pot. Cook on Sauté until the sauce thickens, for 3 minutes. Slice the turkey and serve topped with sauce and parsley.

Homemade Duck & Snow Pea Soup

INGREDIENTS for 4-6 servings

1 cup carrots, diced	1 cup onions, diced
6 cups chicken stock	2 garlic cloves, minced
1 lb duck breast, chopped	2 tbsp duck fat
1 cup celery, chopped	2 tbsp parsley, chopped
1 cup snow peas	Salt and black pepper to taste

DIRECTIONS and total time: approx. 35 minutes

Warm duck fat on Sauté and cook onions, carrots, celery, and garlic for 4 minutes. Add in duck meat and sauté for 3 minutes. Pour in the chicken stock and seal the lid. Select Manual and cook for 20 minutes at High. After the beep, do a quick pressure release. Stir in the peas and cook for 4 minutes on Sauté. Adjust seasoning and serve sprinkled with parsley.

Sriracha Pulled Turkey with Ale Beer

INGREDIENTS for 4 servings

1 lb turkey breast	1 cup ale beer
Salt and black pepper to taste	2 tbsp canola oil

Sriracha sauce:

2 tbsp maple syrup	1 tsp onion powder
½ cup apple cider vinegar	½ cup mustard
1 tsp liquid smoke	1 tbsp Worcestershire sauce
2 tsp sriracha	1 tsp mustard powder
1 tsp garlic powder	2 tbsp olive oil

DIRECTIONS and total time: approx. 40 minutes

Heat canola oil on Sauté and brown turkey on all sides, about 5-6 minutes. Whisk together all the sauce ingredients in a bowl. Add sauce to the pot and stir.

Pour in ale beer, seal the lid and cook for 25 minutes on Manual at High. When ready, release the pressure quickly. Remove the turkey to a plate and shred with two forks. Set the cooker too Sauté and cook until the sauce is reduced and thickened, 3-4 minutes. Return the turkey and stir to coat well. Serve warm.

Buffalo Turkey & Squash Casserole

INGREDIENTS for 4 servings

2 tbsp olive oil	1 garlic clove, minced
4 tbsp buffalo sauce	1 onion, diced
1 lb winter squash, cubed	2 tbsp parsley, chopped
1 lb turkey breast, cubed	Salt and black pepper to taste

DIRECTIONS and total time: approx. 30 minutes

Heat olive oil on Sauté and sauté onion and garlic until soft. Add and cook turkey for 5 minutes. Pour in the remaining ingredients and 1cup water. Seal the lid and cook on Manual for 20 minutes at High. When ready, do a quick pressure release. Top with parsley to serve.

Turkey with Broccoli & Carrots

INGREDIENTS for 4 servings

1 cup carrots, chopped	2 tbsp butter
1 lb turkey breast, sliced	1 cup water
1 cup broccoli florets	Salt and black pepper to taste

DIRECTIONS and total time: approx. 15 minutes

Add water and a steamer basket to your Instant Pot. Place in carrots and broccoli. Seal the lid, press Steam, and cook for 3 minutes at High.

Quick-release the pressure; set aside and wipe clean. Melt butter on Sauté and stir-fry the seasoned turkey for 10 minutes. Serve warm along with the steamed veggies.

Onion Apple Goose

INGREDIENTS for 4 servings

2 cups chicken broth	1 tsp cayenne pepper
2 tbsp butter	2 apples, sliced
1 onion, sliced	¼ tsp garlic powder
1 lb goose breast, chopped	Salt and black pepper to taste
2 tbsp balsamic vinegar	2 tbsp cilantro, chopped

DIRECTIONS and total time: approx. 25 minutes

Melt butter on Sauté and cook goose until golden, 5 minutes; season to taste and set aside. Add onion and apples to the pot and cook for 3 minutes.

Stir in the rest of the ingredients and return the goose. Seal the lid, select Manual and set the timer to 18 minutes at High. When ready, do a quick release. Top with cilantro.

Pork

Pork Chops with Broccoli

INGREDIENTS for 4 servings

1 lb pork chops	1 tbsp arrowroot
1 cup onions, sliced	1 garlic clove, minced
1 cup carrots, sliced	1 cup chicken stock
2 tbsp butter	½ tsp dried thyme
2 cups broccoli florets	Salt and black pepper to taste

DIRECTIONS and total time: approx. 40 minutes

Melt butter on Sauté. Add pork chops and cook on all sides until golden, 5 minutes; transfer to a plate. Add onions, carrots, and garlic and cook for 3 minutes. Return the pork chops to the pot and pour the broth over; add thyme. Seal the lid and cook on Manual at High for 20 minutes. When done, do a quick pressure release. Press Sauté and stir in broccoli for 2-3 minutes. Mix arrowroot with half cup of the cooking liquid in a bowl and pour in the pot. Cook until the sauce thickens, about 3 minutes. Adjust the seasoning and serve hot.

Lemon & Cinnamon Braised Pork

INGREDIENTS for 4-6 servings

2 tbsp olive oil	¼ tsp onion powder
2 lb pork shoulder	1 onion, chopped
1 cinnamon stick	1 serrano pepper, diced
½ cup fresh lemon juice	2 tbsp parsley, chopped
1 tsp cumin	½ tsp oregano
½ tsp garlic powder	Salt and black pepper to taste

DIRECTIONS and total time: approx. 45 minutes

Place half of the olive oil in a small bowl. Add in cumin, garlic and onion powders, oregano, salt, and pepper, and stir to combine. Rub it all over the meat. Heat the remaining oil on Sauté. Add the pork and sear it on all sides until browned, 4-5 minutes. Transfer to a plate. Add onion and serrano pepper and sauté for 2 minutes. Pour in lemon juice and deglaze the bottom with a spatula. Return the pork and add cinnamon stick and 2 cups of water. Seal the lid, select Manual, and cook for 20 minutes at High. When ready, allow for a natural pressure release for 10 minutes. Grab two forks and shred the pork inside the pot. Remove the cinnamon stick and stir. Sprinkle with parsley and serve.

Italian-Style Pancetta & Potato Casserole

INGREDIENTS for 4 servings

½ lb smoked pancetta, chopped	1 cup whipping cream
1 tbsp olive oil	1 tsp Italian seasoning
1 red onion, sliced	4 golden potatoes, chopped
½ cup carrots, sliced	½ cup grated mozzarella
1 cup chicken stock	Salt and black pepper to taste

DIRECTIONS and total time: approx. 40 minutes

Warm olive oil on Sauté and cook pancetta, carrots, and onion for 5 minutes until pancetta is crisp. Stir in potatoes and season with salt, pepper, and Italian seasoning. Transfer to a baking dish and pour in whipping cream and chicken broth; stir to combine. Top with mozzarella cheese. Clean the pot, pour in 1 cup of water and insert a trivet. Place the dish on the trivet and seal the lid. Select Manual and cook for 20 minutes at High. Do a quick pressure release and serve.

Quick Pork Chops with Brussels Sprouts

INGREDIENTS for 4 servings

4 pork chops	2 shallots, chopped
½ lb Brussels sprouts, halved	2 tbsp olive oil
¼ cup sparkling wine	1 cup celery stalk, chopped
2 cups vegetable stock	Salt and black pepper to taste

DIRECTIONS and total time: approx. 35 minutes

Heat olive oil on Sauté mode and cook pork chops until browned on all sides, 3-4 minutes. Stir in Brussels sprouts, celery, and shallots, and stir-fry for 3 minutes. Pour in broth and wine. Seal the lid and cook for 20 minutes on Manual at High. When ready, release the pressure quickly and serve immediately.

Pork & Shallot Frittata

INGREDIENTS for 4 servings

2 tbsp butter, melted	6 eggs
2 shallots, chopped	2 tbsp milk
½ lb ground pork, cooked	Salt and black pepper to taste

DIRECTIONS and total time: approx. 30 minutes

In a bowl, whisk the eggs until frothy. Mix in shallots, ground pork, milk, salt, and pepper. Grease a casserole dish with butter and pour in the egg mixture. Place a trivet in your IP and add in 1 cup of water. Put the dish on the trivet. Seal the lid, select Manual, and cook for 15 minutes at High. Do a quick pressure release.

Tasty Pork with Carrots & Shallots

INGREDIENTS for 4 servings

1 lb pork cutlets	1 cup vegetable broth
1 lb baby carrots	1 tsp garlic powder
2 shallots, sliced	Salt and black pepper to taste
1 tbsp butter	

DIRECTIONS and total time: approx. 35 minutes

Season pork with salt and pepper. Melt butter on Sauté and brown pork on all sides. Stir in carrots and shallots and cook until soft, 2 minutes. Pour in broth and add garlic. Seal the lid and set on Manual for 25 minutes at High. When done, quick-release the pressure.

Spicy Pork Sausage Meatloaf

INGREDIENTS for 4 servings

1 lb ground sausage
½ tsp cayenne powder
½ tsp marjoram
1 egg, beaten
1 tbsp thyme
1 large potato, grated
Salt and black pepper to taste
1 sweet onion, diced
1 tbsp brown sugar
1 cup ketchup

DIRECTIONS and total time: approx. 45 minutes

In a bowl, place ground sausage, egg, cayenne powder, marjoram, thyme, potato, onion, salt, and pepper and mix the ingredients with your hands until well blended. Add and shape the meatloaf mixture in a greased baking dish. Whisk together ketchup and sugar in a bowl and pour over the meatloaf. Place a trivet inside your Instant Pot and pour 1 cup of water. Lay the dish on top, seal the lid, and cook on Manual for 30 minutes at High. When ready, do a quick release. Serve sliced.

Pork Tenderloin in Sweet Ginger Sauce

INGREDIENTS for 4 servings

1 lb pork tenderloin, sliced
12 oz canned pineapple
1 cup vegetable broth
1 tsp brown sugar
2 tbsp olive oil
2 tbsp tomato puree
2 cup shallots, sliced
½ tsp ginger, grated
Salt and black pepper to taste
¼ cup Tamari sauce
¼ cup white wine vinegar
2 tbsp cilantro, chopped

DIRECTIONS and total time: approx. 40 minutes

Heat olive oil on Sauté and fry pork for 4-5 minutes on both sides; reserve. Add shallots to the pot and sauté for 3 minutes. Stir in the rest of the ingredients for 1 minute and return the pork. Seal the lid and cook for 20 minutes on Manual at High. When done, release the pressure quickly. Press Sauté and cook for 2 more minutes until the sauce thickens. Garnish with cilantro.

Fall Pork Stew

INGREDIENTS for 4-6 servings

½ lb pork shoulder, cubed
1 tsp paprika
2 cups diced canned tomatoes
1 head cabbage, shredded
1 celery stalk, diced
1 tbsp cumin
1 cup leeks, chopped
1 carrot, chopped
1 tsp parsley
2 tbsp butter
2 cups chicken broth
Salt and black pepper to taste

DIRECTIONS and total time: approx. 40 minutes

Melt butter on Sauté and cook the pork until browned, about 5 minutes. Add in leeks, celery, cabbage, carrot, cumin, and paprika and cook for another 5 minutes, stirring occasionally. Pour in chicken broth, tomatoes, parsley, salt, and pepper; stir. Seal the lid and cook on Manual for 20 minutes at High. When ready, do a quick release. Ladle into serving bowls to serve.

Pear & Cherry Pork Tenderloin

INGREDIENTS for 4 servings

1 lb pork tenderloin
1 chopped celery stalk
2 cups pears, chopped
½ cup dry cherries, soaked
1 cup vegetable broth
1 onion, chopped
Salt and black pepper to taste
2 tbsp olive oil

DIRECTIONS and total time: approx. 35 minutes

Heat olive oil on Sauté and cook onion and celery for 5 minutes. Season the pork with salt and pepper and add to the pot. Brown for 2-3 minutes per side. Top with pears and cherries, and pour in vegetable broth. Seal the lid and cook on Manual for 20 minutes at High. Once ready, do a quick pressure release. Slice the pork tenderloin and arrange on a serving platter. Spoon pear-cheery sauce over the pork and serve.

Juicy & Tender Pork Loin

INGREDIENTS for 4 servings

2 tbsp olive oil
1 lb pork loin, cut into cubes
2 apples, peeled and chopped
½ tbsp lemon zest
1 onion, diced
1 celery stalk, diced
2 tbsp parsley, chopped
½ cup leeks, sliced
2 cups vegetable broth
½ tsp cumin
½ tsp thyme
Salt and black pepper to taste

DIRECTIONS and total time: approx. 40 minutes

Heat olive oil on Sauté and cook the pork until browned on all sides, 5-6 minutes; set aside. Add leeks, onion, apples, and celery to the pot, and cook for 3 minutes. Add the pork back to the pot, pour in broth, and stir in all herbs and spices. Seal the lid, and cook on Manual at High for 20 minutes. After the beep, do a quick pressure release. Remove the pork to a plate and blitz the sauce with an immersion blender until smooth. Slice the pork and serve topped with the sauce.

Tender BBQ Ribs

INGREDIENTS for 4-6 servings

1 (3 lb) rack pork spare ribs
2 tbsp brown sugar
1 tsp oregano
1 tsp smoked paprika
5 tbsp chili sauce
1 cup vegetable broth
Salt and black pepper to taste
1 tsp mustard powder
1 cup BBQ sauce
2 tbsp balsamic vinegar

DIRECTIONS and total time: approx. 40 minutes

Remove the membrane from the ribs. Cut the rack of ribs into portions. In a bowl, combine sugar, oregano, mustard powder, paprika, salt, and pepper and rub into the ribs. Put the ribs in the inner pot. Combine the remaining ingredients with ½ cup of water in a bowl and pour over the ribs. Seal the lid, select Manual, and cook for 20 minutes at High. When ready, release the pressure naturally for 10 minutes. Serve hot.

Juicy Sweet Pork Ribs

INGREDIENTS for 4 servings

2 tbsp apple cider vinegar	Salt and black pepper to taste
2 lb pork ribs	1 cup pineapple juice
1 tbsp flour	2 tbsp parsley

DIRECTIONS and total time: approx. 40 minutes

Pour pineapple juice and vinegar in your IP and lower a trivet. Season the ribs with salt and pepper, and place them on the trivet. Seal the lid and cook on Manual at High for 20 minutes. Do a natural release for 10 minutes. Place ribs under broiler for 2 minutes to achieve a crispy crust. Mix flour with some cooking juice and pour in the pot; season with salt and pepper. Press Sauté and cook for 2-3 minutes until the sauce thickens. Serve ribs topped with the sauce and parsley.

Pork Shoulder in BBQ Sauce

INGREDIENTS for 4-6 servings

2 lb pork shoulder	1 tsp sweet chili powder
3 tbsp olive oil	2 cups vegetable stock
1 tsp onion powder	6 dates, soaked
1 tsp garlic powder	¼ cup tomato puree
Salt and black pepper to taste	½ cup coconut aminos

DIRECTIONS and total time: approx. 40 minutes

In a small bowl, combine onion, garlic, and sweet chili powders, salt, and pepper. Rub the mixture onto the pork. Heat olive oil on Sauté and cook pork on all sides, about 5 minutes. Pour the stock around the meat, not over it, and seal the lid. Select Manual and set to 20 minutes at High. Release the pressure quickly. Grab two forks and shred the meat inside the pot. Place dates, tomato purre, and coconut aminos in a food processor and pulse until smooth. Pour the sauce over the meat inside the pot. Stir to combine and serve warm.

Grandma's Veggie Ground Pork

INGREDIENTS for 6 servings

1 ¼ lb ground pork	1 red bell pepper, chopped
3 tbsp olive oil	1 green bell pepper, chopped
6 button mushrooms, sliced	1 yellow bell pepper, chopped
½ cup chopped celery	2 cups vegetable broth
1 onion, chopped	1 tsp red pepper flakes
2 large tomatoes, chopped	Salt and black pepper to taste
1 potato, chopped	Chopped parsley for garnish

DIRECTIONS and total time: approx. 40 minutes

Heat olive oil on Sauté and cook the pork until browned, about 5-6 minutes. Stir in the remaining ingredients, except for broth and parsley and sauté for 5 minutes. Pour in vegetable broth. Seal the lid and cook on Manual for 20 minutes at High. Do a quick pressure release. Sprinkle with parsley to serve.

Herby Pork Butt with Potatoes

INGREDIENTS for 4 servings

1 lb pork butt, cubed	¼ tsp parsley
1 lb potatoes, diced	1 ½ tsp sage
2 tsp butter	1 ½ cups vegetable broth
¼ tsp thyme	Salt and black pepper to taste

DIRECTIONS and total time: approx. 40 minutes

Season pork with thyme, sage, parsley, salt, and pepper. Melt the butter on Sauté. Add the pork and brown for 6 minutes. Add the potatoes and pour in the broth. Seal the lid and cook for 20 minutes on Manual at High. When ready, do a quick release, and serve hot.

Rich Parsnip & Mushroom Pork

INGREDIENTS for 4 servings

1 lb pork butt, sliced	1 garlic clove, minced
2 cups mushrooms, sliced	1 cup vegetable broth
1 ½ cups parsnips, chopped	Salt and black pepper to taste
½ cup white wine	2 tbsp olive oil

DIRECTIONS and total time: approx. 45 minutes

Heat olive oil on Sauté and brown pork for 8 minutes. Stir in the remaining ingredients. Season with salt and pepper. Seal the lid and cook for 25 minutes on Manual at High. When done, do a quick release and serve.

Savoy Cabbage with Pancetta

INGREDIENTS for 4-6 servings

1 lb Savoy cabbage, chopped	1 tbsp butter
4 oz pancetta, chopped	Salt and black pepper to taste
2 cups vegetable broth	2 tbsp basil, chopped

DIRECTIONS and total time: approx. 40 minutes

On Sauté, cook pancetta for 5 minutes. Stir in cabbage, salt, pepper, and butter for 5 minutes. Pour in broth and seal the lid. Select Manual and cook for 10 minutes at High. When the cooking is over, release pressure naturally for 10 minutes. Serve hot, topped with basil.

Pork with Shallots & Mushrooms

INGREDIENTS for 4 servings

1 lb lean pork loin, cubed	1 cup sour cream
2 tbsp olive oil	1 cup shallots, chopped
1 ½ cups chicken broth	1 cup mushrooms, sliced
1 garlic clove, minced	Salt and black pepper to taste

DIRECTIONS and total time: approx. 30 minutes

Heat olive oil on Sauté and stir-fry shallots, garlic, mushrooms, and pork for 4-5 minutes. Pour in broth and season with salt and pepper. Seal the lid, select Manual, and cook for 15 minutes at High. Release the pressure quickly. Stir in sour cream and serve.

Sauteed Spinach With Bacon & Chickpeas

INGREDIENTS for 4 servings

2 tbsp olive oil	½ lb bacon slices, chopped
1 tsp oregano	1 onion, chopped
2 garlic cloves, minced	2 cups spinach, chopped
1 cup chickpeas, soaked	2 tbsp parsley, chopped
1 carrot, chopped	Salt and black pepper to taste

DIRECTIONS and total time: approx. 45 minutes

Heat olive oil on Sauté and cook onion, garlic, carrot, oregano, and bacon for 5 minutes. Add chickpeas and 4 cups of water. Seal the lid and cook for 25 minutes on Manual at High. Once done, perform a quick release. Stir in spinach and press Sauté. Cook for 3-4 minutes, adjust the seasoning and serve sprinkled parsley.

Flavorful Pork Roast in Beer Sauce

INGREDIENTS for 4-6 servings

2 lb pork loin roast	1 cup vegetable broth
8 oz white mushrooms, sliced	1 onion, chopped
10 oz root beer	1 carrot, chopped
3 tbsp olive oil	Salt and black pepper to taste

DIRECTIONS and total time: approx. 50 minutes

Heat olive oil on Sauté and brown pork on all sides, about 6 minutes. Add in onion, mushrooms, and carrot, and sauté for 3 minutes. Stir in broth, beer, salt and pepper. Seal the lid and cook on Manual for 40 minutes at High. Do a quick release and remove the pork to a plate. In a blender, pulse the liquid and veggies until smooth. Slice the pork and spoon the sauce over.

Pork and Sauerkraut Goulash

INGREDIENTS for 4 servings

2 tbsp olive oil	1 cup vegetable stock
1 lb ground pork	1 red onion, chopped
4 cups sauerkraut, shredded	2 garlic cloves, minced
1 cup tomato sauce	Salt and black pepper to taste

DIRECTIONS and total time: approx. 45 minutes

Melt butter on Sauté and stir-fry onion and garlic until soft, about 3 minutes. Add in pork and cook for 4 minutes until lightly browned. Stir in the remaining ingredients and season with salt and black pepper. Seal the lid and cook for 15 minutes on Manual at High. When done, release the pressure quickly. Serve warm.

Pork Steaks with Apricot Sauce

INGREDIENTS for 4 servings

2 tbsp olive oil	1 tbsp apricot jelly
4 pork steaks	½ tsp ginger powder
½ cup chicken broth	Salt and black pepper to taste
½ cup white wine	
5 dry apricots, sliced	

DIRECTIONS and total time: approx. 35 minutes

Heat olive oil on Sauté and cook pork for 4-5 minutes on both sides. Pour in the remaining ingredient, except for the jelly. Seal the lid and cook on Manual for 20 minutes at High. Do a quick pressure release. Remove pork and stir jelly in the pot; cook until thickened, 2-3 minutes. Pour sauce over the pork and serve.

Pork in Tomato Buttermilk Sauce

INGREDIENTS for 4 servings

2 tbsp canola oil	½ tbsp cilantro
1 lb pork shoulder, cubed	¼ tsp cumin
1 onion, chopped	¼ tsp cayenne pepper
1 cup buttermilk	1 tsp garlic powder
1 cup tomato sauce	Salt and black pepper to taste

DIRECTIONS and total time: approx. 50 minutes

Heat canola oil on Sauté and cook pork for 5 minutes, stirring occasionally until lightly browned. Add in onion and cook for 3 minutes until fragrant. Stir in the remaining ingredients and seal the lid. Cook for 30 minutes on Manual at High. When it beeps, do a quick pressure release. Serve immediately over cooked rice.

The Best Ever Pineapple Pork Meatballs

INGREDIENTS for 4 servings

1 lb ground pork	1 diced onion
1 tbsp Tamari sauce	1 tsp honey
2 garlic cloves, minced	2 tbsp pineapple juice
½ tsp dried thyme	1 cup breadcrumbs
½ tsp sage	Salt and black pepper to taste

DIRECTIONS and total time: approx. 30 minutes

Whisk honey, tamari, pineapple juice, 1 cup of water, thyme, salt, and pepper inside your IP. Season with salt and pepper. Set to Sauté and cook for 3 minutes. Combine all remaining ingredients in a bowl. Shape meatballs out of the mixture and drop them into the sauce. Seal the lid and cook on Manual for 15 minutes at High. When done, release pressure quickly. Serve.

Pork Rib Chops with Carrots & Parsnips

INGREDIENTS for 4 servings

4 pork rib chops	1 onion, sliced into rings
1 cup carrots, thinly sliced	1 ½ cups bbq sauce
1 cup parsnips, thinly sliced	Salt and black pepper to taste

DIRECTIONS and total time: approx. 35 minutes

Add the pork chops in your IP. In a bowl, combine bbq sauce, 1 cup of water, onion, parsnips, and carrots, and stir. Pour over the pork. Season with salt and pepper. Seal the lid, select Manual, and cook for 20 minutes at High. Once ready, release the pressure quickly. Serve.

Mango Pork Roast with Dijon Mustard

INGREDIENTS for 4-6 servings

2 lb pork roast	1 carrot, chopped
1 mango, chopped	2 garlic cloves, minced
3 tbsp Dijon mustard	2 tbsp olive oil
½ cup white wine	Salt and black pepper to taste

DIRECTIONS and total time: approx. 55 minutes

Brush pork with mustard. Heat olive oil on Sauté and sear the pork on all sides, 8-10 minutes. Add mango, 1 cup of water, and stir in the remaining ingredients. Seal the lid and cook for 30 minutes on Manual at High. When ready, release pressure naturally for 10 minutes.

Peach Short Ribs

INGREDIENTS for 4 servings

1 lb short ribs, cut into pieces	1 garlic clove, minced
18 oz canned peaches	1 tbsp tomato puree
2 tbsp parsley, chopped	3 tsp olive oil
Salt and black pepper to taste	½ cup soy sauce
1 cup onions, sliced	2 tbsp apple cider vinegar
1-inch piece ginger, grated	1 tbsp arrowroot powder

DIRECTIONS and total time: approx. 40 minutes

Heat olive oil on Sauté and cook ribs for 5 minutes, stirring occasionally; set aside. Add onions, ginger, and garlic, and sauté until tender, about 3 minutes. Stir in soy sauce, tomato puree, and 1 cup of water; season to taste. Return the ribs and seal the lid. Press Manual and cook for 20 minutes at High. Once ready, do a quick release. Remove ribs to a plate. Mix arrowroot powder with some of the cooking liquid and pour in the pot. Stir in peaches and vinegar and press Sauté; cook for 2-3 minutes until the sauce thickens. Pour the sauce over the ribs, sprinkle with parsley, and serve.

Green Chili Pork

INGREDIENTS for 4-6 servings

2 lb pork shoulder, cubed	¼ tsp green chili pepper
2 tbsp tomato puree	3 garlic cloves, minced
½ cup sour cream	½ tbsp cilantro
1 cup green onions, chopped	1 bay leaf
2 tbsp olive oil	Salt and black pepper to taste

DIRECTIONS and total time: approx. 50 minutes

Heat olive oil on Sauté and cook pork on all sides for 5-6 minutes; reserve. Add green onions and garlic to the pot and sauté for 3 minutes until softened. Stir in green chili pepper, cilantro, tomato puree, bay leaf, salt, and pepper for 1 minute. Pour in 2 cups water and return the pork. Seal the lid and cook for 30 minutes on Manual at High. Do a quick pressure release. Remove the pork and discard bay leaf. Stir in sour cream. Slice the pork and serve drizzled with the sauce.

Balsamic Pork Tenderloin

INGREDIENTS for 4 servings

1 tsp garlic powder	½ cup balsamic vinegar
2 tbsp olive oil	1 tbsp dry mustard
3 tbsp soy sauce	1 tbsp cornstarch
1 tbsp rosemary	Salt and black pepper to taste
1 lb pork tenderloin	Chopped chives for garnish

DIRECTIONS and total time: approx. 45 minutes

Mix garlic powder, rosemary, dry mustard, salt, and pepper in a bowl. Rub the tenderloin all over with the mixture. Heat olive oil on Sauté and brown the pork on all sides for 5 minutes. Pour in soy sauce, balsamic vinegar, and 1 cup of water. Seal the lid, select Manual, and cook for 20 minutes at High. When done, release the pressure naturally for 10 minutes. Remove pork and let it cool slightly before slicing. Serve topped with fresh chives. Mix cornstarch with some of the cooking liquid until and pour in the pot. Press Sauté and cook the sauce until thickened, about 3 minutes. Pour sauce over the pork and sprinkle with chives to serve.

Orange Cinnamon Ribs

INGREDIENTS for 4 servings

2 lb pork ribs	1 tbsp brown sugar
½ cup orange juice	1 tsp Worcestershire sauce
1 cup barbecue sauce	1 tsp ground cinnamon
1 onion, diced	1 tbsp rosemary for garnish
2 tbsp ground cloves	Salt and black pepper to taste

DIRECTIONS and total time: approx. 40 minutes

Place ribs in your IP. Whisk together all the remaining ingredients with ½ cup of water in a bowl and pour the mixture over. Seal the lid, set to Manual, and cook for 25 minutes at High. When ready, do a natural release for 10 minutes. Serve garnished with rosemary.

Pork Chops with Veggies

INGREDIENTS for 4 servings

1 (14-oz) can diced tomatoes	1 tsp garlic paste
4 bone-in, pork chops	2 tbsp canola oil
1 onion, chopped	2 carrots, chopped
1 cup leeks, sliced	2 tbsp balsamic vinegar
1 celery stalk, diced	1 tsp dried oregano

DIRECTIONS and total time: approx. 35 minutes

Heat canola oil on Sauté and cook the pork chops on both sides for about 5 minutes; reserve. Add carrots, leeks, celery, garlic paste, mushrooms, and onion to the pot and sauté for 5 minutes. Season with salt, pepper, and oregano and pour in tomatoes, balsamic vinegar, and 1 cup of water. Return the chops and seal the lid. Cook on Manual for 15 minutes at High. When done, release the pressure quickly and serve warm.

Chorizo with Bell Peppers & Onions

INGREDIENTS for 4 servings

4 chorizo pork sausages	½ cup vegetable broth
1 onion, sliced	¼ cup white wine
2 red bell peppers, sliced	1 garlic clove, minced
2 tbsp olive oil	Salt and black pepper to taste

DIRECTIONS and total time: approx. 25 minutes

Heat olive oil on Sauté and brown sausages for 5 minutes; remove to a plate. Stir in onion, garlic, and peppers. Stir-fry for 5 minutes until soft. Add back the sausages and pour in vegetable broth and wine; season to taste. Seal the lid and cook for 5 minutes on Manual at High. Once ready, do a quick release. Serve.

Cuban Mojo Pork

INGREDIENTS for 4-6 servings

2 lb pork shoulder roast	4 garlic cloves, minced
1 tsp oregano	¼ tsp red pepper flakes
3 tbsp olive oil	½ cup orange juice
1 tbsp cumin	¼ cup lime juice
1 red onion, chopped	2 tbsp cilantro, chopped
Salt and black pepper to taste	1 avocado, sliced

DIRECTIONS and total time: approx. 55 minutes

Mix cumin, oregano, red flakes, orange and lime juices, salt, and pepper in a bowl. Heat olive oil on Sauté and brown the pork on all sides, about 6 minutes; set aside. Sauté onion and garlic in the pot for 3 minutes; stir in the citrus mixture and 1 cup of water. Return the pork and seal the lid. Select Manual and cook for 30 minutes at High. When done, release the pressure naturally for 10 minutes. Slice the meat. Serve topped with cooking juices and sprinkled with cilantro and avocado slices.

Pork Meatballs with Sour Mushroom Sauce

INGREDIENTS for 4 servings

1 lb ground pork	¼ cup chopped green onions
Salt and black pepper to taste	3 tbsp olive oil
½ cup breadcrumbs	Salt and black pepper to taste
1 egg	1 cup sour cream
1 clove garlic, minced	8 oz mushrooms, sliced

DIRECTIONS and total time: approx. 35 minutes

In a bowl, mix pork, breadcrumbs, egg, garlic, green onions, salt, and pepper and shape into balls. Heat olive oil on Sauté and fry the meatballs on all sides for 3 minutes; reserve. Sauté mushrooms in the pot for 5 minutes and pour 1 cup water; return the meatballs. Seal the lid, select Manual, and cook for 15 minutes at High. When ready, do a quick pressure release. Remove the meatballs. Add in sour cream, stir to combine, and adjust the seasoning. Press Sauté and cook for 3-4 minutes until thickened. Serve meatballs with sauce.

Garlicky BBQ Pork Butt

INGREDIENTS for 6 servings

2 lb pork butt	2 tbsp olive oil
¼ tsp garlic powder	1 tsp tarragon
Salt and black pepper to taste	½ tsp onion powder
1 cup barbecue sauce	1 ½ cups vegetable broth

DIRECTIONS and total time: approx. 50 minutes

In a bowl, combine barbecue sauce and all the spices. Brush the pork with the mixture. Press Sauté and heat olive oil. Add pork and sear on all sides for 6 minutes. Pour the broth around the meat. Seal the lid and cook for 30 minutes on Manual at High. When done, release the pressure naturally for 10 minutes. Serve hot.

Pork with Prune Sauce

INGREDIENTS for 4 servings

1 lb pork tenderloin	1 red onion, chopped
1 chopped celery stalk	Salt and black pepper to taste
1 cup dry prunes, sliced	2 tbsp olive oil
½ cup orange juice	½ cup vegetable broth

DIRECTIONS and total time: approx. 35 minutes

Heat olive oil on Sauté and stir-fry onion and celery for 3 minutes. Season pork with salt and pepper and add to the pot. Brown for 3 minutes per side. Top with prunes, and pour in broth and orange juice. Seal the lid and cook on Manual for 25 minutes at High. Do a quick pressure release. Slice pork and spoon the sauce over.

Pork Chops with Shallots & Carrots

INGREDIENTS for 4 servings

4 pork chops	1 cup vegetable broth
2 carrots, chopped	1 tsp dried rosemary
1 tomato, chopped	2 tbsp olive oil
2 shallots, chopped	1 tbsp flour
2 garlic cloves, minced	1 tbsp tomato puree
¼ cup Merlot red wine	Salt and black pepper to taste

DIRECTIONS and total time: approx. 45 minutes

Heat olive oil on Sauté. In a bowl, mix flour, black pepper, and salt. Coat the pork chops. Place them in the pot and cook for 5-6 minutes on all sides. Add carrots, shallots, garlic, and oregano; cook for 2 minutes. Stir in the remaining ingredients and seal the lid. Cook on Manual for 25 minutes at High. When ready, do a natural pressure release for 10 minutes, and serve.

Juicy Chorizo Sausage with Tater Tots

INGREDIENTS for 4 servings

1 lb chorizo sausage, sliced	10 oz canned mushroom soup
1 lb tater tots	10 oz evaporated milk
½ lb cauliflower florets	Salt and black pepper to taste

DIRECTIONS and total time: approx. 25 minutes

Place ¼ of the sausage slices in the inner pot. In a bowl, whisk together mushroom soup and evaporated milk. Pour some of this mixture over the sausages. Top the sausage slices with ¼ of the cauliflower florets followed by ¼ of the tater tots. Pour some of the soup mixtures again. Repeat the layers until you use up all ingredients. Pour in 1 cup of water, seal the lid and cook on Manual for 15 minutes at High. When ready, do a quick release. Serve warm.

Basil Pork Meatballs

INGREDIENTS for 4 servings

1 lb ground pork	Salt and black pepper to taste
½ cup breadcrumbs	1 ½ cups tomato juice
½ onion, diced	1 cup canned diced tomatoes
1 garlic clove, minced	1 tbsp brown sugar
1 egg	2 tbsp olive oil
1 tsp cumin	2 tbsp basil, chopped

DIRECTIONS and total time: approx. 35 minutes

Combine ground pork, breadcrumbs, onion, garlic, egg, cumin, salt, and pepper in a bowl. Mix well with hands. Shape the mixture into meatballs. Heat olive oil on Sauté and brown meatballs for 6 minutes on all sides. Stir in the remaining ingredients. Seal the lid and cook for 20 minutes on Manual at High. When ready, release the pressure quickly. Serve topped with basil.

Delicious Pork Loin with Turnips & Apples

INGREDIENTS for 4 servings

1 lb pork loin, cut into cubes	1 tbsp vegetable oil
1 onion, diced	1 celery stalk, diced
2 turnips, peeled and diced	1 tbsp dried parsley
1 cup chicken broth	¼ tsp thyme
½ cup white wine	½ tsp cumin
2 apples, diced	¼ tsp lemon zest
½ cup sliced leeks	Salt and black pepper to taste

DIRECTIONS and total time: approx. 35 minutes

Season the pork with salt and pepper. Heat oil on Sauté. Add pork and cook for 5-6 minutes until browned. Stir in onion, apples, and celery and cook for 4 more minutes until soft. Throw in the remaining ingredients. Seal the lid and cook for 15 minutes on Manual at High. When ready, release the pressure quickly. Serve.

Curried Pork Stew with Green Peas

INGREDIENTS for 4 servings

1 lb lean pork loin, cubed	1 bay leaf
1 onion, chopped	2 tbsp olive oil
1 tsp curry powder	2 tbsp chopped chives
1 cup chicken broth	1 cup green peas
Salt and black pepper to taste	2 tomatoes, chopped

DIRECTIONS and total time: approx. 40 minutes

Heat olive oil on Sauté and cook onion, pork, curry powder, salt, and pepper for 5-6 minutes, stirring often. Pour in broth, tomatoes, and bay leaf. Seal the lid, select Manual, and cook for 20 minutes at High. When ready, do a quick release. Discard bay leaf. Stir in the peas and cook for 5 minutes on Sauté to warm through. Ladle into serving bowls and top with chives.

Tarragon Pork with Mushroom Sauce

INGREDIENTS for 4 servings

4 large bone-in pork chops	2 garlic cloves, minced
1 cup tomato sauce	2 tbsp olive oil
1 cup button mushrooms, sliced	Salt and black pepper to taste
2 shallots, chopped	2 tbsp tarragon, chopped

DIRECTIONS and total time: approx. 40 minutes

Heat olive oil on Sauté and stir-fry garlic, shallots, and mushrooms for 4 minutes. Add pork and cook on all sides for 5 minutes. Stir in the remaining ingredients and ½ cup of water. Seal the lid, and cook for 25 minutes on Manual at High. When done, perform a quick pressure release. Top with tarragon and serve.

Jalapeño Pork Stew

INGREDIENTS for 4 servings

1 lb stewed pork, cubed	1 jalapeño pepper, chopped
1 onion, diced	2 cups vegetable broth
1 (14-oz) can tomatoes, diced	1 tsp ground ginger
1 can green peas, drained	2 tsp ground coriander
2 garlic cloves, minced	Salt and black pepper to taste
2 tbsp butter	¼ tsp cayenne pepper

DIRECTIONS and total time: approx. 50 minutes

Melt butter on Sauté. Add onion and garlic cook for 3 minutes until soft. Stir in spices and jalapeño pepper for 1 more minute. Add pork and brown for 6 minutes. Pour in broth, peas, and tomatoes. Seal the lid and cook for 30 minutes on Manual at High. When ready, release the pressure naturally for 10 minutes. Serve hot.

Grandma's Sweet Pork Roast

INGREDIENTS for 4 servings

1 lb sirloin pork roast	2 tbsp olive oil
1 tsp honey	1 ½ cups water
1 tsp cayenne powder	2 tbsp lemon juice
1 tsp oregano	Salt and black pepper to taste

DIRECTIONS and total time: approx. 50 minutes

Combine the spices in a bowl and rub them onto the pork. Heat olive oil on Sauté and sear the pork for 2 minutes per side. Stir in the remaining ingredients. Seal the lid and cook for 30 minutes on Manual at High. Do a natural pressure release for 10 minutes. Serve hot.

Orange Pork Carnitas

INGREDIENTS for 4-6 servings

1 orange, juiced
1 tsp oregano
1 sweet onion, chopped
1 tsp chili powder
Salt and black pepper to taste

2 lb boneless pork shoulder
3 tbsp olive oil
3 garlic cloves, grated
1 jalapeño pepper, minced
Green onions for garnish

DIRECTIONS and total time: approx. 50 minutes

In a bowl, mix oregano, chili powder, salt, and pepper, then rub mixture onto pork. Heat olive oil on Sauté and brown pork on all sides, about 5-6 minutes; reserve. Add onion, garlic, and jalapeño pepper to the pot and sauté for 3 minutes. Stir in orange juice to deglaze the bottom, and return the pork. Pour in 2 cups of water and seal the lid. Select Manual and cook for 30 minutes at High. When ready, release the pressure naturally for 10 minutes. Shred the pork in the pot with two forks and adjust the seasoning. Serve topped with green onions.

Mint & Cilantro Infused Pork

INGREDIENTS for 4-6 servings

3 lb pork shoulder roast
4 cloves garlic, minced
Salt and black pepper to taste
1 tbsp olive oil

½ cup fresh mint leaves
1 cup cilantro
1 tbsp lime juice and zest
Green onions, chopped

DIRECTIONS and total time: approx. 50 minutes

Mix together garlic, olive oil, lime zest and juice, salt, and pepper in a bowl. Cover the pork shoulder with the paste and allow to marinate overnight. Arrange mint and cilantro on the bottom of your IP and lay the marinated pork on top. Pour in 2 cups of water, seal the lid, select Manual, and cook for 30 minutes at High. When ready, release the pressure naturally for 10 minutes. Remove and discard the herbs. Slice the meat and serve topped with cooking sauce and green onions.

BBQ Pulled Pork

INGREDIENTS for 4-6 servings

2 lb boneless pork shoulder
1 tbsp taco seasoning
2 tbsp olive oil
1/3 cup cider vinegar

Salt and black pepper to taste
½ cup brown sugar
Chopped green onions
2 cups barbecue sauce

DIRECTIONS and total time: approx. 45 minutes

Heat olive oil on Sauté and cook pork on all sides for 5-6 minutes. Mix all the remaining ingredients, except for the green onions, in a bowl; add in 1 cup of water. Pour the mixture over the pork in the pot. Seal the lid, select Manual, and cook for 30 minutes at High. When ready, do a quick release. Remove the pork and shred it using two forks, then bring it back to the pot and stir. Serve hot, topped with freshly chopped green onions.

Chorizo Sausage Sandwiches with Gravy

INGREDIENTS for 4 servings

4 English muffins, halved
1 lb chorizo sausages
1 cup milk
2 tbsp olive oil
1 tsp flour

1 cup zucchinis, chopped
1 cup bone broth
Salt and black pepper to taste
2 sprigs dry rosemary
¼ cup grated cheddar

DIRECTIONS and total time: approx. 20 minutes

Heat olive oil on Sauté and stir-fry zucchinis and sausages for 5 minutes. Sprinkle with rosemary and pour in broth. Seal the lid, select Manual, and cook for 5 minutes at High. When ready, do a quick pressure release. Remove the sausages. Blitz zucchini and sauce with an immersion blender. In a bowl, whisk flour and milk and season with salt and pepper. Add the mixture to the pot. Select Sauté and let simmer for 3 minutes. Divide the sausages between muffins and top with cheddar cheese. Spoon over the gravy to serve.

German Pork with Cabbage & Tomatoes

INGREDIENTS for 4-6 servings

3 tbsp olive oil
1 head cabbage, shredded
2 cloves garlic, finely minced
2 red onions, chopped
1 carrot, chopped

1 cup tomato sauce
1 ¼ lb pork shoulder, cubed
1 tsp cumin
1 tbsp paprika
Salt and black pepper to taste

DIRECTIONS and total time: approx. 50 minutes

Heat olive oil on Sauté and brown the pork, stirring periodically for 3-4 minutes; set aside. Sauté garlic, onion, and carrot for 5 minutes. Stir in cabbage, paprika, cumin, salt, and pepper, and cook for another 5 minutes. Pour in tomato sauce and 2 cups of water; return the pork. Seal the lid, press Manual, and cook for 30 minutes at High. Do a quick pressure release.

Sweet Shredded Pork

INGREDIENTS for 4-6 servings

2 tbsp olive oil
2 lb pork shoulder
Salt and black pepper to taste
1 tsp allspice
1 tsp garlic powder

1 tbsp fresh ginger, minced
1 tbsp maple syrup
1 sweet onion, chopped
3 peaches, pitted and sliced
1 cup vegetable broth

DIRECTIONS and total time: approx. 50 minutes

Rub the pork with allspice, salt, pepper, and garlic powder. Heat olive oil on Sauté and cook the pork on all sides for about 5 minutes; set aside. Add onion and ginger, and sauté for 3 minutes. Pour in broth, peaches, and maple syrup and return the pork. Seal the lid, select Manual, and cook for 30 minutes at High. When ready, release the pressure naturally for 10 minutes. Remove the pork and shred it using two forks. Stir and serve.

Oregano Pork with Egg Noodles

INGREDIENTS for 4-6 servings

2 lb boneless pork shoulder	1 cup onion, chopped
3 tbsp olive oil	3 tbsp cornstarch
1 tsp oregano	2 cups chicken broth
16 oz egg noodles	Salt and black pepper to taste

DIRECTIONS and total time: approx. 55 minutes

Cover the noodles with salted water. Seal the lid and cook on Manual for 4 minutes at High. Do a quick release. Drain and reserve. Heat olive oil on Sauté and brown the pork on all sides for 5-6 minutes; set aside. Add onion to the pot and sweat for 3 minutes. Return the pork, pour in chicken broth and season with salt, pepper, and oregano. Seal the lid, select Manual, and cook for 30 minutes at High. Do a quick release. Remove the pork and shred it with two forks. In a bowl, mix the cornstarch with one cup of the cooking liquid and pour in the pot. Cook on Sauté for 2-3 minutes until the sauce thickens. Stir in the pork and noodles.

Garlicky Sweet Pork with Rice

INGREDIENTS for 4-6 servings

4 garlic cloves, sliced	1 cup yellow onions, chopped
1 tsp grated fresh ginger	¼ cup soy sauce
1 lb stewed pork, cubed	1 tsp maple syrup
3 tbsp canola oil	1 cup brown rice
¼ cup white wine	Salt and black pepper to taste

DIRECTIONS and total time: approx. 50 minutes

Heat canola oil on Sauté and brown the pork for 7-8 minutes in total; reserve. Add ginger, onions, and garlic to the pot and sauté for 3 minutes. Stir in rice for 1 minute and add in white wine to deglaze. Pour in soy sauce, maple syrup, and 2 cups of water; return the pork. Seal the lid and cook for 30 minutes on Manual at High. Once ready, do a quick pressure release. Serve.

City Pork with Celery & Carrots

INGREDIENTS for 4 servings

2 tbsp olive oil	Salt and black pepper to taste
1 onion, chopped	2 bay leaves
2 garlic cloves, minced	1 tsp allspice
1 lb stewing pork meat, cubed	1 (14-oz) can tomato sauce
4 potatoes, cubed	3 stalks celery, chopped
1 tbsp Worcestershire sauce	3 carrots, peeled and chopped

DIRECTIONS and total time: approx. 50 minutes

Heat olive oil on Sauté and cook pork, onion, garlic, celery, and carrots for 5 minutes. Stir in the remaining ingredients and pour 1 cup of water. Seal the lid, select Manual, and cook for 30 minutes at High. When done, release the pressure naturally for 10 minutes. Remove the bay leaves and serve in bowls.

Korean-Style Pork

INGREDIENTS for 4 servings

2 tbsp olive oil	1 cup brown sugar
1 lb pork loin, sliced	2 tbsp cornstarch
1 tsp ginger, grated	3 tbsp cold water
2 garlic cloves, minced	2 tbsp gochugaru (Korean chili)
½ cup chicken broth	Chives, chopped, for garnish
1 cup soy sauce	Sesame seeds, for garnish

DIRECTIONS and total time: approx. 50 minutes

Heat olive oil on Sauté and brown the pork for 5 minutes. Add in ginger, garlic, gochugaru, broth, and soy sauce. Mix well and seal the lid. Cook for 20 minutes on Manual at High. When done, release the pressure naturally for 10 minutes. Press Sauté, add brown sugar and mix well. Cook for 2-3 minutes. In a bowl, whisk the cornstarch and cold water until well combined. Add the slurry to the pot and stir well. Cook until the sauce has thickened. Sprinkle with chopped scallions and toasted sesame seeds to serve.

Pork & Rice Stuffed Peppers

INGREDIENTS for 4 servings

4 bell peppers, seeded	2 tomatoes, chopped
2 tbsp olive oil	Salt and black pepper to taste
1 onion, chopped	1 tsp paprika
2 garlic cloves, minced	1 cup cooked rice
1 lb ground pork	2 tbsp dill, chopped

DIRECTIONS and total time: approx. 45 minutes

Heat olive oil on Sauté and cook onion and garlic for 3 minutes until tender. Add in ground pork and cook for 5-6 minutes, crumbling it with a spatula. Stir in paprika for 30 seconds, and add in tomatoes. Season with salt and pepper. Stuff the peppers and transfer them to a greased baking dish. Clean the pot, pour in 1 cup of water, and insert a trivet. Arrange stuffed peppers on the trivet. Seal the lid and cook for 20 minutes at High. When ready, release the pressure naturally for 10 minutes. Sprinkle with dill and serve.

Spicy Pork Chops

INGREDIENTS for 4 servings

4 boneless pork chops	1 tsp basil
2 tbsp butter	1 cup chicken broth
1 tbsp garlic powder	2 garlic cloves, minced
Salt and black pepper to taste	1 tsp paprika
1 tsp oregano	Chopped chives for garnish

DIRECTIONS and total time: approx. 45 minutes

Melt butter on Sauté and brown pork for 3 minutes per side. Add in remaining ingredients. Seal the lid, select Manual, and cook for 30 minutes at High. Release the pressure quickly. Serve garnished with chives.

Green Onion Pork Ribs

INGREDIENTS for 4 servings

1 cup tomato sauce
2 garlic cloves, minced
Salt and black pepper to taste
½ tsp dried sage
2 cups green onions
½ cup carrots, thinly sliced
2 lb cut pork spare ribs
2 tbsp olive oil

DIRECTIONS and total time: approx. 50 minutes

Heat olive oil on Sauté. Season pork ribs with salt and pepper and brown in the pot for 7-8 minutes; reserve. Add green onions, carrots, sage, and garlic to the pot and sauté for 5 minutes. Pour in tomato sauce, 1 cup of water, and return the pork. Seal the lid and cook for 30 minutes on Manual at High. Once ready, do a quick pressure release. Adjust the seasoning and serve.

Saucy Mustard Pork

INGREDIENTS for 4-6 servings

2 tbsp olive oil
¼ tsp garlic powder
1/3 cup mustard
½ tsp cumin
2 lb pork shoulder roast
¼ tsp chili powder
½ tsp smoked paprika
¼ tsp salt
¼ cup apple cider vinegar
2 tbsp parsley, chopped

DIRECTIONS and total time: approx. 50 minutes

In a bowl, mix all the ingredients, except for the pork and parsley. Place the pork into your IP and pour the mixture over. Add 2 cups of water. Seal the lid, select Manual, and cook for 30 minutes at High. When ready, release the pressure naturally for 10 minutes. Shred the meat with two forks. Serve warm topped with parsley.

Pork Ribs with Wine Pecan Sauce

INGREDIENTS for 4 servings

1 lb pork ribs
¼ cup toasted pecans, chopped
2 garlic cloves, minced
1 ½ cups vegetable broth
2 tbsp red wine vinegar
3 tbsp butter
1 tsp brown sugar
½ tsp red pepper flakes
1 tsp sage
Salt and black pepper to taste

DIRECTIONS and total time: approx. 40 minutes

Melt butter on Sauté. Season the ribs with salt, pepper, sage, and red flakes. Place them in the pot and brown for about 5 minutes. Stir in the remaining ingredients. Seal the lid and cook for 30 minutes on Manual at High. When done, release the pressure quickly. Serve.

Creamy Ranch Pork Chops

INGREDIENTS for 4 servings

10 oz condensed cream of mushroom soup
2 tbsp olive oil
Salt and black pepper to taste
1 cup milk
4 boneless pork chops
1 tbsp ranch salad dressing
2 tbsp parsley, chopped

DIRECTIONS and total time: approx. 50 minutes

Heat olive oil on Sauté and brown pork chops on both sides, 3-4 minutes. Combine the remaining ingredients, except for parsley, in a bowl. Pour over the chops and pour ½ cup of water. Seal the lid, select Manual, and cook for 30 minutes at High. When ready, do a natural release for 10 minutes. Top with parsley to serve.

Pork Chops in Onion Sauce

INGREDIENTS for 4 servings

1 tsp Italian seasoning
Salt and black pepper to taste
2 onions, chopped
4 center-cut pork chops
1 cup vegetable broth
½ cup flour
2 tbsp olive oil
2 tbsp chopped cilantro

DIRECTIONS and total time: approx. 50 minutes

In a bowl, combine flour, salt, and pepper. Coat the pork chops in this mixture. Heat olive oil on Sauté and brown the pork for 3 minutes per side; set aside. Sweat onions in the pot for 3 minutes. Stir in broth and Italian seasoning, and return the pork. Seal the lid, select Manual, and cook for 30 minutes at High. When ready, do a quick pressure release; remove the pork. Blitz onions and sauce with an immersion blender. Pour the sauce over pork chops and sprinkle with cilantro.

Sweet & Sour Pork

INGREDIENTS for 4 servings

1 lb pork tenderloin, cubed
1 whole hot red chili pepper
1 cup chicken broth
2 cloves garlic, sliced
1 white onion, chopped
¼ cup soy sauce
1 cup pineapples, diced
1 green bell pepper, diced
1 red bell pepper, diced
1 tbsp potato flour
¼ cup fresh orange juice
½ tsp ground ginger
1 tbsp raw honey
3 tbsp tomato paste

DIRECTIONS and total time: approx. 40 minutes

Add all ingredients to your IP, except for the pineapples, bell peppers, potato flour, and orange juice. Seal the lid, select Manual, and cook for 20 minutes at High. When done, perform a natural release for 10 minutes. Mix the potato flour and orange juice in a mixing bowl, and add to the cooker along with the pineapples and bell peppers. Cook for 2-3 minutes on Sauté. Remove, discard the chili pepper, and serve immediately.

Winter Pork Belly with Red Cabbage

INGREDIENTS for 4 servings

1 lb pork belly, cubed
4 cups red cabbage, shredded
2 tbsp lard
2 cloves garlic, crushed
1 cup carrots, chopped
½ cup celery, chopped
1 onion, sliced
2 cups vegetable stock
1 tsp mustard
Salt and black pepper to taste
½ tsp chili powder
½ cup tomato puree

DIRECTIONS and total time: approx. 50 minutes

Melt lard on Sauté. Add in pork belly, onion, carrots, celery, and garlic and cook for 5 minutes. Pour in cabbage and sauté for another 5 minutes. Stir in chili and mustard powders. Pour in tomato puree and stock. Seal the lid, select Manua,l and cook for 30 minutes at High. Once ready, do a quick pressure release. Serve.

Cheesy Pancetta Penne with Green Peas

INGREDIENTS for 4 servings

16 oz penne pasta	2 tsp olive oil
6 slices pancetta, chopped	1 cup yellow onions, chopped
½ cup Parmesan, grated	2 garlic cloves, finely minced
1 cup cottage cheese	1 cup green peas

DIRECTIONS and total time: approx. 25 minutes

Place penne in your IP and cover with salted water. Seal the lid, select Manual, and cook for 4 minutes at High. Once ready, do a quick pressure release. Drain and set aside, reserving 1 cup of cooking water. Select Sauté and heat olive oil. Cook onions, garlic, and pancetta for 5 minutes. Return the pasta and stir in cottage cheese. Pour in reserved water and peas and cook for 4 minutes on Sauté. Serve topped with Parmesan cheese.

Effortless Pork Chops

INGREDIENTS for 4-6 servings

2 tbsp olive oil	2 lb pork loin chops
½ tsp thyme, dried	1 cup mixed vegetables
2 cups chicken broth	16 oz cornbread stuffing

DIRECTIONS and total time: approx. 40 minutes

Heat olive oil on Sauté and cook the pork until brown for 5-6 minutes. In a bowl, mix the stuffing, thyme, and chicken broth. Pour this mixture over the chops and spread evenly. Arrange the mixed vegetables around the chops. Seal the lid, select Manual, and cook for 20 minutes at High. When done, release the pressure naturally for 10 minutes. Serve immediately.

Pork Chops in Honey & Apple Sauce

INGREDIENTS for 4 servings

2 apples, sliced	¼ cup soy sauce
1 tbsp honey	½ cup chicken broth
4 boneless pork chops	Chopped chives for garnish

DIRECTIONS and total time: approx. 40 minutes

Place half of apple slices at the bottom of your IP. Drizzle the honey over and cover with the pork chops. Spread the remaining apple slices on top. Pour in soy sauce and chicken broth. Seal the lid, select Manual, and cook for 30 minutes at High. When ready, do a quick release. Serve sprinkled with chopped chives.

Sherry Pork Chops with Artichoke Hearts

INGREDIENTS for 4 servings

½ tsp red pepper flakes	1 cup tomato sauce
2 tbsp olive oil	1 tsp garlic, minced
13 oz artichoke hearts	1 tbsp brown sugar
1 tsp Italian seasoning	4 pork chops
2 tbsp cooking sherry	Salt and black pepper to taste

DIRECTIONS and total time: approx. 50 minutes

Heat olive oil on Sauté. Sprinkle the chops with Italian seasoning, salt, and pepper, and brown them in the hot oil on both sides for 3-4 minutes. Pour in the remaining ingredients and one cup of water. Seal the lid, press Manual, and cook for 30 minutes at High. When done, release the pressure naturally for 10 minutes. Serve.

Moo-Shu Wraps

INGREDIENTS for 6 servings

½ cup bamboo shoots, julienned	
2 lb pork tenderloin	2 garlic cloves, minced
Salt and black pepper to taste	6 green onions, chopped
6 flour tortillas, warm	1 tbsp soy sauce
2 tsp minced ginger root	½ cup plum sauce
2 tsp five-spice powder	¾ cup hoisin sauce

DIRECTIONS and total time: approx. 45 minutes

Rub the pork with five-spice powder and garlic. Let the meat absorb the flavors for about 10 minutes. Then, place the pork in the inner pot. In bowl, combine 1 cup of water, plum sauce, ginger root, and soy sauce. Pour the mixture over the pork. Seal the lid, select Manual, and cook for 20 minutes at High. Do a quick release.

Shred the pork using two forks. Add the bamboo shoots and cook for 4 minutes on Sauté. Sprinkle with salt and pepper. Spread hoisin sauce over tortillas and scatter green onions. Top with pork mixture and serve.

Pork Chops Teriyaki Style

INGREDIENTS for 4 minutes

2 tbsp olive oil	4 boneless pork chops
¼ cup teriyaki sauce	2 garlic cloves, minced
½ cup orange juice	2 tbsp cornstarch
2 tbsp brown sugar	½ tsp fresh ginger, minced

DIRECTIONS and total time: approx. 45 minutes

Heat olive oil on Sauté and brown the pork, about 6 minutes. Mix the remaining ingredients, except for the cornstarch, with 1 cup of water in a bowl and pour the mixture over pork chops. Seal the lid, select Manual, and cook for 30 minutes at High. Do a quick pressure release. Dissolve cornstarch in some cooking juices and pour in the pot. Stir for 3 minutes until the sauce thickens. Serve the chops hot, drizzled with the sauce.

Fruit-Stuffed Pork Loin

INGREDIENTS for 4 servings

½ cup pitted dried prunes, soaked and chopped
2 lb boneless pork loin roast | Salt and black pepper to taste
1 tbsp olive oil | ½ tsp dried marjoram
1 cup dry white wine | 1 apple, chopped
2 slices bacon, chopped | 1 cup chicken stock
1 shallot, chopped | 2 tbsp cornstarch

DIRECTIONS and total time: approx. 55 minutes

Heat olive oil on Sauté and cook bacon and shallot for 3-4 minutes, stirring occasionally; remove to a bowl. Add apple, prunes, and marjoram to the pot and cook until soft, about 5 minutes. Remove to the bacon bowl and mix to combine. Cut the center of the roast to make an opening for the stuffing, and push the mixture through. Season the outside of the meat with salt and pepper. Pour the wine in the pot to deglaze, stir for 2 minutes. Add in the pork and chicken broth. Seal the lid, select Manual, and cook for 30 minutes at High. When done, release the pressure quickly. Remove the pork and let it sit for a few minutes before slicing. In a bowl, mix cornstarch with some of the cooking liquid. Add the mixture to the pot and cook for 2-3 minutes on Sauté to thicken. Adjust the seasoning and spoon the gravy over the sliced pork to serve.

Mango Pork Sandwiches

INGREDIENTS for 6 servings

2 lb boneless pork loin roast | 6 hamburger buns, halved
1 tbsp curry powder | 2 jalapeño peppers, diced
1 ½ cups mango chutney | 1 cup mayonnaise
1 cup chicken broth | 1 cup ketchup

DIRECTIONS and total time: approx. 50 minutes

Rub the outside of pork with curry powder. Add pork to the inner pot and pour in the broth, jalapeño peppers, and mango chutney. Seal the lid, select Manual, and cook for 30 minutes at High. When ready, release the pressure quickly. Shred the meat with 2 forks. Divide the pork mixture between bun bottoms and top with ketchup and mayonnaise. Cover with bun tops to serve.

Pulled Pork Mexican-Style

INGREDIENTS for 4-6 servings

2 lb boneless pork shoulder roast | 1 tbsp brown sugar
2 tbsp vegetable oil | A pinch of ground cloves
¼ tsp cinnamon | 1 tsp onion powder
Salt and black pepper to taste | 1 tsp garlic powder
4 tbsp chipotle powder | Chopped green onions

DIRECTIONS and total time: approx. 60 minutes

On Sauté, heat the oil and brown pork for 3-4 minutes. Add in the remaining ingredients and 2 cups of water.

Seal the lid, select Manual at High, and cook for 40 minutes. When done, release the pressure naturally for 10 minutes. Shred the pork with two forks. Serve hot and top with freshly chopped green onions.

Mediterranean Pork Roast

INGREDIENTS for 4-6 servings

2 lb pork roast, boneless | ¼ cup olive oil
¼ cup Chardonnay wine | 1 tsp Greek seasoning
6 garlic cloves, minced | 2 tbsp basil, chopped
¼ cup lemon juice | Salt and black pepper to taste

DIRECTIONS and total time: approx. 60 minutes

Place the pork in a resealable bag, add in garlic, lemon juice, olive oil, and Greek seasoning and toss to coat. Marinate in the fridge for 10 minutes. Remove the meat from the bag and discard the marinade. Place the pork in your IP and pour chardonnay and 1 cup water; season. Seal the lid, select Manual, and cook for 30 minutes at High. Release the pressure naturally for 10 minutes. Serve garnished with basil.

Ribs with Plum Sauce

INGREDIENTS for 4 servings

1 tbsp soy sauce | 1 jar (7-oz) plum sauce
¼ cup orange juice | ½ cup honey
2 tbsp cornstarch | 3 lb pork ribs, cut into servings

DIRECTIONS and total time: approx. 45 minutes

Place the ribs in the inner pot, add in plum sauce, soy sauce, honey, and 1 cup of water. Seal the lid, select Manual, and cook for 20 minutes at High. When done, release the pressure naturally for 10 minutes. Remove the ribs. Dissolve cornstarch in orange juice in a bowl, and pour in the pot. Press Sauté and cook for 3 minutes until the sauce thickens. Pour over the ribs and serve.

Honey-Dijon Pork Chops

INGREDIENTS for 4 servings

4 loin chops, boneless | 2 tbsp water
2 tbsp Dijon mustard | ½ cup chicken broth
1 tbsp cornstarch | ½ cup dry white wine
2 tbsp lemon juice | ¼ cup onion, chopped
2 tbsp honey | 2 tbsp sage, chopped

DIRECTIONS and total time: approx. 50 minutes

Pour wine, onion, broth, and pork chops in the inner pot. Seal the lid, select Manual, and cook for 25 minutes at High. When done, release the pressure naturally for 10 minutes. Transfer the pork to a plate. Press Sauté and add honey, water, mustard, lemon juice, and cornstarch and stir to combine. Cook for 2-3 minutes, stirring often. Serve warm, sprinkled with sage.

Mediterranean Pork Meatballs

INGREDIENTS for 4 servings

1 lb lean ground pork	2 cloves garlic, minced
Salt and black pepper to taste	2 tbsp basil, chopped
2 cups herbed pasta sauce	¼ cup green onions, chopped
16 oz linguine	½ cup ricotta cheese
½ cup breadcrumbs	1 egg
½ tsp ground nutmeg	1 cup spinach, chopped

DIRECTIONS and total time: approx. 35 minutes

Place linguine in your IP and cover with salted water. Seal the lid and cook on Manual for 4 minutes at High. Do a quick release, drain and set aside, reserving 2 cups of cooking water. In a bowl, mix green onions, ricotta, salt, pepper, garlic, egg, ground pork, and spinach and mix to combine. Shape into meatballs. Roll meatballs in breadcrumbs. Pour pasta sauce, reserved cooking water, and meatballs in the pot. Seal the lid, select Manual, and cook for 20 minutes at High. Do a quick release. Pour the sauce over pasta and serve with basil.

Thyme & Green Onion Pork Chops

INGREDIENTS for 4 servings

4 boneless loin chops	4 green onions, sliced
½ cup milk	1 small onion, sliced
1 small rib celery, sliced	1 can cream celery soup
1 tsp dried thyme	Salt and black pepper to taste

DIRECTIONS and total time: approx. 45 minutes

Rub the pork chops with salt, pepper, and thyme. Place in the Instant Pot. Add in green onions and celery on top. Combine milk and soup in a bowl. Pour the mixture over the chops. Pour in ½ cup of water. Seal the lid, press Manual, and cook for 30 minutes at High. When done, release the pressure quickly and serve.

Pork Loin with Mustard Sauce

INGREDIENTS for 4 servings

1 lb boneless pork loin roast	1 tsp yellow mustard
2 tbsp olive oil	1 cup heavy cream
1 cup chicken broth	1 tsp paprika
2 cups onions, chopped	Salt and black pepper to taste

DIRECTIONS and total time: approx. 70 minutes

Heat olive oil on Sauté and cook onions for 3 minutes. Rub pork with salt, pepper, and paprika and transfer it to the pot; sear on all sides for 6 minutes. Pour in broth and seal the lid. Cook on Manual for 30 minutes at High. When done, release the pressure naturally for 10 minutes. Remove the pork and let it rest for 10 minutes before slicing. Blitz the remaining ingredients in the pot with an immersion blender and stir in mustard and heavy cream. Cook for 2-3 minutes on Sauté until thickened. Pour the sauce over the pork to serve.

European Stew

INGREDIENTS for 4 servings

½ lb pork loin, cubed	1 tsp dried marjoram
2 tbsp olive oil	1 garlic clove, minced
½ lb smoked sausages, sliced	1 tsp paprika
1 cup cooked beets, cubed	1 carrot, shredded
Salt and black pepper to taste	1 onion, sliced
1 cup tomato sauce	2 potatoes, chopped
2 tsp dill weed, chopped	4 cups cabbage, shredded

DIRECTIONS and total time: approx. 50 minutes

Heat olive oil on Sauté and cook onion, garlic, carrot, pork, and sausages for 4 minutes, stirring often. Stir in paprika, marjoram, salt, and pepper for 1 minute. Add cabbage and cook for 5-6 minutes until tender. Pour in tomato sauce, beets, potatoes, and 2 cups of water; stir. Seal the lid, select Manual, and cook for 20 minutes at High. When done, release the pressure naturally for 10 minutes. Serve garnished with dill weed.

Pork Stew with Sun-Dried Tomatoes

INGREDIENTS for 4-6 servings

1 ½ lb lean pork, cubed	1 bay leaf
3 tbsp olive oil	1 onion, chopped
6 potatoes, cubed	3 baby carrots, chopped
Salt and black pepper to taste	1 cup sun-dried tomatoes
1 tbsp flour	2 tbsp parsley, chopped

DIRECTIONS and total time: approx. 55 minutes

Soak sun-dried tomatoes in hot water for 10 minutes, then drain and chop them. Heat olive oil on Sauté and stir-fry onion, carrots, tomatoes, and pork for 4-5 minutes. Pour in 3 cups of water, bay leaf, and potatoes; season with salt and pepper. Seal the lid, select Manual, and cook for 20 minutes at High. When done, release the pressure naturally for 10 minutes. Mix ¼ cup of cooking liquid and flour in a bowl and pour it in the pot. Cook for 2-3 minutes on Sauté to thicken the sauce. Discard the bay leaf and serve hot.

Spiced Pork Ribs

INGREDIENTS for 4 servings

2 lb pork ribs	1 tbsp soy sauce
¼ tsp cinnamon	1 tbsp maple syrup
¼ tsp ground ginger	1 onion, chopped
¼ tsp garlic powder	2 tbsp parsley, chopped

DIRECTIONS and total time: approx. 40 minutes

In a bowl, combine all ingredients, except for the pork and parsley. Gently rub the ribs with the spice paste. Transfer to your Instant Pot and add 1 cup of water. Seal the lid, select Manual, and cook for 20 minutes at High. When done, release the pressure naturally for 10 minutes. Serve hot, sprinkled with parsley.

Sausage with Beer & Sauerkraut

INGREDIENTS for 4-6 servings

2 lb kielbasa sausages, sliced
1 (12-oz) bottle beer
1 can (14-oz) diced tomatoes
1 tsp paprika
3 tbsp olive oil
Salt and black pepper to taste
1 (20-oz) can sauerkraut
2 tbsp parsley, chopped

DIRECTIONS and total time: approx. 30 minutes

Heat olive oil on Sauté and cook sausages for 5 minutes. Stir in paprika and add in the remaining ingredients. Pour in 1 cup of water. Seal the lid, select Manual, and cook for 15 minutes at High. Release the pressure quickly. Serve topped with parsley.

Pork Goulash with Spaghetti

INGREDIENTS for 6 minutes

2 lb lean pork loin, cubed
4 oz mushrooms, halved
3 tbsp olive oil
2 small onions, chopped
14 ½ oz canned tomatoes
2 tbsp tomato paste
1 ½ cups vegetable broth
16 oz spaghetti
2 bay leaves
½ cup sour cream
2 tbsp cornstarch
½ tsp fennel seeds
½ tsp caraway seeds
2 tbsp paprika
2 cloves garlic, minced
Salt and black pepper to taste

DIRECTIONS and total time: approx. 40 minutes

Add spaghetti and cover with salted water. Cook on Manual for 4 minutes at High. When done, quick-release the pressure. Drain and set aside. Heat olive oil on Sauté and cook onion, garlic, pork, mushrooms, paprika, salt, and pepper for 5-6 minutes, stirring often. Stir in fennel and caraway seeds for 1 minute, then mix in tomato paste, tomatoes, bay leaves, and broth. Seal the lid, select Manual, and cook for 15 minutes at High. Do a quick pressure release. Mix cornstarch and sour cream and pour in the pot; stir for 2-3 minutes on Sauté. Discard the bay leaves. Spoon goulash over the spaghetti and serve immediately.

Greek-Style Pulled Pork

INGREDIENTS for 4 servings

2 lb pork tenderloin, fat trimmed
2 tbsp Greek seasoning
2 tbsp olive oil
½ cup sliced pepperoncini
2 tbsp fresh dill, chopped

DIRECTIONS and total time: approx. 50 minutes

Sprinkle the pork with Greek seasoning. Heat olive oil on Sauté and brown the pork on all sides for 5-6 minutes. Pour in pepperoncini peppers and 1 cup of water. Seal the lid, select Manual, and cook for 30 minutes at High. Release the pressure naturally for 10 minutes. Remove the pork and shred using two forks. Return to the cooker and stir. Serve with fresh dill.

Chili Pork with Pinto Beans

INGREDIENTS for 4 servings

1 cup green onions, chopped
2 tbsp olive oil
1 large onion, chopped
1 chili, chopped and seeded
1 can (15-oz) pinto beans
1 lb pork loin, cubed
2 garlic cloves, minced
1 tsp oregano
Salt and black pepper to taste
1 cup vegetable broth
2 tsp ground cumin
1 (14-oz) can tomatoes, diced

DIRECTIONS and total time: approx. 45 minutes

Heat olive oil on Sauté and cook pork, onion, chili, and garlic for 5 minutes. Add in the remaining ingredients, except for green onions. Seal the lid, select Manual, and cook for 30 minutes at High. When done, do a quick pressure release. Serve topped with green onions.

Peppered Pork Tenderloin with Rice

INGREDIENTS for 4 servings

1 cup green onions, chopped
2 tbsp olive oil
1 chili, chopped and seeded
1 lb pork tenderloin
2 cups vegetable broth
1 cup brown rice, rinsed
1 tsp garlic powder
Salt and black pepper to taste
2 tbsp parsley, chopped
1 yellow bell pepper, julienned
1 red bell pepper, julienned
1 green bell pepper, julienned

DIRECTIONS and total time: approx. 50 minutes

Heat olive oil on Sauté. Season the pork with salt, pepper, and garlic powder. Add to the pot and cook it on all sides for 5-6 minutes; reserve. Add chili, bell peppers, and green onions to the pot and sauté for 8-10 minutes. Season with salt and pepper and set aside. Pour rice and vegetable rice in the cooker and insert a trivet. Place the pork on the trivet. Seal the lid, select Manual, and cook for 25 minutes at High. Do a quick pressure release. Remove pork to a serving board and let it sit for 5 minutes before slicing. Fluff the rice with two forks and transfer to a plate. Top with bell peppers and sliced pork. Sprinkle with parsley and serve.

Jalapeño Pork with Pico de Gallo

INGREDIENTS for 4 servings

2 tbsp butter
1 lb pork chops
1 bell pepper, sliced
1 onion, chopped
2 garlic cloves, minced
¼ cup white wine
Salt and black pepper to taste
1 (10-oz) jar pico de gallo

DIRECTIONS and total time: approx. 45 minutes

Melt butter on Sauté and sear the pork chops for about 4 minutes on both sides; reserve. Add bell pepper, onion, and garlic to the pot and sauté for 3 minutes. Pour in white wine, 1 cup water and return the pork. Seal the lid, select Manual, and cook for 30 minutes at High. Do a quick pressure release. Serve pork chops topped with pico de gallo salsa and enjoy!

Beef & Lamb

Chili Beef Brisket with Chives

INGREDIENTS for 4 servings

1 ½ lb beef brisket
1 tsp green chili powder
1 tbsp tomato puree
½ cup salsa
1 cup vegetable broth
½ cup chives, chopped
2 tbsp butter
1 onion, sliced
2 garlic cloves, minced
Salt and black pepper to taste

DIRECTIONS and total time: approx. 60 minutes

Season the beef with green chili powder, salt, and pepper. Melt butter on Sauté and brown beef on all sides, for 6 minutes; set aside. Add onion, garlic, and chives to the pot and sauté for 3 minutes until soft. Stir in the remaining ingredients and return the beef. Seal the lid and cook on Manual for 35 minutes at High. When done, do a quick pressure release and serve.

Mount-Watering Beef Ribs with Shiitakes

INGREDIENTS for 4 servings

1 ½ lb beef ribs
2 cups Shiitake mushrooms
1 onion, chopped
¼ cup ketchup
2 cups veggie stock
1 cup carrots, chopped
¼ cup sesame oil
1 tsp garlic, minced
Salt and black pepper to taste
2 tbsp chives, chopped

DIRECTIONS and total time: approx. 50 minutes

Heat olive oil on Sauté. Season the ribs with salt and pepper. Brown them on all sides, about 6 minutes; set aside. Add onion, garlic, carrots, and shiitakes to the pot, and sauté for 5 minutes. Add the ribs back and stir in the remaining ingredients, except for chives. Seal the lid and cook for 30 minutes on Manual at High. When done, do a quick release. Serve with chives.

Thyme Creamy Beef Roast

INGREDIENTS for 4 servings

14 oz canned mushroom soup
1 lb beef roast, cubed
1 onion, diced
1 cup buttermilk
½ tsp cumin
2 tbsp thyme, chopped
1 garlic clove, minced
2 tbsp butter
½ cup vegetable broth
½ tsp green chili powder
Salt and black pepper to taste

DIRECTIONS and total time: approx. 35 minutes

Melt butter on Sauté and cook onion and garlic until soft, about 3 minutes. Add beef and cook until browned, for 5-6 minutes. Pour in mushroom soup, vegetable broth, cumin, green chili powder, salt, and pepper. Seal the lid and cook for 25 minutes on Manual at High. Once done, do a quick release. Stir in buttermilk for 2 minutes on Sauté, and serve topped with thyme.

Holiday Beef Meatloaf

INGREDIENTS for 4 servings

1 lb ground beef
2 garlic cloves, minced
½ cup breadcrumbs
1 egg
½ cup milk
1 onion, finely chopped
½ tsp turmeric powder
½ tsp dried oregano
Salt and black pepper to taste
1 cup ketchup
2 tbsp brown sugar
¼ cup tomato puree
1 tsp garlic powder
½ tsp onion powder
½ tsp cayenne pepper
2 tbsp parsley, chopped

DIRECTIONS and total time: approx. 40 minutes

Mix ground beef, garlic, breadcrumbs, milk, onions, egg, salt, pepper, turmeric, and oregano in a mixing bowl. Use your hands to combine thoroughly. Shape into a loaf and place into a greased baking dish. In another bowl, mix ketchup, brown sugar, tomato puree, garlic and onion powders, and cayenne pepper. Spread the mixture over the meatloaf. Place a trivet in your IP and pour in 1 cup of water. Lower the baking dish onto the trivet. Seal the lid, select Manual, and cook for 25 minutes at High. Once ready, do a quick pressure release. Slice and top with parsley to serve.

Sweet Ginger Beef Ribs

INGREDIENTS for 4-6 servings

3 lb spare ribs, cut into pieces
18 oz canned apricot halves
1 onion, sliced
Salt and black pepper to taste
½ cup tamari sauce
2 tbsp apple cider vinegar
½ cup tomato paste
3 tsp olive oil
¼ tsp ginger powder
2 tbsp cilantro, chopped

DIRECTIONS and total time: approx. 50 minutes

Heat olive oil on Sauté and brown spare ribs on all sides, about 4-5 minutes; reserve. Add onion to the pot and sauté for 3 minutes. Add in apricots, tamari sauce, vinegar, tomato paste, ginger powder, salt, pepper, and 1 cup of water. Return the ribs and seal the lid. Cook for 30 minutes on Manual at High. Use a natural release for 10 minutes and serve topped with cilantro.

Garlic Balsamic Steak

INGREDIENTS for 4 servings

1 lb beef chuck steak, sliced
½ cup agave nectar
½ cup balsamic vinegar
1 cup bone broth
1 tsp garlic paste
Salt and black pepper to taste
2 tbsp olive oil
1 tsp ground ginger

DIRECTIONS and total time: approx. 55 minutes

Heat the olive oil on Sauté, season the beef with salt, pepper, and ginger and brown it on both sides for 5-6 minutes. Add in the remaining ingredients. Seal the lid and cook on Manual for 40 minutes at High. When over, do a quick pressure release, and serve warm.

Sirloin Steak with Gorgonzola Cheese

INGREDIENTS for 4 servings

2 tbsp olive oil	1 cup beef broth
1 lb sirloin steak, cubed	2 cups canned tomatoes
6 oz Gorgonzola, crumbled	1 onion, diced
½ cabbage head, diced	1 garlic clove, minced
1 cup carrots, chopped	1 tsp paprika
2 red bell peppers, chopped	Salt and black pepper to taste

DIRECTIONS and total time: approx. 50 minutes

Heat olive oil on Sauté and brown the sirloin steak on all sides for 7-8 minutes; reserve. Add onion, garlic, carrots, cabbage, and bell peppers and sauté for 5 minutes. Stir in paprika, salt, and pepper for 1 minute, and pour in tomatoes and beef broth; return the meat. Seal the lid and cook on Manual for 40 minutes at High. Once cooking is complete, release the pressure quickly. Stir in blue cheese until melted, and serve.

Beef Sloppy Joes with Coleslaw

INGREDIENTS for 4 servings

1 cup tomatoes, chopped	¼ cup apple cider vinegar
1 onion, chopped	1 tbsp canola oil
1 carrot, chopped	¼ cup tomato sauce
1 lb ground beef	2 tsp garlic powder
1 bell pepper, chopped	1 tbsp Worcestershire sauce
½ cup quinoa flakes	Salt and black pepper to taste

Coleslaw:

3 tbsp extra virgin olive oil	2 tbsp dill
½ red onion, chopped	2 carrots, grated
1 tbsp honey	2 tbsp apple cider vinegar
½ head red cabbage, sliced	1 tbsp Dijon mustard

DIRECTIONS and total time: approx. 35 minutes

Warm canola oil on Sauté and brown the beef for 3-4 minutes. Add in onion, carrot, bell pepper, garlic powder, black pepper, and salt, and cook until soft, about 5 minutes. Stir in tomatoes, vinegar, Worcestershire sauce, 1 cup of water, and tomato sauce. Seal the lid, select Manual, and cook for 25 minutes at High. Do a quick pressure release. Stir in quinoa flakes, press Sauté and cook for 2 minutes. Mix all the slaw ingredients in a large bowl. Serve the sloppy joes with the slaw.

Sunday Beef Garam Masala

INGREDIENTS for 4-6 servings

1 ½ lb beef roast, cubed	1 cup red lentils
2 tbsp ghee	1 tsp mustard powder
1 tbsp tomato puree	½ tsp cayenne pepper powder
½ cup red wine	1 tsp garlic paste
2 tsp soy sauce	¼ tsp Garam masala
1 tsp brown sugar	½ tsp cinnamon
1 tsp balsamic vinegar	1 tsp cilantro
1 onion, chopped	Salt and black pepper to taste

DIRECTIONS and total time: approx. 60 minutes

Melt ghee on Sauté, season the beef with salt and pepper, and brown for 7-8 minutes; set aside. Add onion and garlic paste and sauté for 2 minutes. Add in the remaining ingredients and 2 cups of water; return the beef. Seal the lid and cook on Manual for 30 minutes at High. When ready, quick-release the pressure.

Beef Sausage & Bean Tagliatelle

INGREDIENTS for 4 servings

1 lb beef sausages, chopped	2 tsp olive oil
16 oz tagliatelle pasta	1 cup scallions, chopped
½ cup dry white wine	1 (28-oz) can diced tomatoes
1 clove garlic, minced	¼ tsp crushed red pepper flakes
½ cup green peas	1 cup Grana Padano, grated
1 cup canned black beans	Salt and black pepper to taste
2 yellow bell peppers, chopped	Fresh parsley, for garnish

DIRECTIONS and total time: approx. 45 minutes

Place the paste in the inner pot and cover with salted water. Seal the lid, press Manual, and cook for 4 minutes at High. Drain and set aside reserving the cooking water. Heat olive oil on Sauté. Add in scallions, bell peppers, and garlic, and cook for 3 minutes. Stir in sausages and sear until lightly browned, about 4 minutes. Stir in red flakes, salt, and pepper for 1 minute, then pour in wine, tomatoes, black beans, and 2 cups of the pasta water. Seal the lid, select Manual, and cook for 15 minutes at High. Once ready, do a quick release. Stir in green peas for 3-4 minutes and pour over tagliatelle. Top with Grana Padano and sprinkle with parsley to serve.

Beef & Sauerkraut German Dinner

INGREDIENTS for 4-6 servings

1 ½ lb ground beef	1 cup green onions, chopped
10 oz canned tomato soup	2 tbsp butter
1 cup vegetable broth	1 tsp mustard powder
4 cups sauerkraut	Salt and black pepper to taste

DIRECTIONS and total time: approx. 35 minutes

Melt butter on Sauté and cook the green onions for 3 minutes, add beef and brown for another 4-5 minutes, stirring occasionally. Pour in sauerkraut, broth, tomato soup, and mustard powder and season with salt and pepper. Seal the lid and cook for 20 minutes on Manual at High. When ready, do a quick pressure release.

Saucy Corned Beef Brisket

INGREDIENTS for 4-6 servings

1 ½ lb corned beef brisket	2 tomatoes, diced
2 cups canned celery soup	1 tsp ground bay leaves
2 garlic cloves, minced	2 tsp olive oil
1 red onion, diced	Salt and black pepper to taste

DIRECTIONS and total time: approx. 55 minutes

Season the beef with bay leaves, salt, and pepper. Heat olive oil on Sauté and sweat red onion and garlic for 3 minutes. Add beef and sear on all sides for 8-10 minutes. Pour in celery soup, tomatoes, and 1 cup of water. Seal the lid and cook for 40 minutes on Manual at High. When ready, do a quick release and serve.

Beef with Lemon-Grapefruit Sauce

INGREDIENTS for 4-6 servings

1 lemon, juiced	Salt and black pepper to taste
2 grapefruits, juiced	1 tbsp honey
2 lb flat iron steak	1 tsp soy sauce
3 tbsp butter	2 tsp chili sauce
1 tbsp Italian seasoning	1 tsp cornstarch
1 tsp rosemary	1 cup chicken broth

DIRECTIONS and total time: approx. 60 minutes

Mix salt, pepper, rosemary, and Italian seasoning and rub onto the beef. Let sit for 15 minutes. Melt butter on Sauté and sear the beef on all sides for 5-6 minutes. Dissolve the honey in lemon and grapefruit juices in a bowl. Stir in soy sauce, chili sauce, and broth. Pour the mixture over the beef and seal the lid. Select Manual and cook for 30 minutes at High. When ready, do a quick release. Remove the meat to a cutting board and allow to rest for a few minutes before slicing. Mix cornstarch with some cooking liquid and pour it in the pot. Press Sauté and cook for 2-3 minutes until thickened. Pour sauce over beef and serve.

Beef Roast with Red Potatoes

INGREDIENTS for 6 servings

1 (1-oz) packet dry onion soup mix	
2 lb beef roast	1 tsp cilantro
2 sweet onions, sliced	2 garlic cloves, minced
1 lb red potatoes, chopped	2 tbsp Worcestershire sauce
2 cups beef broth	3 tbsp olive oil
1 cup canned tomatoes	Salt and black pepper to taste

DIRECTIONS and total time: approx. 60 minutes

Warm olive oil on Sauté, season the beef with salt and black pepper and sear it on all sides, about 6-7 minutes; reserve. Add onions and garlic to the pot and sauté for 3 minutes. Stir in the remaining ingredients and return the beef. Seal the lid and cook on Manual for 40 minutes at High. Release the pressure quickly.

Mustardy Beef Steaks with Beer Gravy

INGREDIENTS for 4 servings

4 beef steaks	2 carrots, chopped
12 oz dark beer	1 tbsp tomato puree
2 tbsp Dijon mustard	1 onion, chopped
1 tsp chipotle powder	1 cup vegetable broth
1 tsp sage	Salt and black pepper to taste
1 tbsp flour	2 tbsp olive oil

DIRECTIONS and total time: approx. 50 minutes

Brush the meat with mustard and season with chipotle powder, salt, and pepper. Heat olive oil on Sauté and sear the steaks for 6 minutes in total; reserve. Add onion and carrot to the pot and cook for 3 minutes. Pour in broth to scrape off the bottom of the pot and stir in beer, tomato puree, sage, salt, and black pepper. Return the steak and seal the lid. Cook for 25 minutes on Manual at High. When done, quick-release the pressure. Remove the beef to a serving plate. Whisk flour with some cooking liquids until smooth and pour in the pot. Select Sauté and cook for 2-3 minutes until thickened. Pour the gravy over the meat and serve.

Thyme Pot Roast with Potatoes

INGREDIENTS for 6 servings

3 tbsp olive oil	½ celery stalk, sliced
2 ½ lb beef chuck roast	1 tsp rosemary
1 lb potatoes, chopped	1 tsp sage
2 carrots, chopped	Salt and black pepper to taste
1 parsnip, chopped	2 tbsp tomato puree
1 onion, sliced	1 tsp garlic paste
½ cup red wine	2 cups vegetable broth

DIRECTIONS and total time: approx. 60 minutes

In a bowl, combine sage, rosemary, salt, and pepper and rub the mixture onto the meat. Heat olive oil on Sauté and cook the beef for 5-6 minutes on all sides; reserve. Add onion, carrots, parsnip, celery, and garlic paste to the pot and sauté for 3 minutes. Stir in red wine to deglaze the bottom of the pot. Add in potatoes, tomato puree, and vegetable broth and return the beef. Seal the lid and cook on Manual for 40 minutes at High. Once ready, do a quick pressure release. Serve.

Grandma's Beef with Apple & Vegetables

INGREDIENTS for 4-6 servings

3 tbsp olive oil	1 red cabbage head, shredded
1 green apple, chopped	3 garlic cloves, quartered
½ tsp rosemary	3 turnips, chopped
6 potatoes, quartered	1 cup red wine
2 carrots, cut into pieces	Salt and black pepper to taste
2 lb beef brisket, cubed	2 shallots, chopped

DIRECTIONS and total time: approx. 50 minutes

Heat canola oil on Sauté and cook garlic, shallots, carrots, and beef for 5 minutes. Add in cabbage, rosemary, and apple, and sauté for 5 minutes. Pour in wine, potatoes, turnips, and 2 cups of water. Season with salt and pepper. Seal the lid and cook on Manual for 30 minutes at High. When ready, do a quick release.

Stewed Beef with Vegetables

INGREDIENTS for 4-6 servings

2 lb beef steak, cubed	1 cup tomato sauce
1 sweet onion, chopped	1 tsp paprika
1 cup celery, chopped	1 tbsp sage
1 lb sweet potatoes, diced	1 chicken bouillon cube
1 cup green beans, chopped	Salt and black pepper to taste
3 garlic cloves, minced	3 tbsp olive oil
2 bell peppers, chopped	2 bay leaves

DIRECTIONS and total time: approx. 50 minutes

Heat olive oil on Sauté and sear the meat for 6 minutes, stirring periodically; set aside. Sauté the veggies for 5 minutes. Stir in paprika, sage, salt, and pepper for 1 minute, and pour in tomato sauce, 2 cups of water, and top with the steak. In a bowl, whisk bouillon cube and bay leaves; return the beef. Seal the lid and cook for 30 minutes on Manual at High. When ready, quick-release the pressure. Remove bay leaves and serve.

Beef with Chestnuts & Pearl Onions

INGREDIENTS for 4 servings

2 tbsp olive oil	½ cup chestnuts, sliced
1 lb stewing steak, cubed	2 tomatoes, chopped
1 cup pearl onions	A pinch of allspice
1 cup beef broth	Salt and black pepper to taste
2 garlic cloves, minced	1 tbsp cornflour

DIRECTIONS and total time: approx. 15 minutes

Heat olive oil on Sauté and stir-fry the meat for 6-7 minutes; set aside. Place pearl onions and garlic in the pot to sauté for 3 minutes. Add in chestnuts, tomatoes, broth, allspice, salt and pepper; return the beef and stir well. Seal the lid and cook on Manual for 30 minutes at High. Quick-release the pressure. Beat the cornflour with some cooking liquids and pour in the pot. Press Sauté and cook for 2-3 minutes until the sauce thickens.

Mom's Rump Roast with Potatoes

INGREDIENTS for 4 servings

1 ½ lb rump roast, cubed	2 tbsp butter
6 Yukon gold potatoes, diced	1 carrot, diced
1 onion, diced	1 tsp sage
1 celery stalk, diced	2 bay leaves
½ tbsp Dijon mustard	2 garlic cloves, minced
1 cup beef broth	Salt and black pepper to taste

DIRECTIONS and total time: approx. 55 minutes

Heat olive oil on Sauté and stir-fry onion, garlic, and celery for 3 minutes. Brush mustard over the beef; season with salt and pepper. Sear in the pot for 5 minutes. Stir in the remaining ingredients, seal the lid and cook on Manual for 30 minutes at High. Do a natural release for 10 minutes. Discard bay leaves to serve.

Ground Beef with Zucchini Noodles

INGREDIENTS for 4 servings

1 lb ground beef	2 cups chicken broth
1 cup tomatoes, chopped	2 thyme sprigs, chopped
1 onion, chopped	2 tbsp olive oil
1 carrot, chopped	1 tsp red pepper flakes
1 cup kale, chopped	12 oz zucchini noodles
½ celery stalk, chopped	Parmesan cheese to garnish

DIRECTIONS and total time: approx. 40 minutes

Warm olive oil on Sauté and brown the beef for about 5 minutes. Stir in onions, carrot, and celery and cook for 5 more minutes. Mix in the remaining ingredients, except for the noodles. Seal the lid, press Manual, and cook for 15 minutes at High. When ready, do a quick pressure release. Stir in zucchini noodles and cook for 5 minutes on Sauté. Serve hot, sprinkled with Parmesan.

Quick & Easy Beef Meatloaf

INGREDIENTS for 4 servings

1 lb ground beef	1 tsp garlic, minced
1 carrot, grated	½ tsp sage
1 onion, diced	¼ tsp oregano
½ cup breadcrumbs	Salt and black pepper to taste
1 egg	1 tsp Worcestershire sauce

DIRECTIONS and total time: approx. 30 minutes

Pour in 1 cup of water and insert a trivet. Combine all ingredients in a large bowl. Grease a baking pan with cooking spray and add the mixture, pressing it tightly. Lower the pan on top of the trivet. Seal the lid and cook on Manual for 15 minutes at High. When done, allow a natural release for 10 minutes, and serve warm.

Whiskey-Glazed Meatloaf

INGREDIENTS for 4 servings

Meatloaf:

1 lb ground beef	⅔ cup onion, diced
1 egg white	½ tsp basil
⅔ cup breadcrumbs	1 garlic clove, minced
2 tbsp tomato puree	Salt and black pepper to taste

Whiskey glaze:

1 cup apricot jam	¼ cup honey
½ cup whiskey	1 tbsp hot sauce
½ cup barbecue sauce	¼ cup water

DIRECTIONS and total time: approx. 70 minutes

Combine all meatloaf ingredients in a bowl. Mix and shape into a meatloaf. Place in a greased baking pan. Whisk the glaze ingredients in another bowl. Brush this mixture over the meatloaf. Place a trivet and pour in 1 cup of water. Place baking pan on the trivet and seal the lid. Cook on Manual for 20 minutes at High. When done, do a quick pressure release. Serve warm.

Homemade Beef Minestrone

INGREDIENTS for 4 servings

1 onion, diced	1 carrot, chopped
1 celery stalk, diced	2 garlic cloves, minced
4 cups vegetable broth	¼ cup chopped basil
1 cup canned white beans	1 cup cooked pasta
½ lb ground beef	2 tbsp olive oil
28 oz canned tomatoes	Salt and black pepper to taste

DIRECTIONS and total time: approx. 35 minutes

Heat olive oil on Sauté and brown the beef for 5-6 minutes. Add in onion, celery, carrot, and garlic, and sauté for 2 minutes. Pour in tomatoes, beans, and broth; season with salt and black pepper. Seal the lid, select Manual, and cook for 15 minutes at High. When ready, do a quick release. Stir in pasta just until heated through. Scatter basil over the top and serve hot.

Rosemary Flank Steak

INGREDIENTS for 4 servings

2 lb flank steak	1 carrot, chopped
1 cup beef broth	2 tbsp olive oil
1 onion, diced	2 tbsp rosemary, chopped
1 tbsp potato starch	Salt and black pepper to taste

Mustard marinade:

2 tbsp Dijon mustard	2 garlic cloves, minced
2 tsp fresh lemon juice	½ cup soy sauce
¼ cup red wine vinegar	1 tbsp sesame oil

DIRECTIONS and total time: approx. 65 minutes

Combine all marinade ingredients in a bowl. Add in the beef and let rest for 15 minutes. After, heat olive oil on Sauté and stir-fry onion and carrot for 3 minutes. Add the beef along with the marinade, and brown on all sides for 6-7 minutes. Pour in beef broth. Seal the lid and cook on Manual for 30 minutes at High. When ready, do a quick release. Remove the meat and let it sit for a few minutes before slicing. Mix the potato starch with some cooking liquids and stir to combine. Pour in the pot, press Sauté, and stir for 3-4 minutes until thickened. Adjust the seasoning and pour over the sliced beef. Sprinkle with rosemary and serve.

Sticky Ginger Ale Short Ribs

INGREDIENTS for 4 servings

2 lb beef short ribs, bone-in	12 oz barbecue sauce
2 tsp olive oil	½ tsp onion powder
1 cup ginger ale beer	¼ tsp chipotle powder
Salt and black pepper to taste	¼ tsp garlic powder

DIRECTIONS and total time: approx. 50 minutes

Mix all spices, salt, and pepper in a bowl. Add the short ribs and toss to coat. Heat olive oil on Sauté and sear the ribs for 3 minutes per side, until browned.

Pour in the ale and ½ cup of water. Seal the lid and cook on Manual for 30 minutes at High. Do a quick release. Pour barbecue sauce over the ribs. Press Sauté and simmer for 5 minutes until sticky. Serve hot.

One-Pot Fennel & Parsnip Beef

INGREDIENTS for 4 servings

1 lb beef stew meat, cubed	2 tbsp red wine
2 parsnips, chopped	2 tbsp olive oil
2 fennel bulb, chopped	2 tbsp flour
4 potatoes, diced	1 tsp sage
1 onion, chopped	Salt and black pepper to taste

DIRECTIONS and total time: approx. 45 minutes

In a bowl, mix in flour, salt, and black pepper. Toss the beef to coat. Heat olive oil on Sauté and brown the beef for 8 minutes. Add onion and fennel, and sauté until soft, 3-4 minutes. Stir in the remaining ingredients and 2 cups of water. Seal the lid and cook on Manual for 30 minutes at High. Do a quick pressure release.

Tasty Beef with Carrot-Onion Gravy

INGREDIENTS for 4 servings

4 round steaks	2 tbsp oil
2 onions, sliced	1 carrot, chopped
1 ½ cups beef broth	½ tsp red pepper flakes
1 tsp garlic paste	¼ cup whipping cream
½ tsp thyme	1 tbsp butter
½ tsp rosemary	Salt and black pepper to taste

DIRECTIONS and total time: approx. 40 minutes

Heat olive oil on Sauté and brown steaks for 6 minutes in total; reserve. Stir-fry onions, carrot, and garlic paste for 2 minutes, until fragrant. Stir in salt, pepper, red flakes, rosemary, thyme, and pour in broth; return the steaks. Seal the lid and cook on Manual for 25 minutes at High. When ready, do a quick pressure release. Stir in whipping cream and butter, and cook for 3 minutes until thickened on Sauté. Serve steaks with the gravy.

Easy Beef & Rice Kaiser rolls

INGREDIENTS for 4 servings

1 lb ground beef	1 tsp tomato puree
1 tomato, diced	1 tsp brown sugar
4 Kaiser rolls	½ cup sweet onions
½ cup Arborio rice	½ tsp paprika
½ tsp chipotle powder	½ tsp rosemary
2 tsp canola oil	Salt and black pepper to taste

DIRECTIONS and total time: approx. 30 minutes

Combine all ingredients, except for the rolls, in your IP. Add in 3 cups of water. Seal the lid, set to Manual, and cook for 25 minutes at High. Do a quick pressure release. Divide the mixture between the rolls and serve.

Provençal Meatballs with Cheese Sauce

INGREDIENTS for 4 servings

1 cup canned mushroom soup
3 tbsp olive oil
1 lb ground beef
½ cup onion, diced
1 egg
½ tsp garlic powder

½ cup goat cheese, crumbled
1 tbsp herbes de Provence
½ cup breadcrumbs
Salt and black pepper to taste
½ cup Colby cheese, grated

DIRECTIONS and total time: approx. 40 minutes

In a bowl, combine ground beef, onion, egg, garlic powder, goat cheese, herbes de Provence, breadcrumbs, salt, and pepper. Mix well with hands and shape into meatballs. Heat olive oil on Sauté and brown meatballs on all sides for 5-6 minutes. Pour in ½ cup of water and mushroom soup, seal the lid, and cook for 20 minutes on Manual at High. Do a quick pressure release. Stir in Colby cheese, press Sauté and cook for 3 minutes until the cheese has melted. Serve immediately.

Brussel Sprout & Beef with Red Sauce

INGREDIENTS for 4 servings

1 lb ground beef
1 lb Brussel sprouts, shredded
1 cup leeks, chopped
1 (10.75 oz) can tomato soup
1 tsp thyme

2 garlic cloves, pressed
2 tbsp olive oil
1 tsp mustard powder
1 bay leaf
Salt and black pepper to taste

DIRECTIONS and total time: approx. 55 minutes

Heat olive oil on Sauté and cook leeks and garlic for 5 minutes. Stir in ground beef, mustard, Brussel sprouts, tomato puree, thyme, and bay leaf, and cook for 10 minutes; stir frequently. Season with salt and pepper, add tomato soup and seal the lid. Select Manual and cook for 30 minutes at High. When ready, do a quick pressure release. Discard bay leaf and serve.

Yummy Beef with Vegetables

INGREDIENTS for 4 servings

1 lb butternut squash, cubed
½ cup red wine
2 garlic cloves, minced
½ cup fennel bulb, sliced
Salt and black pepper to taste
1 ½ lb chuck roast, cubed

1 tbsp tomato puree
1 ½ cups beef broth
2 sprigs sage, crushed
2 tsp olive oil
1 red onion, sliced
1 carrot, sliced

DIRECTIONS and total time: approx. 50 minutes

Heat olive oil on Sauté and brown the beef for 5-6 minutes; reserve. Add garlic, fennel, onion, and carrot to the pot and sauté for 3 minutes until tender. Stir in red wine to deglaze the pot and pour in tomato puree, beef broth, squash, sage, salt, and pepper; return the meat. Seal the lid, select Manual, and set to 30 minutes at High. Do a quick pressure release and serve warm.

Chipotle Beef with Wild Rice

INGREDIENTS for 4 servings

2 lb beef sirloin steak, cubed
2 tbsp vegetable oil
1 red onion, chopped
½ tsp chipotle powder
¼ tsp mustard powder

Salt and black pepper to taste
2 garlic cloves, minced
1 cup wild rice
10 ½ oz beef consommé
2 tbsp parsley, chopped

DIRECTIONS and total time: approx. 40 minutes

In a plastic bag, mix mustard powder, salt, pepper, and chipotle powder. Add beef and shake the bag to coat thoroughly. Heat vegetable oil on Sauté, and stir-fry the beef until browned, about 5-6 minutes. Add in onion and garlic and cook for 3 minutes. Stir in rice and beef consommé; season to taste. Seal the lid, press Manual, and cook for 20 minutes at High. When ready, do a quick release. Sprinkle with parsley and serve.

Beef Spaghetti Bolognese

INGREDIENTS for 4 servings

16 oz spaghetti pasta
1 lb ground beef
1 (14.5 oz) can tomatoes
1 onion, finely minced
2 garlic cloves, minced
1 tbsp tomato puree

2 tbsp olive oil
Salt and black pepper to taste
½ tsp red chili flakes
½ tsp Italian seasoning
2 tsp Grana Padano cheese
2 tbsp basil, chopped

DIRECTIONS and total time: approx. 30 minutes

Place spaghetti in your IP and cover with salted water. Seal the lid, press Manual, and cook for 4 minutes at High. Do a quick pressure release. Drain and set aside, reserving the cooking water. Heat olive oil on Sauté and cook onion, garlic, and beef for about 4-5 minutes; season with Italian seasoning, chili flakes, basil, salt, and pepper. Stir in tomato puree and 1 cup of pasta water. Seal the lid, press Manual, and cook for 10 minutes at High. Once ready, do a quick pressure release. Sprinkle with Grana Padano cheese and serve.

Chipotle Beef Curry

INGREDIENTS for 4 servings

1 cup scallions, chopped
1 cup milk
2 carrots, sliced
4 potatoes, chopped
1 cup vegetable broth
1 lb stewed beef, cubed

2 garlic cloves, minced
2 tbsp curry powder
1 tsp oregano
½ tsp chipotle powder
Salt and black pepper to taste
2 tbsp olive oil

DIRECTIONS and total time: approx. 45 minutes

Heat olive oil on Sauté and cook garlic and scallions for 2 minutes. Stir in beef and brown for 5 minutes. Add in the remaining ingredients and stir to combine. Seal the lid, press Manual, and set the timer to 30 minutes at High. Do a quick pressure release. Serve.

Juniper Beef Ragu

INGREDIENTS for 4 servings

7 oz jarred roasted red peppers, chopped	
1 lb beef stew meat, cubed	1 tsp parsley, chopped
1 bay leaf	1 tsp cilantro
2 juniper berries	½ cup beef broth
2 garlic cloves, crushed	2 tbsp olive oil
14 oz canned diced tomatoes	Salt and black pepper to taste

DIRECTIONS and total time: approx. 50 minutes

Season the beef with salt and pepper. Heat oil on Sauté and brown the beef for 6 minutes. Add in the remaining ingredients. Seal the lid, select Manual, and cook for 30 minutes at High. When ready, allow a natural release for 10 minutes. Discard bay leaf and serve.

Spicy Beef with Chickpeas

INGREDIENTS for 4 servings

1 lb ground beef	1 red onion, chopped
1 tsp serrano powder	2 cups beef broth
2 green bell peppers, chopped	2 tbsp grapeseed oil
2 garlic cloves, minced	½ tsp dried oregano
2 tomatoes, chopped	½ tsp dried basil
1 (14 oz) can chickpeas	Salt and black pepper to taste

DIRECTIONS and total time: approx. 35 minutes

Heat grapeseed oil on Sauté and stir-fry onion, garlic, and green peppers for 3-4 minutes. Add in ground beef and brown for 4-5 minutes. Stir in the rest of the ingredients. Seal the lid, select Manual, and cook for 15 minutes at High. Once the cooking is complete, perform a quick pressure release. Serve immediately.

Cajun Beef Ribeye

INGREDIENTS for 4 servings

2 beef ribeye steaks	2 tsp butter
1 sweet onion, chopped	1 tbsp flour
1 cup tomato sauce	1 tsp Cajun seasoning
2 garlic cloves, minced	½ tsp celery seeds
1 carrot, chopped	Salt and black pepper to taste
2 ½ cups beef broth	½ tsp cayenne pepper

DIRECTIONS and total time: approx. 50 minutes

Melt butter on Sauté and brown the beef for 4-6 minutes, turning once; reserve. Add onion, garlic, and carrot, and sauté for 3 minutes. Stir in celery seeds, Italian seasoning, and cayenne pepper, for 1 minute. Pour in beef broth and tomato sauce; return the beef. Seal the lid and cook on Manual for 30 minutes at High. Once ready, do a quick pressure release. Remove the beef. In a bowl, whisk together the flour with ¼ cup of cooking liquid; add to the pot. Press Sauté and stir until thickened, 2-3 minutes. Adjust the seasoning, slice the beef and pour the sauce over to serve.

Beef & Pancetta Bourguignon

INGREDIENTS for 4 servings

1 ½ lb beef brisket, cubed	½ cup Burgundy red wine
2 slices pancetta, diced	1 tbsp flour
2 garlic cloves, minced	½ tsp thyme
2 red bell peppers, diced	2 cups beef stock
1 cup mushrooms, sliced	2 tomatoes, finely chopped
1 tbsp butter, softened	1 tsp chili pepper, minced
2 cups green onions, chopped	Salt and black pepper to taste

DIRECTIONS and total time: approx. 55 minutes

Melt butter on Sauté and cook pancetta for 5 minutes until crispy; set aside. Season the beef with salt and pepper and add to the pot, cook for 5-6 minutes, stirring occasionally; remove. Add garlic, bell peppers, green onions, mushrooms, thyme, and chili pepper to the cooker, and sauté for 3 minutes. Stir in flour for 1-2 minutes, and add in red wine, tomatoes, and beef stock; return beef and pancetta. Seal the lid and cook on Manual for 30 minutes at High. Once cooking is over, do a quick pressure release. Serve hot.

Mexican-Style Ropa Vieja

INGREDIENTS for 4-6 servings

2 lb beef chuck roast	3 tomatoes, chopped
2 cups vegetable broth	1 tsp jalapeño powder
3 cloves garlic, minced	3 cups white rice, cooked
2 limes juiced	Salt and black pepper to taste
1 onion, sliced	2 tbsp fresh cilantro, chopped

DIRECTIONS and total time: approx. 65 minutes

Heat olive oil on Sauté and cook onion and garlic for 3 minutes, stirring often. Add in beef and sear for 5-6 minutes. Pour in broth and tomatoes. Season with salt, pepper, and jalapeño powder. Seal the lid, select Manual, and cook for 40 minutes at High. When ready, release the pressure naturally for 10 minutes. Shred the beef with two forks and stir in lime juice. Pour over the white rice, sprinkle with cilantro and serve.

Caribbean Beef Roast

INGREDIENTS for 4 servings

2 lb beef roast	½ tsp dried sage
½ tsp curcuma	1 tsp garlic powder
½ tsp rosemary	2 tbsp olive oil
1 tsp grated ginger	Salt and black pepper to taste

DIRECTIONS and total time: approx. 70 minutes

Brush the beef with olive oil. Mix curcuma, garlic, rosemary, sage, and ginger in a small bowl, and rub the mixture onto the meat. Place the beef in the inner pot, and pour 1 cup of water around it. Seal the lid and cook on Manual for 50 minutes at High. When ready, do a quick pressure release. Shred the meat and serve.

Italian Beef Stew with Root Vegetables

INGREDIENTS for 4-6 servings

1 tbsp Italian seasoning	2 tbsp olive oil
2 carrots, chopped	1 onion, diced
2 parsnips, chopped	2 bay leaves
2 lb beef roast	2 garlic cloves, minced
2 cups vegetable stock	Salt and black pepper to taste

DIRECTIONS and total time: approx. 55 minutes

Heat olive oil on Sauté and cook onion, garlic, carrots, and parsnips for 5 minutes. Season the beef with pepper and salt, and place on top of the veggies. Pour in stock and bay leaves, and seal the lid. Press Manual and set to 40 minutes at High. When done, do a quick pressure release. Remove the beef and let it sit for a few minutes before slicing. Serve drizzled with cooking juices.

Tasty Beef with Rotini Pasta

INGREDIENTS for 4 servings

1 lb ground beef	2 shallots, chopped
2 cloves garlic, sliced	½ tsp red pepper flakes
1 tbsp tomato puree	2 tbsp vegetable oil
1 tsp dried sage	1 tbsp fresh basil, chopped
Salt and black pepper to taste	16 oz rotini pasta

DIRECTIONS and total time: approx. 40 minutes

Place rotini in inner pot and cover with salted water. Seal the lid, press Manual, and cook for 4 minutes at High. Do a quick pressure release. Drain and set aside, reserving the cooking water. Heat vegetable oil on Sauté and cook shallots and garlic for 3 minutes. Add in beef and season with salt, pepper, and sage. Brown for 5 minutes. Stir in tomato puree, red flakes, and 1 cup of the pasta water. Seal the lid, select Manual, and cook for 15 minutes at High. Do a quick pressure release. Pour over pasta, garnish with basil, and serve.

Picante Beef Stew with Barley

INGREDIENTS for 4 servings

1 lb cubed beef stew meat	1 (14-oz) can diced tomatoes
1 onion, chopped	1 cup barley, rinsed
2 garlic cloves, minced	1 tsp oregano
1 tsp paprika	½ tsp red pepper flakes
2 cups beef stock	Salt and black pepper to taste

DIRECTIONS and total time: approx. 45 minutes

Select Sauté and brown the beef for 5 minutes, stirring occasionally; reserve. Add onion and garlic to the pot, and sauté for 3 minutes. Stir in barley, paprika and oregano for 1 minute. Pour in tomatoes and broth, and return the beef. Taste and adjust the seasoning. Seal the lid, press Manual, and cook for 30 minutes at High. When ready, do a quick pressure release. Fluff barley with a fork and sprinkle with red pepper flakes.

Beef with Garlic & Honey

INGREDIENTS for 4-6 servings

3 lb beef chuck roast, halved	tsp brown sugar
2 tbsp olive oil	6 cloves garlic, minced
1 ½ cups vegetable stock	2 tbsp soy sauce
1 tsp honey	2 tbsp chopped chives

DIRECTIONS and total time: approx. 60 minutes

Place beef in inner pot. In a bowl, mix together the remaining ingredients, except for the chives, and stir well. Pour the mixture over the beef. Seal the lid, select Manual, and cook for 40 minutes at High. When ready, release the pressure naturally for 10 minutes. Remove and shred the beef using two forks. Drizzle the cooking juices over and top with chopped chives to serve.

Zucchini Rump Steak

INGREDIENTS for 4 servings

2 tbsp olive oil	1 onion, chopped
2 bay leaves	2 zucchinis, chopped
2 lb beef rump steak	14 oz canned tomato sauce
1 cup celery, diced	1 ½ cups vegetable broth
Salt and black pepper to taste	½ cup dry red wine

DIRECTIONS and total time: approx. 50 minutes

Warm olive oil on Sauté and brown the beef on all sides, about 5-6 minutes; set aside. Add onion, celery, zucchinis, salt, and black pepper to the pot, and sauté for 3 minutes. Deglaze with red wine, and pour in vegetable broth, tomato sauce, and bay leaves; return the beef. Seal the lid and cook on Manual for 30 minutes at High. When ready, do a quick release. Remove the beef to a cutting board and let it sit for 10 minutes before slicing. Blitz the sauce in the pot with an immersion blender and pour over the beef to serve.

Smoked Beef Steak

INGREDIENTS for 4 servings

2 lb beef eye round steak, sliced	
2 tbsp olive oil	½ cup carrots, sliced
Salt and black pepper to taste	½ cup onions, sliced
1 can (14-oz) tomatoes, diced	1 cup celery, sliced
2 garlic cloves, diced	1 ½ cups beef broth
1 bay leaf	1 tbsp liquid smoke
½ cup bell peppers, chopped	Chopped green onions

DIRECTIONS and total time: approx. 1 hour and 19 minutes

Heat olive oil on Sauté and stir-fry onions, bell peppers, celery, garlic, carrots, salt, and pepper for 5 minutes. Add in beef and brown it for 5-6 minutes on both sides. Pour in beef broth, bay leaf, liquid smoke, and tomatoes. Seal the lid, select Manual, and cook for 40 minutes at High. When ready, release the pressure quickly; discard the bay leaf. Serve with green onions.

Dinner Ribs with Beets & Potatoes

INGREDIENTS for 4-6 servings

2 lb short ribs, excess fat trimmed
1 ½ cups beef broth | 1 (14-oz) can diced tomatoes
½ lb small potatoes | 2 sprigs rosemary, chopped
3 tsp butter | ½ lb beets, thinly sliced
2 red onions, chopped | Salt and black pepper to taste
½ tsp thyme | 2 cloves garlic, minced

DIRECTIONS and total time: approx. 50 minutes

Rub the ribs with salt and black pepper. Melt butter on Sauté and sear the ribs on all sides, about 5-6 minutes; reserve. Add beets, garlic, and onion to the pot, and stir-fry for 4-5 minutes. Return the ribs and stir in the remaining ingredients. Seal the lid and cook on Manual for 30 minutes at High. Once cooking is complete, perform a quick pressure release. Serve immediately.

Beef with Pearl Onions & Mushrooms

INGREDIENTS for 4 servings

2 lb beef shoulder, cubed | 3 tbsp olive oil
16 oz pearl onions | ½ cup white wine
1 ½ cups beef stock | 2 garlic cloves, minced
2 bell peppers, chopped | 1 tbsp flour
8 oz mushrooms, sliced | 1 tsp thyme
1 carrot, chopped | Salt and black pepper to taste

DIRECTIONS and total time: approx. 50 minutes

Season the beef with salt and pepper, and coat with flour. Heat olive oil on Sauté and brown the beef on all sides, about 7-8 minutes; set aside. Add pearl onions, garlic, mushrooms, carrot, and bell peppers to the pot, and sauté for 3 minutes. Deglaze with wine and stir for 1 minute. Add in beef stock, thyme, and the reserved beef. Seal the lid and cook on Manual for 30 minutes at High. When cooking is over, release the pressure quickly. Adjust the seasoning and serve.

Cheesy Beef Tortilla Pie

INGREDIENTS for 4 servings

4-6 corn tortillas | 12 oz Colby cheese
2 tbsp taco seasoning | ¼ cup refried beans
1 lb ground beef | Salt and black pepper to taste

DIRECTIONS and total time: approx. 20 minutes

Pour 1 cup of water in inner pot and insert a trivet. Mix ground beef with taco seasoning, salt, and pepper. Place 1 tortilla on the bottom of a greased baking pan. Top with some beans, beef mixture, and cheese. Top with another tortilla. Repeat until you've use up all ingredients. The final layer should be a tortilla. Lower the pan on the trivet. Seal the lid and cook on Manual for 12 minutes at High. When ready, do a quick pressure release. Remove the pan and serve with guacamole.

Barbecued Brisket with Tagliatelle

INGREDIENTS for 6 servings

3 lb beef brisket, fat trimmed | ¼ cup red wine vinegar
2 cups barbecue sauce | ½ tsp nutmeg
1 celery stalk, chopped | Salt and black pepper to taste
2 medium onions, sliced | ½ tsp ginger powder
16 oz tagliatelle | 1 tsp garlic paste
¼ cup light brown sugar | 2 tbsp parsley, minced

DIRECTIONS and total time: approx. 60 minutes

Place tagliatelle in inner pot and cover with salted water. Seal the lid, press Manual, and cook for 4 minutes at High. Do a quick pressure release. Drain and set aside, reserving the cooking water. Mix nutmeg, ginger, garlic, parsley, salt, and pepper in a bowl and stir to combine. Rub the brisket with the spice mix and place inside the pot. Combine 1 cup of pasta water, vinegar, sugar, celery, onions, and barbecue sauce in small bowl. Place on top of the brisket. Seal the lid, select Manual, and cook for 30 minutes at High. When ready, release the pressure naturally for 10 minutes. Remove the brisket to a platter and let it stand for 10 minutes. Slice and serve over tagliatelle topped with parsley.

Beef & Vegetable Casserole

INGREDIENTS for 4 servings

1 lb beef flank steak, sliced | 1 cup green beans, sliced
1 red onion, sliced | 2 cloves garlic, sliced
1 lb mushrooms, sliced | 1 carrot, diced
2 tbsp olive oil | 1 cup tomato sauce
2 bell peppers, sliced | Salt and black pepper to taste

DIRECTIONS and total time: approx. 45 minutes

Heat olive oil on Sauté and brown the beef on both sides, about 7-8 minutes; reserve. Lay vegetables at the bottom of the cooker and place the steak on top. Pour over the remaining ingredients and 1 cup of water. Seal the lid, select Manual, and cook for 30 minutes at High. When ready, do a quick pressure release and serve.

Cilantro Vegetable Beef Soup

INGREDIENTS for 6 servings

½ lb beef stew meat, cubed | 1 carrot, diced
2 tbsp olive oil | 1 cup green onions, chopped
½ lb russet potatoes, diced | 6 cups beef broth
2 tomatoes, chopped | Salt and black pepper to taste
1 celery stalk, chopped | ½ cup fresh cilantro, chopped

DIRECTIONS and total time: approx. 50 minutes

Heat olive oil on Sauté and cook green onion and garlic for 3 minutes. Add in the remaining ingredients, except for cilantro. Seal the lid, select Manual, and cook for 30 minutes at High. Once done, allow a natural release for 10 minutes. Stir in cilantro, and serve warm.

Country Beef Stew with Sweet Potatoes

INGREDIENTS for 4-6 servings

1 onion, diced	1 tsp garlic paste
2 sweet potatoes, cubed	1 ½ cups vegetable broth
½ tsp basil, chopped	1 tbsp tomato paste
½ tsp parsley, chopped	1 bell pepper, chopped
½ tsp oregano, chopped	1 tbsp canola oil
2 lb cubed stew beef meat	Salt and black pepper to taste

DIRECTIONS and total time: approx. 50 minutes

Heat canola oil on Sauté and cook bell pepper, garlic paste, and onion for 3 minutes. Add the beef and brown on all sides, about 5-6 minutes. Stir in the remaining ingredients. Seal the lid and cook on Manual for 30 minutes at High. When ready, do a quick release. Serve.

Curried Beef Stew with Green Peas

INGREDIENTS for 4 servings

2 lb beef stew meat, cubed	2 bay leaves
3 tbsp olive oil	Salt and black pepper to taste
1 onion, chopped	10 oz frozen green peas
1 tsp curry powder	1 large tomato, chopped
2 cups vegetable broth	Chopped fresh parsley

DIRECTIONS and total time: approx. 50 minutes

Heat olive oil on Sauté, season the beef with salt and pepper, and brown it for 5-6 minutes on all sides; reserve. Add onion to the pot and sauté for 2 minutes. Stir in curry powder, bay leaves, and tomato for 1 minute. Pour in vegetable broth and return the beef; season with salt and pepper. Seal the lid, select Manual, and cook for 30 minutes at High. When ready, do a quick release. Discard bay leaves. Add peas and cook for 4 minutes on Sauté. Serve sprinkled with parsley.

Burrito Beef

INGREDIENTS for 4 servings

2 large scallions, chopped	2 tbsp green taco sauce
2 lb beef steak	1 garlic clove, minced
1 jalapeño pepper, minced	2 tbsp olive oil
Salt and black pepper to taste	½ cup green onions, chopped
1 tsp chili powder	2 cups salsa verde
½ tsp cumin	2 tbsp cilantro, chopped

DIRECTIONS and total time: approx. 56 minutes

Heat olive oil on Sauté. Remove excess fat from steak and cook the meat on all sides for 5-6 minutes. In a bowl, mix jalapeño pepper, salsa verde, green onions, garlic, chili powder, cumin, salt, and pepper. Add the mixture to the pot and stir well. Pour in 1 cup of water. Seal the lid, select Manual, and cook for 20 minutes at High. When ready, release the pressure naturally for 10 minutes. Remove the beef and shred it using two forks. Serve warm in burritos topped with green taco sauce.

Malaysian Beef Curry

INGREDIENTS for 4-6 servings

2 lb beef stew meat, cubed	1 tsp coriander, ground
3 tbsp olive oil	4 cloves garlic, minced
1 onion, quartered	½ tsp cinnamon, ground
1 cup coconut cream	½ tsp chili powder
4 cups spinach, chopped	½ tsp ginger powder
1 tsp turmeric	1 tsp cardamom, ground
1 tsp cumin, ground	Salt and black pepper to taste

DIRECTIONS and total time: approx. 56 minutes

Mix all the spices in a bowl and add in the beef; toss to coat. Heat olive oil on Sauté and cook the beef and onion for 5-6 minutes, stirring occasionally. Pour in 2 cups of water. Seal the lid, select Manual, and cook for 15 minutes at High. When ready, release the pressure quickly. Stir in spinach and coconut cream, press Sauté, and cook until the spinach wilts, 3-4 minutes. Serve.

Stewed Beef Oxtails

INGREDIENTS for 4 servings

2 lb beef oxtails, chopped into chunks

2 cups beef broth	2 tbsp butter, melted
1 garlic clove, minced	Salt and black pepper to taste
1 tsp onion powder	1 tsp dried thyme
2 tbsp tomato paste	½ tsp ground ginger
1 tbsp fish sauce	½ tbsp cornstarch
2 tbsp soy sauce	2 tbsp parsley, chopped

DIRECTIONS and total time: approx. 50 minutes

Place all the ingredients, except for the beef oxtails, parley, and cornstarch in your IP, and stir to combine. Seal the lid, select Manual, and cook for 40 minutes at High. When ready, release the pressure quickly. Remove oxtails to a serving plate. Whisk cornstarch with some cooking liquids and pour in the pot. Press Sauté and stir to make gravy, about 2-3 minutes. Pour the gravy over the beef and serve topped with parsley.

Speedy Meatballs

INGREDIENTS for 4 servings

3 tbsp olive oil	Salt and black pepper to taste
1 lb ground beef	½ tsp oregano
1 onion, grated	1 cup cranberry sauce
½ cup breadcrumbs	2 tsp yellow mustard
1 egg	½ cup chili sauce

DIRECTIONS and total time: approx. 40 minutes

Combine all ingredients, except for cranberry and chili sauces, in a bowl and shape into balls. Heat olive oil on Sauté and fry meatballs for 6-7 minutes on all sides. Add in cranberry and chili sauces and 1 cup of water; stir to coat. Seal the lid, select Manual, and cook for 20 minutes at High. Quick-release the pressure, and serve.

Shiitake & Baby Carrot Beef Stew

INGREDIENTS for 4 servings

½ tsp marjoram, dried	1 pound stewing beef, cubed
1 ½ cups beef broth	1 cup Shiitake, sliced
1 tbsp paprika	1 cup baby carrots, chopped
2 bay leaves	½ cup flour
1 cup tomatoes, chopped	2 tbsp olive oil
1 onion, chopped	Salt and black pepper to taste

DIRECTIONS and total time: approx. 60 minutes

Heat olive oil on Sauté, season the beef with salt and pepper, and coat in flour. Brown in the oil for 4-5 minutes, stirring often; set aside. Add onion, carrots, tomatoes, and Shiitake mushrooms to the pot, and sauté for 4 minutes. Stir in paprika, bay leaves, marjoram, salt, and pepper. Pour in beef broth and return the beef. Seal the lid, select Manual, and cook for 30 minutes at High. When ready, release the pressure naturally for 10 minutes. Discard the bay leaves and serve.

Beef Paprikash

INGREDIENTS for 4 servings

2 lb beef stew meat, cubed	1 tbsp tomato paste
½ cup flour	1 tsp Hungarian paprika
1 cups red onions, chopped	2 bay leaves
2 tbsp olive oil	3 tbsp old bay seasoning
½ cup sour cream	3 red bell peppers, chopped
2 tbsp chopped parsley	Salt and black pepper to taste

DIRECTIONS and total time: approx. 55 minutes

Coat the beef in flour and season with salt and pepper. Heat the olive oil on Sauté and cook onions and bell peppers for 2 minutes. Add in the beef and stir-fry for 5 minutes. Stir in paprika, tomato paste, and old bay seasoning. Pour in 1 cup of water and bay leaves. Seal the lid, select Manual, and cook for 30 minutes at High. When ready, release the pressure naturally for 10 minutes. Remove bay leaves and stir in sour cream for 2 minutes. Adjust the seasoning, and top with parsley.

Beef & Rutabaga Stew

INGREDIENTS for 4-6 servings

2 lb stew beef meat, cubed	1 rutabaga, chopped
3 tbsp butter	Salt and black pepper to taste
1 tsp ground cumin	2 celery stalks, sliced
1 cup beef broth	2 bay leaves
1 can (14-oz) tomatoes	5 potatoes, cubed
2 cloves garlic, minced	1 tsp paprika
1 onion, chopped	Chopped parsley for garnish

DIRECTIONS and total time: approx. 47 minutes

Melt butter on Sauté and cook celery, garlic, and onion for 3 minutes. Add in the beef and cook for 5-6 minutes until brown. Stir in paprika and cumin for 1 minute.

Add in tomatoes, beef broth, bay leaves, rutabaga, potatoes, salt, and pepper. Seal the lid, select Manual, and cook for 18 minutes at High. When ready, do a quick release. Serve hot garnished with parsley.

Herby Beef Stroganoff

INGREDIENTS for 4 servings

2 lb beef stew meat, cubed	½ tsp dried thyme
2 tbsp olive oil	½ tsp dried basil
1 cup mushrooms, halved	½ tsp dried rosemary
1 cup sour cream	½ tsp dried parsley
1 onion, chopped	Salt and black pepper to taste
1 tbsp Maggi seasoning	Chopped chives for garnish

DIRECTIONS and total time: approx. 47 minutes

Heat olive oil on Sauté and cook the beef, mushrooms, and onions for 5-6 minutes in total. Mix dry herbs and Maggi seasoning in 1 cup of water and stir to combine. Pour over the beef and mushrooms. Seal the lid, select Manual, and cook for 15 minutes at High. When ready, do a quick release. Stir in sour cream for 2 minutes. Adjust the taste and serve topped with fresh chives.

Korean Beef Brisket

INGREDIENTS for 4-6 servings

3 lb beef brisket, quartered	1 tbsp ginger paste
1 tbsp Korean gochugaru	1 tbsp fish sauce
3 tbsp sesame oil	Salt and black pepper to taste
2 tbsp soy sauce	3 tbsp cilantro, chopped
4 garlic cloves, minced	1 red chili, seeded and diced
1 tsp brown sugar	1 onion, chopped

DIRECTIONS and total time: approx. 60 minutes

Rub the beef with gochugaru, salt, and pepper. Heat sesame oil on Sauté and brown the beef on all sides for 6-7 minutes; reserve. Add onion, garlic, ginger, and red chili and sauté for 3 minutes. Stir in soy and fish sauces, and brown sugar for 1 minute. Return the beef and pour in 2 cups of water. Seal the lid, select Manual, and cook for 40 minutes at High. Allow a natural release for 10 minutes. Top with cilantro and serve.

Parsley Buttered Beef

INGREDIENTS for 4 servings

1 package dry onion soup mix	
2 lb stew beef meat, cubed	2 tbsp parsley, chopped
½ cup butter	Salt and black pepper to taste

DIRECTIONS and total time: approx. 45 minutes

Melt butter on Sauté and cook beef for 4-5 minutes, stirring occasionally. Sprinkle with onion soup mix and add 2 cups of water. Seal the lid, select Manual, and cook for 30 minutes at High. Do a quick release. Adjust seasoning and serve garnished with parsley.

Tarragon Beef & Prune Casserole

INGREDIENTS for 4 servings

1 lb stew beef meat, cubed
2 cloves garlic, minced
½ cup dried prunes, chopped
1 tbsp flour
2 tbsp olive oil
2 cups beef broth
¼ cup vermouth
3 celery stalks, chopped
Salt and black pepper to taste
1 tsp paprika
2 carrots, chopped
1 yellow onion, chopped
2 tbsp tarragon, chopped
2 tomatoes, chopped

DIRECTIONS and total time: approx. 45 minutes

Heat olive oil on Sauté and cook the beef for 6-7 minutes; reserve. Add onion, garlic, celery, and carrots and sauté for 3 minutes until softened. Stir in flour, paprika and prunes for 1 minute. Deglaze with vermouth and pour in tomatoes, broth, salt, and pepper and return the beef. Seal the lid, select Manual at High, and cook for 30 minutes. When ready, allow a natural release for 10 minutes. Serve topped with tarragon.

Easy Beef Stew

INGREDIENTS for 4 servings

1 ½ lb beef stew meat, cubed
2 garlic cloves, minced
2 tbsp olive oil
2 tomatoes, chopped
2 sweet potatoes, cubed
2 celery stalks, chopped
1 tbsp red wine vinegar
2 cups vegetable broth
½ tsp thyme
½ tsp rosemary
Salt and black pepper to taste
1 yellow onion, chopped
2 bay leaves
1 carrot, sliced
1 tbsp flour
2 tbsp parsley, chopped

DIRECTIONS and total time: approx. 50 minutes

Heat olive oil on Sauté and cook beef for 5-6 minutes; reserve. Add garlic, celery, onion, carrot, thyme, rosemary, salt, and pepper to the pot, and sauté for 3 minutes. Pour in tomatoes, broth, red wine vinegar, potatoes, and bay leaves; remove the beef. Seal the lid, select Manual, and cook for 30 minutes at High. When ready, do a quick release. In a bowl, mix flour with 2 tbsp of cooking liquid and stir in the pot for 2 minutes on Sauté until thickened. Serve garnished with parsley.

Zucchini & Potato Beef Stew

INGREDIENTS for 4 servings

1 lb beef round steak, sliced
1 garlic clove, minced
2 tbsp olive oil
1 cup tomato sauce
1 tbsp cornstarch
3 shallots, chopped
2 zucchinis, sliced
2 potatoes, chopped
1 tsp red chili powder
2 cups vegetable broth
Salt and black pepper to taste
2 tbsp dill, chopped

DIRECTIONS and total time: approx. 65 minutes

Heat olive oil on Sauté and stir-fry beef, shallots, and garlic for 5 minutes. Stir in chili powder, salt, and pepper, and pour in broth, tomato sauce, and potatoes.

Seal the lid, select Manual, and cook for 20 minutes at High. When ready, release the pressure quickly. Stir in zucchinis for 4-5 minutes on Sauté. In a bowl, mix cornstarch with some cooking liquid. Add to the pot and stir for 2 minutes on Sauté to thicken. Serve hot.

Beef & Bean Goulash

INGREDIENTS for 4 servings

½ lb beef round steak, cubed
2 tbsp olive oil
2 cups beef broth
1 red bell pepper, sliced
1 carrot, chopped
2 potatoes, cubed
1 onion, chopped
Salt and black pepper to taste
½ cup sour cream
1 tsp dried thyme
2 tsp crushed caraway seeds
2 garlic cloves, minced
1 tsp paprika
1 (14-oz) can white beans

DIRECTIONS and total time: approx. 40 minutes

Heat olive oil on Sauté. Add in beef, onion, garlic, carrot, bell pepper, salt, and black pepper, and stir-fry for 5 minutes. Stir in paprika, caraway seeds, and thyme for 1 more minute. Pour in beef broth, potatoes, and white beans. Seal the lid, select Manual, and cook for 25 minutes at High. When ready, do a quick pressure release. Serve topped with sour cream.

Chipotle Shredded Beef

INGREDIENTS for 4-6 servings

1 can (14-oz) diced tomatoes
2 tbsp olive oil
2 lb beef chuck roast
1 cup chipotle sauce
1 tsp honey
3 garlic cloves, minced
2 tbsp chili powder
3 jalapeno peppers, chopped
Salt and black pepper to taste
2 cups beef broth
1 tsp cumin, ground
2 tbsp cilantro, chopped

DIRECTIONS and total time: approx. 69 minutes

Rub the meat with chili powder, cumin, salt, and pepper. Heat olive oil on Sauté and sear beef for 6-7 minutes on all sides; reserve. Add garlic, jalapeño peppers, and cumin, and sauté for 3 minutes. Pour in the remaining ingredients except for the parsley, and return the beef. Seal the lid, select Manual, and cook for 40 minutes at High. When ready, do a quick pressure release. Remove the meat and shred it with two forks. Stir back to the pot. Sprinkle with cilantro and serve hot.

Polish-Style Beef & Cabbage Pot

INGREDIENTS for 4 servings

½ lb stew beef meat, cubed
1 tsp thyme
2 bay leaves
1 carrot, chopped
½ parsnip, chopped
1 onion, sliced
½ head cabbage, shredded
1 beet, chopped
1 can (14-oz) diced tomatoes
5 whole peppercorns
4 cups vegetable broth
Salt to taste
3 tbsp red wine vinegar
1 celery stalk, chopped

DIRECTIONS and total time: approx. 45 minutes

Heat olive oil on Sauté. Add in beef, carrot, onion, beet, celery, and parsnip, and cook for 5-6 minutes. Stir in cabbage for 2-3 minutes and pour in vegetable broth, tomatoes, peppercorns, salt, thyme, and bay leaves. Seal the lid, select Manual, and cook for 25 minutes at High. When ready, do a quick release. Stir in red wine vinegar and discard bay leaves. Serve hot.

Parsley Beef Roast with Mushrooms

INGREDIENTS for 4 servings

2 cups tomato and basil pasta sauce	
1 ½ lb beef rump roast	1 onion, sliced
½ cup red wine	1 cup mushrooms, sliced
2 tbsp olive oil	16 oz linguine
½ tsp garlic pepper seasoning	2 tbsp chopped parsley

DIRECTIONS and total time: approx. 50 minutes

Place rotini pasta in inner pot and cover with salted water. Seal the lid, press Manual, and cook for 4 minutes at High. Do a quick pressure release. Drain and set aside, reserving the cooking water. Rub garlic pepper seasoning onto beef roast. Heat olive oil on Sauté and cook the roast on all sides, about 6-7 minutes; reserve. Add mushrooms and onion, and sauté for 3 minutes. Pour in wine, pasta sauce, and 1 cup of the pasta water. Seal the lid, select Manual at High, and cook for 30 minutes. When ready, do a quick release. Slice the roast and serve on a pasta bed. Top with fresh parsley.

Beef Stew with Tomatoes

INGREDIENTS for 4 servings

2 tbsp olive oil	1 tsp rosemary
2 lb beef stew meat, cubed	1 bay leaf
6 potatoes, cubed	1 onion, chopped
1 cup celery, chopped	1 cup carrots, chopped
Salt and black pepper to taste	1 cup tomatoes, chopped
1 tbsp flour	2 tbsp parsley

DIRECTIONS and total time: approx. 28 minutes

Heat olive oil on Sauté and stir-fry beef for 5-6 minutes; reserve. Add celery, onion, and carrots to the pot, and sauté for 4 minutes. Stir in flour for 1 minute and pour in tomatoes, potatoes, rosemary, bay leaf, and 2 cups of water, salt, and pepper; return the beef. Seal the lid, select Manual, and cook for 30 minutes at High. When ready, do a quick release. Remove and discard bay leaf and serve sprinkled with parsley.

Beef & Jalapeño Curry

INGREDIENTS for 4 servings

1 lb beef stew meat	4 cups beef broth
2 tbsp olive oil	1 onion, chopped
1 can (14.5-oz) tomatoes	1 tbsp curry powder
1 tsp fresh ginger, minced	Salt and black pepper to taste
1 jalapeño pepper, chopped	2 tbsp cilantro, chopped

DIRECTIONS and total time: approx. 48 minutes

Heat olive oil on Sauté. Season the beef with salt and pepper and brown for about 5-6 minutes on both sides; set aside. Add jalapeño pepper, onion, garlic, and ginger to the pot, and sauté for 3 minutes. Stir in curry, tomatoes and beef broth; return the beef. Seal the lid, select Manual, and cook for 30 minutes at High. When ready, do a quick release. Top with cilantro and serve.

Beef & Cavolo Nero Pot

INGREDIENTS for 4 servings

4 cups cavolo nero (curly kale), diced	
1 cup carrots, chopped	2 bay leaves
1 lb cubed stew beef meat	1 cup red pepper, chopped
1 tsp rosemary	2 tsp garlic paste
1 cup heavy cream	1 tsp paprika
2 cups chopped tomatoes	2 tbsp tomato paste
2 cups chicken stock	2 tbsp olive oil
1 cup daikon, chopped	1 yellow onion, diced

DIRECTIONS and total time: approx. 50 minutes

Heat olive oil on Sauté and cook beef for 5-6 minutes, stirring often; reserve. Add onion, red pepper, carrots, and garlic paste to the pot, and sauté for 3 minutes. Stir in paprika, tomato paste, tomatoes, daikon, bay leaves, and chicken stock and return the beef. Seal the lid, select Manual at High, and cook for 30 minutes. Do a quick release. Discard the bay leaves and stir in cavolo nero. Press Sauté and cook for 2-3 minutes, then mix in heavy cream. Top with rosemary to serve.

Saucy Beef Short Ribs

INGREDIENTS for 4 servings

2 lb beef short ribs, cut into pieces	
Salt and black pepper to taste	3 tbsp oil
1 onion, chopped	½ tbsp tomato puree
½ cup red wine	2 carrots, sliced

DIRECTIONS and total time: approx. 60 minutes

Rub ribs with salt and pepper. Heat olive oil on Sauté and brown ribs on all sides, 8 minutes; reserve. Add onion to the pot and cook for 3 minutes. Pour in wine and deglaze by scraping any browned bits from the bottom of the pot. Cook for 2 minutes until wine has reduced. Return ribs and add carrots, tomato puree and 2 cups water. Seal the lid, select Manual, and cook for 30 minutes at High. Let the pressure release naturally for 10 minutes. Transfer the ribs to a baking sheet and place under the broiler for 4 minutes until crispy. Blitz the remaining ingredients in the pot with an immersion blender until smooth. Pour the sauce over the ribs.

Melt-in-Your-Mouth Beef with Vegetables

INGREDIENTS for 4-6 servings

2 lb boneless beef chuck roast, trimmed and cubed
2 carrots, chopped
2 lb red potatoes, chopped
1 cup beef broth
2 garlic cloves, minced
3 tsp olive oil
1 celery stalk, chopped
2 bell peppers, sliced

1 tbsp tomato puree
2 sweet onions, chopped
½ cup dry white wine
1 tbsp flour
½ tsp dried basil
2 sprigs dried sage, crushed
Salt and black pepper to taste

DIRECTIONS and total time: approx. 50 minutes

Heat olive oil on Sauté and brown the beef for 5-6 minutes on all sides; reserve. Stir in onions, garlic, carrots, and bell peppers, and sauté for 3 minutes. Deglaze with the beef broth. Stir in the remaining ingredients, except for flour, and pour in 1 cup of water. Seal the lid, select Manual, and cook for 30 minutes at High. Once the cooking is over, do a quick pressure release. Make the slurry by whisking the flour with 1 tbsp of water. Add to the pot and press Sauté. Let simmer for about 5 minutes until thickened and serve.

Beef Brisket with Vegetables

INGREDIENTS for 4 servings

1 tbsp demi-glace sauce mix
2 lb beef brisket, cubed
6 red potatoes, chopped
1 cup scallions, chopped
2 bay leaves
2 tbsp olive oil
1 carrot, chopped

2 garlic cloves, minced
3 tbsp Worcestershire sauce
2 celery stalks, chopped
2 bok choy, chopped
Salt and black pepper to taste
1 cup vegetable broth

DIRECTIONS and total time: approx. 60 minutes

Season the beef with black pepper. Heat olive oil on Sauté and cook scallions, carrot, garlic, and celery until softened, 3 minutes. Add beef to the pot and cook until browned on all sides, 6-7 minutes. Pour in broth, bay leaves, and Worcestershire sauce. Seal the lid and cook on Manual for 40 minutes at High. When ready, do a quick pressure release. Discard bay leaves. Whisk demi-glace sauce mix with some cooking liquid and pour in the pot. Add in the boy choy, press Sauté and simmer for 5 minutes until thickened. Serve warm.

Winter Beef with Vegetables

INGREDIENTS for 4 servings

10 oz pumpkin, chopped
1 cup leeks, chopped
2 tbsp olive oil
2 carrots, chopped
½ tsp thyme
1 garlic clove, minced
1 parsnip, chopped
1 lb stewing beef meat, cubed

1 ½ cups green beans
1 cup mushrooms, sliced
3 cups beef stock
Salt and black pepper to taste
1 onion, sliced
1 turnip, cubed
½ tsp garlic powder
Chopped parsley for garnish

DIRECTIONS and total time: approx. 40 minutes

Heat olive oil on Sauté and cook onion, leeks, carrots, parsnip, mushrooms, turnip, beef, and garlic for 5 minutes, stirring periodically. Pour in the remaining ingredients except for the parsley, and stir to combine. Seal the lid, select Manual, and cook for 30 minutes at High. Do a quick release. Serve garnished with parsley.

Beef Soup with Red Potatoes & Pancetta

INGREDIENTS for 4-6 servings

5 cups beef broth
1 tsp thyme
1 carrot, sliced
1 celery stalk, sliced
1 onion, sliced
2 garlic cloves, minced

4 red potatoes, cubed
1 cup tomato sauce
½ lb beef stew meat, cubed
6 pancetta slices, chopped
Salt and black pepper to taste
2 tbsp parsley, chopped

DIRECTIONS and total time: approx. 45 minutes

Set your IP to Sauté and cook pancetta for 5 minutes; set aside. Add in beef, thyme, carrot, celery, onion, and garlic and cook for 5 minutes. Pour in broth, potatoes, tomato sauce, and bay leaves. Seal the lid, select Manual, and cook for 25 minutes at High. Do a quick release. Discard bay leaves. Adjust the seasoning and serve sprinkled with parsley and pancetta.

Beef Sausage & Spinach Stew

INGREDIENTS for 4 servings

2 lb spinach, shredded
1 lb beef sausage, sliced
2 cloves garlic, minced
1 ½ cups canned tomatoes
1 cup cooked white rice

1 tsp fennel seeds, cooked
1 cup scallions, chopped
Salt and black pepper to taste
½ cup fresh parsley, chopped
1 cup beef broth

DIRECTIONS and total time: approx. 30 minutes

In a bowl, stir in spinach and fennel seeds. Spread half of this mixture on the bottom of your Instant Pot. In another bowl, mix cooked rice, beef sausage, parsley, scallions, garlic, salt, and black pepper. Ladle half of this mixture over the spinach mixture and then top with another layer of the remaining spinach mixture. Finish with the meat mixture. In a large-sized bowl, whisk tomatoes and broth. Pour over the mixture. Seal the lid, select Manual, and cook for 20 minutes at High. Once the cooking is complete, do a quick pressure release. Serve in individual bowls topped with parsley.

Savory Beef Roast in Passion Fruit Gravy

INGREDIENTS for 4 servings

2 lb beef roast
1 onion, quartered
1 tbsp cornstarch
1 cup passion fruit juice

2 garlic cloves, minced
1 tsp rosemary
2 tbsp olive oil
Salt and black pepper to taste

DIRECTIONS and total time: approx. 60 minutes

Season the beef with salt, rosemary, and pepper. Warm olive oil on Sauté and brown the beef on all sides for 5-6 minutes; reserve. Add onion and garlic in the pot and sauté for 2 minutes. Pour passion fruit juice to deglaze the bottom of the pot. Return the beef, add in 1 cup of water and seal the lid. Select Manual and cook for 40 minutes at High. Do a quick release. Remove the roast to a plate. Whisk cornstarch with some cooking liquid and stir in the pot. Simmer until the gravy thickens, 2-3 minutes. Slice the meat and serve drizzled with gravy.

Beat Lamb Stew with Kale & Peaches

INGREDIENTS for 4 servings

1 lb lamb, cubed	3 cups chopped kale
4 dried peaches, diced	2 cups tomatoes, chopped
1 tsp garlic paste	½ tsp cinnamon
1 onion, diced	1 tsp thyme
2 potatoes, chopped	½ tsp ginger powder
2 carrots, chopped	Salt and black pepper to taste
2 cups chicken broth	2 tbsp olive oil

DIRECTIONS and total time: approx. 45 minutes

Heat olive oil on Sauté and cook lamb on all sides, about 4-5 minutes; reserve. Add onion, garlic paste, and carrots, and sauté for 3 minutes. Stir in the remaining ingredients except for kale, and return the lamb. Seal the lid, press Manual, and cook for 20 minutes at High. When done, do a quick pressure release. Stir in kale and press Sauté. Cook for 5 minutes until the kale wilts.

Lamb Shanks in Port Wine

INGREDIENTS for 4 servings

2 lb lamb shanks	8 whole garlic cloves, peeled
2 tbsp olive oil	½ cup chicken broth
½ cup Port wine	½ tsp oregano
1 tbsp tomato puree	½ tsp dried rosemary
1 carrot, chopped	Salt and black pepper to taste

DIRECTIONS and total time: approx. 50 minutes

Season lamb shanks with salt and pepper. Warm olive oil on Sauté and brown lamb on all sides, about 4-5 minutes. Add garlic and cook for 2 minutes. Stir in the rest of the ingredients. Seal the lid and cook on Manual for 30 minutes at High. Do a quick pressure release. Remove lamb shanks and let the sauce boil for 5 minutes on Sauté. Serve lamb drizzled with gravy.

Effortless Lamb with Green Onions

INGREDIENTS for 4 servings

2 lb lamb chops	5 green onions, chopped
1 cup vegetable broth	1 rosemary spring, crushed
2 tbsp olive oil	1 bay leaf
2 tsp dried tarragon	Salt and black pepper to taste

DIRECTIONS and total time: approx. 45 minutes

Heat olive oil on Sauté and cook green onions for 3 minutes. Season lamb with salt, pepper, rosemary, and tarragon. Add to the pot and brown for 2-3 minutes per side. Pour in vegetable broth and bay leaf. Seal the lid and cook on Manual for 30 minutes at High. Do a quick pressure release. Discard the bay leaf and serve hot.

Herby Lamb with Vegetables

INGREDIENTS for 4 servings

1 lb lamb, cubed	2 garlic cloves, minced
3 potatoes, chopped	1 cup vegetable broth
1 cup carrots, chopped	Salt and black pepper to taste
½ cup turnips, chopped	2 tbsp canola oil
2 cups tomato sauce	1 tbsp cilantro
1 onion, diced	1 tsp mint

DIRECTIONS and total time: approx. 45 minutes

Heat canola oil on Sauté and cook lamb until browned on all sides, 6-7 minutes; reserve. Add onion, garlic, and carrots to the pot and sauté for 3 minutes. Mix in the remaining ingredients; return the lamb. Seal the lid, select Manual and cook for 30 minutes at High. Do a natural pressure release for 10 minutes. Serve hot.

Lamb & Bok Choy Curry

INGREDIENTS for 4 servings

2 tbsp olive oil	1 tbsp grated ginger
1 lb cubed stewing lamb meat	1 tsp ground cumin
1 onion, chopped	Salt and black pepper to taste
1 carrot, sliced	2 tomatoes, chopped
3 garlic cloves, minced	1 cup bok choy, chopped

DIRECTIONS and total time: approx. 35 minutes

Heat olive oil on Sauté and cook lamb, garlic, onion, ginger, and carrots for 6 minutes. Stir in tomatoes, spices, and 2 cups water. Seal the lid, select Manual, and cook for 20 minutes at High. Do a quick pressure release. Stir in bok choy for 4-5 minutes and serve.

Lamb Stew

INGREDIENTS for 4 servings

2 tbsp olive oil	1 carrot, chopped
1 lb lamb stew meat, cubed	1 celery stalk, chopped
1 tbsp flour	2 garlic cloves, minced
Salt and black pepper to taste	1 sprig rosemary
1 tbsp tomato puree	2 potatoes, cubed
1 onion, chopped	2 cups vegetable stock

DIRECTIONS and total time: approx. 45 minutes

Dust lamb with flour, salt, and pepper. Heat oil on Sauté and brown lamb for 7 minutes. Stir in the remaining ingredients. Seal the lid, press Manual, and cook for 30 minutes at High. Do a quick pressure release. Serve.

Lamb & Mushroom Ragout

INGREDIENTS for 4 servings

2 lb lamb, bone-in
2 tbsp butter
4 tomatoes, chopped
1 tbsp tomato puree
1 cup mushrooms, sliced
2 garlic cloves, minced
1 yellow onion, chopped
1 tsp rosemary
Salt and black pepper to taste
Fresh mint leaves, chopped

DIRECTIONS and total time: approx. 45 minutes

Season lamb with salt and pepper. Melt butter on Sauté and brown lamb on all sides, about 6-7 minutes. Stir in tomatoes, tomato puree, mushrooms, garlic, onion, carrots, and rosemary. Pour in 2 cups of water. Seal the lid, press Manual, and cook for 45 minutes at High. When ready, do a natural pressure release for 10 minutes. Discard bones from lamb, and using two forks, shred it. Bring the lamb back to the pot and stir. Serve garnished with freshly chopped mint leaves.

Lamb Roast with Turnips

INGREDIENTS for 4 servings

2 lb lamb steaks
½ tsp dried sage
½ tsp dried marjoram
1 bay leaf, crushed
3 garlic cloves, minced
4 cups turnips, cut into pieces
2 tbsp olive oil
3 tbsp arrowroot powder
2 cups chicken broth
Salt and black pepper to taste

DIRECTIONS and total time: approx. 45 minutes

Combine the herbs with salt and pepper, and rub the mixture onto meat. Melt butter on Sauté and brown the lamb on all sides, about 3-4 minutes. Pour in chicken broth, bay leaf, and turnips. Seal the lid and cook on Manual for 30 minutes at High. When done, release the pressure quickly. Remove and discard the bay leaf. Whisk the arrowroot with some cooking liquid and stir the mixture in the pot. Press Sauté and cook for 2 minutes until thickened. Serve immediately.

Lamb with Green Onions

INGREDIENTS for 4 servings

1 lb lamb chops
Salt and black pepper to taste
1 cup tomatoes, chopped
4 cups green onions, chopped
2 garlic cloves, minced
2 cups chicken stock
1 tsp paprika
2 tbsp mint, chopped
2 tbsp parsley, chopped
2 tbsp olive oil

DIRECTIONS and total time: approx. 45 minutes

Heat olive oil on Sauté and cook green onions and garlic for 4 minutes until soft. Add in lamb and cook for 6 minutes on both sides. Season with salt, pepper, add paprika and stir. Pour in chicken stock, tomatoes, and mint. Seal the lid, select Manual, and cook for 30 minutes at High. Once cooking is over, do a quick pressure release. Serve garnished with fresh parsley.

Thyme Braised Lamb

INGREDIENTS for 4 servings

4 lamb shanks
2 carrots, sliced
2 cups canned tomato, diced
1 tbsp thyme
1 garlic clove, minced
1 tbsp chopped fresh oregano
¼ cup flour
2 tsp olive oil
1 onion, chopped
¾ cup red wine
¼ cup beef broth
Salt and black pepper to taste

DIRECTIONS and total time: approx. 50 minutes

In a plastic bag, place lamb and flour; shake to coat. Remove lamb and discard excess flour. Heat oil on Sauté and brown lamb for 4-5 minutes; reserve. Add onion, garlic, and carrots to the pot and sauté for 4 minutes. Deglaze with wine and add in tomatoes, broth, and thyme. Return the lamb. Seal the lid, select Manual, and cook for 30 minutes at High. Do a quick pressure release. Sprinkle with oregano and serve.

Chili Lamb with Carrots & Celery

INGREDIENTS for 4 servings

1 lb ground lamb
2 carrots, chopped
2 celery stalks, chopped
1 bell pepper, chopped
1 onion, diced
1 jalapeño pepper, minced
1 tsp rosemary
1 tsp garlic paste
14 oz canned diced tomatoes
1 tbsp chili powder
1 tsp cumin
2 cups chicken broth
Salt and black pepper to taste
2 tbsp olive oil

DIRECTIONS and total time: approx. 55 minutes

Heat olive oil on Sauté and stir-fry onion and garlic for 3 minutes. Stir in ground lamb and cook until lightly browned for 5-6 minutes. Add in the remaining ingredients and give it a good stir. Seal the lid, select Manual, and cook for 30 minutes at High. When ready, do a natural pressure release for 10 minutes. Serve.

Lamb Cacciatore

INGREDIENTS for 4 servings

1 lb lamb chops
Salt and black pepper to taste
2 tbsp olive oil
1 red bell pepper, sliced
1 onion, chopped
1 cup mushrooms, sliced
2 garlic cloves, minced
½ cup dry white wine
2 cans (14-oz) diced tomatoes
2 tbsp black olives, pitted
1 cup spinach, chopped
½ tsp dried oregano

DIRECTIONS and total time: approx. 50 minutes

Season lamb with salt and pepper. Select Sauté and heat oil. Cook lamb for 8 minutes; set aside. Add garlic, bell pepper, onion, and mushrooms to the pot and sauté for 5 minutes. Deglaze with wine and mix in tomatoes, olives, spinach, and oregano; return lamb. Pour in 1 cup water. Seal the lid, select Manual, and cook for 30 minutes at High. Do a quick pressure release. Serve.

Vegetarian & Vegan

Cauliflower "Risotto" with Mushrooms

INGREDIENTS for 4 servings

2 cauliflower heads	1 cup veggie broth
2 cups mushrooms, sliced	1 tbsp olive oil
1 garlic clove, minced	3 tbsp chives
1 tsp dried oregano	½ onion, diced
1 carrot, grated	Salt and black pepper to taste

DIRECTIONS and total time: approx. 15 minutes

Cut the cauliflower into pieces and place in a food processor. Process until ground, rice like consistency. Heat olive oil on Sauté and cook carrot, garlic, and onion for 3 minutes. Stir in the remaining ingredients. Seal the lid, cook on Manual for 5 minutes at High. When ready, do a quick pressure release. Serve warm.

Vegetable & Peanut Pilaf

INGREDIENTS for 4 servings

2 shallots, cut into wedges	2 tbsp olive oil
2 carrots, julienned	2 tbsp toasted peanuts, chopped
2 eggplants, chopped	1 cup brown rice, rinsed
2 tbsp parsley	2 garlic cloves, minced
Salt and black pepper	1 heat broccoli, grated
2 tsp allspice	½ cup Greek yogurt

DIRECTIONS and total time: approx. 30 minutes

Heat olive oil on Sauté and cook shallots, eggplants, and garlic for 3 minutes. Stir in allspice and brown rice for 1 minute. Add in broccoli and 2 cups of water; season to taste. Seal the lid and cook on Manual for 20 minutes at High. Do a quick pressure release. Fluff rice with a fork, top with parsley, and serve with yogurt.

Mom's Carrots with Walnuts & Berries

INGREDIENTS for 4 servings

2 lb carrots, cut into rounds	¼ cup dried cranberries
½ cup walnuts, chopped	Salt and black pepper to taste
2 tbsp butter	1 tbsp vinegar

DIRECTIONS and total time: approx. 15 minutes

Select Sauté, melt the butter and cook carrots for 5 minutes until tender. Add cranberries, 1 cup of water, and salt. Seal the lid, press Manual, and set to 3 minutes at High. When ready, do a quick pressure release. Stir in vinegar and black pepper. Scatter walnuts all over.

Lemon Asparagus

INGREDIENTS for 4 servings

1 lb asparagus, ends cut off	Salt to taste
8 oz Monterey Jack cheese	1 lemon, sliced

DIRECTIONS and total time: approx. 10 minutes

Pour 1 cup of water into your IP. Slice the cheese in enough strips to wrap around each asparagus spear. Arrange wrapped asparagus inside a steamer basket and place the basket in the cooker. Seal the lid and cook on Manual for 4 minutes at High. Release the pressure quickly. Garnish with lemon and serve.

Grana Padano Green Risotto

INGREDIENTS for 4 servings

2 cups veggie broth	3 tbsp butter
1 cup spinach, chopped	2 tsp olive oil
1 cup kale, chopped	1 cup Arborio rice
¼ cup Grana Padano, grated	4 sun-dried tomatoes, chopped
1 diced onion	Salt and black pepper to taste

DIRECTIONS and total time: approx. 25 minutes

Heat olive oil on Sauté and sweat onion until soft, about 3 minutes. Add in rice and cook for 1 minute. Pour in broth. Seal the lid, and cook on Manual for 12 minutes at High. Do a quick pressure release. Stir in the remaining ingredients. Cover with the lid and leave for 3-4 minutes until the greens wilt a bit. Serve hot.

Savory Spinach & Leek Relish

INGREDIENTS for 4 servings

½ lb leeks, chopped	1 tsp dry sage
3 cups spinach, chopped	2 tbsp olive oil
2 cups stock	1 tsp nutmeg
1 onion, chopped	Salt and black pepper to taste
2 cloves garlic, minced	2 tbsp parsley, chopped

DIRECTIONS and total time: approx. 20 minutes

Heat olive oil on Sauté and fry leeks, garlic, and onion for 5 minutes. Add in the remaining ingredients, except for the parsley, and seal the lid. Select Manual and cook for 5 minutes at High. Do a quick release the pressure. Top with parsley to serve.

Parmesan Zoodle Soup

INGREDIENTS for 4 servings

2 cups zoodles	½ celery stalk, chopped
1 onion, chopped	1 carrot, chopped
2 garlic cloves, minced	2 tbsp chopped basil
4 cups vegetable broth	2 tbsp Parmesan, grated
2 tbsp olive oil	Salt and black pepper to taste

DIRECTIONS and total time: approx. 20 minutes

Heat olive oil on Sauté and cook onion, garlic, carrot, and celery for 3 minutes. Add in the broth and seal the lid. Cook on Manual for 8 minutes at High. Do a quick pressure release. Stir in zoddles and press Sauté to cook for 3-4 minutes. Adjust the seasoning, sprinkle with Parmesan cheese and basil, and serve.

Chickpea & Bean Hummus

INGREDIENTS for 4-6 servings

1 onion, quartered	¼ cup chopped parsley
2 tbsp soy sauce	1 tsp cumin
¼ cup tahini	Juice of 1 lemon
¾ cup chickpeas, soaked	Salt and black pepper to taste
¼ cup dried soybeans, soaked	2 garlic cloves, minced

DIRECTIONS and total time: approx. 40 minutes

Add chickpeas and soybeans to your IP. Pour enough water over to cover them by one inch. Seal the lid, press Manual for 30 minutes at High. When ready, release pressure naturally for 10 minutes. Drain the beans and save the cooking liquid. Place the beans along with the remaining ingredients and some of the cooking liquid into a food processor, and process until smooth. Serve.

Vegan Shepherd's Pie

INGREDIENTS for 4 servings

2 tbsp anise, ground	1 cup grated potatoes
1 cup diced onions	½ cup diced carrots
2 cups cauli rice	½ cup frozen corn
2 tbsp olive oil	½ cup frozen peas
1 ¾ cups veggie broth	Salt and black pepper to taste
1 cup diced tomatoes	

DIRECTIONS and total time: approx. 35 minutes

Heat olive oil on Sauté and stir-fry onions, carrots, and anise for 3 minutes. Stir in potatoes, corn, peas, and veggie broth. Seal the lid, cook on Manual for 10 minutes at High. When ready, do a quick release. Stir in tomatoes. Divide the mixture between 4 ramekins. Top each ramekin with ½ cup of cauli rice. Pour 1 cup of water into your IP and fit in a trivet. Arrange the ramekins on the trivet. Seal the lid and cook on Manual for 5 minutes at High. Do a quick pressure release.

Broccoli, Cauliflower & Zucchini Cakes

INGREDIENTS for 4 servings

1 zucchini, peeled and grated	½ onion, diced
3 cups cauliflower florets	½ tsp turmeric powder
1 carrot, grated	4 tbsp olive oil
1 cup veggie broth	1 tsp sage
2 cups broccoli florets	Salt and black pepper to taste

DIRECTIONS and total time: approx. 25 minutes

Heat half of olive oil on Sauté and stir-fry onion and carrot for 3 minutes. Pour in the remaining vegetables, seal the lid, and cook on Manual for 5 minutes at High. Do a quick pressure release. Mash veggies with a potato masher and stir in the seasonings. Let cool for a few minutes, and make burger patties out of the mixture. Heat the remaining oil on Sauté. Cook the patties for 5-6 minutes, flipping once. Serve hot.

Garden Vegetable Spaghetti

INGREDIENTS for 4 servings

16 oz spaghetti	1 tsp dried oregano
1 cup broccoli florets	10 oz canned tomatoes
1 carrot, chopped	½ cup mushrooms
2 garlic cloves, minced	1 zucchini, chopped
1 tbsp tomato puree	½ cup grated Parmesan
1 tsp agave nectar	Salt and black pepper to taste

DIRECTIONS and total time: approx. 20 minutes

Place spaghetti in your IP and cover with salted water. Seal the lid, press Manual, and cook for 4 minutes at High. Do a quick pressure release. Drain and set aside, reserving the cooking water. Add broccoli, mushrooms, zucchini, garlic, and carrots to a food processor, and process until finely ground. Transfer to the pot. Stir in tomato puree, tomatoes, agave nectar, oregano, salt, and pepper. Pour in cup 1 of pasta water. Seal the lid and cook on Manual for 5 minutes at High. When ready, release the pressure quickly. Pour the sauce over spaghetti, top with Parmesan cheese and serve warm.

Herby Vegetables

INGREDIENTS for 6 servings

2 lb yellow bell peppers, sliced	3 tbsp butter, melted
2 tbsp tomato paste	1 tsp fresh basil, chopped
½ cup vegetable broth	1 tsp fresh oregano, chopped
½ tbsp miso paste	1 tsp fresh thyme, chopped
1 tsp garlic paste	Salt and black pepper to taste
½ cup green onions, chopped	2 tbsp white wine

DIRECTIONS and total time: approx. 20 minutes

Melt butter on Sauté and stir-fry green onions and garlic paste until soft, about 3 minutes. Pour in broth, tomato paste, miso, basil, oregano, thyme, salt, and pepper and stir. Seal the lid, press Manual, and cook for 10 minutes at High. When ready, do a quick release. Serve warm, drizzled with white wine.

Cottage Cheese Deviled Eggs

INGREDIENTS for 4-6 servings

10 large eggs	¼ tsp garlic powder
¼ cup cottage cheese	1 tsp shallot powder
¼ cup mayonnaise	Salt and black pepper to taste

DIRECTIONS and total time: approx. 15 minutes

Pour 1 cup of water and insert a steamer basket in your IP. Put eggs in the steamer basket. Seal the lid and cook on Manual for 5 minutes at High. Once ready, do a quick pressure release. Transfer the eggs to cold water to cool. Peel, slice the eggs in half and remove the yolks to a bowl. Mash them with a fork and add the remaining ingredients. Split the mixture on the egg whites and arrange on a serving plate.

Tahini Tofu with Cauliflower & Potatoes

INGREDIENTS for 4 servings

1 lb tofu, cubed	1 cup vegetable stock
2 garlic cloves, minced	1 onion, sliced
2 tbsp soy sauce	2 cups cauliflower florets
2 tbsp sesame seeds, toasted	1 cup diced potatoes
2 tsp sesame oil	2 tbsp Tabasco sauce
2 tbsp tahini	Salt and black pepper to taste
1 tbsp rice vinegar	2 tbsp chives, chopped

DIRECTIONS and total time: approx. 25 minutes

Heat olive oil on Sauté and cook onion, garlic, and potatoes for 4 minutes. Stir in soy sauce, vegetable stock, tofu, and vinegar. Seal the lid, select Manual, and cook for 8 minutes at High. Do a quick pressure release. Add in cauliflower florets and press Sauté; cook for 3-4 minutes. Stir in tahini and Tabasco sauce. Sprinkle with sesame seeds and serve.

Niçoise-Style Ratatouille

INGREDIENTS for 4 servings

1 zucchini, sliced	1 tsp herbes de Provence
2 tomatoes, sliced	2 tbsp olive oil
1 tbsp balsamic vinegar	¼ fennel bulb, chopped
1 eggplant, sliced	2 garlic cloves, minced
1 onion, sliced	Salt and black pepper to taste

DIRECTIONS and total time: approx. 25 minutes

Spread garlic and fennel on a greased springform pan. Arrange the veggie slices in a circle. Sprinkle with herbes de Provence, salt, and pepper, and top with olive oil and balsamic vinegar. Pour 1 cup of water in your IP and insert a trivet. Place the pan on the trivet. Seal the lid and cook on Manual for 6 minutes at High. When done, release pressure naturally for 10 minutes.

Chipotle Soybeans

INGREDIENTS for 4 servings

1 tsp chipotle powder	1 jalapeño pepper, chopped
1 tsp curry powder	2 garlic cloves, minced
1 cup soybeans, soaked	2 tbsp olive oil
1 onion, diced	1 tsp cumin seeds
1 tsp turmeric	2 tomatoes, chopped
Juice of 1 lime	Salt and black pepper to taste

DIRECTIONS and total time: approx. 35 minutes

Heat olive oil on Sauté and cook cumin seeds for a minute. Add in onion, garlic, and jalapeño pepper and sauté for 3 minutes. Stir in curry powder, turmeric, chipotle powder, salt, and pepper for 1 minute. Mix in tomatoes and soybeans. Pour water to cover the ingredients by at least 2 inches. Seal the lid, cook on Manual for 25 minutes at High. Do a quick pressure release. Sprinkle with lime juice and serve hot.

Emmental Baked Eggs

INGREDIENTS for 4 servings

8 eggs	4 tbsp spring onions, chopped
8 slices Parmesan cheese	2 tbsp cilantro, chopped
4 slices Emmental cheese	Salt and black pepper to taste
2 tbsp butter, softened	1 cup water

DIRECTIONS and total time: approx. 15 minutes

Pour the water in the inner pot and fit in a trivet. Coat the bottom and sides of 4 ramekins with butter. Place two slices of Parmesan cheese at the bottom of each ramekin, and crack two eggs into each one. Add 1 tbsp of onions and top with a slice of Emmental cheese. Repeat for all ramekins. Lower the ramekins onto the trivet and cover with aluminum foil. Seal the lid, select Manual, and cook for 5 minutes at High. Once done, do a quick pressure release. Remove the aluminium foil, invert onto plates and serve garnished with cilantro.

Turmeric Vegan Sausage Casserole

INGREDIENTS for 4 servings

4 vegan sausage links, sliced	2 tbsp grated cheddar
3 large potatoes, diced	1 cup veggie stock
2 bell peppers, chopped	½ tsp cumin
1 onion, chopped	Salt and black pepper to taste
1 eggplant, chopped	¼ tsp turmeric powder
1 carrot, chopped	2 tbsp olive oil

DIRECTIONS and total time: approx. 20 minutes

Heat olive oil on Sauté and stir-fry onion, bell peppers, eggplant, and carrot for 5 minutes until tender. Add sausages and cook until browned, about 3-4 minutes. Transfer to a baking dish. Stir in cumin, turmeric powder, stock, and potatoes; season. To the pot, pour 1 cup of water and insert a trivet. Place the dish on the trivet. Seal the lid and cook on Manual for 5 minutes at High. Do a quick release. Top with cheese to serve.

Monterey Jack Vegetable Casserole

INGREDIENTS for 4 servings

1 ½ lb potatoes, chopped	½ cup sour cream
1 onion, chopped	1 cup Monterey Jack, grated
1 cup carrots, chopped	1 tsp thyme
1 cup bell peppers, chopped	3 tbsp olive oil
1 cup panko breadcrumbs	Salt and black pepper to taste

DIRECTIONS and total time: approx. 25 minutes

Heat olive oil on Sauté and cook all veggies for 5 minutes; transfer to a baking pan. Stir in sour cream, ½ cup of water, thyme, salt, and pepper. Sprinkle with Monterey Jack cheese and breadcrumbs. Pour 1 cup of water in the pot and insert a trivet. Place the pan on the trivet and seal the lid. Cook on Manual for 10 minutes at High. When ready, do a quick release. Serve sliced.

Blue Cheese Potatoes

INGREDIENTS for 4 servings

1 ½ lb fingerling potatoes	4 tbsp butter
1 cup blue cheese, crumbled	½ tsp thyme
Salt and pepper to taste	½ tsp cayenne pepper

DIRECTIONS and total time: approx. 25 minutes

Pour 1 cup of water in the inner pot and insert a steamer basket. Place the potatoes in the basket and seal the lid. Cook on Manual for 10 minutes at High. Discard the water and press Sauté. Melt butter and add the potatoes to stir-fry for 5-6 minutes, until browned. Season with thyme, cayenne, salt, and pepper. Top with blue cheese.

Penne with Pepperoncini Sauce

INGREDIENTS for 10 servings

1 pickled pepperoncini pepper, chopped	
16 oz penne pasta	1 cup milk
12 oz Pecorino Romano, grated	1 tbsp dill
1 ½ tbsp flour	½ tsp chili pepper
1 cup tomato sauce	2 tbsp basil, chopped
2 tsp olive oil	Salt and black pepper to taste

DIRECTIONS and total time: approx. 20 minutes

Place penne in the inner pot and cover with salted water. Seal the lid, press Manual, and cook for 4 minutes at High. Do a quick pressure release. Drain and set aside, reserving the cooking water. Heat olive oil on Sauté. Slowly stir in flour, and keep stirring until you obtain a paste. Pour the milk and stir until the mixture thickens. Add in pepperoncini, dill, chili, and tomato sauce. Stir for 3-4 minutes. Pour over penne, top with Pecorino cheese and sprinkle with basil to serve.

Basil Buttered Corn on the Cob

INGREDIENTS for 4 servings

4 corn on the cob, husked	Salt to taste
½ cup butter, softened	2 tbsp chopped fresh basil

DIRECTIONS and total time: approx. 10 minutes

Place a trivet into your pressure cooker. Pour in 1 cup of water and lower the corn on the trivet. Seal the lid, set to Steam, and cook for 3 minutes at High. Quick-release the pressure. Sprinkle the corn with salt, then brush with butter, and top with basil. Serve warm.

Quick Veggie Meal

INGREDIENTS for 4 servings

2 tomatoes, chopped	2 tbsp olive oil
2 carrots, chopped	1 tbsp ketchup
1 cup peas	¼ tsp cayenne pepper
2 onions, chopped	Salt and black pepper to taste
4 potatoes, diced	1 cup veggie stock

DIRECTIONS and total time: approx. 20 minutes

Heat olive oil on Sauté and cook onions and carrots for 4 minutes. Stir in the remaining ingredients. Seal the lid and cook on Manual for 10 minutes at High. When ready, do a quick pressure release. Serve warm.

Cheesy Spinach with Eggs

INGREDIENTS for 4 servings

8 eggs	1 ½ cups spinach, chopped
1 ¼ cups Gruyere, shredded	2 shallots, chopped
½ cup ricotta, crumbled	½ tsp dried thyme
1 cup sour cream	Salt and black pepper to taste

DIRECTIONS and total time: approx. 20 minutes

In a deep bowl, whisk eggs, 4 tbsp of water, and sour cream. Stir in the remaining ingredients until well mixed. Transfer the mixture into a heat-proof dish and cover with aluminum foil. Add 1 cup of water in your IP and fit in a trivet. Lower the dish onto the trivet. Select Manual, seal the lid, and cook for 15 minutes at High. When ready, do a quick release and serve.

Creamy Leek Potatoes

INGREDIENTS for 4 servings

1 lb potatoes, peeled and sliced	½ cup milk
½ cup half-and-half	1 cup vegetable broth
1 tbsp potato starch	Salt and black pepper to taste
1 cup chopped leeks	2 tbsp olive oil

DIRECTIONS and total time: approx. 20 minutes

Heat olive oil on Sauté and cook leeks for 3 minutes. Add in potatoes and vegetable broth; season to taste. Seal the lid and cook on Manual for 10 minutes at High. Do a quick pressure release. With a perforated spoon, remove the potatoes to a serving plate. Whisk the remaining ingredients in the pot. Select Sauté and cook for 2 minutes, stirring constantly, until you obtain sauce texture. Pour the sauce over potatoes and serve.

Tempeh Stir-Fry with Sherry & Parsley

INGREDIENTS for 4 servings

12 oz tempeh, chopped	2 tsp sherry
2 shallots, diced	¼ cup parsley, chopped
1 tomato, diced	1 tsp garlic paste
1 cup turnips, chopped	Salt and black pepper to taste
2 tbsp olive oil	1 cup vegetable broth

DIRECTIONS and total time: approx. 15 minutes

Heat olive oil on Sauté and cook shallots, turnips, garlic, and tomato for 3 minutes, stirring occasionally. Stir in tempeh, sherry, and vegetable broth; season to taste. Seal the lid and cook on Manual for 4 minutes at High. Do a quick release. Serve topped with parsley.

Cheesy Pumpkin Chutney

INGREDIENTS for 4 servings

1 cup Grana Padano, grated
¼ cup milk
1 tsp sesame seeds, toasted
Salt and black pepper to taste

½ cup butter, melted
1 lb pumpkin, sliced
2 tbsp apple cider vinegar
2 tbsp olive oil

DIRECTIONS and total time: approx. 15 minutes

Add 1 cup of water in your IP and insert a trivet. Place the pumpkin on the trivet, drizzle with butter and seal the lid. Cook on Steam for 10 minutes at High. When done, quick-release the pressure. Transfer pumpkin to a food processor along with Grana Padano cheese and milk, and blend until smooth. Then, slowly add the vinegar and olive oil while the machine is running. Season to taste and sprinkle with sesame seeds to serve.

Peas, Sweet Potatoes & Spinach Pot

INGREDIENTS for 4 servings

1 cup canned black-eyed peas
1 lb sweet potatoes, diced
1 onion, chopped
2 cups spinach, chopped
2 garlic cloves, minced
1 tbsp tomato paste

2 tbsp olive oil
½ tsp ground coriander
½ tsp cumin
½ tsp thyme
Salt and black pepper to taste

DIRECTIONS and total time: approx. 30 minutes

Heat olive oil on Sauté and cook onion and garlic for 3 minutes until soft and fragrant. Stir in tomato paste and spices. Pour in 1 cup of water and stir to combine. Add sweet potatoes and peas, and seal the lid. Cook on Manual for 14 minutes at High. When ready, do a quick pressure release. Stir in spinach and press Sauté. Cook until it wilts for about 4-5 minutes. Serve warm.

Simple Sweet Potatoes

INGREDIENTS for 4 servings

1 tsp dried thyme
2 tbsp olive oil
1 cup veggie broth

1 onion, finely chopped
2 lb sweet potatoes, cubed
Salt and black pepper to taste

DIRECTIONS and total time: approx. 30 minutes

Heat olive oil on Sauté and cook onion for 3 minutes. Add potatoes, broth, thyme, salt, and pepper. Seal the lid and cook on Manual for 15 minutes at High. Once ready, do a quick pressure release and serve warm.

Sweet Tomato Sauce

INGREDIENTS for 6-8 servings

3 lb tomatoes, peeled and diced
1 cup red onions, chopped
¼ cup olive oil
2 tsp brown sugar

½ tsp dried basil
½ tsp dried oregano
2 cloves garlic, minced
Salt and black pepper to taste

DIRECTIONS and total time: approx. 20 minutes

Heat olive oil on Sauté and cook onions and garlic until tender, about 3 minutes. Add in the remaining ingredients and ½ cup of water. Seal the lid, select Manual, and cook for 10 minutes at High. When ready, do a quick pressure release. Let cool before serving.

Zucchini Pomodoro Pasta

INGREDIENTS for 4 servings

2 zucchini, spiralized
½ onion, diced
3 tsp garlic, minced
1 tbsp olive oil

1 cup tomatoes, diced
1 tbsp tomato puree
1 tbsp basil, chopped
1 red bell pepper, chopped

DIRECTIONS and total time: approx. 20 minutes

Heat olive oil on Sauté and cook onion, garlic, and bell pepper for 3 minutes. Stir in tomatoes, ½ cup of water, and tomato puree. Seal the lid and cook on Manual for 3 minutes at High. Release the pressure quickly. Stir in zoodles and season with salt and pepper. Cook for 3 minutes on Sauté. When done, top with basil to serve.

Mushroom & Bell Pepper Bruschettas

INGREDIENTS for 4 servings

1 baguette, cut into 4 bruschettas
1 cup mushrooms, chopped
1 onion, chopped
1 carrot, chopped
2 green bell peppers, chopped

2 tomatoes, chopped
1 garlic clove, minced
2 tbsp olive oil
1 cup vegetable stock
Salt and black pepper to taste

DIRECTIONS and total time: approx. 15 minutes

Heat olive oil on Sauté and stir-fry onion, garlic, mushrooms, carrot, and bell peppers for 5 minutes. Stir in tomatoes, vegetable stock, salt, and pepper and seal the lid. Cook on Manual for 6 minutes at High. Release the pressure quickly and remove to a food processor; pulse until smooth. Spread mixture over bruschettas.

Spinach & Feta Pie Sandwiches

INGREDIENTS for 4 servings

4 eggs
1 salad tomato, sliced
2 cups baby spinach
8 oz feta, crumbled

4 brioche buns, halved
1 tbsp brown mustard
½ tsp chipotle powder
Salt and black pepper to taste

DIRECTIONS and total time: approx. 25 minutes

In a bowl, whisk all ingredients, except for the buns and tomato, until combined. Pour the mixture in a greased baking dish. Pour 1 cup of water in the inner pot and insert a trivet. Place the dish on the trivet. Seal the lid and cook on Manual for 15 minutes at High. When done, release the pressure quickly. Slice the pie. Divide tomato and pie slices between buns and serve.

Vegan Burrito Bowls

INGREDIENTS for 4 servings

2 tbsp sesame oil	½ tsp cumin
½ cup spring onions, chopped	½ tsp chili powder
½ red bell pepper, chopped	¼ tsp kosher salt
2 cloves garlic, minced	1 cup vegetable broth
1 cup canned black beans	2 tbsp coconut cream
½ cup white rice, rinsed	2 tbsp chopped cilantro
½ cup corn	1 jalapeño pepper, sliced
½ cup kale	½ cup hot sauce
½ cup red salsa	1 avocado, sliced

DIRECTIONS and total time: approx. 10 minutes

Heat sesame oil on Sauté and cook green onions, garlic, and bell pepper for 3 minutes. Stir in rice, cumin, chili powder, salt, and red salsa. Pour in broth, black beans, and corn. Seal the lid and cook on Manual for 4 minutes at High. When done, release the pressure quickly. Stir in kale for 3-4 minutes until wilts on Sauté. Divide the mixture between bowls and top with coconut cream, hot sauce, jalapeño pepper, and cilantro to serve.

Kalamata & Zucchini Toast

INGREDIENTS for 4 servings

4 bread sliced, toasted	4 tbsp olive oil
2 zucchinis, peeled and sliced	1 tbsp tahini
1 red bell pepper, sliced	Juice from 1 lemon
2 garlic cloves	A pinch of red pepper flakes
10 kalamata olives, chopped	Salt and black pepper to taste

DIRECTIONS and total time: approx. 10 minutes

Combine 1 cup of water, bell pepper and zucchini in your IP. Seal the lid and cook on Manual for 3 minutes at High. When ready, do a quick pressure release. Drain and place in a food processor. Add in lemon juice, olive oil, olives, tahini, garlic, salt, pepper, and red flakes. Pulse until smooth. Spread the mixture over the toasted bread and serve warm.

Pumpkin & Lentil Dhal

INGREDIENTS for 4-6 servings

4 ½ cups vegetable broth	1 tsp ground turmeric
1 ½ cups tomatoes, diced	Juice from 1 lemon
1 ½ cups red lentils, rinsed	Salt and black pepper to taste
1 tsp garlic paste	2 lb pumpkin, chopped
1 onion, diced	2 tsp Garam masala
3 tbsp olive oil	½ cup cilantro, chopped
½ tsp cayenne pepper	½ cup yogurt, for garnish

DIRECTIONS and total time: approx. 30 minutes

Warm olive oil on Sauté and stir-fry garlic and onion for 3 minutes until soft. Add in pumpkin, Garam masala, cayenne, turmeric, salt, and pepper. Cook for 3 more minutes. Stir in broth, lentils, and tomatoes. Seal the lid, select Manual and cook for 15 minutes at High.

Do a quick pressure release. Stir in lemon juice. Ladle dhal into bowls and garnish with cilantro and yogurt.

Scallion & Tofu Bowl

INGREDIENTS for 4 servings

20 oz firm tofu, crumbled	1 tbsp tamari
2 garlic cloves, minced	1 tsp rosemary
1 onion, chopped	2 tbsp white wine
2 tbsp scallions, chopped	2 tsp vegetable oil
1 tsp ginger, minced	Salt and black pepper to taste
2 cups vegetable broth	1 cup rice

DIRECTIONS and total time: approx. 30 minutes

Heat vegetable oil on Sauté and cook garlic, onion, and ginger for 3-4 minutes. Stir in tamari, rosemary, white wine, and rice for 1 minute, and pour in vegetable broth Season to taste. Seal the lid and cook on Manual for 15 minutes at High. When done, release the pressure quickly. Top with tofu and scallions and serve in bowl.

Garlic Kale Hummus

INGREDIENTS for 6 servings

2 tbsp tahini	1 cup green garlic, minced
Salt and black pepper to taste	2 tbsp olive oil
1 cup chickpeas	2 cups kale, chopped

DIRECTIONS and total time: approx. 30 minutes

Pour 3 cups of water in your IP and add the chickpeas. Seal the lid and cook on Manual for 30 minutes at High. Do a quick release and drain them. Transfer to a food processor along with kale, garlic, salt, pepper, and tahini. Pour the oil gradually while the machine is running, until everything is well incorporated.

Simple Herby Potatoes

INGREDIENTS for 4 servings

2 lb potatoes, quartered	¼ tsp rosemary
Salt and black pepper to taste	¼ tsp dried basil
2 tbsp sesame oil	¼ tsp dried oregano

DIRECTIONS and total time: approx. 15 minutes

Fit a trivet in the inner pot and pour 1 in cup of water. Lay the potatoes on the trivet, seal the lid and select Steam mode for 10 minutes at High. When ready, do a quick release. Remove the potatoes to a bowl. Add the remaining ingredients and lightly toss to coat. Serve.

Pecan & Mashed Potato Bake

INGREDIENTS for 4 servings

4 potatoes	½ cup chopped pecans
2 tbsp breadcrumbs	1 tbsp butter, melted
¼ tsp cinnamon	2 tbsp fresh lemon juice
2 tbsp milk	Salt and black pepper to taste

DIRECTIONS and total time: approx. 30 minutes

Place potatoes in the inner pot and cover with water. Seal the lid, select Manual, and cook for 12 minutes at High. Do a quick pressure release. Drain, peel, and put in a bowl. Mash them with potato mash and add in milk, cinnamon, lemon juice, and butter. Mix until the well incorporated. Press the mixture firmly at the bottom of a greased baking dish. Top with pecans and sprinkle with breadcrumbs. Pour 1 cup of water in the pot and lower a trivet. Place baking dish on the trivet. Seal the lid, and cook on Manual at High for 7 minutes. When ready, do a quick pressure release. Serve warm.

Veggie Flax Patties

INGREDIENTS for 4 servings

1 large head cauliflower, cut into florets
2 tbsp canola oil   1 tbsp cumin
1 cup pumpkin puree   1 cup flax meal
Salt and black pepper to taste   2 tbsp parsley, chopped

DIRECTIONS and total time: approx. 20 minutes

Pour 1 cup of water in your IP and insert a steamer basket. Add in the florets, sprinkle with salt and seal the lid. Cook on Manual for 3 minutes at High. After the timer goes off, do a quick pressure release. Remove and put in a bowl. Mash them with a potato masher. Stir in cumin, pumpkin puree, flax meal, parsley, salt, and pepper. Shape the mixture into 4 patties. Wipe the pot clean, and heat canola oil on Sauté. Cook the veggie burgers for 6 minutes, flipping once halfway. Serve.

Winter Root Vegetable Pot

INGREDIENTS for 4 servings

1 onion, diced   1 tsp sage
1 parsnip, chopped   1 tsp dried parsley
2 lb baby potatoes, halved   2 tbsp olive oil
2 carrots, chopped   1 cup vegetable broth
1 tsp garlic, minced   Salt and black pepper to taste

DIRECTIONS and total time: approx. 20 minutes

Heat oil on Sauté and cook onion, carrots, parsnip, and garlic for 5 minutes until tender. Stir in the rest of the ingredients. Seal the lid, Press Manual, and cook for 10 minutes at High. Release the pressure quickly.

Snow Pea & Raisin Salad

INGREDIENTS for 4-6 servings

1 cup cannellini beans, soaked   2 tbsp olive oil
1 cup dried raisins   1 tbsp white wine vinegar
1 cup frozen snow peas   ¼ cup tamari sauce
1 cup scallions, chopped   1 tsp chili paste
1 tomato, thinly sliced   Salt and black pepper to taste
2 garlic cloves, minced   ½ tsp red pepper flakes

DIRECTIONS and total time: approx. 35 minutes

In a bowl, whisk tamari sauce, olive oil, vinegar, chili paste, and garlic, and mix to combine; set aside. Place the beans in your IP and pour enough water to cover them. Seal the lid, select Manual and cook for 30 minutes at High. Once the cooking is complete, do a quick pressure release. Drain the beans and transfer to a serving bowl. Add in the remaining ingredients, and toss with the dressing until well coated.

Catalan Vegetable Samfaina

INGREDIENTS for 4 servings

1 eggplant, sliced   1 zucchini, sliced
1 cup tomatoes, crushed   1 purple onion, chopped
3 Roma tomatoes, sliced   ¼ cup grated Manchego cheese
¼ tsp apple cider vinegar   Salt and black pepper to taste
2 tbsp parsley, chopped   1 garlic clove, minced

DIRECTIONS and total time: approx. 45 minutes

Spread the crushed tomatoes on the bottom of a greased baking dish. In a bowl, mix the remaining ingredients, except for the Roma tomatoes and parsley. Cover the crushed tomatoes with the mixture and top with tomato slices. Scatter Manchego cheese all over. Pour 1 cup of water in your IP and insert a trivet. Place the dish on the trivet. Seal the lid and cook on Manual for 10 minutes at High. After cooking, do a natural pressure release for 10 minutes. Sprinkle with parsley and serve.

Green Chili Buttered Corn

INGREDIENTS for 4 servings

4 ears shucked corn   ½ tsp green chili powder
6 tbsp butter, melted   2 tbsp parsley, minced
Salt to taste

DIRECTIONS and total time: approx. 10 minutes

Pour 1 cup of water in your IP and insert a trivet. Place corn on top of the trivet and seal the lid. Select Steam for 3 minutes at High. Do a quick pressure release. In a bowl, combine butter, salt, parsley, and green chili powder and pour over the corn. Serve immediately.

Awesome Candied Potatoes

INGREDIENTS for 4 servings

4 sweet potatoes, cubed   1 tsp cinnamon
4 tbsp butter   2 tsp cornstarch
¼ cup maple syrup   ½ cup walnuts, chopped
1 tsp brown sugar

DIRECTIONS and total time: approx. 10 minutes

Combine all ingredients in your Instant Pot. Pour in 1 cup of water. Seal the lid and cook on Manual at High for 5 minutes. Release the pressure quickly and serve.

Gingery Sweet Potato & Kale Bowl

INGREDIENTS for 4 servings

1 lb sweet potatoes, cubed	1 tsp lemon juice
1 onion, chopped	1 tsp ground ginger
2 cups kale	½ tsp cayenne pepper
2 garlic cloves, minced	½ tbsp sesame oil
½ cup veggie broth	Salt and black pepper to taste

DIRECTIONS and total time: approx. 20 minutes

Heat sesame oil on Sauté, add onion, garlic, ginger, cayenne, salt, and pepper, and cook for 2 minutes. Add the sweet potatoes and cook for another minute. Pour in broth and lemon juice. Seal the lid, select Manual for 10 minutes at High. Release the pressure quickly. Stir in kale for 3-4 minutes until wilts on Sauté. Serve.

Spicy Red Lentils with Yogurt

INGREDIENTS for 4 servings

1 cup red lentils, soaked	½ tsp cayenne pepper
1 onion, chopped	½ tsp ground bay leaves
2 garlic cloves, minced	1 tsp parsley
2 tsp olive oil	2 tbsp chopped fresh cilantro
Salt and black pepper to taste	½ cup yogurt
1 tbsp cumin seeds	1 sliced jalapeño

DIRECTIONS and total time: approx. 20 minutes

Heat olive oil on Sauté and cook onion, cumin seeds, garlic, cayenne pepper, ground bay leaves, parsley, salt, and pepper for 3 minutes. Add in lentils and 3 cups of water. Seal the lid and cook on Manual for 10 minutes at High. Do a quick pressure release. Serve garnished with fresh cilantro, jalapeño slices, and yogurt.

Tasty Mac & Cheese

INGREDIENTS for 4 servings

16 oz macaroni	1/2 cup heavy cream
¾ cup Cheddar cheese, shredded	Salt and black pepper to taste

DIRECTIONS and total time: approx. 15 minutes

Place macaroni in your IP and cover with salted water. Seal the lid and cook on Manual for 4 minutes at High. When ready, do a quick pressure release. Stir in heavy cream and cheddar cheese until melted and combined on Sauté. Let sit for 2 minutes until the sauce thickens. Adjust the seasoning with salt and pepper and serve.

Tomato & Broccoli Casserole

INGREDIENTS for 4-6 servings

1 head broccoli, cut into florets	2 tbsp tomato paste
3 tomatoes, diced	1 tsp chili powder
½ cup hot water	2 tbsp olive oil
1 lemon, grated, juiced	Salt and black pepper to taste
1 tbsp parsley, chopped	2 garlic cloves, minced

DIRECTIONS and total time: approx. 20 minutes

Pour 1 cup of water in the IP and insert a trivet. Place all the ingredients in a baking dish, stir to combine, and put the dish on the trivet. Seal the lid, select Manual, and cook for 3 minutes at High. When done, release the pressure naturally for 10 minutes. Serve hot.

Cannellini Beans Ragout

INGREDIENTS for 4 servings

1 tomato, chopped	½ tsp cayenne pepper
2 tbsp olive oil	Salt and black pepper to taste
1 bell pepper, sliced	1 cup cannellini beans, soaked
2 garlic cloves, minced	1 handful parsley, chopped,
1 cup celery stalk, chopped	1 cup carrots, chopped
1 tbsp tomato puree	2 small onions, chopped

DIRECTIONS and total time: approx. 40 minutes

Heat oil on Sauté and cook onions, celery, and garlic for 3 minutes. Add the remaining ingredients, except for parsley. Pour in 3 cups of water, seal the lid, and set on Manual for 30 minutes at High. When ready, do a quick pressure release. Sprinkle with parsley to serve.

Oregano & Parmesan Zucchini Noodles

INGREDIENTS for 4 servings

½ cup tomato paste	2 tbsp fresh basil, chopped
2 (16-oz) packets zoodles	1 tsp fresh parsley, chopped
2 garlic cloves, minced	Salt and black pepper to taste
¼ cup veggie broth	½ tsp oregano
2 cups canned tomatoes, diced	1 cup Parmesan, grated

DIRECTIONS and total time: approx. 15 minutes

Place all ingredients in your Instant Pot, except for Parmesan cheese and basil. Seal the lid, select Manual, and cook for 3 minutes at High. Do a quick pressure release. Serve topped with Parmesan cheese and basil.

Apples in Cranberry Sauce

INGREDIENTS for 4 servings

1 lb apples, cored and halved	2 tsp cornstarch
2 ½ cups cranberries	¼ tsp grated nutmeg
1 tsp vanilla paste	½ tsp ground cardamom
½ cup granulated sugar	1 tbsp mint, chopped

DIRECTIONS and total time: approx. 30 minutes

Throw all ingredients, except for sugar and cornstarch, into your IP. Pour in 1 ½ cups of water. Select Manual and cook for 10 minutes at High. Do a quick pressure release. Remove the apples with a spoon that has long, narrow holes. Then, mash the berries with a heavy spoon. Combine the sugar and cornstarch with 2 tbsp of water. Stir into pot and let simmer for 5 minutes on Sauté until the sauce thickens. Serve the apples topped with cranberry sauce.

Morning Blueberry Oatmeal with Peaches

INGREDIENTS for 2 servings

1 cup blueberries
1 ¼ cups steel-cut oats
½ cup milk
3 tbsp pecans, chopped

1 cup peaches, pitted and diced
1 tsp vanilla extract
½ tsp ground cinnamon

DIRECTIONS and total time: approx. 20 minutes

Place all ingredients, except for blueberries and pecans, in your Instant Pot. Pour in 1 ½ cups water. Seal the lid and cook on Manual for 10 minutes at High. Release the pressure quickly. Ladle the oatmeal in two serving bowls and top with blueberries and chopped pecans.

Brussel Sprouts & Apple Lunch

INGREDIENTS for 4 servings

1 lb Brussel sprouts, shredded
½ cup red wine
1 cup apples, diced
1 cup onions, diced
1 tsp thyme
1 tsp sage

1 ½ cups vegetable stock
1 tbsp olive oil
1 ½ tbsp cornstarch slurry
1 ½ tbsp flour
Salt and black pepper to taste
½ tsp brown sugar

DIRECTIONS and total time: approx. 30 minutes

Warm olive oil on Sauté, add onions and apples, and cook for 5 minutes until lightly browned. Stir in the remaining ingredients, except for the slurry. Cook for 20 minutes, and bring the mixture to a boil. Stir in the slurry and cook on Sauté until thickened, 2 minutes.

Vegetable Medley with Brazil Nuts

INGREDIENTS for 4 servings

3 cups cremini mushrooms, sliced
¾ cup Brazil nuts, chopped
½ cup basil, chopped
2 garlic cloves, minced
½ cup olive oil
1 cup vegetable broth

3 zucchinis, chopped
½ tsp red pepper flakes
1/3 cup nutritional yeast
1 lb grape tomatoes, diced
Salt and black pepper to taste

DIRECTIONS and total time: approx. 16 minutes

Heat olive oil on Sauté and cook zucchini, mushrooms, and garlic for 5 minutes. Add the remaining ingredients, except for nuts and basil, and stir. Seal the lid, press Manual, and cook for 6 minutes at High. Do a quick pressure release. Serve sprinkled with basil and nuts.

Bolognese Sauce Vegan-Style

INGREDIENTS for 4 servings

3 garlic cloves, minced
2 tbsp balsamic vinegar
1 tbsp basil
2 cups carrots, chopped
28 oz crushed tomatoes

2 eggplants, chopped
1 tbsp agave nectar
1 cup mushrooms, chopped
1 head cauliflower, chopped
1 cup vegetable stock

DIRECTIONS and total time: approx. 30 minutes

In a food processor, place all the vegetables, except for tomatoes, and pulse until rice-like consistency. Add them to the inner pot along with salt, pepper, agave nectar, stock, tomatoes, and balsamic vinegar. Mix to combine. Seal the lid and press Manual. Cook for 10 minutes at High. After cooking, do a natural pressure release for 10 minutes. Serve topped with basil.

Spicy Eggplants

INGREDIENTS for 4 servings

1 tsp Garam masala
¼ tsp cayenne pepper
3 eggplants, chopped
1 tbsp olive oil

1 tsp ginger, grated
1 cup onions, diced
1 can (14-oz) diced tomatoes
3 garlic cloves, minced

DIRECTIONS and total time: approx. 35 minutes

Stir garlic, garam masala, cayenne, olive oil, ginger, salt, pepper, half of tomatoes, and onions into the cooker; place eggplant pieces on top. Cover with the remaining tomatoes and add ¼ cup of water. Seal the lid, select Manual, and cook for 8 minutes at High. When done, do a natural release for 10 minutes. Serve.

Carrot & Zucchini Spirals with Avocado

INGREDIENTS for 2 servings

2 zucchinis
2 carrots
2 avocados, chopped
2 tbsp olive oil
1 tbsp lemon juice

1 tbsp almonds, thinly sliced
Salt and black pepper to taste
2 tsp dry basil
2 garlic cloves, minced
2 tomatoes, diced

DIRECTIONS and total time: approx. 15 minutes

Using a spiral vegetable slicer, make carrot and zucchini noodles. Add all ingredients to the inner pot, except for almonds and avocado, and mix well. Pour in 1 cup of water. Seal the lid, press Manual and set on High for 3 minutes. After cooking, do a quick pressure release. Serve hot topped with almonds and avocado.

Mint & Parmesan Zucchini

INGREDIENTS for 2 servings

2 zucchini, spiralized
1 tsp lime zest
2 tbsp lime juice
2 tbsp mint, chopped

2 tbsp olive oil
1 tsp garlic, minced
Salt and black pepper to taste
½ cup Parmesan, shaved

DIRECTIONS and total time: approx. 10 minutes

Heat olive oil on Sauté and cook garlic and lime zest for about 30 seconds. Add the rest of the ingredients, stir well to combine, and cook for 2 minutes only. Divide the mixture among two serving bowls. Top with shaved Parmesan, lemon juice, and mint.

Easy Vegetable Roast

INGREDIENTS for 4 servings

2 parsnips, chopped
2 tbsp olive oil
2 tbsp honey
2 tbsp olive oil
1 onion, thinly sliced

1 carrot, chopped
1 head cauliflower, chopped
1 tsp cumin
Salt and black pepper to taste
¾ cup vegetable broth

DIRECTIONS and total time: approx. 35 minutes

Pour 1 cup of water in the IP and insert a trivet. Place all ingredients in a baking dish, stir to combine, and place on top of the trivet. Seal the lid, press Manual and cook at High for 15 minutes. After cooking, do a natural pressure release for 10 minutes. Serve hot.

Yellow Split Peas with Cilantro & Spinach

INGREDIENTS for 4 servings

3 tomatoes, diced
2 cups spinach, chopped
¾ tsp paprika
1 cup yellow split peas
2 tbsp olive oil

4 garlic cloves, minced
1 tsp coriander seeds
1 purple onion, sliced
¼ cup cilantro, chopped
Salt and black pepper to taste

DIRECTIONS and total time: approx. 40 minutes

Heat olive oil on Sauté and cook onion and garlic for 3 minutes. Stir in mustard and coriander seeds, paprika, salt, and black pepper for 30 seconds. Pour in 3 cups of water, split peas, and tomatoes. Seal the lid, press Manual, and cook for 12 minutes at High. After cooking, do a quick pressure release. Stir in spinach and let sit covered for 4-5 minutes until the spinach wilts. Sprinkle with cilantro and serve in bowls.

Lime & Ginger Eggplants

INGREDIENTS for 4 servings

1 lb eggplants, chopped
2 tsp minced ginger
1 onion, chopped
½ lime, zested and juiced
1 tsp tomato paste
2 tbsp olive oil

½ tsp paprika
½ tsp cumin
½ tsp cilantro
½ tsp turmeric
Salt and black pepper to taste
1 cup vegetable broth

DIRECTIONS and total time: approx. 25 minutes

Heat olive oil on Sauté and cook onion, ginger, and eggplants for 5 minutes. Add the remaining ingredients. Seal the lid, press Manual, and cook for 10 minutes at High. After cooking, do a quick pressure release.

Paleo Crusted Veggie Quiche

INGREDIENTS for 4 servings

4 oz goat cheese, crumbled
6 eggs
2 cups mushrooms, sliced

1 ½ cups kale, chopped
1 tbsp butter, melted
Salt and black pepper to taste

DIRECTIONS and total time: approx. 25 minutes

In a bowl, whisk eggs, black pepper and salt until smooth. Grease a baking dish with melted butter and add mushrooms and kale. Pour the egg mixture over and top with goat cheese. Add 1 cup of water and fit in a trivet inside the IP. Place the dish on the trivet. Seal the lid, select Manual at High, and cook for 15 minutes. When done, release the pressure naturally for 5 minutes. Serve hot.

Balls of Zucchini in Ginger Sauce

INGREDIENTS for 2 servings

2 tbsp olive oil
1 can (14.5-oz) tomatoes
1 cup heavy cream
1 tsp chili powder
2 garlic cloves
1/3 cup flour

3 spring onions, chopped
3 zucchinis, shredded
1 tsp ginger, grated
¼ tsp turmeric
1 tsp cumin
¼ tsp salt

DIRECTIONS and total time: approx. 20 minutes

Make ginger sauce by blending ginger, garlic, heavy cream, tomatoes, and spring onions with 1 cup of water in a food processor; set aside. In a bowl, add zucchinis, flour, chili, turmeric, salt, and cumin and mix to combine. Shape the mixture into balls. Heat oil on Sauté and cook the balls on all sides for 5-6 minutes. Pour in the previously prepared ginger sauce. Seal the lid, press Manual, and cook for 8 minutes at High. After cooking, do a quick pressure release. Serve.

Mango Okra Gumbo

INGREDIENTS for 4 servings

1 lb okra, sliced
2 tbsp olive oil
½ tsp mango powder
3 green chili peppers, sliced
1 tsp cumin
2 tomatoes, diced
2 cups vegetable broth

2 garlic cloves, minced
½ tsp turmeric
1 tsp ginger, grated
1 cup canned black beans
1 onion, finely chopped
Salt and black pepper to taste
1 tbsp cilantro, chopped

DIRECTIONS and total time: approx. 15 minutes

Heat olive oil on Sauté and cook onion, ginger, and garlic for 3 minutes. Add the remaining ingredients, except for cilantro, and stir to combine. Seal the lid, press Manual, and cook for 5 minutes at High. After cooking, do a quick pressure release. Serve hot sprinkled with cilantro.

Garlic Mushrooms with Wine & Parsley

INGREDIENTS for 4 servings

1 lb button mushrooms, sliced
2 tbsp olive oil
½ cup white wine
½ cup vegetable broth

4 cups fresh parsley, chopped
3 garlic cloves, minced
Salt and black pepper to taste

DIRECTIONS and total time: approx. 20 minutes

Heat olive oil on Sauté and cook garlic and mushrooms for 5 minutes. Stir in the remaining ingredients, except for the parsley. Seal the lid, press Manual, and cook for 10 minutes at High. When ready, do a quick pressure release. Serve hot sprinkled with parsley.

Cilantro Cauli Rice with Carrots & Kale

INGREDIENTS for 4 servings

2 tbsp oil	2 cups kale, chopped
1 onion, chopped	2 tsp cilantro, chopped
1 cup veggie broth	1 carrot, chopped
4 cups cauliflower rice	Salt and black pepper to taste
2 large tomatoes, chopped	¼ tsp garlic powder

DIRECTIONS and total time: approx. 15 minutes

Heat olive oil on Sauté and cook onion and carrot for 3 minutes. Stir in tomatoes, cauliflower, cumin, salt, pepper, and garlic powder, and sauté for 1-2 minutes. Pour the broth over, seal the lid, press Manual and cook for 3 minutes at High. After you hear the beep, release the pressure quickly. Stir in kale for 3-4 minutes until wilted, and serve garnished with cilantro.

Mozzarella Broccoli with Hazelnuts

INGREDIENTS for 4 servings

1 head broccoli, cut into florets	¼ cup grated mozzarella
1 onion	1 cup hazelnuts, chopped
2 tbsp butter	1 garlic clove, minced
¼ tbsp flour	Black pepper and salt to taste

DIRECTIONS and total time: approx. 25 minutes

Melt butter on Sauté and cook onion and garlic for 3 minutes. Season with salt and pepper, and stir in the flour for 1 minute. Whisk in 1 cup of water and add in broccoli. Transfer to a greased baking dish and top with cheese. Pour 1 cup of water in the pot and insert a trivet. Place the dish on the trivet. Seal the lid, press Manual, and cook for 10 minutes at High. When ready, do a quick release. Serve sprinkled with hazelnuts.

Spaghetti Squash with Kale & Broccoli

INGREDIENTS for 4 servings

4 garlic cloves, minced	1 cup kale, chopped
3 cups broccoli, florets	Salt and black pepper to taste
½ lb spaghetti squash	2 tbsp olive oil
3 cups mushrooms, sliced	1 cup vegetable broth

DIRECTIONS and total time: approx. 15 minutes

Mix all ingredients in the IP, except for kale. Seal the lid, press Manual and cook for 4 minutes at High. When ready, do a quick pressure release. Stir in kale, press Sauté and cook for 3 minutes until the kale wilts.

Palak Paneer

INGREDIENTS for 4-6 servings

1 ½ cups paneer cubes	2 tomatoes, chopped
½ cup whipping cream	1 lb spinach, chopped
Salt and black pepper to taste	1 yellow onion, chopped
1 tsp ground turmeric	½ jalapeño pepper, chopped
2 tsp garam masala	1 tbsp fresh ginger, chopped
½ tsp cayenne pepper	5 cloves garlic, chopped
2 tsp ground cumin	2 tsp olive oil

DIRECTIONS and total time: approx. 23 minutes

Heat olive oil on Sauté and cook jalapeño, garlic, and ginger for 3 minutes. Add in the remaining ingredients, except for whipping cream. Pour 1 cup of water, seal the lid, press Manual, and cook for 10 minutes at High. When ready, do a quick release. Puree the mixture using an immersion blender. Gently stir in the paneer. Serve warm, topped with a dollop of whipping cream.

Green Chili & Cheese Frittata

INGREDIENTS for 4 servings

1 cup shredded Mexican blend cheese	
1 can (10-oz) green chilies, chopped	
6 eggs	Salt and black pepper to taste
2 tbsp butter, melted	1 cup half-and-half
½ tsp cumin	¼ cup chopped cilantro

DIRECTIONS and total time: approx. 30 minutes

In a bowl, beat the egg, then stir in chilies, half-and-half, salt, cumin, and the shredded cheese. Pour the mixture in a greased with butter baking pan and cover with aluminum foil. Pour 1 cup of water in your IP, fit in a trivet and place the baking dish on top. Seal the lid and cook on Manual for 15 minutes, at High. Allow a natural release for 10 minutes; remove the foil. Using a knife, carefully loosen the frittata on the pan side. Then, hold a plate on top and carefully invert. Serve garnished with fresh cilantro.

Fennel & Zucchini with Mushrooms

INGREDIENTS for 4 servings

3 zucchinis, sliced	1 cup milk
2 cups mushrooms, chopped	½ fennel bulb, chopped
2 tbsp olive oil	2 cups cherry tomatoes
2 garlic cloves, minced	Salt and black pepper to taste
1 sweet onion, sliced	1 tsp turmeric

DIRECTIONS and total time: approx. 30 minutes

Heat olive oil on Sauté. Add the mushrooms, onion, zucchinis, fennel, and garlic and cook for 5 minutes. Add in the remaining ingredients and stir to combine. Pour in 1 cup of water. Seal the lid, select Manual at High, and cook for 6 minutes. When done, release pressure naturally for 10 minutes and serve.

Curry Spaghetti Squash

INGREDIENTS for 4 servings

2 tbsp butter
1 cup tomato sauce
2 tbsp curry powder
2 lb squash
3 cups spinach, chopped
Salt and black pepper to taste

DIRECTIONS and total time: approx. 30 minutes

Slice the squash lengthwise, then scoop out the seeds. Put 1 cup of water and fit a trivet inside your IP. Put the squash on the trivet. Seal the lid, select Manual, and cook for 6 minutes at High. When done, release the pressure naturally for 10 minutes. Allow to cool. Then, make spaghetti noodles by scrapping off the flesh with a fork. Melt butter on Sauté and cook spinach for 2-3 minutes until wilted. Stir in curry powder, salt, and pepper and pour in tomato sauce. Simmer for 5 minutes. Pour the sauce over squash spaghetti to serve.

Green Beans with Fresh Garlic

INGREDIENTS for 2 servings

1 lb green beans, chopped
2 tbsp olive oil
1 cup fresh garlic cloves, minced
Salt and black pepper to taste
¼ cup pomegranate seeds
1 tsp onion powder

DIRECTIONS and total time: approx. 20 minutes

Heat olive oil on Sauté and cook garlic and green beans for 5 minutes. Season with onion powder, salt and pepper and stir. Pour in 1 cup of water, seal the lid, press Manual, and cook for 5 minutes at High. After cooking, do a quick pressure release. Serve topped with pomegranate seeds.

Cauliflower Mac & Cheese

INGREDIENTS for 4 servings

2 cups cauliflower rice
Salt and pepper as needed
½ cup cheddar cheese, grated
½ cup half-and-half
2 tbsp cream cheese2
2 tbsp parsley, chopped

DIRECTIONS and total time: approx. 20 minutes

In a baking dish, mix cream cheese, cauliflower rice, cheddar cheese, half-and-half, parsley, pepper, and salt. Cover the bowl with aluminum foil. Pour 1 cup of water in the inner pot and insert a trivet. Place the dish on top. Seal the lid and cook on Manual for 5 minutes at High. When ready, do a natural release for 5 minutes.

Vegan Broccoli with Tahini Sauce

INGREDIENTS for 4 servings

1 broccoli head, cut into florets
1 tbsp lime juice
Salt and black pepper to taste
3 tbsp olive oil
¼ cup pistachios, crushed
1 tsp paprika
2 roasted garlic cloves, crushed
2 tbsp tahini sauce
1 tbsp lime juice
1 tbsp olive oil

DIRECTIONS and total time: approx. 25 minutes

Set to Sauté and heat 2 tbsp of olive oil. Add paprika, pistachios, salt, and pepper and stir-fry for 2-3 minutes. Add in broccoli and 1 cup of water. Seal the lid, select Manual, and cook for 3 minutes at High. When done, release the pressure naturally for 10 minutes. Mix garlic, tahini, lime juice, and remaining oil in a small bowl. Drizzle over the cooked broccoli. Serve warm.

Poblano Pepper & Sweet Corn Side Dish

INGREDIENTS for 4 servings

2 tbsp vegetable oil
1 cup heavy cream
1 tsp cumin
Salt and black pepper to taste
1 cup corn
1 sliced red onion
2 poblano peppers, sliced
2 tbsp lemon juice

DIRECTIONS and total time: approx. 15 minutes

Heat oil on Sauté and stir-fry peppers and onion for 6 minutes. Stir in corn and heavy cream for 3-4 minutes. Season with salt, pepper and cumin, and drizzle with lemon juice to serve.

Mushroom & Eggplant Mix

INGREDIENTS for 4 servings

2 cups Portobello mushrooms, sliced
2 eggplants, sliced
2 tbsp olive oil
2 garlic cloves, minced
½ cup tomatoes, diced
1 tsp rosemary
Salt and black pepper to taste

DIRECTIONS and total time: approx. 30 minutes

Heat olive oil on Sauté and cook garlic, mushrooms, and eggplant for 5 minutes. Stir in rosemary, tomatoes and ½ cup of water; season to taste. Seal the lid, select Manual, and cook for 6 minutes at High. When done, release pressure naturally for 10 minutes. Serve hot.

Stewed Vegetables

INGREDIENTS for 4 servings

3 zucchinis, sliced
2 eggplants, sliced
2 green peppers, sliced
2 tbsp basil, chopped
Salt and black pepper to taste
1 yellow onion, chopped
1 (14-oz) can tomatoes, diced
2 garlic cloves, minced
½ cup olive oil
1 cup vegetable broth

DIRECTIONS and total time: approx. 30 minutes

Heat olive oil on Sauté and fry zucchinis and eggplants, for 7-8 minutes; reserve. Add onion, garlic, and green peppers to the pot, and sauté for 2 minutes. Stir in tomato, salt, and pepper. Return zucchinis and eggplants, and pour in 1 cup of water. Seal the lid, select Manual, and cook for 6 minutes at High. When done, release pressure naturally for 10 minutes. Serve garnished with basil.

Mirin Tofu Bowl

INGREDIENTS for 4-6 servings

20 oz smoked tofu, sliced	1 onion, chopped
2 ½ tbsp oyster sauce	1 cup basmati rice
2 tbsp mirin wine	1 tsp rosemary
3 garlic cloves, minced	2 tbsp fresh chives, chopped
2 tsp olive oil	Salt and black pepper to taste
2 cups vegetable broth	1-inch piece ginger, grated

DIRECTIONS and total time: approx. 20 minutes

Heat olive oil on Sauté and stir-fry tofu until slightly browned; reserve. Place the rice and vegetable broth in the pot and seal the lid; cook on Manual for 6 minutes at High. Do a quick pressure release. In a blender, add the remaining ingredients and pulse until you obtain a smooth paste. Stir in rice and top with tofu to serve.

Quick Indian Creamy Eggplants

INGREDIENTS for 4 servings

4 cups eggplants, chopped	1 onion, thinly sliced
¼ tsp turmeric, ground	¼ tsp cayenne pepper
¼ tsp garam masala	¼ cup heavy cream
1 tomato, chopped	¼ tsp goda masala
2 tsp peanut oil	Salt and black pepper to taste

DIRECTIONS and total time: approx. 30 minutes

Grease a baking dish with peanut oil. Add tomato and onion, then place eggplants on top. Sprinkle with turmeric, pepper, salt, goda masala, garam masala, and cayenne; do not stir. Top with heavy cream. Pour 1 cup of water in your IP and insert a trivet. Put the dish on the trivet. Seal the lid, press Manual, and cook for 10 minutes at High. Do a quick pressure release and serve.

Lemon Artichokes

INGREDIENTS for 4 servings

2 fresh lemons, sliced thinly	3 cloves garlic, minced
4 artichokes	Salt and black pepper to taste

DIRECTIONS and total time: approx. 30 minutes

Add 1 cup of water and fit a trivet. Season the artichokes with garlic, salt, and black pepper, and place them on the trivet. Seal the lid, select Manual, and cook for 12 minutes at High. When done, release the pressure naturally for 10 minutes. Serve topped with lemon.

Heavenly Black Bean & Bell Pepper Chili

INGREDIENTS for 4 servings

1 tsp chili pepper, minced	1 cup black beans, soaked
1 cup red bell peppers, sliced	½ tsp celery seeds
2 garlic cloves, minced	1 tbsp tomato puree
2 tbsp vegetable oil	½ cup green onions, chopped
1 cup carrots, chopped	Salt and black pepper to taste

DIRECTIONS and total time: approx. 35 minutes

Heat vegetable oil on Sauté and stir-fry garlic, green onions, chili pepper, bell peppers, and carrots for 3-4 minutes. Stir in tomato puree, celery seeds, 2 cups of water, salt, and pepper. Seal the lid, press Manual and cook for 30 minutes at High. Serve hot.

Power Green Minestrone Stew with Lemon

INGREDIENTS for 4 servings

1 head cauliflower, cut into florets	
2 green bell peppers, sliced	4 cups vegetable broth
2 celery stalks, chopped	1 bunch kale, chopped
1 tsp garlic, minced	2 tsp fresh lemon juice
1 tsp olive oil	Salt and black pepper to taste
4 spring onions, chopped	Grated Grana Padano

DIRECTIONS and total time: approx. 25 minutes

Heat olive oil on Sauté and stir-fry spring onions and garlic until tender, about 2 minutes. Add in the remaining ingredients, except for the kale and Grana Padano cheese. Seal the lid, press Manual and cook for 10 minutes at High. Once the cooking is over, do a quick release. Add in kale. Cook for 4-5 minutes until tender on Sauté, stirring occasionally. Divide between bowls and serve sprinkled with Grana Padano cheese.

Vegetable One-Pot

INGREDIENTS for 4 servings

1 zucchini, sliced	½ lb sweet potatoes, cubed
2 tbsp olive oil	¼ cup fresh parsley, chopped
Salt and black pepper to taste	2 carrots, chopped
2 tomatoes, chopped	1 garlic paste
½ lb green beans	1 onion, chopped

DIRECTIONS and total time: approx. 35 minutes

Heat olive oil on Sauté and cook onion, zucchini, carrots, and garlic for 5 minutes. Add in the remaining ingredients, except for parsley, and 1 cup of water. Seal the lid, select Manual, and cook for 10 minutes at High. When done, release the pressure naturally for 10 minutes. Sprinkled with parsley and serve.

Garlic Green Peas with Zucchini

INGREDIENTS for 4 servings

14 oz milk	1 onion, chopped
1 cup green peas	2 garlic cloves, minced
4 zucchinis, chopped	2 tbsp curry powder
Salt and black pepper to taste	¼ cup vegetable broth

DIRECTIONS and total time: approx. 30 minutes

Place all ingredients in inner pot and stir to combine. Seal the lid and press Manual. Cook for 15 minutes at High. After cooking, do a natural pressure release for 10 minutes. Serve immediately.

Jalapeño Tofu Stew with Vegetables

INGREDIENTS for 4 servings

1 jalapeño pepper, minced	½ cup barbecue sauce
2 cups tofu cubes	2 carrots, chopped
2 bell peppers, diced	4 sweet potatoes, diced
2 ripe tomatoes, chopped	1 tbsp vegetable oil
2 white onions, chopped	2 tbsp tomato puree
1 cup turnips, chopped	⅓ tsp Gochugaru chile flakes
1 cup green peas	Salt and black pepper to taste

DIRECTIONS and total time: approx. 25 minutes

Heat olive oil on Sauté and stir-fry onions, carrots, turnips, jalapeño and bell peppers until soft, 5 minutes. Add the rest of the ingredients and pour enough water to cover by an inch. Seal the lid, and cook on Manual for 10 minutes at High. Do a quick pressure release.

Braised Red Cabbage & Cherry Stew

INGREDIENTS for 4 servings

2 tbsp olive oil	1 tbsp grated ginger
2 carrots, chopped	2 tbsp dried cherries, sliced
1 red cabbage, shredded	4 cups vegetable broth
1 apple, diced	2 tbsp parsley, chopped
1 onion, diced	Salt and black pepper to taste

DIRECTIONS and total time: approx. 30 minutes

Heat olive oil on Sauté and cook carrots, apple, onion, ginger for 5 minutes. Stir in cabbage for another 5 minutes. Pour in vegetable broth and dried cherries; season to taste. Seal the lid, press Manual, and cook for 20 minutes at High. When done, do a quick pressure release. Sprinkle with parsley and serve.

Pinto Bean & Sweet Potato Chili

INGREDIENTS for 4 servings

2 cups vegetable broth	1 green bell pepper, chopped
2 cups canned diced tomatoes	1 tbsp olive oil
1 cup canned pinto beans	1 tbsp chili powder
2 sweet potatoes, chopped	¼ tsp cinnamon
1 red onion, chopped	1 tsp cayenne pepper
1 red bell pepper, chopped	Salt and black pepper to taste

DIRECTIONS and total time: approx. 25 minutes

Heat olive oil on Sauté and cook onion, peppers, and potatoes for 4 minutes. Stir in the rest of the ingredients. Seal the lid and cook on Manual for 16 minutes at High. Once ready, do a quick pressure release. Serve.

Brown Rice and Kidney Beans Casserole

INGREDIENTS for 4 servings

1 cup kidney beans, soaked	1 cup brown rice
1 tsp onion powder	1 tbsp tomato puree
2 tsp serrano chili powder	2 tbsp olive oil

2 garlic cloves, minced	1 tsp cumin
Salt and black pepper to taste	1 tsp parsley

DIRECTIONS and total time: approx. 40 minutes

Heat olive oil on Sauté and cook all the ingredients for 3-4 minutes. Pour in 4 cups of water. Seal the lid, select Manual, and cook for 30 minutes at High. When ready, do a quick pressure release. Serve warm.

Raclette Soup with Tortillas

INGREDIENTS for 4 servings

6 corn tortillas, cut into wide strips
Grated raclette cheese for serving

2 tbsp butter	1 cup zucchini, chopped
4 cups vegetable stock	3 garlic cloves, minced
1 cup shallots, chopped	2 ripe tomatoes, chopped
1 cup green peas	½ tsp ground cumin
1 ½ cups pumpkin puree	Salt and black pepper to taste
½ habanero pepper, diced	½ tsp chili powder
1 green bell pepper, diced	½ tsp oregano

DIRECTIONS and total time: approx. 35 minutes

Preheat oven to 400 F. Line a baking sheet with parchment paper. Lightly spray both sides of each tortilla with cooking spray. Spread the tortilla strips onto the baking sheet. Bake until they are crisp, turning once halfway through baking, about 7-8 minutes.

Melt butter on Sauté and cook shallots, zucchini, bell and habanero peppers, and garlic for 3 minutes. Stir in cumin, chili, and oregano and add tomatoes, pumpkin puree, and vegetable stock. Seal the lid, press Manual, and cook for 10 minutes at High. Do a quick release. Stir in peas for 3 minutes and adjust the seasoning. Divide the soup between bowls and top with crushed tortilla chips and raclette cheese to serve.

Ricotta Stuffed Potatoes

INGREDIENTS for 4 servings

1 lb potatoes	1 cup ricotta cheese
1 tsp chili powder	2 tbsp butter, melted
½ tsp onion powder	2 spring onions, chopped
½ tsp garlic powder	Salt and black pepper to taste

DIRECTIONS and total time: approx. 30 minutes

Pour 1 cup of water in your IP and insert a trivet. Place the potatoes on the trivet and seal the lid. Cook on Manual for 15 minutes at High. When ready, do a quick pressure release.

Half the potatoes lengthwise and scoop out pulp. Mash the pulp in a bowl with potato mash and add in butter, ricotta cheese, onion and garlic powders, and chili powder and mix well. Fill the potato shells and top with spring onions to serve.

Soups, Stews & Chilis

Basil Cherry Tomato Soup

INGREDIENTS for 4 servings

1 lb cherry tomatoes, halved	4 cups vegetable broth
2 tbsp whipping cream	1 onion, chopped
1 tbsp tomato purée	2 tbsp olive oil
1 garlic clove, minced	½ tsp red chili flakes
2 tbsp chopped basil leaves	Salt and black pepper to taste
1 carrot, chopped	A pinch of sugar

DIRECTIONS and total time: approx. 25 minutes

Warm olive oil on Sauté and cook onion, garlic, and carrot for 3 minutes. Add in tomato puree, cherry tomatoes, red chili flakes, sugar, and broth. Seal the lid, select Manual, and cook for 10 minutes at High. Once done, quick-release the pressure. Blend soup inside the pot with an immersion blender until smooth; adjust the seasoning. Ladle into soup bowls and top with a swirl of whipping cream and basil to serve.

Tuscan Vegetable Tortellini Soup

INGREDIENTS for 4-6 servings

1 onion, diced	1 tsp sugar
2 carrots, diced	2 celery stalks, sliced
1 garlic clove, minced	Salt and black pepper to taste
2 cups chopped spinach	1 tsp Italian seasoning
2 tbsp olive oil	1 tsp tomato puree
4 cups vegetable broth	8 oz dry cheese tortellini
1 cup tomato sauce	2 tbsp grated Parmesan

DIRECTIONS and total time: approx. 15 minutes

Heat olive oil on Sauté and cook onion, garlic, celery, and carrots until soft, about 3 minutes. Stir in the rest of the ingredients, except for cheese. Seal the lid, and cook on Manual for 5 minutes at High. When ready, do a quick pressure release. Adjust the seasoning and sprinkle with Parmesan cheese. Serve hot.

Mom's Vegetable Soup

INGREDIENTS for 4 servings

1 cup canned diced tomatoes	2 tbsp olive oil
1 cup celery stalks chopped	Salt and black pepper to taste
½ lb green beans, chopped	1 cup vermicelli
4 cups vegetable broth	1 cup onions, cut into rings
1 tsp dill	1 cup fresh corn kernels

DIRECTIONS and total time: approx. 15 minutes

Heat olive oil on Sauté and stir-fry onions and celery for 3 minutes. Add in vegetable broth, tomatoes, corn, vermicelli, dill, and green beans. Season to taste, seal the lid and cook on Manual for 5 minutes at High. Once ready, do a quick pressure release. Serve warm.

Moroccan Chicken Soup

INGREDIENTS for 4 servings

½ lb chicken breasts, cubed	1 tsp cinnamon
1 cup canned chickpeas	Salt and black pepper to taste
2 cups collard greens, torn	1 tomato, finely chopped
2 tbsp olive oil	1 red onion, sliced
1 bay leaf	½ cup celery, chopped
1 tsp paprika	4 cups vegetable stock
1 tsp cumin	2 tbsp cilantro, chopped

DIRECTIONS and total time: approx. 30 minutes

Heat olive oil on Sauté and stir-fry chicken, onion, and celery for 3 minutes. Add in paprika, cumin, and cinnamon and stir for 1 minute. Pour in tomato, stock, chickpeas, and bay leaf. Seal the lid, select Manual, and cook for 15 minutes at High. Once ready, do a quick pressure release. Remove bay leaf and stir in collard greens. Cook for 3 minutes on Sauté and adjust the seasoning. Divide soup among bowls and sprinkle with cilantro to serve.

White Bean & Pancetta Soup

INGREDIENTS for 4 servings

4 oz cubed pancetta	2 cups spinach, chopped
2 tbsp olive oil	2 tbsp chopped parsley
1 cup white beans, soaked	1 cup tomato sauce
1 onion, chopped	1 celery stalk, chopped
2 carrots, sliced	2 garlic cloves, minced
½ chopped green bell pepper	Salt and black pepper to taste

DIRECTIONS and total time: approx. 40 minutes

Heat olive oil on Sauté and cook pancetta, onion, garlic, carrots, celery, salt, and bell pepper for 5 minutes until tender. Pour in tomato sauce, beans, and 4 cups of water; season with salt and pepper. Seal the lid and cook on Manual for 25 minutes at High. When ready, do a quick release. Stir in spinach and press Sauté. Cook for 2-3 minutes until the spinach wilt. Sprinkle with parsley and serve.

Winter Squash & Chickpea Soup

INGREDIENTS for 4 servings

2 red bell peppers, chopped	1 cup winter squash, diced
½ cup chickpeas, soaked	2 tsp olive oil
4 ½ cups vegetable stock	Salt and black pepper to taste
2 shallots, thinly sliced	2 tbsp tamari sauce
1 cup fresh chives, sliced	1 garlic clove, minced

DIRECTIONS and total time: approx. 40 minutes

Heat olive oil on Sauté and cook shallots and garlic until translucent, 2-3 minutes. Add the rest of the ingredients, except for the chives. Seal the lid, press Manual, and cook for 30 minutes at High. Once done, do a quick pressure release. Serve topped with chives.

Sage Zucchini & Navy Bean Soup

INGREDIENTS for 4 servings

1 lb zucchini, cut into strips	½ cup navy beans, soaked
1 tbsp sage	Salt and black pepper to taste
1 leek, chopped	2 tsp olive oil
1 garlic clove, minced	4 cups vegetable broth

DIRECTIONS and total time: approx. 15 minutes

Warm olive oil on Sauté and stir-fry leek, garlic, and zucchini for 4-5 minutes. Add in the remaining ingredients, seal the lid and cook on Manual for 15 minutes at High. When ready, do a quick release.

Chicken Enchilada Soup

INGREDIENTS for 4 servings

1 cup pumpkin, cubed	Salt and black pepper to taste
½ lb chicken breasts, cubed	2 russet potatoes, quartered
8 oz canned tomato soup	2 garlic cloves, minced
½ tsp cumin	3 cups chicken broth
1 onion, chopped	1 cup canned black beans
2 tbsp chopped cilantro	2 green chiles, chopped
½ cup red taco sauce	1 avocado, sliced

DIRECTIONS and total time: approx. 35 minutes

Heat olive oil on Sauté and stir-fry chicken, onion, green chiles, and garlic for 5 minutes. Pour in tomato soup, black beans, red taco sauce, pumpkin, potatoes, cumin, and broth. Seal the lid, select Manual, and cook for 15 minutes on High. When it beeps, do a quick pressure release. Remove the chicken to a bowl and shred with two forks; return to the soup. Adjust the seasoning, top with cilantro and avocado to serve.

"Eat-me" Ham & Pea Soup

INGREDIENTS for 4 servings

2 tbsp olive oil	1 celery stalk, diced
1 onion, diced	½ lb ham chunks
½ lb yellow split peas	½ tsp dried sage
2 carrots, diced	Salt and black pepper to taste

DIRECTIONS and total time: approx. 25 minutes

Heat olive oil on Sauté and stir-fry onion, carrots, celery, and ham for 3-4 minutes. Stir in the remaining ingredients and pour in 4 cups of water. Seal the lid, select Manual, and cook for 15 minutes at High. Once over, do a quick pressure release and serve.

Apple-Butternut Squash Soup

INGREDIENTS for 4 servings

2 lb butternut squash, diced	4 apples, chopped
2 tbsp butter	1 white onion, chopped
1 tsp cumin	Salt and black pepper to taste
1 tsp hot paprika	4 tbsp whipping cream

DIRECTIONS and total time: approx. 25 minutes

Melt butter on Sauté and cook onion for 3 minutes. Pour in the remaining ingredients, except for whipping cream, and pour in 4 cups of water. Seal the lid, select Manual at High, and cook for 12 minutes. When done, release the pressure quickly. Puree the soup with an immersion blender until smooth. Stir in whipping cream and serve.

Japanese-Style Tofu Soup

INGREDIENTS for 4 servings

½ cup corn	2 celery stalks, chopped
2 tbsp miso paste	2 carrots, chopped
1 onion, sliced	Salt and black pepper to taste
1 tsp wakame flakes	Soy sauce to taste
1 cup silken tofu, cubed	2 tsp dashi granules

DIRECTIONS and total time: approx. 15 minutes

Add all ingredients except for miso paste and soy sauce to the inner pot. Pour in 4 cups of water. Seal the lid, select Manual, and cook for 7 minutes at High. When ready, do a quick pressure release. Mix miso paste with 1 cup of cooking broth. Stir it into the soup along with soy sauce. Serve warm.

Cheddar Cheese & Broccoli Soup

INGREDIENTS for 4 servings

4 cups vegetable broth	2 tbsp olive oil
1 onion, chopped	1 cup bell peppers, chopped
½ cup parsnips, chopped	1 cup fennel bulb, sliced
1 cup carrots, sliced	2 cups broccoli florets
Salt and black pepper to taste	½ cup cheddar cheese, grated

DIRECTIONS and total time: approx. 20 minutes

Heat olive oil on Sauté and stir-fry onion, parsnips, carrots, bell peppers, and fennel for about 4-5 minutes. Place in the remaining ingredients, except for cheddar cheese and seal the lid. Select Manual and cook for 8 minutes at High. When ready, do a quick pressure release. Puree soup with a hand blender. Serve soup topped with freshly grated cheddar cheese.

Curry Zucchini Soup

INGREDIENTS for 4 servings

3 cups vegetable broth	1 garlic clove, minced
1 lb zucchini, chopped	1 onion, chopped
1 cup milk	Salt and black pepper to taste
1 carrot, chopped	2 tbsp butter, softened
1 tbsp curry paste	Crème fraîche for garnish

DIRECTIONS and total time: approx. 20 minutes

Melt butter on Sauté and cook onion, garlic, carrot, and zucchini for about 4-5 minutes. Stir in curry paste and vegetable broth and seal the lid; select Manual.

Cook for 10 minutes at High. When over, do a quick pressure release. Remove the ingredients to a deep bowl, add milk, and blend with an immersion blender; adjust the taste. Serve garnished with crème fraîche.

Lentil & Bacon Soup

INGREDIENTS for 4 servings

4 bacon slices, chopped	1 red bell peppers chopped
4 garlic cloves, minced	1 cup dry lentils
1 tsp cumin	1 bay leaf
4 cups vegetable broth	1 tsp paprika
1 onion, chopped	½ cup tomato sauce
2 celery stalks, chopped	2 tbsp olive oil
2 carrots, chopped	Salt and black pepper to taste

DIRECTIONS and total time: approx. 35 minutes

Heat olive oil on Sauté and cook bacon, onion, garlic, celery, bell pepper, and carrots for 3 minutes. Stir in paprika and cumin for 1 minute and pour in tomato sauce, lentils, broth, and bay leaf. Seal the lid, set on Manual for 12 minutes. When it beeps, do a natural release for 10 minutes. Adjust the seasoning and serve.

Oregano Pearl Barley & Chorizo Soup

INGREDIENTS for 4 servings

6 oz chorizo sausages, sliced	2 tbsp oregano
1 cup pearl barley	2 tsp olive oil
½ lb zucchini, sliced	2 garlic cloves, minced
1 red onion, chopped	4 cups vegetable broth
1 tsp red pepper flakes, crushed	Salt and black pepper to taste

DIRECTIONS and total time: approx. 15 minutes

Select Sauté and heat olive oil. Cook chorizo, garlic, zucchini, and onion for 4-5 minutes. Add the remaining ingredients, except for oregano. Seal the lid and cook for 12 minutes on Manual at High. Once cooking is over, release the pressure quickly. Remove the lid and add the oregano, stir, and serve hot.

Thyme Potato & Pumpkin Cream Soup

INGREDIENTS for 4 servings

2 cups pumpkin, cubed	1 tbsp whipping cream
1 lb potatoes, cubed	4 cups vegetable broth
2 tbsp olive oil	A pinch of thyme
1 onion, diced	Salt and black pepper to taste

DIRECTIONS and total time: approx. 35 minutes

Warm olive oil on Sauté and cook onion for 3 minutes. Stir in potatoes and pumpkin, and cook for an additional minute. Pour broth over and stir in thyme. Seal the lid, choose Manual for 10 minutes at High. When done, do a natural pressure release for 10 minutes. Blend the soup with an immersion blender and stir in whipping cream. Adjust the seasoning and serve.

Spiced Sweet Potato Soup

INGREDIENTS for 4 servings

1 chipotle pepper, minced	Salt and black pepper to taste
4 cups vegetable broth	1 lb sweet potatoes
2 tbsp olive oil	1 garlic clove, minced
1 yellow onion, chopped	½ tsp allspice
2 tbsp fresh cilantro, chopped	2 tbsp pumpkin seeds
½ tsp cayenne pepper	1 cup whipping cream

DIRECTIONS and total time: approx. 25 minutes

Warm olive oil on Sauté and cook garlic and onion until brown, about 3-4 minutes. Add in chipotle pepper, allspice, salt, cayenne and black peppers and cook for another 2 minutes. Stir in sweet potatoes and vegetable broth. Seal the lid, press Manual, and cook for 12 minutes at High. Once ready, do a quick pressure release. Transfer the soup to a food processor. Blend until smooth and creamy and stir in whipping cream. Sprinkle with pumpkin seeds and cilantro to serve.

Greek Chicken Soup with Olive Tapenade

INGREDIENTS for 4 servings

1 cup marinated artichoke hearts, chopped	
2 chicken breasts	1 onion, chopped
2 tbsp chopped oregano	2 tbsp olive oil
4 cups chicken broth	2 large potatoes, diced
4 tbsp olive tapenade	2 baby carrots, diced
¼ tsp lemon pepper	Juice of 1 lemon
¼ tsp ground coriander	3 garlic cloves, minced

DIRECTIONS and total time: approx. 40 minutes

Heat olive oil on Sauté and cook onion, carrots, and garlic for 3 minutes. Stir in lemon pepper and ground coriander for 1 minute. Stir in chicken broth, artichokes, and potatoes. Seal the lid, select Manual, and cook for 15 minutes at High. When ready, do a quick release. Stir in lemon juice and adjust the seasoning. Top with olive tapenade and oregano. Serve in bowls.

Pumpkin & Pearl Barley Soup

INGREDIENTS for 4 servings

½ cup pearl barley, rinsed	1 turnip, chopped
1 lb pumpkin, cubed	2 tsp olive oil
1 carrot, chopped	Salt and black pepper to taste
2 shallots, chopped	½ tsp cayenne pepper
1 tbsp fennel seeds	2 tbsp parsley, chopped

DIRECTIONS and total time: approx. 25 minutes

Heat olive oil on Sauté and cook shallots for 3 minutes. Stir in fennel seeds, cayenne pepper, barley, pumpkin, carrot, turnip, and 4 cups of water; season with salt and pepper. Seal the lid, press Manual, and cook for 12 minutes at High. Once cooking is over, do a quick pressure release. Top with parsley and serve.

Udon Noodle Chicken Soup

INGREDIENTS for 4 servings

2 cups shiitake mushrooms, sliced
1 lb boneless skinless chicken thighs
1 garlic head, cut in half   1 cup snow peas
4 green onions, chopped   7 oz udon noodles
1 (4-inch) piece Kombu   1 carrot, sliced
1 (2-inch) piece fresh ginger   1 tbsp fish sauce
2 tsp sesame seeds   3 tbsp Mirin wine
2 tsp sesame oil   3 tbsp tamari sauce

DIRECTIONS and total time: approx. 45 minutes

Soak kombu in 4 cups of water for 10 minutes. Add garlic, green onions, ginger, fish and tamari sauces, mirin wine, sesame oil, and kombu with water in your Instant Pot. Seal the lid, select Manual, and cook for 10 minutes at High. When ready, do a quick release. Strain to discard the solids and return the broth to the cooker. Add in chicken, mushrooms, and carrots and seal the lid. Select Manual and cook for 12 minutes at High. Do a quick pressure release. Stir in snow peas and noddles and press Sauté. Cook for 2-3 minutes to warm through. Garnish with sesame seeds and serve.

Beer Cheese Potato Soup

INGREDIENTS for 4 servings

2 tbsp olive oil   1 celery stalk, chopped
4 potatoes, chopped   1 garlic clove, minced
1 cup heavy cream   1 yellow onion, chopped
Salt and black pepper to taste   8 oz shredded cheddar cheese
½ cup beer   Chives, chopped for garnish

DIRECTIONS and total time: approx. 30 minutes

Heat olive oil on Sauté and cook onion, garlic, and celery for 3 minutes. Pour in beer, potatoes, and 4 cups of water; season with salt and pepper. Seal the lid, select Manual, and cook for 12 minutes at High. When ready, do a quick release. Transfer 1/3 of the potatoes to a blender, along with heavy cream, and process until smooth. Add to the pot along with cheese and stir. Cook for 3 minutes on Sauté until the cheese has melted completely. Serve warm, topped with chives.

Beef, Potato & Carrot Soup

INGREDIENTS for 4 servings

½ lb ground beef   1 tsp rosemary
1 cup tomato sauce   2 cups cubed potatoes
1 cup fresh corn   1 onion, chopped
Salt and black pepper to taste   ½ tsp hot pepper sauce
1 carrot, chopped   2 tbsp vegetable oil

DIRECTIONS and total time: approx. 25 minutes

Heat olive oil on Sauté and brown beef for 3-4 minutes. Add in onion and carrot and sauté for 2 more minutes.

Stir in the remaining ingredients, and pour in 3 cups of water. Seal the lid and cook on Manual at High for 15 minutes. Once done, do a quick release. Serve warm.

Coconut Pumpkin Soup

INGREDIENTS for 4-6 servings

1 ½ lb pumpkin, cubed   4 tsp olive oil
1 carrot, chopped   2 garlic cloves, minced
5 cups vegetable broth   Salt and black pepper to taste
2 shallots, diced   ½ tsp cayenne pepper
1 cup coconut milk   2 tbsp chopped cilantro

DIRECTIONS and total time: approx. 25 minutes

Press Sauté and warm oil. Cook shallots until tender, about 3 minutes. Add pumpkin, carrot, garlic, salt, black pepper, and cayenne; sauté for 4 minutes. Pour in broth. Seal the lid, select Manual, and cook for 10 minutes at High. When ready, do a quick release. Add coconut milk and puree the soup using an immersion blender. Divide between bowls and top with cilantro.

Cabbage & Carrot Soup with Bacon

INGREDIENTS for 4 servings

2 cups cabbage, shredded   1 tsp cayenne pepper
1 red onion, sliced   1 tsp olive oil
1 cup carrot, chopped   Salt and black pepper to taste
2 potatoes, chopped   1 garlic clove, minced
4 oz bacon, chopped   4 cups vegetable broth

DIRECTIONS and total time: approx. 30 minutes

Heat olive oil on Sauté and cook bacon for 5 minutes until crispy; reserve. Add onion, carrot, and garlic to the pot and sauté for 3-4 minutes. Stir in cabbage and cayenne; cook for 5 minutes. Pour in broth and potatoes, seal the lid, press Manual, and cook for 10 minutes at High. Once ready, do a quick pressure release. Adjust seasoning and top with bacon to serve.

Smoked Turkey & Bean Soup

INGREDIENTS for 6 servings

1 (1.5-lb) piece smoked turkey leg, halved
2 tbsp olive oil   ½ lb white beans, soaked
1 celery stalk, chopped   2 tsp fresh oregano, chopped
1 onion, chopped   1 tsp cumin
1 bell pepper, chopped   6 cups vegetable broth

DIRECTIONS and total time: approx. 35 minutes

Heat olive oil on Sauté and cook onion, celery, and bell pepper for 3 minutes. Stir in cumin, beans, and broth. Add in turkey and seal the lid. Select Manual and cook for 25 minutes at High. When ready, do a quick pressure release. Transfer turkey to a plate; remove and discard the skin. Discard the bone, shred the meat, and return to pot; stir. Top with oregano and serve.

Mexican Chicken & Corn Chowder

INGREDIENTS for 4 servings

1 cup Mexican four-cheese blend, shredded
2 chicken breasts
2 cups canned corn
1 onion, diced
½ cup heavy cream
1 tbsp roasted green chile
4 cups chicken broth
1 garlic clove, minced
½ tsp cumin
A pinch of red pepper flakes
2 tbsp butter
2 tbsp chopped cilantro
1 lime, juiced

DIRECTIONS and total time: approx. 35 minutes

Melt butter on Sauté and fry chicken for 2 minutes per side; reserve. Add onion and garlic in the pot and sauté for 3 minutes. Stir in cumin, red pepper flakes, and roasted green chili for 1 minute. Pour in chicken broth and return the chicken. Seal the lid and cook on Manual for 15 minutes at High. When it beeps, do a quick pressure release. Remove chicken to a cutting board and shred it using two forks. Add back to the pot and stir in heavy cream, corn, and cheese. Press Sauté and cook for 2-3 minutes until the cheese melts. Top with cilantro and lime juice and serve hot.

Cheesy Tomato Soup

INGREDIENTS for 4 servings

3 lb tomatoes, peeled and diced
1 carrot, diced
1 onion, diced
1 cup heavy cream
1 tsp sugar
2 tbsp butter
Salt and black pepper to taste
2 cups chicken broth
½ cup Grana Padano, grated
1 garlic clove
2 tbsp basil, chopped
½ tsp cumin

DIRECTIONS and total time: approx. 20 minutes

Melt butter on Sauté and stir-fry onion, garlic, and carrot until soft, 3 minutes. Add in tomatoes, sugar, cumin, and chicken broth. Seal the lid, select Manual, and cook for 8 minutes at High. When it goes off, do a quick pressure release. Blitz with an immersion blender and stir in heavy cream; adjust the seasoning. Top with Grana Padano cheese and basil. Serve warm.

Nutmeg Chicken Gnocchi Soup

INGREDIENTS for 4 servings

½ lb chicken breasts, cubed
10 oz gnocchi
A pinch of nutmeg
1 onion, chopped
2 tbsp olive oil
1 cup diced carrots
4 cups chicken broth
1 cup diced celery
2 tbsp sage, chopped
1 tbsp butter
Salt and black pepper to taste
2 tbsp grated Parmesan

DIRECTIONS and total time: approx. 30 minutes

Heat olive oil on Sauté and stir-fry chicken, onion, garlic, celery, and carrot for 3 minutes. Add in nutmeg and chicken broth. Seal the lid and press Manual.

Cook for 15 minutes at High. After cooking, do a quick pressure release. Stir in gnocchi and butter and press Sauté. Cook for 3-4 minutes until gnocchi cooks through. Top with Parmesan cheese and sage to serve.

South American Chicken & Lentil Soup

INGREDIENTS for 4 servings

4 cups chicken stock
3 green onions, chopped
2 tbsp cilantro, chopped
3 cups spinach
1 cups frozen corn
½ lb chicken breasts, cubed
½ cup dry green lentils
Salt and black pepper to taste
2 tsp garlic powder
1 cup milk
½ tsp ground cumin
Crushed tortilla chips

DIRECTIONS and total time: approx. 30 minutes

Heat olive oil on Sauté and cook chicken and green onions for 4 minutes. Stir in cumin, garlic powder, corn, milk, and chicken broth. Seal the lid, select Manual at High, and cook for 15 minutes. When ready, do a quick release. Stir in spinach and press Sauté; cook for 4 minutes until wilted. Adjust seasoning and sprinkle with cilantro and crushed tortilla chips to serve.

Lentil Soup with Persillade Topping

INGREDIENTS for 4-6 servings

1 cup lentils, rinsed
½ tsp peppercorns, cracked
1 onion, chopped
1 carrot, diced
2 stalks celery, diced
6 cups vegetable broth
2 tbsp olive oil
1 tsp oregano, dried
Salt to taste
4 tsp red wine vinegar
4 garlic cloves, minced
1 cup parsley, chopped

DIRECTIONS and total time: approx. 25 minutes

Heat olive oil on Sauté and stir-fry carrot, celery, and onion for 3 minutes. Stir in oregano, peppercorns, lentils, and broth. Seal the lid, select Manual, and cook for 12 minutes at High. When ready, do a quick release. Adjust the seasoning. In a bowl, mix red wine vinegar, garlic, and parsley. Pour over the soup and serve hot.

Turmeric Chicken & Broccoli Soup

INGREDIENTS for 4 servings

1 broccoli head, chopped
½ lb chicken meatballs
½ tsp turmeric powder
1 sweet potato, diced
1 onion, diced
1 carrot, diced
Salt and black pepper to taste
1 tsp parsley
3 cups vegetable broth
2 tbsp olive oil

DIRECTIONS and total time: approx. 25 minutes

Warm olive oil on Sauté and stir-fry onion and carrot until tender, 3-4 minutes. Season with salt and pepper. Add the rest of the ingredients and stir to combine. Seal the lid, cook on Manual for 15 minutes at High. When ready, do a quick pressure release. Serve warm.

Vegetable Soup with Parsley Croutons

INGREDIENTS for 4 servings

2 pickled chili peppers, chopped
4 cups vegetable stock
1 onion, chopped
½ tsp ground cumin
2 tbsp parsley, chopped
1 cup parsnips, chopped

Salt and black pepper to taste
2 tbsp olive oil
1 cup carrots, chopped
½ cup fennel bulb, chopped
2 cubed bread slices

DIRECTIONS and total time: approx. 30 minutes

In a small bowl, mix olive oil with parsley and pour inside your Instant Pot; press Sauté to heat up. Add in the bread cubes and stir-fry for 3-4 minutes; reserve. Add fennel, parsnips, carrots, onion, and chili peppers to the pot and sauté for 5 minutes. Stir in the remaining ingredients. Seal the lid, press Manual, and cook for 15 minutes at High. Once ready, do a quick release. Ladle the soup into bowls and serve garnished with croutons.

Hearty Sausage Soup

INGREDIENTS for 6 servings

1 lb Italian sausages, chopped
2 tbsp olive oil
6 cups chicken broth
1 garlic clove, minced
1 tsp cumin

Salt and black pepper to taste
1 red bell pepper, chopped
3 cups kale, chopped
4 green onions, chopped
1 leek, chopped

DIRECTIONS and total time: approx. 25 minutes

Heat olive oil on Sauté and cook green onions, leek, garlic, and bell pepper for 3 minutes. Add in sausages; stir-fry for 5 minutes. Add in the rest of the ingredients, except for the kale; stir. Seal the lid, select Manual, and cook for 5 minutes at High. When done, perform a quick pressure release. Add in kale and cook for another 5 minutes on Sauté. Serve hot in soup bowls.

Spicy Haricot Vert & Potato Curry

INGREDIENTS for 4 servings

2 cups haricots verts
2 potatoes, chopped
1 bay leaf
1 onion, chopped
¼ tsp mustard seeds
2 tbsp olive oil
3 green chilies, chopped
½ tsp nutmeg

½ tsp coriander powder
3 tomatoes, chopped
2 tbsp cilantro, chopped
½ tsp cinnamon
½ tsp cardamom
½ tsp grated ginger
2 whole cloves
¼ tsp turmeric

DIRECTIONS and total time: approx. 20 minutes

In a blender, puree chilies, cloves, tomatoes, garlic, ginger, cardamom, and cinnamon. Heat oil on Sauté and stir-fry onion and blended mixture for 3 minutes. Add in the remaining ingredients and 2 cups water. Seal the lid, press Manual, and cook for 8 minutes at High. After cooking, do a quick pressure release. Serve.

Cheeseburger Soup

INGREDIENTS for 4 servings

2 russet potatoes, diced
2 tbsp butter
8 oz ground beef
4 cups chicken broth
1 tsp garlic powder
1 tsp parsley
1 tsp basil

1 shredded carrot
1 celery stalk, chopped
1 brown onion, diced
4 green onions, chopped
½ cup shredded cheddar
¼ cup sour cream
1 cup half-and-half

DIRECTIONS and total time: approx. 25 minutes

Melt butter on Sauté and brown beef for 5 minutes. Add in carrot, celery, and onion, and sauté for 3 minutes. Stir in parsley, garlic powder, basil, and potatoes and pour in chicken broth. Seal the lid, select Manual, and cook for 10 minutes at High. When done, release the pressure quickly. Stir in half-and-half and sour cream. Add in cheese and cook on Sauté until heated through. Serve topped with green onions.

Tradicional Indian Chicken Curry

INGREDIENTS for 4 servings

2 tbsp ghee
1 lb chicken breasts, cubed
2 garlic cloves, minced
1 white onion, chopped
1 cup tomatoes, chopped
½ tbsp ginger, grated
½ tsp garam masala

½ tbsp ground turmeric
½ tbsp ground cumin
½ tbsp cayenne pepper
½ tbsp ground coriander
¼ cup cilantro, chopped
½ tsp smoked paprika
1 cup coconut milk

DIRECTIONS and total time: approx. 40 minutes

Melt ghee on Sauté and brown chicken for 6 minutes, stirring occasionally; set aside. Add onion, garlic, tomatoes, and ginger to the pot and sauté for 3 minutes. Mix in all the spices and cook for 1-2 minutes. Pour in coconut milk and 1 cup of water, and return the chicken. Seal the lid, press Manual and cook for 15 minutes at High. When done, release the pressure naturally for 10 minutes. Press Sauté and cook the curry until it has thickened, about 3-4 minutes. Serve hot.

Pork & Canadian Bacon Soup

INGREDIENTS for 4 servings

4 cups chicken stock
2 tbsp olive oil
½ tsp thyme
1 celery stick, sliced
1 carrot, sliced
1 onion, chopped
1 clove garlic, minced

2 bay leaves
2 cups red potatoes, cubed
½ cup dry red wine
1 (14-oz) can tomato sauce
½ lb pork loin, cubed
6 oz Canadian bacon, diced
Salt and black pepper to taste

DIRECTIONS and total time: approx. 35 minutes

Heat olive oil on Sauté and cook onion, garlic, celery, carrot, bacon, and pork and cook for 4-5 minutes.

Pour in stock, tomato sauce, bay leaves, thyme, potatoes, and wine. Seal the lid, select Manual, and cook for 20 minutes at High. When ready, do a quick release. Discard bay leaves, adjust seasoning and serve.

Simple Pumpkin Soup

INGREDIENTS for 4 servings

2 tbsp olive oil	2 lb pumpkin, cubed
2 shallots, chopped	2 tbsp celery leaves, chopped
2 garlic cloves, minced	Salt and black pepper to taste
1 cup milk	½ tsp nutmeg
4 cups vegetable broth	

DIRECTIONS and total time: approx. 30 minutes

Heat olive oil on Sauté and sweet shallots and garlic for 4 minutes until softened. Stir in pumpkin for 4-5 minutes, and pour in vegetable broth and cumin. Seal the lid, select Manual, and cook for 10 minutes at High. When done, release the pressure naturally for 10 minutes. Add milk to the pot and puree the soup with an immersion blender until smooth. Top with chopped celery leaves and serve warm.

Red Lentil Soup

INGREDIENTS for 4 servings

½ cup red lentils	3 tsp ground cumin
4 cups vegetable stock	2 tsp olive oil
1 brown onion, chopped	2 garlic cloves, sliced
3 tbsp fresh cilantro	2 celery stalks, sliced
1-inch piece ginger, chopped	2 carrots, diced
½ cup plain Greek yogurt	Garlic naan bread for serving

DIRECTIONS and total time: approx. 20 minutes

Heat olive oil on Sauté and cook carrots, garlic, and onion for 3 minutes. Pour in cumin, lentils, and stock. Seal the lid, select Manual, and cook for 12 minutes at High. Do a quick release. Ladle soup into bowls and top with yogurt and cilantro. Serve with naan bread.

Red Cabbage & Beet Borscht

INGREDIENTS for 4 servings

2 tbsp olive oil	1 garlic clove, diced
3 cups red cabbage, shredded	4 cups vegetable stock
1 beet, diced	2 carrots, diced
2 tbsp dill, chopped	4 tbsp crème fraîche
1 onion, diced	Salt and black pepper to taste

DIRECTIONS and total time: approx. 40 minutes

Heat olive oil on Sauté and stir-fry onion, garlic, and carrots for 4 minutes. Add in red cabbage and sauté for another 4-5 minutes. Pour in vegetable stock and seal the lid. Select Manual and set to 20 minutes at High. When done, release the pressure quickly. Serve borscht with a drizzle of crème fraîche and dill.

Chorizo & Black Bean Stew with Potatoes

INGREDIENTS for 4 servings

1 lb chorizo sausages, sliced	3 potatoes, diced
2 olive oil	2 tbsp fresh parsley, chopped
1 cup pearl onions	2 tomatoes, chopped
1 cup black beans, soaked	3 cups vegetable stock
1 bunch broccoli rabe, chopped	1 tsp fennel seeds
2 carrots, diced	Salt and black pepper to taste

DIRECTIONS and total time: approx. 35 minutes

Heat olive oil on Sauté and brown chorizo for 3-4 minutes, stirring often. Add in pearl onions, carrots, and fennel seeds, and sauté for 3 minutes. Stir in the remaining ingredients, except for the broccoli rabe and parsley. Seal the lid, select Manual, and cook for 25 minutes at High. When ready, do a quick pressure release. Stir in broccoli rabe and cook for 2-3 minutes on Sauté; adjust the seasoning. Top with parsley and ladle in serving bowls to serve.

Spanish Pisto Manchego

INGREDIENTS for 4 servings

2 zucchini, chopped	2 garlic cloves, minced
1 green bell pepper, chopped	1 yellow onion, diced
1 eggplant, chopped	¼ cup olive oil
1 red bell pepper, chopped	Salt and black pepper to taste
1 (15-oz) can tomatoes, diced	4 eggs

DIRECTIONS and total time: approx. 45 minutes

Heat olive oil on Sauté and stir-fry onion, garlic, bell peppers, eggplant, and zucchini for 5-6 minutes. Pour in tomatoes and sauté for another 5-6 minutes; season with salt and pepper. Transfer the mixture to a baking dish and carefully crack the eggs on top; season. Pour 1 cup of water in the pot and insert a trivet. Place the dish on the trivet and seal the lid. Select Manual, and cook for 15 minutes at High. When ready, release the pressure naturally for 10 minutes. Serve hot.

Basil Lentil & Barley with Mushrooms

INGREDIENTS for 4 servings

2 cups fresh mushroom mix, chopped	
2 cups vegetable broth	½ cup lentils, rinsed
2 tbsp basil, chopped	½ cup pearl barley, rinsed
4 garlic cloves, minced	Salt and black pepper to taste
¼ cup dried onion flakes	½ grated white cheese

DIRECTIONS and total time: approx. 30 minutes

Heat olive oil on Sauté and cook garlic and mushrooms for 3-4 minutes. Stir in onion flakes and barley for 1 minute, and pour in vegetable broth and lentils. Seal the lid, select Manual, and cook for 15 minutes at High. When ready, release the pressure naturally for 10 minutes. Top with white cheese and basil to serve.

Beef & Portobello Stew

INGREDIENTS for 4 servings

½ lb Portobello mushrooms, sliced
2 tbsp canola oil
2 tbsp chopped parsley
1 onion, chopped
1 ½ lb beef, cut into pieces

4 potatoes, cut into chunks
2 carrots, cut into chunks
2 cups beef broth
Salt and black pepper to taste

DIRECTIONS and total time: approx. 30 minutes

Heat olive oil on Sauté and brown the beef for 2-3 minutes per side. Stir in the remaining ingredients, except for the parsley. Seal the lid, select Manual, and cook for 20 minutes at High. When it beeps, do a quick pressure release. Serve topped with parsley.

Harissa Potato & Spinach Stew

INGREDIENTS for 4 servings

6 potatoes, halved lengthwise
1 onion, chopped
½ lb spinach, chopped
¼ tsp chipotle powder
2 tsp Harissa paste

2 cups vegetable broth
2 tbsp olive oil
1 can (14-oz) diced tomatoes
2 garlic cloves, chopped
Salt and black pepper to taste

DIRECTIONS and total time: approx. 25 minutes

Heat olive oil on Sauté and stir-fry onion and garlic for 3 minutes until softened. Stir in the remaining ingredients, except for the spinach, and seal the lid. Cook on Manual for 12 minutes at High. Once ready, do a quick pressure release. Stir in spinach and cook for 3-4 minutes until wilted on Sauté. Serve warm.

Yummy Lamb Stew

INGREDIENTS for 4 servings

1 lb cubed lamb stew meat
1 onion, sliced
2 tbsp cornstarch
2 tbsp olive oil
2 yams, cut into cubes

3 carrots, chopped
2 ½ cups veggie broth
½ tsp sage
Salt and black pepper to taste
2 tbsp mint leaves, chopped

DIRECTIONS and total time: approx. 35 minutes

Season lamb with salt and pepper. Heat olive oil on Sauté and sear lamb for 5 minutes on all sides. Stir in the remaining ingredients, except for cornstarch and mint. Seal lid and cook on Manual for 20 minutes at High. When ready, do a quick release. Whisk cornstarch with some of the cooking liquid and stir in the pot on Sauté for 3 minutes. Top with mint and serve.

Chicken & Mushroom Stew with Spinach

INGREDIENTS for 4 servings

2 portobello mushrooms, sliced
4 chicken fillets
Black pepper and salt to taste

4 cups baby spinach, chopped
½ cup chives, chopped
4 tbsp olive oil

DIRECTIONS and total time: approx. 35 minutes

Heat olive oil on Sauté and brown the chicken for 5 minutes in total. Stir in vegetables and pour in 1 cup of water; season. Seal the lid, select Manual, and cook for 15 minutes at High. When ready, release the pressure naturally for 10 minutes. Serve garnished with chives.

Rosemary Beef Stew

INGREDIENTS for 4 servings

2 tbsp olive oil
3 cups beef stock
1 onion, chopped
1 lb potatoes
2 lb cubed stewing beef
2 carrots, chopped
1 (14-oz) diced tomatoes

1 celery stalk, chopped
2 garlic cloves, minced
2 bay leaves
1tsp Hungarian paprika
2 tbsp chopped rosemary
Salt and black pepper to taste
1 tbsp arrowroot powder

DIRECTIONS and total time: approx. 35 minutes

Heat olive oil on Sauté and brown the beef for 5-6 minutes, stirring occasionally; set aside. Add onion, carrots, celery, and garlic to the pot and sauté for 3 minutes. Stir in paprika and pour in tomatoes, beef broth, and bay leaves; return beef. Seal the lid, select Manual, and cook for 20 minutes at High. When ready, do a quick release. Discard bay leaves and adjust the seasoning. In a bowl, mix arrowroot powder with some cooking liquid and pour in the cooker on Sauté for 2-3 minutes until thickened. Top with rosemary and serve.

Mushroom Lentil Stew

INGREDIENTS for 4 servings

3 cups vegetable broth
1 cup lentils
1 cups mushrooms, sliced
2 tbsp olive oil
Salt and black pepper to taste
1 cup tomato juice

2 celery stalks, chopped
1 sweet onion, diced
4 carrots, sliced
½ tsp paprika
½ tsp oregano
4 garlic cloves, sliced

DIRECTIONS and total time: approx. 20 minutes

Heat olive oil on Sauté and stir-fry sweet onion, garlic, celery, carrots, and mushrooms for 5 minutes until tender. Stir in paprika and oregano. Pour in vegetable broth, tomato sauce, and lentils. Seal the lid, select Manual, and cook for 10 minutes at High. When ready, do a quick release. Adjust the seasoning and serve hot.

Rosemary Butternut Squash Stew

INGREDIENTS for 4 servings

1 cup button mushrooms, sliced
2 tbsp olive oil
2 cups collard greens
Salt and black pepper to taste
1 leek, chopped
1 tsp paprika

2 garlic cloves, minced
1 lb butternut squash, cubed
3 cups vegetable broth
3 tomatoes, chopped
½ tsp rosemary

DIRECTIONS and total time: approx. 30 minutes

Heat olive oil on Sauté and cook leek, mushrooms, and butternut squash for 5 minutes until softened. Stir in rosemary, paprika, and garlic for 1 minute. Pour in tomatoes and vegetable broth. Seal lid, select Manual, and cook for 8 minutes at High. When ready, release the pressure naturally for 10 minutes. Stir in collard greens, press Sauté, and cook for 2-3 minutes until wilted. Adjust the seasoning and serve hot.

Leftover Turkey Stew

INGREDIENTS for 4 servings

1 lb leftover roast turkey, shredded	
2 tbsp olive oil	½ tsp crushed chilies
1 onion, diced	2 cups diced canned tomatoes
2 garlic cloves, minced	2 baby carrots
3 cups chicken broth	2 potatoes, chopped
2 tbsp cilantro, chopped	1 cup black pitted olives

DIRECTIONS and total time: approx. 25 minutes

Heat olive oil on Sauté and cook onion, garlic, and carrots for 5 minutes. Pour in the remaining ingredients, except for cilantro, and seal the lid. Select Manual, and cook for 10 minutes at High. When ready, do a quick release. Sprinkle with cilantro and serve hot.

North African Chicken Stew

INGREDIENTS for 4 servings

3 cups chicken broth	2 onions, chopped
2 tomatoes, chopped	1 ½ tsp ras el hanout
Salt and black pepper to taste	1 tsp red chili flakes
1 lb cubed butternut squash	2 cloves garlic, minced
1 cup canned chickpeas	2 tbsp olive oil
2 lb chicken breasts, chopped	2 tbsp cilantro, chopped

DIRECTIONS and total time: approx. 40 minutes

Heat olive oil on Sauté and brown the chicken for 4-5 minutes, stirring occasionally; set aside. Add onions, butternut squash, and garlic to the pot and sauté for 5 minutes. Stir in ras el hanout, red chili flakes, tomatoes, chickpeas, and chicken broth; return the chicken. Seal the lid, select Manual, and cook for 20 minutes at High. Do a quick release. Serve hot sprinkled with cilantro.

Spicy Chicken & Mixed Vegetable Stew

INGREDIENTS for 4 servings

1 carrot, chopped	¼ tsp cayenne pepper
2 tbsp olive oil	1 (29-oz) can pumpkin puree
2 onions, diced	1 tbsp flour
2 russet potatoes, cubed	½ tsp oregano
2 cloves garlic, minced	1 lb baby spinach, chopped
1 celery stalk, chopped	2 cups cooked chicken, cubed
2 cups bone broth	Chopped chives for garnish
Salt and black pepper to taste	

DIRECTIONS and total time: approx. 25 minutes

Heat olive oil on Sauté. Add onions, carrots, celery, and garlic and cook for 5 minutes. Pour in the remaining ingredients and stir to combine. Seal the lid, select Manual, and cook for 12 minutes at High. Do a quick pressure release. Top with chopped chives and serve.

Turnip & Chickpea Stew

INGREDIENTS for 4 servings

2 cups vegetable broth	1 onion, diced
½ tsp red pepper flakes	16 oz canned chickpeas
2 garlic cloves, minced	1 cup baby spinach, chopped
14 oz canned tomatoes, chopped	½ tsp ground cumin
2 carrots, chopped	Salt and black pepper to taste
2 turnips, chopped	2 tbsp parsley, chopped

DIRECTIONS and total time: approx. 35 minutes

Heat olive oil on Sauté and add in onion, garlic, carrots, and turnips; stir-fry for 5 minutes. Pour in broth, chickpeas, and tomatoes. Season with salt, pepper, red pepper flakes, and cumin. Seal the lid, select Manual, and cook for 10 minutes at High. Once done, perform a quick pressure release. Add spinach. Cook for 3 minutes on Sauté. Top with parsley and serve.

Fall Bean Chili

INGREDIENTS for 4 servings

4 cups vegetable stock	1 onion, chopped
1 tsp red pepper flakes, crushed	2 tbsp cilantro
1 cup tomatoes, chopped	Salt and black pepper to taste
1 carrot, chopped	1 cup white beans, soaked
1 celery stick, chopped	1 cup potato, chopped
2 garlic cloves, minced	3 tbsp olive oil

DIRECTIONS and total time: approx. 30 minutes

Heat olive oil on Sauté and stir-fry garlic and onion for 3 minutes. Add in beans along with the remaining ingredients, except for the cilantro. Seal the lid, press Manual, and cook for 20 minutes at High. Once ready, do a quick pressure release. Garnish with cilantro.

Chickpea & Spinach Chili

INGREDIENTS for 4 servings

1 tbsp olive oil	1 cup chickpeas, soaked
1 onion, diced	4 cups chicken broth
28 oz canned tomatoes	2 cups spinach, chopped

DIRECTIONS and total time: approx. 45 minutes

Heat oil on Sauté and cook onion for 3 minutes. Pour in broth and chickpeas. Seal the lid, press Manual, and cook for 30 minutes at High. Once done, release the pressure quickly. Stir in spinach and cook for 5 minutes until wilted on Sauté. Serve hot.

Beef Stew with Carrots & Parsnips

INGREDIENTS for 4-6 servings

2 tbsp olive oil	2 tbsp tomato paste
2 lb cubed beef chuck roast	1 tbsp flour
1 lb parsnips, chopped	1 tsp smoked paprika
3 garlic cloves, minced	Salt and black pepper to taste
½ lb carrots, chopped	4 green onions chopped

DIRECTIONS and total time: approx. 45 minutes

Heat olive oil on Sauté and brown the beef for 4-5 minutes, stirring occasionally; set aside. Add green onions and garlic to the pot and sauté for 3 minutes. Stir in smoked paprika and flour for 1-2 minutes. Mix in tomato paste and 2 cups of water. Pour in carrots, parsnips, and return the beef; season. Seal the lid, select Manual, and cook for 20 minutes at High. When ready, do a natural pressure release for 10 minutes. Serve hot.

Lamb Shanks & Root Vegetable Stew

INGREDIENTS for 4 servings

4 lamb shanks	2 cloves garlic, minced
1 celery stalk, chopped	1 carrot, sliced
4 cups vegetable broth	1 lb potatoes, chopped
½ tsp coriander	1 rutabaga, chopped
½ tsp cayenne pepper	1 (15-oz) can tomatoes, diced
Salt and black pepper to taste	1 tbsp olive oil
2 onions, diced	2 tbsp mint leaves, chopped

DIRECTIONS and total time: approx. 29 minutes

Heat olive oil on Sauté and brown lamb all over for 4-5 minutes, turning once; reserve. Add onions, garlic, and spices to the pot and sauté for about 3-4 minutes. Add the remaining ingredients, except for the mint leaves, and return the lamb. Seal the lid, select Manual, and cook for 20 minutes at High. Do a quick release. Adjust the seasoning, top with mint leaves and serve.

Beef Stew with Bacon & Avocado

INGREDIENTS for 4 servings

2 strips bacon, chopped	1 jalapeño pepper, chopped
1 tbsp olive oil	14 oz canned diced tomatoes
2 avocados, cubed	2 lb ground beef
1 carrot, chopped	1 tsp cumin
1 celery stalk, chopped	2 cups beef broth
1 tsp chili powder	Salt and black pepper to taste
1 onion, diced	2 tbsp chopped oregano

DIRECTIONS and total time: approx. 45 minutes

Heat oil on Sauté and cook bacon for 5 minutes; set aside. Add carrot, celery, onion, jalapeño and beef and cook for 8 minutes. Stir in chili powder and cumin. Pour in tomatoes and broth. Seal the lid, select Manual, and cook for 20 minutes at High. Do a quick release. Adjust seasoning and add bacon. Top with avocado to serve.

Mediterranean Vegetable Stew

INGREDIENTS for 4 servings

1 (10-oz) package frozen okra, thawed	
10 pimiento-stuffed olives, chopped	
1 lb sweet potatoes, cubed	1 onion, chopped
½ tsp turmeric	1 cup canned tomato sauce
3 garlic cloves, minced	2 zucchinis, cubed
1/3 cup raisins	1 eggplant, sliced
2 cups vegetable broth	¼ tsp crushed red pepper
1 carrot, sliced	¼ tsp paprika
2 ripe tomatoes, chopped	Goat cheese for garnish

DIRECTIONS and total time: approx. 35 minutes

Heat olive oil on Sauté and stir-fry onion, zucchini, eggplant, garlic, and carrot for 5 minutes. Stir in turmeric, paprika, red pepper, and raisins for 2 minutes. Pour in the remaining ingredients, except for the cheese, and seal the lid. Select Manual and cook for 8 minutes at High. When ready, release the pressure naturally for 10 minutes. Top with goat cheese to serve.

Caribbean Black-Eyed Pea Stew

INGREDIENTS for 4 servings

1 chipotle in adobo sauce, diced	
2 tbsp olive oil	1 cup canned tomatoes
1 onion, diced	Salt and black pepper to taste
2 carrots, sliced	2 cups vegetable broth
1 celery stalk, diced	1 tsp chili powder
1 sweet potato, diced	1 tsp sage
1 green bell pepper, diced	1 tsp ground cumin
1 cup canned black-eyed peas	2 tbsp chopped cilantro

DIRECTIONS and total time: approx. 20 minutes

Heat olive oil on sauté and cook onion, carrots, celery, and bell pepper for 5 minutes. Pour in the remaining ingredients, except for the cilantro. Give it a good stir. Seal the lid, select Manual, and cook for 10 minutes at High. Do a quick pressure release. Adjust taste with salt and pepper. Top with cilantro and serve hot.

Ground Beef & Tomato Chili

INGREDIENTS for 4 servings

1 lb ground beef	½ tsp cumin
1 cup beef broth	1 tbsp chili powder
1 onion, diced	1 tsp garlic powder
2 tbsp olive oil	1 tsp tomato paste
3 cups tomatoes, chopped	Salt and black pepper to taste

DIRECTIONS and total time: approx. 50 minutes

Heat olive oil on Sauté and cook the beef for about 5 minutes. Add onion, cumin, chili, garlic, tomato paste, and cook for 4 more minutes. Stir in tomatoes and beef broth and season to taste. Seal the lid and cook on Manual for 30 minutes at High. Do a quick release.

Snacks & Appetizers

Jamón Serrano & Parmesan Egg Muffins

INGREDIENTS for 4 servings

8 slices Spanish jamón serrano
8 medium-sized eggs
4 slices Parmesan cheese
2 tbsp butter, softened
4 tbsp green onions, chopped

DIRECTIONS and total time: approx. 15 minutes

Pour 1 cup of water in inner pot and place in a trivet. Coat the bottom and sides of 4 ramekins with butter. Place 2 slices of jamón on each ramekin bottom and crack in two eggs. Sprinkle with green onions and top with a slice of Parmesan. Lower the ramekins onto the trivet and seal the lid. Select Manual and cook for 10 minutes at High. Do a quick pressure release. Serve.

Bacon & Cheese Eggs with Chives

INGREDIENTS for 4 servings

8 eggs
8 bacon slices
4 Parmesan cheese slices
4 tbsp chives, chopped
2 tbsp fresh parsley, chopped
2 tbsp butter, melted
Salt and black pepper to taste

DIRECTIONS and total time: approx. 25 minutes

Pour 1 cup of water in inner pot and lower a trivet. Coat 4 ramekins with butter. Break 2 eggs into each ramekin and top with chives. Cover with 2 bacon slices and top with a slice of Parmesan cheese. Sprinkle with parsley. Cover the ramekins with foil and place on the trivet. Seal the lid and cook on Manual for 10 minutes at High. Do a natural release for 10 minutes and serve.

Duck Legs with Serrano Pepper Sauce

INGREDIENTS for 4-6 servings

1 ½ lb duck legs
1 tbsp maple syrup
1 tbsp tomato puree
1 tsp basil
1 tbsp cumin
Salt and black pepper to taste
½ cup whipping cream
½ cup chopped parsley
¼ cup olive oil
2 tbsp lemon juice
2 serrano peppers, chopped
1 garlic clove

DIRECTIONS and total time: approx. 40 minutes

Pour 1 cup of water in inner pot and fit in a trivet. Arrange the duck on a greased baking pan. In a bowl, combine maple syrup, tomato puree, basil, cumin, salt, and pepper, and rub the mixture onto duck. Put the pan on top of the trivet and seal the lid. Cook on Manual for 20 minutes at High. When ready, do a natural release for 10 minutes. Pulse whipping cream, parsley, olive oil, lemon juice, serrano pepper, and garlic in a food processor until smooth. Serve the duck with the sauce.

Italian-Style Mushrooms with Sausage

INGREDIENTS for 4 servings

2 cups mushrooms
1 cup marinara sauce
¼ cup Parmesan, shredded
Salt and black pepper to taste
1 lb Italian sausages, sliced
1 clove garlic, finely diced
1 onion, diced
½ tbsp olive oil

DIRECTIONS and total time: approx. 35 minutes

Clean the mushrooms, then cut off stems. Set aside the caps on a paper towel to drain. Mince the stems in a bowl. Set the cooker to Sauté and heat olive oil. Add garlic, onion, and minced mushroom stems and cook for 5 minutes until softened; set aside. Add in sausages to brown for 3-4 minutes. Remove to a bowl and sprinkle with Parmesan cheese; mix well. Carefully spoon the sausage mixture into the mushroom caps. Pour marinara sauce into the pot and place mushrooms over. Add in 1 cup of water. Seal the lid, select Manual, and cook for 8 minutes at High. When done, release the pressure naturally for 10 minutes. Serve.

Mayonnaise & Bacon Stuffed Eggs

INGREDIENTS for 4 servings

8 eggs
2 oz bacon, chopped
Salt and black pepper to taste
1 tsp mayonnaise
¼ tsp oregano
Chopped chives for garnish

DIRECTIONS and total time: approx. 23 minutes

Place eggs in inner pot and cover with water. Seal the lid and press Manual. Cook for 8 minutes at High. After cooking, do a quick pressure release. Remove eggs and carefully put them in a bowl of ice water for 5 minutes. Discard the water from the pot and press Sauté. Fry the bacon for 5 minutes until crispy; set aside. Peel off the eggshells. Cut eggs in half and remove the yolks to a bowl. Add in mayonnaise, oregano, salt, pepper, and cooled bacon, and stir to combine. Fill the egg white with the mixture and top with chives. Serve.

Mushroom & Sesame Pâté

INGREDIENTS for 4 servings

1 lb cremini mushrooms, sliced
1 tbsp sesame paste
1 tbsp sesame seeds
1 tbsp lemon juice
1 garlic clove, minced
1 tsp cumin
3 tbsp olive oil
Salt and black pepper to taste

DIRECTIONS and total time: approx. 15 minutes

Heat olive oil on Sauté and cook garlic and mushrooms for 3 minutes. Pour in 1 cup of water and seal the lid. Cook on Manual for 4 minutes at High. Do a quick pressure release. Drain the mixture and transfer to a food processor. Add in lemon juice, cumin, olive oil, salt, pepper, and sesame paste. Process until smooth, and stir in the sesame seeds. Ready to serve.

Lemony Carrot Sticks with Nuts

INGREDIENTS for 4 servings

2 tbsp olive oil	1 tbsp orange juice
1 lb carrots, cut into sticks	1 tsp lemon juice
¼ cup chopped walnuts	½ tsp onion powder
½ tbsp balsamic vinegar	Salt and black pepper to taste

DIRECTIONS and total time: approx. 10 minutes

Combine 2 cups of water and carrots in your Instant Pot. Seal the lid, select Manual, and cook for 5 minutes at High. When it goes off, do a quick release. Drain the carrots and place on a serving plate. In a bowl, whisk together vinegar, orange juice, lemon juice, onion powder, and olive oil. Pour the mixture over the carrots and toss to coat well. Sprinkle with walnuts to serve.

Hot Buffalo Chicken Balls

INGREDIENTS for 4 servings

1 tbsp buffalo sauce	½ tsp paprika
1 lb ground chicken	Salt and black pepper to taste
1 onion, grated	½ tsp garlic powder
1 tbsp flour	1 egg

DIRECTIONS and total time: approx. 30 minutes

Beat the egg in a bowl and mix with ground chicken and garlic. Add flour, paprika, onion, salt, and pepper; mix to combine. Shape the mixture into balls. Add 1 cup of water to your Instant Pot and fit in a trivet. In a heat-proof bowl, place chicken balls on top of the trivet and sprinkle them with buffalo sauce. Seal the lid and press Manual. Cook for 20 minutes at High. After cooking, do a quick pressure release. Serve warm.

Herby Cipollini Onions

INGREDIENTS for 4-6 servings

1 ½ lb cipollini onions, peeled	2 bay leaves
2 tbsp lemon juice	1 tsp lemon zest
3 tbsp olive oil	2 tbsp fresh parsley
½ tsp rosemary, chopped	Salt and black pepper to taste

DIRECTIONS and total time: approx. 15 minutes

Combine 1 cup of water, onions, and bay leaves in your IP. Seal the lid, press Manual, and cook for 6 minutes at High. Do a quick release. Drain the onions and transfer to a cutting board to cut into quarters. Whisk together the remaining ingredients and pour over the onions.

Pumpkin Hummus

INGREDIENTS for 4-6 servings

2 lb pumpkin, chopped	½ tsp garlic powder
1 tbsp pumpkin seeds	3 tbsp olive oil
Salt to taste	2 tsp tahini sauce
½ tsp cayenne pepper	1 cup water

DIRECTIONS and total time: approx. 25 minutes

Pour water in inner pot and insert a trivet. Place the pumpkin in a greased baking pan. Put the pan on the trivet, seal the lid, and press Manual. Cook for 15 minutes at High. After cooking, do a quick pressure release. Let the pumpkin cool for a few minutes. Transfer to a food processor and add olive oil and tahini; blend until smooth. Mix in garlic, cayenne pepper, and salt. Serve topped with pumpkin seeds.

Party Egg Custard

INGREDIENTS for 4 servings

1 egg + 2 yolks	½ tsp rum extract
1 ½ cups milk	¾ cup sugar
2 cups whipping cream	1 tsp anise seeds

DIRECTIONS and total time: approx. 25 minutes

Beat eggs and yolks in a bowl. Beat in milk, rum, and whipping cream. Whisk in star anise and sugar. Divide the mixture between 4 ramekins. Pour 1 cup of water in your IP. Place the ramekins on top of the trivet. Seal the lid and cook on Manual for 10 minutes at High. Allow a natural pressure release for 10 minutes. Serve.

Smoked Paprika Potato Chips

INGREDIENTS for 4 servings

4 russet potatoes, sliced	Salt and black pepper to taste
1 tsp smoked paprika	2 tbsp olive oil

DIRECTIONS and total time: approx. 20 minutes

Place the potatoes in your Instant Pot and pour enough water to cover them. Seal the lid, select Manual, and cook for 10 minutes at High. When done, release the pressure quickly. Drain potatoes and discard water. Wipe the pot clean. Heat olive oil on Sauté and sprinkle potatoes with paprika, salt, and pepper; toss to combine. Fry potatoes for 1 minute per side. Serve.

Cheese Fondue

INGREDIENTS for 4-6 servings

1 cup Swiss cheese, shredded	1/3 cup white wine
1 tsp cayenne pepper	4 oz cream cheese
1 garlic clove, minced	½ tbsp flour

DIRECTIONS and total time: approx. 15 minutes

In a glass pan, mix Swiss cheese and flour. Add in cream cheese and mix well. Stir in wine and garlic, and cover with aluminium foil. Pour 1 cup of water in inner pot and fit in a trivet. Place the pan on the trivet. Seal the lid and press Manual. Cook for 5 minutes at High. After cooking, do a quick pressure release. Season with cayenne pepper. When the fondue begins to thicken, merely add more wine and stir. Serve.

Best Bacon Wrapped Mini Smokies

INGREDIENTS for 4-6 servings

1 lb bacon slices	2 tbsp vinegar
1 lb mini smokie sausages	1 tbsp brown sugar

DIRECTIONS and total time: approx. 35 minutes

Cut the bacon slices in half. Wrap a slice of bacon around each sausage. Put the seam side facing down in a greased baking dish. In a bowl, mix vinegar and sugar. Drizzle this mixture over smokies in the dish. Place in the fridge for 10 minutes. Pour 1 cup of water into the IP and fit in a trivet. Remove the smokies from the refrigerator and place the dish on the trivet. Seal the lid, press Manual, and cook for 20 minutes at High. After cooking, do a quick release. Serve warm.

Bacon Asparagus Wraps

INGREDIENTS for 4 servings

1 lb asparagus, trimmed	Salt and black pepper to taste
3 oz bacon slices	

DIRECTIONS and total time: approx. 15 minutes

Pour 1 cup of water in your IP and insert a trivet. Season the asparagus with salt and pepper, then wrap in bacon slices. Place wraps on the trivet and seal the lid. Press Manual and cook for 4 minutes at High. After cooking, do a quick pressure release. Serve warm.

Hot Chicken Dip

INGREDIENTS for 4 servings

2 chicken breasts, cubed	1 cup ranch dressing
5 oz hot sauce	16 oz cream cheese
2 tbsp olive oil	Salt to taste

DIRECTIONS and total time: approx. 20 minutes

Add chicken, hot sauce, salt, and 1 cup of water in your Instant Pot. Drizzle with the olive oil. Seal the lid, press Manual, and cook for 15 minutes at High. After cooking, do a quick pressure release. Remove and blend the chicken in a food processor. Mix in ranch dressing and cream cheese until creamy. Serve.

Cauliflower Popcorn

INGREDIENTS for 4 servings

1 head cauliflower, cut into florets	
2 tbsp olive oil	Salt and black pepper to taste

DIRECTIONS and total time: approx. 15 minutes

Sprinkle florets with salt, pepper, and oil. Add 1 cup water in your IP and place a trivet. Put florets in a greased baking pan and place on top of the trivet. Seal the lid, press Manual and set to 5 minutes at High. When ready, do a quick pressure release. Serve.

Party Mix

INGREDIENTS for 4-6 servings

2 ½ cups assorted cereals	1/8 cup butter, melted
¼ tsp garlic powder	¾ cup mixed nuts
½ tsp onion powder	¾ cup sesame sticks
½ tsp hot pepper sauce	¾ cup small pretzels
2 tbsp Worcestershire sauce	Salt and black pepper to taste

DIRECTIONS and total time: approx. 20 minutes

In a bowl, combine butter, hot sauce, Worcestershire sauce, garlic powder and onion powder. Add in cereals, sesame sticks, pretzels, and mixed nuts. Pour into a greased baking dish. Insert a trivet in your IP and add 1 cup of water. Put the dish on the trivet. Seal the lid, select Manual, and cook for 5 minutes at High. When done, do a natural pressure release for 10 minutes.

Hard-Boiled Eggs

INGREDIENTS for 2 servings

4 eggs	Salt and paprika to taste

DIRECTIONS and total time: approx. 20 minutes

Cover eggs with enough water inside the pot. Seal the lid, press Manual and cook at High for 6 minutes. After cooking, do a quick pressure release. Remove the eggs and place them in a bowl with chilled water, for 5 minutes. After, peel off the shells and cut in half. Sprinkle with paprika and salt and serve.

Cheesy Potato Hash Brown

INGREDIENTS for 4 servings

1 lb potatoes, grated	Salt and black pepper to taste
1 tsp chili powder	2 tbsp olive oil
¼ tsp smoked paprika	2 cups cheddar, shredded

DIRECTIONS and total time: approx. 20 minutes

Heat olive oil on Sauté and add potatoes and cheddar cheese. Season with spices and stir to combine. Press them with a spatula and cook for 8-12 minutes. Flip over once. Divide between 4 plates and serve.

Jalapeño Chicken Dip

INGREDIENTS for 4 servings

2 jalapeno peppers, diced	16 oz cream cheese
10 oz green chilies, diced	1 cup cooked chicken, chopped
2 cups chicken broth	Salt and black pepper to taste

DIRECTIONS and total time: approx. 10 minutes

Place all ingredients in your IP, except for cream cheese; stir to combine. Seal the lid, press Manual, and cook for 5 minutes at High. After cooking, do a quick pressure release. Blend with an immersion blender. Stir in cream cheese and adjust the seasoning. Serve.

Spinach Dip

INGREDIENTS for 4 servings

2 cups spinach, chopped
1 garlic clove, minced
1/3 cup milk
1 oz cooked bacon, chopped
1/3 white onion, chopped
½ cup of water

DIRECTIONS and total time: approx. 15 minutes

Add spinach, garlic, onion, bacon, milk, and water to your IP. Seal the lid and press Manual. Cook at High for 4 minutes. Do a quick pressure release. Transfer to a food processor and pulse until smooth. Serve.

Crispy Sweet Potato Sticks

INGREDIENTS for 4 servings

4 sweet potatoes, cut into sticks
1 cup olive oil
Salt and black pepper to taste
1 cup flour
½ tsp paprika
2 tbsp rosemary, chopped

DIRECTIONS and total time: approx. 20 minutes

Combine flour with paprika, salt, and pepper in a bowl. Coat the potato sticks in the flour. Press Sauté on your IP and add the olive oil to heat. Fry the potatoes for 6-7 minutes on all sides. Sprinkle with rosemary to serve.

Reuben Dip

INGREDIENTS for 4-6 servings

1/8 cup Thousand Island dressing
1 tsp caraway seeds, crushed
6 oz cream cheese
½ cup Swiss cheese, grated
¾ cup sauerkraut, drained
½ cup corn beef, chopped
Salt and black pepper to taste

DIRECTIONS and total time: approx. 30 minutes

In a greased baking dish, combine all ingredients. Pour 1 cup of water in inner pot and insert a trivet. Put the dish on the trivet. Seal the lid, select Manual, and cook for 15 minutes at High. When done, release the pressure naturally for 10 minutes. Serve.

Cannellini Bean & Chili Salad

INGREDIENTS for 6 servings

4 oz cream cheese
1 shallot, sliced
½ tsp red pepper sauce
1 tsp crushed red pepper
1 garlic clove, minced
2 oz diced green chilies
1 cup Cannellini beans, soaked
¼ cup Parmesan, grated
2 tbsp olive oil
2 tbsp parsley, chopped

DIRECTIONS and total time: approx. 40 minutes

Put the beans and 3 cups of water in inner pot. Seal the lid, press Manual, and cook for 30 minutes at High. After cooking, do a quick pressure release. Drain and place in a bowl. Add in the remaining ingredients, except for Parmesan cheese; mix to combine. Serve topped with Parmesan cheese and fresh parsley.

Buffalo Chicken Wings with Cheese Dip

INGREDIENTS for 4 servings

1 ½ lb chicken wings
Salt and black pepper to taste
½ tbsp white vinegar
2 tbsp butter
2 tbsp hot pepper sauce
1 cup chicken broth

Blue Cheese Dip:
¾ tbsp red wine vinegar
½ tsp celery seeds
Dash of cayenne pepper
Salt and black pepper to taste
1/3 cup mayonnaise
2 tbsp blue cheese, crumbled

DIRECTIONS and total time: approx. 30 minutes

In inner pot, mix butter, vinegar, and hot pepper sauce. Press Sauté and cook for 2 minutes. Season chicken wings with pepper and salt. Add to the pot and cook for 4 minutes per side. Pour in chicken broth, seal the lid and press Manual. Cook for 20 minutes at High. After cooking, do a quick pressure release. Combine the blue cheese dip ingredients in a bowl. Once the wings are cooked, serve with the dip and enjoy!

Eggplant Caviar

INGREDIENTS for 4-6 servings

2 large eggplants
Salt and black pepper to taste
2 tbsp lemon juice
1 tsp oregano
4 tbsp olive oil
6 garlic cloves, minced
½ cup yogurt
½ cup onion, finely chopped
1 cup tomato, finely chopped
1 cup water

DIRECTIONS and total time: approx. 20 minutes

Pour water in inner pot and insert a trivet. Use a fork to poke the eggplants all over, then place on the trivet. Seal the lid, select Manual and cook for 6 minutes at High. When ready, do a quick pressure release. Slice the eggplants in half and spoon out the pulp into a bowl. Mash the pulp and combine it with onion, yogurt, tomato, garlic, olive oil, and oregano. Mix well. Season with lemon juice, pepper, and salt. Serve.

Celery & Chicken Casserole

INGREDIENTS for 4 servings

1 lb chicken breasts
13 oz crackers
1 celery stalk, chopped
2 cups cheddar, shredded
¾ cup tabasco pepper sauce
1 cup ranch dressing
16 oz mascarpone cheese
2 tbsp olive oil

DIRECTIONS and total time: approx. 25 minutes

Heat olive oil on Sauté and cook the chicken for 2-3 minutes per side. Remove to a baking dish. Add tabasco sauce, ranch dressing, and mascarpone cheese to the pot and mix well. Stir in the shredded cheese. Pour 1 cup of water in the pot and insert a trivet. Lay the dish on the trivet. Seal the lid, select Manual, and cook for 8 minutes at High. When ready, do a natural release for 10 minutes. Serve garnished with celery.

Cheesy Hamburger Tortillas

INGREDIENTS for 4 servings

1 lb ground beef	1 cup Velveeta cheese, cubed
1 onion, finely chopped	16 oz chunky salsa
4 tortilla chips	2 tbsp olive oil

DIRECTIONS and total time: approx. 40 minutes

Heat olive oil on Sauté and brown the beef for 5-6 minutes. Add in onion and cook for 3 more minutes, stirring often. Add in salsa, 1 cup of water, and cheese cubes and stir. Seal the lid, press Manual, and cook for 20 minutes at High. After cooking, do a quick pressure release. Serve with tortilla chips.

Garlic Buttered Almonds

INGREDIENTS for 4-6 servings

3 cups whole almonds	2 tbsp butter
2 cloves garlic, minced	½ tsp black pepper

DIRECTIONS and total time: approx. 10 minutes

Melt butter on Sauté, add almonds and toss to coat. Stir in garlic and pepper, and cook for another 5 minutes. Set aside and allow cooling before serving.

Sausage & Cream Cheese Dip

INGREDIENTS for 6 servings

1 can (14.5-oz) tomatoes with chilies	
1 lb bulk sausages	2 tbsp olive oil
8 oz cream cheese	2 tbsp parsley

DIRECTIONS and total time: approx. 25 minutes

Heat olive oil on Sauté and brown the sausages for 5-6 minutes. Stir in the tomatoes and cream cheese. Add in 1 cup of water. Seal the lid, press Manual, and cook for 10 minutes at High. After cooking, do a quick pressure release. Top with parsley and serve with crackers.

Rolled Chicken with Asparagus & Prosciutto

INGREDIENTS for 4 servings

8 slices Prosciutto	Salt and black pepper to taste
4 chicken breasts, halved	1 bunch asparagus, trimmed
2 garlic cloves, minced	Parsley, chopped for garnish

DIRECTIONS and total time: approx. 30 minutes

Use a mallet to flatten the chicken slices. Rub them with garlic, salt, and pepper. Take 3 pieces of asparagus and roll the chicken around it. Roll Prosciutto around the chicken and use toothpicks to secure in place. Repeat the process with the rest of the ingredients. Pour 1 cup of water in the pot and insert a trivet. Place the rolls on the trivet, seal the lid, select Manual and cook for 15 minutes at High. When ready, release the pressure naturally for 10 minutes. Serve warm.

Sticky Sweet Chicken Wings

INGREDIENTS for 4-6 servings

2 pounds chicken wings	2 tbsp balsamic vinegar
Salt and black pepper to taste	1/3 cup soy sauce
3 garlic cloves, minced	1 tsp Sriracha sauce
1 tbsp fresh lime juice	1 tsp ground coriander
¼ cup chicken broth	1 tbsp potato starch
¼ cup raw honey	2 tbsp chopped cilantro

DIRECTIONS and total time: approx. 30 minutes

Season the chicken wings with salt and black pepper and place inside the pot. In a bowl, combine honey, broth, vinegar, soy sauce, garlic, lime juice, coriander, and sriracha sauce, and mix well. Pour mixture over the wings and toss to coat. Seal the lid, select Manual, and cook for 20 minutes at High. When doner, perform a natural release for 10 minutes and remove chicken wings to a plate. Whisk potato starch with 2 tbsp of cold water and stir in the pot. Cook for 2-3 minutes on Sauté. Pour over wings and serve topped with cilantro.

Spicy-Sweet Meatballs

INGREDIENTS for 4 servings

1 lb ground beef	½ tsp Worcestershire sauce
4 tbsp olive oil	Salt and black pepper to taste
½ cup breadcrumbs	2 tbsp parsley, chopped
½ tbsp brown sugar	1 egg
¼ cup honey	¼ cup milk
1 cup chili sauce	1 onion, chopped

DIRECTIONS and total time: approx. 20 minutes

In a bowl, mix beef, onion, milk, egg, parsley, salt, pepper, Worcestershire sauce, and breadcrumbs. Shape into balls. Set the pot to Sauté and brown meatballs for 10 minutes; set aside. To the pot, add sugar, chili sauce, and honey, and stir frequently until melted. Return the meatballs and mix to coat. Pour in ½ cup of water, seal the lid, select Manual, and cook for 4 minutes at High. When done, quick-release the pressure.

Beef Ribs Texas BBQ Style

INGREDIENTS for 4 servings

2 lb beef ribs, cut into 2-bone pieces	
1 cup BBQ sauce	2 tbsp olive oil
2 tbsp Ancho chili powder	½ yellow onion, diced
½ tbsp garlic powder	Salt and black pepper to taste

DIRECTIONS and total time: approx. 55 minutes

Heat olive oil on Sauté. Rub the beef with salt, pepper, garlic, and chili powder and brown on all sides for 5-6 minutes; reserve. Add onion to the pot and sweat for 3 minutes. Return the beef, pour in BBQ sauce, and ½ cup water. Seal the lid, select Manual, and cook for 30 minutes at High. Release the pressure quickly. Serve.

Sticky BBQ Chicken Drumsticks

INGREDIENTS for 4 servings

1 lb chicken drumsticks	1 tbsp maple syrup
2 garlic cloves, minced	1 tbsp chili sauce
Salt and black pepper to taste	1 cup barbecue sauce

DIRECTIONS and total time: approx. 25 minutes

Arrange the drumsticks on the bottom of inner pot. Add chili sauce, barbecue sauce, maple syrup, garlic, salt, and pepper in a bowl; mix well. Pour the mixture over the drumsticks inside the pot. Add in ½ cup of water, seal the lid, press Manual and set to 15 minutes at High. When ready, do a quick pressure release. Serve.

Teriyaki Chicken in Lettuce Wrap

INGREDIENTS for 6 servings

2 tbsp olive oil	½ cup coconut milk
½ tbsp ground ginger	½ cup honey
3 garlic cloves, minced	1 onion, chopped
4 chicken breasts, cubed	1 ¼ cups water
¼ tbsp red wine vinegar	6 lettuce leaves
1 tbsp arrowroot powder	Shredded cheddar for garnish

DIRECTIONS and total time: approx. 40 minutes

Heat olive oil on Sauté and cook chicken, ginger, garlic, and onion for 5-6 minutes, stirring often. Pour in red wine to deglaze and add in coconut milk, honey, and water. Seal the lid, select Manual, and cook for 15 minutes at High. When ready, release the pressure naturally for 10 minutes. Remove the chicken to a plate. In a bowl, mix arrowroot with some of the cooking liquid, pour in the pot and cook for 3 minutes on Sauté. Add chicken back to pot and stir. Serve on lettuce leaves topped with cheddar cheese.

Pizza Marguerite with Cauliflower Crust

INGREDIENTS for 4 servings

1 egg	2 tbsp flour
1 ½ cups cauli rice	½ tsp garlic powder
1 cup mozzarella, shredded	½ tsp sea salt
2 tomatoes, sliced	2 tbsp basil, chopped

DIRECTIONS and total time: approx. 30 minutes

Line a baking dish with parchment paper. Pour 1 cup of water in your IP and insert a trivet. Add egg, cauli rice, flour, garlic powder and salt in a bowl, and mix until pizza dough is formed. Spread the dough on the baking dish and put on the trivet. Seal the lid, press Manual, and cook for 10 minutes at High. After cooking, do a quick release. Sprinkle mozzarella cheese over the crust and top with tomato slices. Seal the lid again, press Manual, and cook for 5 minutes at High. After cooking, do a quick release. Serve topped with basil.

Orange Tofu & Broccoli Cups

INGREDIENTS for 6 servings

14 oz firm tofu, cubed	12 lettuce leaves
2 tbsp sweet chili sauce	1 chili pepper, minced
10 oz broccoli florets	1 cup chicken broth
2 tbsp sesame oil	2 tbsp chopped scallions
1 tsp ginger paste	1 tsp orange zest

DIRECTIONS and total time: approx. 15 minutes

Heat sesame oil on Sauté and stir-fry tofu, chili pepper, and ginger for 3-4 minutes. Add in sweet chili sauce, broccoli, and broth, and give it a stir. Transfer to a baking dish. Pour 1 cup of water in the pot and insert a trivet. Lower the dish on the trivet. Seal the lid and cook on Manual for 3 minutes at High. When ready, do a quick release. Divide the mixture between lettuce leaves, sprinkle with orange zest and scallions to serve.

Cheesy Sausage with Potatoes

INGREDIENTS for 4 servings

1 lb smoked chicken sausages, sliced	
1 lb russet potatoes, diced	1 (10.75-oz) can chicken soup
1 green bell pepper, diced	2 tbsp olive oil
1 red bell pepper, diced	½ cup sour cream
2 tbsp parsley, chopped	1 ½ cups cheddar, shredded
Salt and black pepper to taste	1 onion, diced

DIRECTIONS and total time: approx. 25 minutes

Heat olive oil on Sauté and cook onion, bell peppers, and sausages for 4-5 minutes. Add in potatoes, parsley, chicken soup, sour cream, and ½ cup of water. Stir and season with salt and pepper. Transfer to a baking dish and sprinkle with cheddar cheese. Pour 1 cup of water in the pot and fit in a trivet. Lower the dish on the trivet. Seal the lid and cook on Manual for 10 minutes at High. When ready, do a quick release. Serve hot.

Dijon Deviled Eggs

INGREDIENTS for 4 servings

4 eggs	1 tbsp balsamic vinegar
1 tsp chili pepper	Salt and black pepper to taste
1 tbsp mayonnaise	2 tbsp chopped parsley
1 tsp Dijon mustard	2-3 lettuce leaves

DIRECTIONS and total time: approx. 20 minutes

Add a trivet and pour 1 cup water in your IP. Place the eggs on the trivet. Seal the lid and cook on Manual for 8 minutes at High. Do a quick pressure release. Remove eggs to an ice bath and let cool. Peel and cut them in half. Remove yolks to a dish and mash with a fork; add the remaining ingredients, excluding the parsley and lettuce, and give it a stir. Fill the egg halves with the yolk mixture. Put the lettuce on a serving platter and arrange the stuffed eggs on top. Sprinkle with parsley.

Colby Asparagus with Anchovy Dressing

INGREDIENTS for 4-6 servings

5 sun-dried tomatoes in oil, chopped
12 oz asparagus, trimmed
½ cup frozen green peas
5 anchovy fillets in oil
2 tbsp oil from anchovies

2 tbsp oil from tomatoes
2 tbsp lemon juice
1 cup grated Colby cheese
Salt and black pepper to taste

DIRECTIONS and total time: approx. 20 minutes

Insert a trivet in your IP and pour 1 cup water. Place asparagus on the trivet. Seal the lid and cook on Manual for 3 minutes at High. Do a quick pressure release. Remove asparagus and trivet. Pour green peas in the water inside the pot and let them sit for 5 minutes; drain and set aside. Blitz in a blender anchovy fillets, sun-dried tomatoes, lemon juice, anchovy oil and tomato oil until a dressing texture is formed; adjust the seasoning. Arrange asparagus on a platter and scatter the green peas over. Season with salt and pepper. Drizzle with the dressing and top with Colby cheese.

Yummy Smoked Sausage Bites

INGREDIENTS for 4 servings

2 tbsp olive oil
1 lb smoked sausage, sliced
½ cup brown sugar

1 onion, diced
½ cup ketchup
2 tbsp parsley, chopped

DIRECTIONS and total time: approx. 25 minutes

Heat olive oil on Sauté and sweat onion for 4 minutes. Add in sausages and brown for 6 minutes, stirring often. In a bowl, mix together ketchup, sugar, and 1 cup of water, and pour over the sausages; stir to coat. Seal the lid, press Manual, and cook for 3 minutes at High. After cooking, do a quick pressure release. Remove the sausage and press Sauté; cook the sauce until thickened, about 3-4 minutes. Pour the sauce over sausages and top with parsley to serve.

Thyme Tomato Dip Sauce

INGREDIENTS for 4-6 servings

2 lb tomatoes, peeled and diced
1 cup green onions, chopped
¼ cup olive oil
1 tsp brown sugar
½ tsp basil

1 green chili, chopped
½ tsp dried oregano
2 cloves garlic, minced
½ tsp thyme
Salt and black pepper to taste

DIRECTIONS and total time: approx. 30 minutes

Select Sauté and heat the oil. Cook the green onions and garlic until tender, for about 3 minutes. Add the remaining ingredients and ½ cup of water. Seal the lid, select Manual, and cook for 10 minutes at High. When ready, do a quick pressure release. Select Sauté and cook for 10 minutes until thickened. Blitz with an immersion blender in the pot. Let cool before serving.

Potato Balls with Walnut-Yogurt Sauce

INGREDIENTS for 4 servings

4 tbsp olive oil
1 leek, sliced
1 lb potatoes, chopped
½ cup flour
¼ tsp onion powder
¼ tsp paprika

½ cup natural yogurt
1 garlic clove, minced
2 tbsp ground walnuts
1 tsp chopped dill
¼ tsp garlic powder
Salt and black pepper to taste

DIRECTIONS and total time: approx. 30 minutes

Place the potatoes inside your IP and cover them with salted water. Seal the lid and cook on Manual for 12 minutes at High. Do a quick release. Drain and mash with a potato mash. Add in leek, flour, onion and garlic powders; season with salt and pepper. Stir until well combined. Shape the mixture into small patties. Heat 3 tbsp of olive oil on Sauté and brown the patties for 6-8 minutes on all sides. Whisk together yogurt, remaining olive oil, dill, minced garlic, and walnuts until well mixed. Drizzle potato balls with the sauce and serve.

Camembert Root Vegetable Mix

INGREDIENTS for 4 servings

2 oz Camembert cheese, cubed
3 mixed bell peppers, diced
½ fennel bulb, sliced
3 carrots, julienned
1 parsnip, julienned
1 daikon, julienned
1 orange, sliced

1 garlic clove, minced
2 tbsp hazelnuts, chopped
1 cup pearl onions
½ cup vegetable broth
2 tbsp olive oil
Salt and black pepper to taste

DIRECTIONS and total time: approx. 25 minutes

Mix all ingredients, except for the cheese and orange, in a baking dish and toss to coat. Pour 1 cup of water in your IP and insert a trivet. Place the dish on the trivet. Seal the lid, press Manual, and cook for 10 minutes at High. After cooking, do a quick pressure release. Arrange the cheese cubes and orange slices on top of the vegetable mixture and place under the broiler for 4 minutes on high until the cheese melts. Serve warm.

Potato & Parsnip Mix

INGREDIENTS for 4 servings

4 potatoes, chopped
2 parsnips, chopped
2 purple onions, chopped
2 cups vegetable broth

1 carrot, chopped
Salt and black pepper to taste
1 tsp oregano
2 tbsp olive oil

DIRECTIONS and total time: approx. 25 minutes

Heat olive oil on Sauté and cook onions and carrot for 3-4 minutes. Add in the remaining ingredients and stir to combine. Seal the lid, select Manual at High and cook for 12 minutes. When done, release the pressure naturally for 10 minutes. Serve hot.

Mashed Garlic Cauliflower Dish

INGREDIENTS for 4 servings

1 head cauliflower, chopped	2 tbsp butter
Salt and black pepper to taste	¼ cup sour cream
1 tbsp parsley, chopped	6 garlic cloves, minced

DIRECTIONS and total time: approx. 15 minutes

Add all the ingredients, except for sour cream, in your IP and stir to combine. Pour in 2 cups of water. Seal the lid, select Manual, and set to 3 minutes at High. When done, release the pressure quickly. Blend in a food processor along with sour cream until smooth. Serve.

Pineapple & Soda-Glazed Ham

INGREDIENTS for 6 servings

1 (15 ¼-oz) can pineapple rings with juice
2.5 lb pork picnic ham   1 can cola-flavored soda

DIRECTIONS and total time: approx. 33 minutes

Add the ham to inner pot with the fattier side facing downwards. Place the pineapple rings over the ham, attach them with toothpicks. Pour soda and pineapple juice all over the ham. Seal the lid, select Manual, and cook for 8 minutes at High. When ready, release the pressure naturally for 5 minutes. Serve hot.

Cheese Sweet Corn

INGREDIENTS for 4-6 servings

Juice of 2 limes	6 tbsp yogurt
1 cup Grana Padano, grated	½ tsp garlic powder
6 ears sweet corn	Salt and black pepper to taste

DIRECTIONS and total time: approx. 10 minutes

Pour in 1 cup of water and add a trivet. Put the corn on top. Seal the lid, and cook on Steam for 3 minutes at High. Combine the remaining ingredients, except for the cheese, in a bowl. Once ready, do a quick pressure release. Let cool for a couple of minutes. Remove husks from the corn and brush them with the mixture. Sprinkle Grana Padano cheese on top and serve.

Garlicky Potato & Rutabaga Mash

INGREDIENTS for 4 servings

3 tbsp butter	1 rutabaga, chopped
3 garlic cloves, minced	1 lb potatoes, chopped
2 tbsp chopped chives	½ cup milk

DIRECTIONS and total time: approx. 20 min

Pour 1 cup of water in inner pot and add in potatoes and rutabaga. Seal the lid, and cook on Manual for 12 minutes at High. When ready, do a quick pressure release. Transfer to a bowl and mash them with potato mash. Stir in butter and milk. Serve topped with chives.

Zesty Carrots with Pistachios

INGREDIENTS for 4 servings

1 lb carrots, cut into rounds	¼ cup raisins
½ cup pistachios, chopped	Salt and black pepper to taste
2 tbsp butter	1 tbsp vinegar

DIRECTIONS and total time: approx. 15 minutes

Select Sauté and melt the butter. Add in carrots and cook for 5 minutes until tender. Add raisins, ½ cup of water, and salt. Seal the lid, press Manual, and cook for 3 minutes at High. When ready, do a quick pressure release. Pour in vinegar and black pepper, and give it a good stir. Scatter the pistachios over the top and serve.

Zucchini & Potato Patties

INGREDIENTS for 4 servings

¼ cup coconut flakes	½ tsp ground cumin
¼ cup flour	2 tbsp chopped parsley
1 lb potatoes, chopped	Salt and black pepper to taste
1 large zucchini, shredded	2 tbsp olive oil

DIRECTIONS and total time: approx. 30 minutes

Cover potatoes salted water in your IP. Seal the lid and cook on Manual for 12 minutes at High. Do a quick release. Drain and mash with a potato mash. Add in the remaining ingredients, except for olive oil, and mix with hands until fully incorporated. Shape the mixture into patties. Press Sauté and heat olive oil. Cook the patties for 3 minutes per side until browned. Serve.

Swiss Chard Crisps with Orange Juice

INGREDIENTS for 4 servings

1 lb Swiss chard, stems removed
Salt and black pepper to taste   2 tbsp olive oil
2 garlic cloves, minced   2 tbsp orange juice

DIRECTIONS and total time: approx. 10 minutes

Heat olive oil on Sauté and cook garlic for 1 minute. Add in Swiss chard and ½ cup water; season. Seal the lid and cook on Manual for 3 minutes at High. Do a quick pressure release and drizzle with orange juice.

Basil Infused Avocado Dip

INGREDIENTS for 4 servings

2 avocados, sliced	4 tsp lemon juice
¼ cup basil leaves	Salt and black pepper to taste

DIRECTIONS and total time: approx. 35 minutes

Arrange basil leaves on the bottom of your IP. Sprinkle avocado with lemon juice, salt, and pepper. Lay on top of the basil. Add ½ cup of water. Seal the lid, press Manual, and cook for 5 minutes. Do a quick pressure release. Discard basil and blend the mixture. Serve.

Desserts

Chocolate-Strawberry Bars

INGREDIENTS for 6 servings

½ cup flour
½ cup cocoa powder
½ cup brown sugar
½ cup butter, softened
2 cups strawberries
2 tbsp mint leaves, chopped

DIRECTIONS and total time: approx. 30 minutes

Pour 1 cup of water in your IP and insert a trivet. Line a baking pan with parchment paper. In a bowl, mix flour, half of the brown sugar, cocoa powder, and butter, and stir until a dough is formed. Spread on the baking pan and sprinkle with the remaining sugar. Top with strawberries. Place the pan on the trivet. Seal the lid, select Manual, and cook for 15 minutes at High. When it goes off, do a quick release. Let cool for a few minutes, top with mint, and cut into squares to serve.

Delightful Tiramisu Cake

INGREDIENTS for 12 servings

1 tbsp chocolate-flavored liqueur
1 ½ cups ladyfingers, crushed
1 tbsp granulated espresso
1 tbsp butter, melted
16 oz whipping cream
8 oz mascarpone cheese
2 eggs
2 tbsp powdered sugar
½ cup white sugar
1 tbsp cocoa powder
1 tsp vanilla extract

DIRECTIONS and total time: approx. 50 min + chilling time

In a bowl, beat whipping cream, mascarpone, and sugar. Whisk in eggs, powdered sugar, and vanilla. Combine liqueur, ladyfingers, granulated espresso, and butter in another bowl. Press the ladyfinger crust at the bottom of a greased baking pan. Pour the egg mixture over. Cover the pan with aluminum foil. Pour 1 cup of water in your IP and lower a trivet. Place the pan inside and seal the lid. Select Manual and set to 35 minutes at High. Wait for about 10 minutes before releasing the pressure quickly. Let cool completely and serve.

Homemade Raspberry Compote

INGREDIENTS for 4 servings

2 cups frozen raspberries
¾ cup sugar
Juice of ½ lemon
1 tbsp mint leaves, chopped

DIRECTIONS and total time: approx. 15 min + chilling time

Place raspberries, lemon juice, ½ cup of water, and sugar in your IP. Seal the lid, cook on Manual for 1 minute at High. Once ready, allow a natural pressure release for 10 minutes. Press Sauté and stir in mint; cook until the mixture thickens. Transfer the compote to a bowl and let chill completely before serving.

Silky Lemon Cheesecake with Blueberries

INGREDIENTS for 6 servings

2 cups graham cracker crumbs
1 cup blueberries
3 cups cream cheese
1 tbsp fresh lemon juice
3 eggs
½ stick butter, melted
¾ cup sugar
1 tsp vanilla paste
1 tsp finely grated lemon zest
1 cup water

DIRECTIONS and total time: approx. 25 min + chilling time

Insert a trivet into the pressure cooker and add the water. Mix in graham cracker crumbs with sugar and butter in a bowl. Press the mixture to form a crust at the bottom of a greased springform. Blend the blueberries and cream cheese with an electric mixer. Crack in the eggs and keep mixing until well combined. Mix in the remaining ingredients and stir. Pour the mixture over the crust and cover the pan with aluminium foil. Lay pan on the trivet, seal the lid, press Manual and cook for 20 minutes at High. Once the cooking is over, do a quick pressure release. Refrigerate before serving.

Holiday Almond Cake

INGREDIENTS for 4 servings

3 eggs, yolks & whites separated
¾ cup flour
½ tsp almond extract
1 ½ cups warm milk
½ cup sugar
2 tbsp powdered sugar
2 tbsp butter, melted

DIRECTIONS and total time: approx. 60 minutes

In a bowl, beat the egg yolks along with the sugar. In a separate bowl, beat the whites until soft form peaks. Stir in almond extract and butter. Gently fold in the flour. Line a baking dish and pour in the batter. Cover with aluminum foil. Pour 1 cup of water in your IP and add a trivet. Lower the dish onto the trivet. Seal the lid, select Manual, and cook for 40 minutes at High. Do a quick pressure release. Invert onto a wire rack, sprinkle with powdered sugar and let it cool for a few minutes before slicing and serving.

Lemony Berry Cream

INGREDIENTS for 2 servings

½ cup blueberries
½ cup strawberries, chopped
½ cup raspberries
1 cup milk
¼ tsp vanilla extract
¼ tsp lemon zest

DIRECTIONS and total time: approx. 10 min + chilling time

Place all ingredients, except for the vanilla extract, inside your Instant Pot. Seal the lid, select Steam, and set the timer to 3 minutes at High. When it goes off, do a quick pressure release. Remove to a blender. Add vanilla extract and pulse until smooth. Divide between two serving glasses and refrigerate before serving.

Pineapple Chocolate Pudding

INGREDIENTS for 4 servings

3 eggs, yolks & whites separated
1 lime, zested
½ cup pineapple juice
2 oz chocolate, chopped
¼ cup sugar
2 tbsp butter, softened
¼ cup cornstarch
1 cup milk
½ tsp ginger powder

DIRECTIONS and total time: approx. 35 minutes

Combine sugar, cornstarch and butter in a bowl. Mix in pineapple juice and lime zest. Add in egg yolks, ginger, milk, and whisk to mix well. Stir in egg whites. Pour this mixture into custard cups and cover with aluminium foil. Add 1 cup of water in your IP and insert a trivet. Lower the cups onto the trivet. Seal the lid, select Manual, and cook for 25 minutes at High. Once the cooking is over, do a quick pressure release. Stir in chocolate and serve chilled.

Poppy Seed & Lemon Bars

INGREDIENTS for 8 servings

1 ½ tbsp vanilla
1 tbsp egg yolks
1 tsp vanilla extract
1 lemon, zested
3 tbsp lemon juice
1/3 cup vanilla
2 cups flour
1 tbsp poppy seeds
½ tsp baking powder
½ tsp baking soda
½ cup sugar
¼ cup olive oil

DIRECTIONS and total time: approx. 30 minutes

Line a baking dish with foil. In a bowl, combine all dry ingredients. In a separate bowl, mix all wet ingredients with a blender. Gradually stir in the dry ingredients. Pour the mixture in the baking dish, pour 1 cup of water in your IP and insert a trivet. Place the dish on the trivet, seal the lid, select Manual at High, and cook for 20 minutes. When ready, do a quick pressure release. Let cool and cut into bars before serving.

Savory Blueberry Curd

INGREDIENTS for 4-6 servings

12 oz blueberries
2 tbsp butter
Juice of 2 lemons
1 cup sugar
2 egg yolks
1 tsp lemon zest

DIRECTIONS and total time: approx. 5 min + chilling time

Add blueberries, sugar, and lemon juice in your IP. Seal the lid and cook on Manual for 2 minutes at High. Once ready, do a quick pressure release. With a hand mixer, puree the blueberries. Whisk the yolks in a bowl. Slowly combine the yolks with the hot blueberry puree. Pour the mixture in the pot. Press Sauté and cook for a minute. Stir in butter and lemon zest; cook for a couple more minutes until thickened. Refrigerate for 2 hours before consuming.

Tasty Honey Pumpkin Pie

INGREDIENTS for 4 servings

1 lb pumpkin, diced
1 egg
¼ cup honey
½ cup milk
½ tsp cinnamon
½ tbsp cornstarch
A pinch of sea salt
1 cup water

DIRECTIONS and total time: approx. 30 minutes

Pour the water in your IP and add a trivet. Lay pumpkin on top of the trivet. Seal the lid and cook on Manual for 5 minutes at High. When ready, do a quick release. Remove the pumpkin and set aside. Whisk the remaining ingredients in a bowl. Add in the pumpkin and stir to combine. Pour the batter into a greased baking dish. Place on the trivet and seal the lid. Cook for 10 minutes Manual at High. Do a quick release. Transfer pie to a wire rack to cool. Slice and serve.

Authentic Spanish Crema Catalana

INGREDIENTS for 4 servings

½ tsp vanilla paste
1 cinnamon stick
1 ½ cups milk
2 tbsp cornstarch
1 tsp rum
3 large-sized egg yolks
1 cup + 2 tbsp sugar
Lemon rind from ½ lemon

DIRECTIONS and total time: approx. 35 min + chilled time

In a saucepan over medium heat, warm milk with vanilla paste, cinnamon stick, and lemon rind. In a bowl, whisk egg yolks with 1 cup of sugar, rum, and cornstarch. When the milk starts to boil, turn off the heat and strain the milk. Slowly pour in the yolk mixture, stirring constantly until creamy. Fill 4 ramekins with this mixture and wrap with foil. Pour 1 cup of water into your IP. Add a trivet and lay the ramekins on top. Seal the lid, press Manual, and cook for 12 minutes at Low. Once the cooking is over, allow a natural pressure release for 10 minutes. Remove the ramekins and let them cool. Sprinkle each ramekin with the remaining sugar and caramelize with a kitchen blow torch. Serve cool. Refrigerate for at least 2 hours.

Pumpkin Custard

INGREDIENTS for 6 servings

2 eggs + 2 yolks
2 cups pumpkin puree
½ tsp vanilla extract
1 pinch nutmeg
1 pinch cinnamon powder
1 pinch salt
2 tbsp brown sugar
1 cup condensed milk

DIRECTIONS and total time: approx. 40 minutes

In a bowl, combine all the ingredients. Pour the mixture in a greased baking dish. Add 1 cup of water in your IP and insert a trivet. Put dish on the trivet. Seal the lid, select Manual, and cook for 30 minutes at High. When ready, do a quick pressure release. Serve chilled.

Sweet Milk Balls

INGREDIENTS for 6-8 servings

2 ½ cups sugar
2 tbsp white wine vinegar

6 cups milk
1 tsp ground cardamom

DIRECTIONS and total time: approx. 10 min + chilling time

On Sauté, pour milk and bring to a boil; add in vinegar. Stir for 2 minutes and strain mixture through a cheesecloth-lined colander. Drain as much liquid as you can. Place the obtained paneer on a smooth surface. Form a ball and shape into 20 equal dumplings. Pour 4 cups of water in the pot and bring to a boil on Sauté. Stir in sugar and cardamom. Add in the dumplings. Seal the lid and cook on Manual for 5 minutes at High. Once done, do a quick pressure release. Let cool.

Ice Cream Topped Brownie Cake

INGREDIENTS for 6 servings

3 large eggs, lightly beaten
1 ½ sticks butter, melted
2/3 cup cocoa powder
1 ½ cups sugar

1 tsp pure vanilla extract
½ cup chocolate chips
A pinch of salt
Vanilla ice cream for serving

DIRECTIONS and total time: approx. 50 minutes

Line a baking dish with a piece of foil. Cover the foil with some butter. In a bowl, whisk the remaining butter, flour, cocoa powder, eggs, salt, vanilla, and sugar. Fold in the chocolate chips. Pour the batter in the baking dish. Add 1 cup of water in your IP and insert a trivet. Put the dish on the trivet. Seal the lid, select Manual, and cook for 30 minutes at High. When done, do a quick pressure release. Serve topped with ice cream.

Butter-Lemon Pears

INGREDIENTS for 2 servings

2 pears, cut into wedges
½ cup lemon juice

½ tsp cinnamon
1 tbsp butter, melted

DIRECTIONS and total time: approx. 10 minutes

Combine lemon juice and 1 cup of water in your IP. Place the pear wedges in a steamer basket and lower the basket into the pot. Seal the lid, select Manual, and cook for 3 minutes at High. When done, release the pressure quickly. Transfer the pear wedges to a bowl. Drizzle with butter and sprinkle with cinnamon. Serve.

Christmas Banana Bread

INGREDIENTS for 6-8 servings

3 ripe bananas, mashed
1 ¼ cups sugar
1 cup milk
2 cups all-purpose flour
1 tsp baking powder

1 tbsp pineapple juice
1 stick butter, softened
A pinch of salt
¼ tsp cinnamon
½ tsp vanilla extract

DIRECTIONS and total time: approx. 45 minutes

In a bowl, mix together flour, baking powder, sugar, vanilla, and salt. Add in bananas, cinnamon, and pineapple juice. Slowly stir in butter and milk until everything is well combined. Pour the batter into a baking pan. Place a trivet your IP and fill with 1 cup of water. Place the pan on the trivet. Seal the lid, select Manual, and cook for 40 minutes at High. Do a quick pressure release. Let cool before slicing, and serve.

Lemon & Cinnamon Poached Pears

INGREDIENTS for 4 servings

4 pears, halved
1 tsp powdered ginger
1 tsp nutmeg

1 lemon, juiced
2 tsp cinnamon
¼ cup sugar

DIRECTIONS and total time: approx. 20 minutes

Place 1 cup of water, lemon juice, sugar, and spices in your IP and bring to a boil on Sauté. Add in the pears. Seal the lid and cook on Manual for 4 minutes at High. When ready, do a quick release. Remove pears to a serving plate. Cook the sauce on Sauté until reduced by half, about 8 minutes. Pour over the pears and serve.

Party Cinnamon & Yogurt Cheesecake

INGREDIENTS for 6-8 servings

1 ½ cups graham cracker crumbs
2 eggs
¼ cup sugar
1 ½ cups yogurt

1 tsp cinnamon
4 oz cream cheese, softened
4 tbsp butter, melted

DIRECTIONS and total time: approx. 40 min + chilling time

Mix butter and cracker crumbs, and press the mixture onto the bottom of a springform pan. In a bowl, beat cream cheese with yogurt, cinnamon, and sugar. Whisk in the eggs one at a time. Spread the filling on top of the crust. Pour 1 cup of water in your IP and add a trivet. Lower the pan onto the trivet. Seal the lid and cook on Manual for 35 minutes at High. When ready, do a quick release. Let cool before slicing, and serve.

Simple Poached Apricots

INGREDIENTS for 4 servings

½ cup black currants
4 apricots, pits removed

1 cup orange juice
1 cinnamon stick

DIRECTIONS and total time: approx. 15 minutes

Place black currants and orange juice in a blender. Blend until smooth. Pour the mixture in your IP and add in cinnamon stick. Add the apricots to a steamer basket and then insert it into the pot. Seal the lid, select Manual, and set to 5 minutes at High. When ready, do a quick pressure release. Serve drizzled with sauce.

Almond Butter Bars

INGREDIENTS for 6 servings

1 cup flour
1 egg
½ cup almond butter, softened
½ cup butter, softened
1 cup oats
½ tsp baking soda
½ cup white sugar
½ cup brown sugar

DIRECTIONS and total time: approx. 40 minutes

Beat the eggs, almond butter, butter, white and brown sugar in a bowl. Fold in oats, flour, and baking soda. Press the batter into a greased baking pan. Pour 1 cup of water in your IP and add a trivet. Lower the pan onto the trivet. Seal the lid, press Manual and cook for 30 minutes at High. When ready, do a quick release. Invert onto a plate, cut into bars, and serve cooled.

Party Cherry Pie

INGREDIENTS for 6 servings

1 (9-inch) double pie crust
½ tsp vanilla extract
4 cups cherries, pitted
¼ tsp coconut extract
4 tbsp quick tapioca
1 cup sugar

DIRECTIONS and total time: approx. 25 minutes

Pour 1 cup of water in your IP and fit in a trivet. Combine cherries with tapioca, sugar, vanilla and coconut extracts in a bowl. Place one pie crust on the bottom of a greased baking pan. Spread the cherry mixture and top with the other crust. Lower the pan onto the trivet. Seal the lid, cook on Manual for 18 minutes at High. Once done, do a quick pressure release. Let cool on a cooling rack. Slice to serve.

Raisin Chocolate Cookies

INGREDIENTS for 2 servings

¼ cup whole wheat flour
¼ cup oats
1 tbsp butter
2 tbsp sugar
½ tsp vanilla extract
1 tbsp honey
2 tbsp milk
2 tsp olive oil
3 tbsp chocolate chips
1 cup raisins

DIRECTIONS and total time: approx. 35 minutes

Mix all ingredients in a bowl. Line a baking pan with parchment paper. Shape lemon-sized cookies out of the mixture and flatten onto the lined pan. Pour 1 cup of water and add a trivet. Lower the baking pan on the trivet. Seal the lid and cook on Manual for 15 minutes at High. When cooking is over, do a quick pressure. Let cool for 15 minutes and serve.

Apple Coconut Dessert

INGREDIENTS for 2 servings

¼ cup flour
1 cup milk
2 apples, peeled and diced
¼ cup shredded coconut

DIRECTIONS and total time: approx. 10 minutes

Combine all ingredients in your IP. Seal the lid, select Manual, and set the timer to 5 minutes at High. When ready, do a quick pressure release. Serve in bowls.

Speedy Nectarines with Blueberry Sauce

INGREDIENTS for 4 servings

½ vanilla bean, sliced lengthwise
8 nectarines, cored and halved
2 cups blueberries
¼ cup honey
1 ½ tbsp cornstarch
¼ tsp ground cardamom
½ cinnamon stick

DIRECTIONS and total time: approx. 20 minutes

Add blueberries, cardamom, vanilla bean, and 1 cup of water to your IP. Place a trivet on top. Arrange the nectarines on the trivet and seal the lid. Select Manual and cook for 5 minutes at High. Do a quick pressure release. Remove the nectarines to serving plates and discard vanilla bean. Blitz the blueberry mixture with an immersion blender and mix in honey and cornstarch. Press Sauté and let simmer until the sauce thickens, about 5 minutes. Pour the sauce over nectarines to serve.

Awesome Chocolate Lava Cake

INGREDIENTS for 4 servings

2 tbsp butter, melted
1 cup chocolate, melted
6 tbsp flour
1 tsp vanilla extract
3 eggs plus
1 yolk, beaten
¾ cup sugar
1 cup water

DIRECTIONS and total time: approx. 15 minutes

Combine all ingredients in a bowl. Grease 4 ramekins with cooking spray. Divide the filling between the ramekins. Pour the water in the Instant Pot and fit in a trivet. Place the ramekins on the trivet. Seal the lid and cook on Manual for 10 minutes at High. When ready, do a quick pressure release. Serve warm or chilled.

Orange Crème Caramel

INGREDIENTS for 4 servings

2 eggs
7 oz condensed milk
½ cup milk
½ tsp cinnamon
4 tbsp caramel syrup
1 tbsp orange zest

DIRECTIONS and total time: approx. 20 minutes

Divide caramel syrup between 4 ramekins. Pour 1 cup of water in the IP and add a trivet. In a bowl, beat with a whisk the remaining ingredients. Divide between the ramekins. Cover with foil and lower onto the trivet. Seal the lid and cook on Manual for 13 minutes at High. When ready, do a quick pressure release; let cool. To unmold the flan, insert a spatula along the ramekins' sides and flip onto a dish.

Scrumptious Stuffed Pears

INGREDIENTS for 4-6 servings

½ cup dried apricots, chopped
3 lb pears, cored
¼ cup sugar
¼ cup walnuts, chopped
¼ tsp cardamom
½ tsp grated nutmeg
½ tsp ground cinnamon
1 ¼ cups red wine
¼ cup graham cracker crumbs

DIRECTIONS and total time: approx. 20 minutes

Lay the pears on the bottom of your IP and pour in the red wine. In a bowl, mix the other ingredients, except for the crackers and walnuts, and pour over pears. Seal the lid and cook on Manual for 15 minutes at High. Once ready, do a quick pressure release. Top with graham cracker crumbs and walnuts and serve.

Easy Peach Cobbler

INGREDIENTS for 6 servings

6 oz brown sugar
3 ½ oz rolled oats
20 oz frozen peach slices
¼ cup unsalted butter
¼ tsp kosher salt
½ tsp nutmeg, freshly grated
½ tsp allspice, freshly ground
½ tsp baking powder
4 oz flour
1 cup water

DIRECTIONS and total time: approx. 35 minutes

Combine baking powder, sugar, oats, flour, nutmeg, allspice, and salt in a bowl. Add butter and beat it into the ingredients until there is a crumbly texture. Fold in the peach slices. Grease the bottom as well as the sides of a baking dish with butter. Add in the mixture. Pour the water in your IP and fit in a trivet. Place the baking dish on the trivet. Seal the lid, press Manual and cook for 15 minutes at High. After cooking, do a quick pressure release. Let cool and serve.

Hazelnut & Apple Delight

INGREDIENTS for 4 servings

4 apples, peeled and diced
½ cup hazelnuts, chopped
½ cup milk
¼ tsp cinnamon

DIRECTIONS and total time: approx. 10 minutes

Place apples, milk, cinnamon, and ¼ cup of water in inner pot. Seal the lid and cook on Manual for 5 minutes at High. When ready, do a quick release. Blitz with an immersion blender and divide the mixture among 4 serving bowls. Sprinkle with hazelnuts to serve.

Simple Cranberry Peach Biscuits

INGREDIENTS for 4 servings

4 peaches, halved lengthwise
8 dried cranberries, soaked
4 tbsp pecans, chopped
1 cup crumbled cookies
1 tsp cinnamon powder
¼ tsp grated nutmeg
¼ tsp ground cloves
1 cup water

DIRECTIONS and total time; approx. 20 minutes

Pour the water in your IP and add a trivet. Arrange the peaches on a greased baking dish cut-side-up. Mix all of the remaining ingredients in a bowl. Stuff the peaches with the mixture. Lower the dish onto the trivet. Seal the lid, press Manual, and cook for 15 minutes at High. When ready, do a quick pressure release. Serve cooled.

Pineapple Upside Down Cake

INGREDIENTS for 6 servings

1 tbsp chopped maraschino cherries
Some whole maraschino cherries for garnish
1 cup flour
½ cup pecans, chopped
½ tsp ground cinnamon
¾ tsp baking powder
½ cup light brown sugar
10 tbsp butter, softened
¼ tsp grated nutmeg
¼ tsp fine salt
2/3 cup sugar
1 tbsp confectioners' sugar
½ cup heavy cream
2 tbsp milk
1 tsp pure vanilla extract
2 large eggs
2 tbsp dark rum
½ ripe pineapple, sliced

DIRECTIONS and total time: approx. 50 min + chilling time

Grease a baking dish with cooking spray. Line it with a double layer of foil, then grease the foil. Add in brown sugar and rum. Arrange the pineapple slices on the bottom of the baking dish, pressing into the sugar mixture. In a bowl, mix flour, pecans, baking powder, cinnamon, nutmeg, and salt. In another bowl, combine sugar and butter, and using a mixer, beat until fluffy.

Scrape down sides of a bowl with butter mixture, then whisk in the eggs and vanilla. Add in the milk and continue beating until smooth. Spread the batter over the pineapples. Pour 1 cup of water in the IP and insert a trivet. Put the dish on the trivet. Seal the lid, select Manual, and cook for 30 minutes at High. When done, perform a natural pressure release for 10 minutes, then a quick pressure release to let out the remaining steam. Allow the cake to rest for 20 minutes. Carefully, invert cake onto a platter and peel off the foil. Whip the cream until peaks form. Fold in the confectioners' sugar and chopped cherries. Serve cake slices with a nice dollop of whipped cream and a whole cherry on top.

Apple Cacao Dessert

INGREDIENTS for 2 servings

1 tbsp cinnamon
1 cup apples, chopped
½ cup milk
1 tbsp cacao powder
1 tbsp lemon juice

DIRECTIONS and total time: approx. 13 minutes

Place apples, cinnamon, lemon juice, and ½ cup of water in your IP. Seal the lid, select Manual, and cook for 3 minutes at High. When ready, do a quick pressure release. Mix in cacao powder and blend well. Serve.

Summer Berry Cobbler

INGREDIENTS for 6 servings

Berry filling:

2 tbsp lemon juice
¼ cup cornstarch

5 cups frozen mixed berries
2/3 cup sugar

Biscuit Topping:

3 tbsp sugar
1 ¼ cups flour
1 tsp baking powder
A pinch of salt

4 tbsp butter, cubed
¾ cup milk
¼ tsp ground cinnamon

Whipped sour cream topping:

2 tbsp confectioners' sugar
¼ cup sour cream

½ cup heavy cream

DIRECTIONS and total time: approx. 40 minutes

In a bowl, whisk cornstarch, lemon juice, and 2 tbsp water. Add in berries and sugar; toss. Pour the mixture into a greased baking dish. Whisk flour, 2 tbsp sugar, baking powder, and salt in a bowl. Add butter and rub mixture with fingers to form a coarse meal. Add the milk and stir to form a wet dough. Drop spoonful of dough on top of berry mixture. Mix the remaining 1 tbsp sugar and cinnamon, then sprinkle over dough. Pour 1 cup of water in the IP and insert a trivet. Put the baking dish on the trivet. Seal the lid, select Manual, and cook for 15 minutes at High. When done, release the pressure naturally for 10 minutes. Beat the topping ingredients in a bowl using an electric mixer until it forms peaks. Serve cobbler with sour cream topping.

Pumpkin Cake

INGREDIENTS for 6 servings

1/3 cup flour
¾ cup honey
1 cup raw cashews, chopped
1 tsp ground ginger
½ tsp nutmeg
1 tsp cinnamon

1 cup pumpkin puree
1 tsp almond extract
2 tbsp butter, melted
4 large eggs
2 tsp baking powder
½ tsp vanilla extract

DIRECTIONS and total time: approx. 40 minutes

Grease a baking pan with butter. Mix all the ingredients in a bowl. Gently spread the batter onto the bottom of the pan. Add 1 cup of water in the pot and insert a trivet. Put the dish on the trivet. Seal the lid, select Manual, and cook for 20 minutes at High. When done, allow a natural release for 10 minutes. Serve sliced.

Apricots & Pecans with Mascarpone

INGREDIENTS for 4 servings

1 lb apricots, halved
½ cup orange juice
4 tbsp honey
¾ cup mascarpone cheese

½ cup pecans, chopped
¼ tsp grated nutmeg
½ tsp ground cinnamon
½ tsp vanilla extract

DIRECTIONS and total time: approx. 10 minutes

Add all ingredients, except for cheese and pecans, to your IP. Pour in ½ cup of water. Seal the lid, select Manual, and cook for 5 minutes at High. When ready, do a quick pressure release. Remove apricots to serving plates and top with cheese and pecans to serve.

Quinoa Energy Bars

INGREDIENTS for 6 servings

1 cup milk
2 tbsp maple syrup
2 tbsp butter, melted
½ tsp cinnamon
2 large eggs, beaten

1/3 cup almonds, chopped
½ cup raisins
1 cup quinoa, uncooked
2 tbsp chia seeds
1/3 cup dried apples, chopped

DIRECTIONS and total time: approx. 35 minutes

Lightly grease your IP with cooking spray. In a bowl, mix butter and maple syrup until smooth. Stir in milk and cinnamon. Add in the remaining ingredients and 1 cup of water; give it a stir. Carefully pour the mixture into the pot. Seal the lid, select Manual, and cook for 15 minutes at High. When ready, do a quick release. Place in the fridge to set. Cut into bars and serve.

Chocolate Pudding Cake

INGREDIENTS for 8 servings

1 box (19-oz) chocolate fudge cake mix
1 (14-oz) package chocolate instant pudding
3 cups milk   1 cup fresh strawberries
1 cup whipped cream

DIRECTIONS and total time: approx. 35 minutes

In a bowl, mix together milk and pudding mix until smooth. Add the mixture to a greased baking dish. Prepare the cake batter according to the box directions. Pour it over the pudding, do not stir. Add 1 cup of water in your IP and insert a trivet. Put the dish on the trivet. Seal the lid, select Manual, and cook for 25 minutes at High. When ready, do a quick release and let cool. Top with whipped cream and strawberries and slice.

Walnut Fudge

INGREDIENTS for 2 servings

½ cup milk
¼ cup honey
1 tsp vanilla

3 tbsp olive oil
¾ cup walnuts, chopped
A pinch of salt

DIRECTIONS and total time: approx. 10 min + chilling time

Mix olive oil, honey, and milk in your IP. Press Sauté and cook until the mixture is well combined. Add in vanilla and walnuts, and stir. Pour the mixture in a lined with foil baking sheet. Place in the fridge for at least 1 hour until firm. Cut before serving.

Mom's Banana Cake

INGREDIENTS for 6 servings

6 tbsp butter, melted	¼ tsp ground nutmeg
6 bananas, halved lengthwise	2 tbsp milk
3 tbsp dark rum	1 egg yolk
¾ cup dark brown sugar	2/3 cups white sugar
¾ tsp baking soda	4 tbsp butter, softened
¾ cups cake flour	¼ tsp fine salt
½ tsp cinnamon	Ice cream for serving

DIRECTIONS and total time: approx. 55 minutes

Line a baking pan with foil. Sprinkle with melted butter, rum, and brown sugar. Cover with banana halves, cut side down; set aside. Sift flour, baking powder, cinnamon, nutmeg, and salt into a large bowl; whisk to combine. In another bowl, beat the remaining butter and white sugar with an electric mixer until light and fluffy. Add in egg yolk and beat until well blended. Fold in flour mixture. Add in milk in 2 parts and mix at medium speed to make a smooth batter. Pour batter over bananas and smooth with a spatula. Pour 1 cup of water in your IP and insert a trivet. Put the pan on the trivet. Seal the lid, select Manual, and cook for 30 minutes at High. When done, release the pressure naturally for 10 minutes. Let cool. Carefully invert the cake onto a serving platter. Serve with ice cream.

Vanilla & Fruit Compote

INGREDIENTS for 4-6 servings

1 ½ cups apricots, dried	½ cup white wine
4 ripe pears, chopped	1 1/3 cups sugar
Pinch of salt	2 ¼ cups hot water
¼ tsp vanilla extract	1 cup cherries, dried
1 tsp orange zest	

DIRECTIONS and total time: approx. 20 minutes

Mix sugar, water, zest, vanilla, wine, and salt in your IP until the sugar is dissolved. Gently stir in the fruits, and make sure not to squish the pears. Seal the lid, select Manual at High, and cook for 10 minutes. When ready, do a quick release. Allow to cool and serve.

Coconut Stuffed Apples

INGREDIENTS for 4 servings

2 tbsp cinnamon	½ cup heavy cream
1 cup butter	4 apples, cored
4 tbsp shredded coconut	A pinch of nutmeg

DIRECTIONS and total time: approx. 25 minutes

Mix all ingredients, except the apples, in a bowl. Stuff the apples with this mixture. Place the stuffed apples in the pot, pour 1 cup of water and seal the lid. Select Manual, and cook for 6 minutes at High. When done, release pressure naturally for 10 minutes. Serve warm.

Grandma's Pear & Peach Compote

INGREDIENTS for 4 servings

2 ½ cups peaches, chopped	2 tbsp cornstarch
2 cups pears, diced	¼ tsp cinnamon
Juice of 1 orange	2 tbsp brown sugar

DIRECTIONS and total time: approx. 15 min + chilling time

Place peaches, pears, ½ cup of water, and orange juice in your IP. Stir to combine, seal the lid, select Manual and, cook for 3 minutes at High. When ready, do a quick release. Press Sauté and whisk in sugar, cornstarch and cinnamon. Cook until the compote thickens, about 5 minutes. Refrigerate for a few hours, before serving.

Blueberry Clafoutis

INGREDIENTS for 4-6 servings

1 ½ cups fresh blueberries	2/3 cups milk
1 tsp butter	¼ tsp lemon zest
2 eggs	Confectioner's sugar
½ cup sugar	½ cup pancake mix

DIRECTIONS and total time: approx. 35 minutes

Coat the inside of a baking dish with butter and some pancake mix. Gently pour in the blueberries. In a bowl, whisk sugar, salt, eggs, and pancake mix. Add in milk, lemon zest, and vanilla extract; beat until smooth. Pour over the blueberries, but do not stir. Add 1 cup of water in your IP and fit in a trivet. Place the baking dish on the trivet. Seal the lid, select Manual, and cook for 20 minutes at High. When ready, do a quick release. Serve warm with a sprinkling of confectioner's sugar on top.

Classic Vanilla Cheesecake

INGREDIENTS for 8 servings

4 oz graham crackers	¼ cup whipping cream
1 tsp cinnamon	2 eggs
3 tbsp butter, melted	1 tsp vanilla extract
1 lb cream cheese	1 tsp orange zest
¾ cup granulated sugar	1 tbsp orange juice

DIRECTIONS and total time: approx. 50 minutes

Mix graham crackers and cinnamon in a blender and blitz until the mixture resembles wet sand. Add butter and blend a few more times. Pour crumbs into the bottom of a baking dish in a single layer; set aside. Beat whipping cream, sugar, and cream cheese with an electric mixer until creamy and fluffy. Add in eggs, vanilla extract, orange zest, and orange juice and continue beating until the color is solid, about 2 minutes. Spread the mixture over the crust in the baking dish. Pour 1 cup of water into your IP and lower a trivet. Place the baking dish on the trivet. Seal the lid, and cook on Manual for 30 minutes at High. Once ready, do a quick pressure release. Serve cooled.

Orange Cheesecake

INGREDIENTS for 4 servings

For the crust:

1 ¾ cups crumbled crackers	¼ cup sugar
½ cup butter, melted	A pinch salt

For the filling:

2 eggs	2 tbsp orange zest
8 oz heavy cream	¼ cup orange juice
½ cup sugar	3 tbsp cornstarch
1 ¾ cups cold milk	2 cups water

Topping:

3 oranges, sliced thinly

DIRECTIONS and total time: approx. 45 min + chilling time

Line the bottom of a cake pan with foil, then grease with cooking spray. In a bowl, mix the crust ingredients. Spoon the crust into the cake pan and press firmly into the bottom. Chill for 20 minutes in the freezer. In a bowl, beat eggs with heavy cream and sugar. Whisk in milk, orange zest, orange juice, and cornstarch until smooth. Remove the crust from the fridge and pour the filling over. Pour 1 cup of water in your IP and insert a trivet. Place the cake pan on top. Seal the lid, select Manual for 25 minutes at High. When ready, naturally release the pressure for 10 minutes. Let cool at room temperature, then refrigerate. Top with blood orange slices and slice into wedges to serve.

Fruit Mix with Almonds

INGREDIENTS for 2 servings

1 cup mango chunks	¼ cup almonds, chopped
1 cup berry mix	¼ cup fresh orange juice
2 apples, peeled and diced	1 tbsp olive oil

DIRECTIONS and total time: approx. 10 minutes

Pour ½ cup of water, orange juice, and fruits in your IP. Give it a good stir and seal the lid. Press Manual and set the timer to 5 minutes at High. When it goes off, release the pressure quickly. Blend the mixture with a hand blender and immediately stir in the olive oil. Serve sprinkled with chopped almonds.

Cinnamon-Flavored Apple Sauce

INGREDIENTS for 4 servings

12 apples, chopped	½ tsp nutmeg
1 tsp cinnamon	½ lemon, sliced

DIRECTIONS and total time: approx. 20 minutes

Add apples, lemon slices, and ½ cup of water in your IP. Sprinkle with nutmeg and cinnamon. Seal the lid, select Manual, and cook for 3 minutes at High. When done, release the pressure naturally for 10 minutes. Puree the mixture using an immersion blender. Serve.

Apple & Cinnamon Cake

INGREDIENTS for 4 servings

2 cups baking mix	1 tsp ground cinnamon
2/3 cup applesauce	2 apples, peeled and diced
¼ cup milk	2 tbsp butter, melted
1 egg	2 tbsp sugar
1 tsp vanilla extract	

Topping:

¼ cup baking mix	2 tbsp butter, softened
¼ cup nuts, chopped	¼ cup brown sugar

DIRECTIONS and total time: approx. 35 minutes

Combine applesauce, milk, baking mix, sugar, butter, apples, vanilla, cinnamon, and egg in a bowl; mix until thick and lumpy. In another bowl, combine the topping ingredients. Pour the batter into a greased baking dish and spread the topping evenly. Pour 1 cup of water in your IP and insert a trivet. Place the dish on top. Seal the lid, select Manual, and cook for 20 minutes at High. When ready, do a quick pressure release and let cool for a few minutes before serving.

Tasty Apple Risotto

INGREDIENTS for 8 servings

¼ cup butter	1 ½ tsp cinnamon
1/3 cup brown sugar	3 apples, peeled and diced
1 ½ cups rice	3 cups milk
1/8 tsp nutmeg	2 tbsp lemon zest

DIRECTIONS and total time: approx. 40 minutes

Turn your IP on Sauté and melt the butter. Add in rice and stir, making sure to coat it evenly. Add in apples, sugar, lemon zest, nutmeg, milk, and 1 cup of water and stir. Seal the lid, select Manual, and cook for 20 minutes at High. When ready, perform natural pressure release for 10 minutes. Serve sprinkled with cinnamon.

Mango Tarts

INGREDIENTS for 6 servings

15 medium phyllo shells, thawed	
2 cups cubed mango + extra for garnish	
½ cup orange juice	2 tbsp water
¼ tsp mint, chopped	1 ½ tbsp butter
½ cup sugar	½ tsp vanilla extract
2 tbsp cornstarch	1 ¼ cups whipped cream

DIRECTIONS and total time: approx. 10 min + cooling time

Select Sauté and pour in mango, orange juice, and sugar. Combine cornstarch with water and stir into the pot. Bring to a boil, stirring occasionally. Cook for 1 minute. Stir in butter and vanilla. Remove and allow slight cooling. Spoon 2 tbsp into each phyllo shells and refrigerate for 2 hours. Remove the tarts, top with whipped cream, reserved mango and mint and serve.

White Chocolate Cake in a Cup

INGREDIENTS for 2 servings

5 tbsp flour	2 tbsp cocoa powder
3 tbsp sugar	4 tbsp white chocolate chips
2 tbsp vanilla	4 tbsp milk
1 tsp ginger powder	3 tbsp vegetable oil

DIRECTIONS and total time: approx. 15 minutes

Pour 1 cup of water in your IP and insert a trivet. In a bowl, combine flour, sugar, vanilla, ginger powder, milk, oil, and cocoa powder and mix well. Stir in chocolate chips. Divide the mixture between two mugs and place on the trivet.

Seal the lid, press Manual, and cook for 10 minutes at High. When ready, do a quick pressure release. Let cool before serving.

Quick Rum Egg Custard

INGREDIENTS for 4 servings

1 egg + 2 egg yolks	2 cups heavy cream
½ cup sugar	½ tsp pure rum extract
½ cups milk	½ tsp vanilla extract

DIRECTIONS and total time: approx. 15 minutes

Beat egg and yolks in a bowl. Gently add rum and vanilla extracts. Mix in milk and heavy cream. Add sugar and stir. Divide this mixture between 4 ramekins.

Add 1 cup of water in your IP and insert a trivet. Lay the ramekins on the trivet. Select Manual and cook for 10 minutes at High. Do a quick pressure release.

Coconut White Chocolate Fondue

INGREDIENTS for 12 servings

10 oz white chocolate, chopped	¼ tsp cinnamon powder
2 tsp coconut liqueur	A pinch of salt
8 oz heavy cream	1 cup water

DIRECTIONS and total time: approx. 15 minutes

Pour the water in your IP and insert a trivet. Place all the ingredients, except for the liqueur, in a glass recipient that fits inside the pot and place on top of the trivet. Press Sauté and cook for 7-8 minutes, stirring occasionally until the chocolate is smooth. Remove from the cooker and mix in coconut liqueur. Serve.

Beery Chocolate Cups

INGREDIENTS for 6 servings

3 eggs	2 tsp vanilla extract
2 ½ cups all-purpose flour	1 cup milk
1 tbsp baking soda	1 cup blackberries
1 ½ cup sugar	¾ dark chocolate chips
¾ cup butter, melted	2 cups water

DIRECTIONS and total time: approx. 25 min + cooling time

In a bowl, mix flour, baking soda, and sugar. Stir in butter, eggs, vanilla extract, and milk until well combined. Fold in blackberries and half of the chocolate chips. Share the mixture into a 12-holed silicone egg mold and scatter the remaining chocolate chips on top.

Pour 1 cup of water in your IP and lower a trivet; place the egg mold on top. Seal the lid, select Manual, and cook for 8 minutes at High. Once done, perform a natural pressure release for 10 minutes. Serve the muffins after slightly cooled.

Peanut Pear Wedges

INGREDIENTS for 4 servings

2 pears, cut into wedges	2 tbsp olive oil
3 tbsp peanuts, chopped	1 cup water

DIRECTIONS and total time: approx. 20 minutes

Pour the water in your IP. Place the pears in a steamer basket and then insert the basket in the pot. Seal the lid and cook on Manual for 2 minutes at High.

When the timer goes off, do a natural pressure release for 10 minutes. Remove the basket, discard water, and wipe the cooker clean. Press Sauté and heat olive oil. Add the pear wedges and cook until browned. Top with peanuts and serve.

Cinnamon & Raisin Muffins

INGREDIENTS for 4 servings

2 eggs	1 tsp vanilla extract
½ cup butter, softened	¼ tsp nutmeg powder
1 cup sugar	2 cups all-purpose flour
¼ tsp salt	¼ cup raisins
½ tsp cinnamon	A pinch salt
½ tsp baking powder	1 cup water

For the streusel topping:

¾ cup all-purpose flour	4 tbsp sugar
½ tsp cinnamon powder	¼ cup butter softened

DIRECTIONS and total time: approx. 45 minutes

In a bowl, beat eggs, butter, and sugar. Mix in salt, cinnamon, baking powder, vanilla extract, nutmeg, flour, and raisins. In another bowl, combine the topping ingredients. Divide the cake batter into silicon muffin cups and sprinkle with the topping.

Open the pot, pour in the water, insert a trivet, and place the muffin cups on top. Seal the lid and select Manual and cook for 20 minutes at High. Once done, do a natural pressure release. Let cool and serve.

My 50 Favorite Recipes

Cheesy Mushroom Cakes

INGREDIENTS for 4 servings

5 oz oyster mushrooms, sliced	¼ cup dry white wine
2 tbsp melted butter, divided	1 sheet puff pastry, thawed
1 small white onion, sliced	1 cup shredded Swiss cheese
Salt and black pepper to taste	2 sliced green onions

DIRECTIONS and total time: approx. 45 minutes

Melt butter on Sauté and cook onion and mushrooms for 5 minutes. Season with salt and pepper, pour in wine and cook until evaporated, 2 minutes; set aside. Unwrap the puff pastry and cut into 4 squares. Pierce the dough with a fork and brush both sides with the remaining butter. Share half of the Swiss cheese evenly over the puff pastry squares. Also, share the mushroom mixture over the pastry squares and top with the remaining cheese. Place in a greased baking pan.

Pour 1 cup of water in your IP and fit a trivet. Lay the pan on top of the trivet. Seal the lid, select Manual and cook for 20 minutes at High. After cooking, do a natural pressure release for 10 minutes. Transfer the tart to a plate. Garnish with green onions and serve.

Creamy Pumpkin & Ginger Soup

INGREDIENTS for 4 servings

2 lb pumpkin, cubed	4 cups vegetable stock
2 tbsp parsley, chopped	½ cup sour cream
1 onion, chopped	½ cup pumpkin seeds toasted
¼ tsp cumin	Salt and black pepper to taste
½ inch piece ginger, sliced	2 tbsp olive oil

DIRECTIONS and total time: approx. 25 minutes

Warm olive oil on Sauté. Add in onion, parsley, salt, and pepper, and cook for 3 minutes until soft. Place in pumpkin and brown for 5 minutes, stirring often. Add in ginger, cumin, and vegetable stock and stir. Seal the lid, select Manual, and set time to 10 minutes at High. When ready, do a quick release. Pour the mixture into a blender and blitz until smooth. Add in sour cream and stir. Serve garnished with pumpkin seeds.

Colorful Pasta with Pine Nuts

INGREDIENTS for 4 servings

1 lb tri-color rotini pasta	2 tbsp olive oil
1 onion, chopped	¼ cup grated Parmesan
3 cloves garlic, minced	¼ cup pine nuts
12 white mushrooms, sliced	6 cups baby spinach
1 zucchini, sliced	1 cup chicken stock
1 tsp basil	½ cup tomato paste
Salt and black pepper to taste	3 tbsp light soy sauce

DIRECTIONS and total time: approx. 30 minutes

Heat olive oil on Sauté. Place in onion and garlic and stir-fry until fragrant, 3 minutes. Season with salt and black pepper. Put in mushrooms, zucchini, and basil and cook for 3 minutes, until tender. Pour in stock, rotini pasta, tomato paste, 2 cups of water, and soy sauce, and stir to combine. Seal the lid, select Manual at High, and set time to 4 minutes. When ready, do a natural release for 10 minutes. Top with Parmesan cheese and pine nuts, and serve immediately.

Cheesy Mushroom Risotto

INGREDIENTS for 4 servings

1 ½ lb fresh mixed mushrooms, sliced	
2 cups vegetable stock	1 cup arborio rice,
1 oz dried porcini mushrooms	1 tbsp miso paste
4 tbsp olive oil	1 cup dry white wine
4 tbsp butter	¼ cup heavy cream
Salt and black pepper to taste	2 tbsp mascarpone cheese
1 onion, chopped	1 oz grated Parmesan cheese
2 cloves garlic, minced	2 tbsp minced chervil

DIRECTIONS and total time: approx. 40 minutes

Soak porcini mushrooms in 1 cup of hot water for 20 minutes. Drain, reserve the liquid, and chop; set aside. Set your IP to Sauté and heat butter and olive oil. Place in fresh mushrooms, salt, and pepper and cook for 5 minutes. Add in onion, garlic, chopped porcini and cook for 5 minutes until onion is fragrant. Put in rice and miso paste and cook for 1 minute. Pour in wine and scrape off any browned bits at the bottom of the pot. Add in reserved mushroom liquid, and stock. Seal the lid, select Manual, and set time to 15 minutes on High. When ready, do a quick release. Stir in heavy cream, mascarpone and Parmesan cheeses, and chervil. Serve.

Jalapeño Haddock with Samfaina

INGREDIENTS for 4 servings

15 oz canned diced tomatoes	2 garlic cloves, minced
4 haddock fillets	1 eggplant, cubed
Salt and black pepper to taste	1 bell pepper, chopped
3 tbsp olive oil	½ tsp basil
½ small onion, sliced	½ cup sliced green olives
1 jalapeño, seeded and minced	3 tbsp capers

DIRECTIONS and total time: approx. 20 minutes

Season the fish with salt and pepper; set aside. Press Sauté and heat olive oil. Cook onion, eggplant, bell pepper, jalapeño, and garlic for 5 minutes. Stir in tomatoes, basil, and olives. Lay the fish on top of the vegetables. Seal the lid, select Manual, and set time to 3 minutes at High. After cooking, do a quick pressure release. Transfer the fish to a serving platter and spoon the sauce over. Sprinkle with the chervil and capers.

Broccoli & Potatoes with Gruyere

INGREDIENTS for 4 servings

1 head broccoli, cut into florets ¾ cup half and half
2 cups Gruyere cheese, grated 2 tbsp butter
4 small russet potatoes 1 tsp cornstarch

DIRECTIONS and total time: approx. 25 minutes

Pour 1 cup of water in inner pot and fit in a steamer basket. Place the broccoli inside the basket. Seal the lid, select Manual and set time to 1 minute at High. When ready, do a quick release. Remove broccoli to a bowl. Put the potatoes in the steamer basket. Seal the lid again, select Manual and set time to 15 minutes at High. When ready, do a quick pressure release. Let the potatoes cool. Take out the basket and discard water. Press Sauté and warm half and half and butter. In a bowl, mix cheese with cornstarch, and pour it into pot. Stir until the cheese is melted. Toss broccoli with cheese sauce. Cut a slit into each potato and stuff with the broccoli mixture. Scatter with chives. Serve warm.

Minestrone al Pesto with Cheese Bread

INGREDIENTS for 4 servings

¼ cup grated Pecorino Romano cheese
1 Pecorino Romano rind 1 large carrot, chopped
1 lb yellow squash, chopped 1 cup chopped zucchini
1 (14-oz) can diced tomatoes 1 tsp mixed herbs
1 cup canned cannellini beans ¼ tsp cayenne pepper powder
3 tbsp butter, softened Salt to taste
3 tbsp vegetable oil 1 garlic clove, minced
1 red onion, chopped 4 slices white bread
1 celery stalk, chopped 1/3 cup pesto

DIRECTIONS and total time: approx. 35 minutes

On Sauté, heat olive oil and cook onion, celery, and carrot for 5 minutes, until softened. Stir in yellow squash, tomatoes, beans, 4 cups of water, zucchini, mixed herbs, cayenne pepper, salt, and Pecorino Romano rind. Seal the lid, select Manual for 4 minutes at High. In a bowl, mix butter, Pecorino Romano cheese, and garlic. Spread the mixture on bread slices. Place under the broiler for 4 minutes at High. After cooking the soup, perform a natural pressure release for 10 minutes. Adjust the taste and drizzle the pesto over. Serve with the garlic toasts.

Crunchy Cod with Quinoa

INGREDIENTS for 4 servings

1 tbsp olive oil 4 tbsp melted butter
2 cups quinoa ¼ cup minced fresh cilantro
1 yellow bell pepper, chopped 1 tsp lemon zest
1 red bell pepper, chopped 1 lemon, juiced
4 cups vegetable broth Salt to taste
1 cup panko breadcrumbs 4 cod fillets

DIRECTIONS and total time: approx. 20 minutes

Combine oil, quinoa, bell peppers, and broth in Instant Pot. Seal the lid, select Manual, and set time to 6 minutes at High. When ready, do a quick release. Remove quinoa. In a bowl, whisk breadcrumbs, half of the butter, cilantro, lemon zest, lemon juice, and salt. Coat the cod fillets with the the breadcrumb mixture. Wipe the pot clean. Press Sauté, heat in the remaining butter, and fry cod fillets for 2-3 minutes per side. Share the quinoa into plates and top with the cod to serve.

Habanero Beef Tortilla Tart

INGREDIENTS for 4 servings

2 ½ cups shredded Monterrey Jack cheese
1 lb ground beef 2 tbsp olive oil
3 tbsp taco seasoning 4 flour tortillas
1 cup water ¼ cup habanero hot sauce
1½ cups canned refried beans 1 red onion, sliced
1/3 cup salsa 1 large tomato, sliced

DIRECTIONS and total time: approx. 35 minutes

Set to Sauté and warm olive oil. Add in beef and cook for 7 minutes, stirring occasionally; sprinkle with the taco seasoning and stir; remove to a plate. Wipe the inner pot clean, pour in water, and fit in a trivet. In a bowl, mix refried beans and salsa. In a greased baking pan, lay one flour tortilla, ½ cup of the bean mixture, 1 cup of ground beef, a little bit of habanero sauce, and 1 cup of cheese. Repeat these steps for the 3 layers. Top with the fourth tortilla and cover with foil. Place the pan on the trivet. Seal the lid, select Manual, and set timer to 15 minutes at High. When ready, do a quick pressure release. Serve warm topped with the remaining cheese, red onion, and tomato slices.

Saucy Seafood Penne with Chorizo

INGREDIENTS for 4 servings

8 oz shrimp, peeled and deveined
12 clams, cleaned and debearded
1 tbsp olive oil 3 cups fish broth
1 onion, chopped 1 chorizo, sliced
1 garlic, chopped Salt and black pepper to taste
16 oz penne pasta 8 oz scallops
1 (24-oz) jar Arrabbiata sauce 2 tbsp parsley, chopped

DIRECTIONS and total time: approx. 25 minutes

Warm olive oil on Sauté and cook chorizo, onion, and garlic for 5 minutes. Stir in pasta, Arrabbiata sauce, and fish broth. Seal the lid, select Manual and cook for 4 minutes. Do a quick pressure release. Stir in shrimp, scallops, and clams. Cook for 5 minutes on Sauté until the clams have opened and the shrimp and scallops are opaque. Discard any unopened clams. Adjust the seasoning and serve sprinkled with parsley.

Herby Cavatappi Pasta Siciliana

INGREDIENTS for 4 servings

½ cup Parmigiano Reggiano shavings
2 tbsp olive oil
4 shallots, chopped
2 cloves minced garlic
3 cups mushrooms, sliced
½ tsp dried parsley
½ tsp dried basil
¼ tsp dried oregano

¼ tsp red pepper flakes
3 cups water
2 cups milk
¼ cup flour
16 oz cavatappi pasta
2 cups frozen peas, thawed
1 cup canned pinto beans

DIRECTIONS and total time: approx. 20 minutes

Warm olive oil on Sauté. Add mushrooms, garlic, parsley, basil, oregano, red pepper flakes, and shallots and cook until tender, 5 minutes. Stir in water, milk, and flour. Place in the remaining ingredients, except for Parmigiano Reggiano shavings and pinto beans. Seal the lid, select Manual at High, and set time to 8 minutes. When ready, do a quick release. Stir in pinto beans and cook until everything heats up on Sauté. Scatter with Parmigiano Reggiano shavings and serve.

Garlic Tilapia in Tomato-Olives Sauce

INGREDIENTS for 4 servings

2 tilapia fillets
Salt and black pepper to taste
4 sprigs fresh thyme
4 lemon slices

2 tbsp butter
2 garlic cloves, thinly sliced
16 cherry tomatoes, halved
2 tsp green olives, sliced

DIRECTIONS and total time: approx. 25 minutes

Rub the fish with salt and pepper. Transfer to a foil-lined baking dish and top each fillet with 2 spring of thyme and 2 slices of lemon. Melt butter on Sauté and cook garlic for 30 seconds until fragrant. Stir in cherry tomatoes and olives and sauté for 3 minutes. Pour the mixture over the fish. Wipe the pot clean, pour in 1 cup water and fit in a trivet. Place the dish on top. Seal the lid, select Manual, and cook for 10 minutes at High. Do a quick release. Top tilapia with the sauce and serve.

Easy Mac´n´Cheese with Sriracha Sauce

INGREDIENTS for 4 servings

1 ½ cups Gruyere cheese, grated
A pinch of salt
1 lb elbow macaroni
2 large eggs

1 tsp ground mustard
1 tsp sriracha sauce
1 ½ cups half and half

DIRECTIONS and total time: approx. 15 minutes

Cover macaroni with salted water inside your Instant Pot. Seal the lid and cook on Manual for 4 minutes at High. When ready, do a quick release. In a bowl, whisk the eggs with ground mustard, sriracha sauce, and half and half. Set the pot to Sauté. Toss in the egg mixture, stir in Gruyere cheese until melted, and serve warm.

Canadian-Style Succotash with Fish

INGREDIENTS for 4 servings

1 tbsp olive oil
½ small onion, chopped
1 garlic clove, minced
1 red chili, chopped
1 cup frozen corn
1 cup mixed green beans
1 cup butternut squash, cubed
1 bay leaf
¼ tsp cayenne pepper

¼ cup chicken stock
½ tsp Worcestershire sauce
Salt and black pepper to taste
4 firm white fish fillets
¼ cup mayonnaise
1 tbsp Dijon mustard
1 ½ cups breadcrumbs
1 tomato, chopped
¼ cup chopped fresh basil

DIRECTIONS and total time: approx. 25 minutes

Season the fish fillets with salt and pepper. In a bowl, mix mayonnaise and mustard. In a separate bowl, pour the breadcrumbs and basil. Spread the mayo mixture on both sides of the fish and dredge each piece in the basil breadcrumbs. Warm olive oil on Sauté and fry the fish for 6-7 minutes in total; set aside. Add onion, garlic, and chili pepper to the pot and sauté for 4 minutes. Stir in corn, butternut squash, green beans, bay leaf, cayenne pepper, chicken stock, and Worcestershire sauce. Seal the lid, select Manual, and cook for 5 minutes at High. Once the succotash is ready, do a quick release. Stir in tomato and remove the bay leaf. Serve warm.

Chili Chicken Carnitas

INGREDIENTS for 4 servings

½ cup cherry tomatoes, halved
1 lb chicken breast
8 corn tortilla shells

1 avocado, sliced

Filling

1 can (10-oz) fire-roasted tomatoes, chopped
½ yellow onion, chopped
1 garlic clove, minced
1 tbsp olive oil
½ cup chicken broth

½ tbsp chili powder
1 tbsp taco seasoning
Salt and black pepper to taste
¼ tsp ground coriander

DIRECTIONS and total time: approx. 30 minutes

Add the chicken to your IP. In a bowl, mix all filling ingredients. Pour the mixture over the chicken. Seal the lid, select Manual, and cook for 15 minutes at High. Do a quick pressure release. Remove the chicken to a cutting board and let it cool for a few minutes. Shred-it and return to the pot; stir. Warm tortillas in the microwave. Divide the chicken mixture between tortillas, top with cherry tomatoes and avocado, and wrap to serve.

Mashed Potatoes & Celeriac with Chives

INGREDIENTS for 4 servings

1 cup water
Salt and black pepper to taste
1 lb potatoes, chopped
½ lb celeriac, chopped

1/3 cup milk
3 tbsp butter, softened
1 garlic clove, minced
¼ handful chives, chopped

DIRECTIONS and total time: approx. 30 minutes

Place water, salt, celeriac, and potatoes into your IP. Seal the lid, select Steam, and set the time to 10 minutes at High. When ready, do a natural pressure release for 10 minutes. Drain celeriac and potatoes. Use a masher to mash the potatoes, and slowly pour in the milk until uniform and smooth. Add in butter, pepper, and garlic and whisk until you get the desired texture. Adjust the seasoning. Serve scattered with a handful of chives.

Shrimp Paella with Andouille Sausage

INGREDIENTS for 4 servings

1 lb jumbo shrimp, peeled and deveined
1 tbsp melted butter
1 lb andouille sausage, sliced
1 white onion, chopped
4 garlic cloves, minced
½ cup dry white wine
1 cup Spanish rice

2 cups chicken stock
1 ½ tsp sweet paprika
1 tsp turmeric powder
Salt and black pepper to taste
1 lb baby squid, cut into rings
1 red bell pepper, chopped

DIRECTIONS and total time: approx. 30 minutes

Melt butter on Sauté and cook sausage until browned, 3 minutes; set aside. Sauté onion, garlic, bell pepper, and squid in the same fat for 5 minutes. Pour in white wine. Scrape off any browned bits from the bottom and cook for 2 minutes until wine reduces by half. Stir in rice and chicken broth, season with paprika, turmeric, salt, and pepper. Seal the lid, select Manual, and set time to 5 minutes at High. When ready, do a quick pressure release. Select Sauté and add in shrimp. Stir gently without mashing the rice. Cook for 6 minutes, until the shrimp are pink and opaque. Return the sausage to the pot and stir. Warm for 2 minutes and serve.

Italian-Style Chicken

INGREDIENTS for 4 servings

2 lb boneless, skinless chicken breasts, halved lengthwise
½ cup sun-dried tomatoes, chopped
¾ cup Parmesan, grated
1 tbsp Italian seasoning
Salt and black pepper to taste
1 tbsp garlic powder

2 tbsp butter
1 cup chicken broth
¾ cup heavy cream
2 cups spinach, chopped

DIRECTIONS and total time: approx. 30 minutes

Flatten the chicken breasts with a meat mallet. Season with Italian seasoning, salt, pepper, and garlic powder. Set the pot to Sauté and melt the butter. Add in chicken and brown for 4 minutes on both sides. Pour in broth, seal the lid, select Manual, and cook for 10 minutes at High. When ready, do a quick release and remove the chicken. Select Sauté and stir in heavy cream, sun-dried tomatoes, and spinach for 5 minutes until the spinach is wilted. Return the chicken to the pot. Sprinkle with Parmesan cheese and serve.

Carrot & Potato Crispy Chicken

INGREDIENTS for 4 servings

4 bone-in chicken thighs
Salt and black pepper to taste
2 tbsp melted butter
2 tsp Worcestershire sauce
2 tsp turmeric powder
1 tsp dried oregano
½ tsp dry mustard

½ tsp garlic powder
¼ tsp sweet paprika
2 tsp chili sauce
1 cup chicken stock
1 tbsp olive oil
1 lb potatoes, quartered
2 carrots, sliced into rounds

DIRECTIONS and total time: approx. 30 minutes

In a bowl, mix butter, Worcestershire sauce, turmeric, oregano, mustard, garlic powder, paprika, and chili sauce until well combined, and stir in chicken stock. Heat olive oil on Sauté and fry the thighs for 4-5 minutes until browned. Season with salt and pepper; reserve. Add potatoes, carrots, and half of the spicy sauce to the pot and mix to coat. Put the chicken thighs on top and drizzle with the remaining sauce. Seal the lid, select Manual, and cook for 15 minutes at High. After cooking, do a quick pressure release. Serve.

Salmon with Hot-Garlic Sauce

INGREDIENTS for 4 servings

2 salmon fillets   Salt and black pepper to taste
For sauce:
1 tbsp chili garlic sauce
½ lemon juiced
2 cloves garlic minced
1 tbsp honey

1 tbsp olive oil
1 tbsp hot water
1 tbsp chopped cilantro
½ tsp cumin

DIRECTIONS and total time: approx. 15 minutes

In a bowl, combine all the sauce ingredients; set aside. Pour 1 cup of water in the pot and fit in a trivet. Place salmon on the trivet and sprinkle with salt and pepper. Seal lid, select Steam, and cook for 5 minutes at High. When ready, do a quick pressure release. Transfer the salmon to a plate, drizzle with the sauce and serve.

Chicken Wings in Hot Sauce

INGREDIENTS for 4 servings

24 chicken wings
2 tbsp sesame oil
2 tbsp hot sauce

2 tbsp honey
2 garlic cloves, minced
1 tbsp toasted sesame seeds

DIRECTIONS and total time: approx. 20 minutes

Pour 1 cup of water in inner pot and fit in a trivet. Place the chicken wings on the trivet. Seal the lid, select Manual, and cook for 10 minutes at High. After cooking, do a quick release. Remove the trivet from the pot and discard water. In a bowl, whisk sesame oil, hot sauce, honey, and garlic. Toss the wings in the sauce and put them in the pot. Press Sauté and cook for 5 minutes. Sprinkle with the sesame seeds and serve.

Chicken Meatballs in Tomato Sauce

INGREDIENTS for 4 servings

1 lb ground chicken	2 1/3 tbsp Parmesan, grated
3 tbsp breadcrumbs	2 tbsp olive oil
2 1/3 tbsp whole milk	2 tbsp white wine
1 garlic clove, minced	½ can (14.5 oz) tomato sauce
1 egg, beaten	Salt and black pepper to taste

DIRECTIONS and total time: approx. 25 minutes

In a bowl, mix ground chicken, breadcrumbs, garlic, salt, pepper, egg, and Parmesan cheese. Shape the mixture into medium-sized balls. Set the pot to Sauté and heat olive oil. Brown the meatballs for 5-6 minutes on all sides; reserve. Pour in white wine to scrape off any browned bits from the bottom. Stir in tomato sauce and ½ cup of water and return the meatballs. Seal the lid, select Manual and cook for 10 minutes at High. When done, perform a quick pressure release. Serve.

Green Onion & Walnut Salmon Pilaf

INGREDIENTS for 4 servings

1 smoked salmon fillet, flaked	1 cup frozen corn, thawed
4 green onions, chopped	Salt and black pepper to taste
½ cup walnuts, chopped	2 tsp prepared horseradish
1 tbsp canola oil	1 tomato, chopped
1 cup basmati rice	2 cups water

DIRECTIONS and total time: approx. 25 minutes

Heat canola oil on Sauté and stir-fry green onions for 3 minutes. Stir in rice and cook for 2 minutes. Add in water, salt, and pepper. Seal the lid, select Manual and cook for 5 minutes at High. After cooking, do a natural pressure release for 10 minutes. Fluff the rice with a fork. Stir in flaked salmon, corn, horseradish, and tomato and let warm. Top with walnuts and serve.

Egg Noodles with Sausage & Pancetta

INGREDIENTS for 4 servings

3 oz pancetta, chopped	Salt and black pepper to taste
1 tbsp olive oil	5 oz wide egg noodles
1 onion, sliced	4 cups shredded cabbage
½ cup dry white wine	1 lb smoked sausage, sliced
2 cups chicken stock	2 tbsp parsley, chopped

DIRECTIONS and total time: approx. 20 minutes

Heat olive oil on Sauté and cook pancetta for 6 minutes. Transfer to a paper towel-lined plate. Add onion to the pot and sauté for 3 minutes. Pour in wine and simmer until reduced by half. Stir to scrape the bottom off any browned bits. Pour in chicken stock and noodles. Add in cabbage and sausages on top of cabbage. Seal the lid, select Manual and set the timer to 8 minutes at High. When ready, do a quick release. Adjust the seasoning and top with pancetta Serve warm.

Paprika & Leek Chicken Pilaf

INGREDIENTS for 4 servings

1 lb boneless chicken thighs, skin on	
2 tbsp olive oil	¼ tsp ground coriander
1 leek, chopped	1 ½ cups chicken stock
1 cup rice, rinsed	1 carrot, chopped
Salt and black pepper to taste	1 celery stick, chopped
¼ tsp smoked paprika	2 garlic cloves, minced

DIRECTIONS and total time: approx. 40 minutes

Heat olive oil on Sauté and cook chicken for 5 minutes per side or until golden brown; reserve. Put in leek, carrot, celery, and garlic and cook for 3 minutes until softened. Stir in rice, salt, black pepper, cumin, smoked paprika, and coriander. Cook for 2 minutes. Pour in chicken stock and stir; return the chicken. Seal the lid, select Manual and set time to 15 minutes at High. When ready, do a natural pressure release for 10 minutes. Fluff the rice with a fork and serve.

Mexican-Style Green Chili Chicken

INGREDIENTS for 4 servings

½ cup shredded cheddar	1 ½ lb chicken breasts
2 tbsp olive oil	2 jalapeños, chopped
12 oz plum tomatoes, halved	1 serrano pepper, chopped
1 cup chicken stock	2 garlic cloves, minced
Salt and black pepper to taste	1 onion, sliced
½ tsp ground cumin	¼ cup minced fresh cilantro
1 tsp Mexican seasoning mix	½ lime, juiced

DIRECTIONS and total time: approx. 40 minutes

Heat olive oil on Sauté and cook chicken for 5-6 minutes on all sides; reserve. Add onion and jalapeño and serrano peppers to the pot and sauté for 3 minutes. Stir in cumin, Mexican seasoning, salt, and pepper for 1 minute and pour in tomatoes; cook for 3 minutes. Add in stock and return the chicken. Seal the lid, select Manual and cook for 15 minutes. Do a quick pressure release. Remove the chicken and purée the remaining ingredients with an immersion blender. Shred the chicken and return it to the pot. Drizzle with lime juice. Top with cheddar cheese and cilantro to serve.

Spicy Baby Back Ribs

INGREDIENTS for 4 servings

1 rack (2 lb) baby back ribs, quartered	
2 tbsp oil	Hoisin sauce

Rub

1 tbsp salt	1 tbsp white sugar
2 tbsp smoked paprika	½ tbsp ground mustard
1 tbsp black pepper	½ tsp cayenne pepper
1 tbsp garlic powder	½ tsp cumin
1 tbsp onion powder	½ tsp ground fennel seeds
1 tbsp chili powder	½ tsp dried rosemary

DIRECTIONS and total time: approx. 30 min + chilling time

In a bowl, combine all the rub ingredients. Coat the ribs with the mixture. Cover with plastic wrap and let sit in the fridge overnight. Heat oil on Sauté and brown the ribs meat-side down for 5 minutes. Remove to a plate. Pour 1 cup water in the pot and fit in a trivet. Arrange the ribs on the trivet. Seal the lid, select Manual, and cook for 20 minutes at High. When done, perform a quick release and transfer the ribs to a foil-lined baking dish. Brush with hoisin sauce and set under the broiler for 4 minutes until a nice crust is formed. Serve warm.

Saucy Turkey with Green Peas

INGREDIENTS for 4 servings

1 (1 oz) package onion soup	1 onion, chopped
2 tbsp olive oil	1 cup chicken broth
1 lb turkey breast, sliced	1 tbsp cornstarch
2 ribs celery, chopped	1 cup green peas

DIRECTIONS and total time: approx. 55 minutes

Heat olive oil on Sauté. Add celery, onion, salt and pepper, and stir-fry for 3 minutes. Rub the turkey with onion soup mix and add to the pot. Cook for 5 minutes, stirring occasionally. Pour in broth, seal the lid, select Manual, and cook for 20 minutes at High. When done, perform a quick release. Remove to a plate. In a bowl, combine cornstarch and some liquid from the pot. Stir until dissolved. Set the pot to Sauté, pour in the slurry and cook for 3 minutes until reduced to a thick consistency. Stir in green peas and cook for 3 minutes. Top the turkey with the sauce and serve.

Mushroom & Potato Beef Stew

INGREDIENTS for 4 servings

2 tbsp olive oil	1 garlic clove, minced
1 lb beef stew meat, cubed	¼ cup red wine
2 tbsp flour	1 bay leaf
Salt and black pepper to taste	1 tbsp dry thyme
½ tbsp paprika	4 potatoes, cubed
1 onion, chopped	1 cup canned tomatoes
1 carrot, chopped	1 cup mushrooms, sliced
1 celery stalk, chopped	2 cups beef stock

DIRECTIONS and total time: approx. 70 minutes

Set to Sauté and heat the oil. Toss the beef with salt, pepper, and flour until completely coated. Place into the pot and brown for 5-6 minutes, stirring occasionally; set aside. Add onion, carrot, celery, garlic, and mushroom and cook for 5 minutes, until tender. Pour in the remaining ingredients and stir to combine. Seal the lid, select Meat/Stew, and set the time to 35 minutes at High. When ready, do a natural pressure release for 10 minutes. Remove and discard the bay leaf. Ladle the stew into bowls to serve.

Jalapeño Chicken Quesadillas with Kale

INGREDIENTS for 4 servings

½ cup grated Pecorino Romano cheese	
1 lb chicken breasts	
¼ cup butter, softened	3 oz cottage cheese
2 cups baby kale, chopped	2 tsp Mexican seasoning mix
1 jalapeño pepper, minced	6 oz shredded cheddar cheese
1 onion, chopped	4 medium flour tortillas

DIRECTIONS and total time: approx. 30 minutes

Melt 2 tbsp of the butter on Sauté and cook chicken for 5-6 minutes on all sides. Season with salt and pepper, and pour in 1 cup water. Seal the lid, select Manual, and cook for 15 minutes. Do a quick pressure release. Remove the chicken. Clean the pot and warm 1 tbsp of butter. Add kale, jalapeño pepper, and onion and cook for 5 minutes, stirring occasionally. Remove to a bowl. Shred the chicken with 2 forks and add it to the kale mixture. Stir in cottage and cheddar cheeses and Mexican seasoning. Place a tortilla on a clean flat surface. Brush the top with some butter and sprinkle 1 tsp of Pecorino Romano cheese on top. Press the cheese down with the palm of your hand to stick to the tortilla. Spread about a 1/3 cup of kale mixture over half of the tortilla. Fold the other half over the filling and press. Repeat the process with the remaining tortillas. Serve.

Pork with Mushrooms & Tomato Sauce

INGREDIENTS for 4 servings

1 ½ tbsp cornstarch mixed with 2 tbsp water	
4 boneless pork loin chops	2 tbsp peanut oil
1 onion, sliced	1 tbsp white sugar
4 garlic cloves, minced	1 tsp tabasco sauce
8 mushrooms, sliced	Salt and black pepper to taste
2 tbsp tomato paste	2 tbsp ketchup

Marinade

2 sambal oelek ground fresh chili paste	
½ tsp brown sugar	1 ½ tbsp soy sauce
1 tsp sesame oil	2 tbsp light soy sauce

DIRECTIONS and total time: approx. 45 minutes

Using a meat mallet, flatten the pork chops. In a bowl, combine brown sugar, soy sauce, sesame oil, salt, and chili paste. Stir in pork chops, cover, and marinate for 10 minutes. Heat peanut oil on Sauté. Place in the marinated chops and cook for 2 minutes per side; reserve. Add onion, garlic, and mushrooms to the pot and cook for 3 minutes. Pour in 1 cup water to scrape off any browned bits from the bottom. Add in ketchup, white sugar, tabasco sauce, and tomato paste and stir; return the chops. Seal the lid, select Manual, and set timer to 15 minutes at High. When ready, do a natural release for 10 minutes, and remove the chops. Select Sauté and stir in the cornstarch slurry. Cook until a thick sauce is obtained. Adjust the seasoning and serve.

Easy Mango-Teriyaki Chicken

INGREDIENTS for 4 servings

1 lb bone-in, skin-on chicken thighs
1 cup canned mango chunks, drained
Salt to taste
2 tbsp sesame oil
½ cup chicken broth
¼ cup teriyaki sauce

2 tbsp soy sauce
1 red bell pepper, chopped
1 tsp sesame seeds
2 tbsp cilantro, chopped

DIRECTIONS and total time: approx. 40 minutes

Season chicken thighs with salt. Set the pot to Sauté and warm sesame oil. Cook the chicken for 4 minutes on all sides; reserve. Add bell pepper to the pot and sauté for 3-4 minutes. Pour in broth to scrape off any browned bits from the bottom. Stir in 2 tbsp of teriyaki sauce and soy sauce; return the chicken. Seal the lid, select Manual, and cook for 15 minutes at High. When done, perform a quick pressure release. Transfer the chicken to a baking sheet. Drizzle with the remaining teriyaki sauce and place under the broiler for 4 minutes, until golden brown. Add mango chunks to the pot. Press Sauté and cook for 3 minutes until the sauce is thickened. Divide the chicken among serving plates and spoon the sauce over. Sprinkle with sesame seeds and cilantro. Serve warm.

Beef Sloppy Joes with BBQ Sauce

INGREDIENTS for 4 servings

1 onion, chopped
2 tbsp olive oil
1 lb ground beef
1 red pepper, chopped
1 celery stick, chopped
¼ cup beef broth
1 garlic clove, minced

1 tbsp tomato purée
1 tbsp yellow mustard
2 tsp brown sugar
2 tsp BBQ sauce
Salt and black pepper to taste
4 seeded burger buns, halved
4 lettuce leaves

DIRECTIONS and total time: approx. 25 minutes

Set to Sauté and warm the olive oil. Brown beef for 4 minutes, breaking it with a wooden spatula. Stir in onion, red pepper, garlic, and celery and sauté for 3 minutes. Stir in tomato puree, mustard, sugar, and BBQ sauce. Pour in beef broth; season. Seal the lid, select Manual and cook for 12 minutes at High. When ready, do a quick release and adjust the seasoning. Arrange lettuce leaves on the bottom bun halves, top with meat and sauce, and cover with the other top bun halves.

Pearl Onion & Squash Beef Stew

INGREDIENTS for 6 servings

2 tbsp olive oil
1 (3-pound) chuck roast
½ cup dry red wine
1 cup beef broth
1 tsp oregano

1 bay leaf
Salt and black pepper to taste
2 lb butternut squash, chopped
2 carrots, chopped
1 cup pearl onions

DIRECTIONS and total time: approx. 55 minutes

Heat olive oil on Sauté. Season the beef with salt and pepper and add to the pot. Cook for 3 minutes per side; reserve. Add squash, pearl onions, and carrots to the pot and sauté for 3 minutes. Pour in wine and scrape the bottom of the pot off any browned bits. Bring to a boil and cook for 2 minutes, until the wine has reduced by half. Mix in broth, oregano, and bay leaf. Stir to combine and add beef with its juices. Seal the lid, select Manual and set the timer to 35 minutes at High. After cooking, do a quick release. Remove the beef and slice. Remove and discard the bay leaf. Taste the meal and adjust the seasoning. Transfer to a serving plate and top with beef slices to serve.

Hispanic Chicken & Rice

INGREDIENTS for 4 servings

1 onion, chopped
4 tbsp olive oil
3 chicken breasts, cubed
Salt and black pepper to taste
1 red bell pepper, chopped
2 garlic cloves, minced
1 cup white rice

1½ cups chicken broth
½ cup dry white wine
2 tbsp drained Spanish capers
1 (14-oz) can tomatoes
1 cup frozen peas
½ cup green olives
¼ cup parsley, for garnishing

DIRECTIONS and total time: approx. 35 minutes

Heat olive oil on Sauté. Sprinkle the chicken with salt and pepper, and cook in the pot for 5 minutes or until browned, stirring occasionally; remove to a plate. To the pot, add and sauté onion, bell pepper and garlic for 3 minutes. Stir in rice for 1 minute. Pour in broth, white wine, capers, tomatoes, peas, and olives. Bring back the chicken, seal the lid, select Manual, and set timer to 15 minutes at High. When ready, do a quick pressure release. Garnish with parsley and serve.

Beef Stew with Fennel & Red Wine

INGREDIENTS for 4 servings

3 lb stewing beef, cubed
¾ cup flour
Salt and pepper to taste
1 lb red potatoes, cubed
1 tbs tomato paste
2 carrots, peeled and chopped

½ cup red wine
½ fennel bulb, sliced
1 onion, chopped
2 ½ cups beef stock
3 tbs olive oil
2 tbsp chopped parsley

DIRECTIONS and total time: approx. 50 minutes

Season the beef with salt and pepper, then roll in the flour. Set the pot to Sauté and heat olive oil. Cook the beef for 8 minutes, stirring often; reserve. Add onion, carrots, and fennel to the pot, and sauté for 3 minutes. Pour in red wine to deglaze and cook until reduced by half. Return the meat and add in potatoes, tomato paste, and stock. Seal the lid, select Manual, and cook for 30 minutes at High. Sprinkle with parsley and serve.

French Cheesy Beef Baguettes

INGREDIENTS for 6 servings

1 (10-oz) can condensed onion soup
6 small French Baguettes, halved lengthwise

1 onion, chopped	1 tbsp soy sauce
1 garlic clove, minced	1 ½ cups beef broth
1 tbsp olive oil	2 bay leaves
3 lb beef chuck roast	6 Fontina cheese slices
Salt and black pepper to taste	2 tbsp Dijon mustard

DIRECTIONS and total time: approx. 50 minutes

Warm olive oil on Sauté. Rub the roast with salt and brown for 5 minutes per side; reserve. Add garlic and onion to the pot and sauté for 3 minutes. Pour in soy sauce, onion soup, beef broth, and bay leaves; return the beef. Seal the lid, select Manual and cook for 30 minutes at High. Do a quick pressure release. Transfer the beef to a plate. Let cool slightly before shredding it with 2 forks. Remove and discard the bay leaves from the sauce and adjust the seasoning. Divide Fontina cheese and mustard among the baguettes, top with shredded meat, and serve with cooking sauce.

Empanadas Filled with Beef & Olives

INGREDIENTS for 4 servings

1 cup olive oil	Salt and black pepper to taste
1 garlic clove, minced	¼ tsp paprika
1 white onion, chopped	2 small tomatoes, chopped
1 lb ground beef	8 square wonton wrappers
¼ tsp cumin powder	1 egg, beaten
⅛ tsp cinnamon powder	6 green olives, chopped

DIRECTIONS and total time: approx. 35 minutes

Heat 2 tbsp olive oil on Sauté and cook garlic, onion, and ground beef for 5 minutes, stirring occasionally, until the beef is no longer pink. Stir in olives, cumin, cinnamon, and paprika for an additional 1 minute. Pour in tomatoes and 1 cup of water. Season with salt and pepper. Seal the lid, select Manual, and set to 12 minutes at High. After cooking, do a quick pressure release. Remove and let cool for a few minutes. Lay the wonton wrappers on a flat surface. Place 2 tbsp of beef mixture in the middle of each wrapper. Brush the edges of the wrapper with egg and fold in half to form a triangle. Pinch the edges together to seal. Wipe the inner pot clean, heat the remaining oil and fry the empanadas in a single layer, about 20 seconds per side. Remove to paper towels to soak up excess fat. Serve.

Bacon & Mozzarella Egg Bites

INGREDIENTS for 4 servings

¾ cup shredded mozzarella	4 large eggs
½ cup ricotta cheese	¼ cup heavy cream
¼ cup crumbled cooked bacon	½ tsp salt

DIRECTIONS and total time: approx. 20 minutes

Mix eggs, mozzarella, ricotta, heavy cream and salt in a bowl. Divide the bacon among ramekins, then fill with the cheese mixture, and cover with foil. Pour 1 cup of water in your Instant Pot and fit in a trivet. Place ramekins on the trivet. Seal the lid, select Manual and set timer to 8 minutes at High. When done, perform a natural pressure release for 10 minutes. Serve warm.

Pork Ragu with Rigatoni

INGREDIENTS for 6 servings

4 oz Italian sausages, casings removed

½ cup grated Parmesan cheese	1 celery stalk, chopped
1 (28-oz) can diced tomatoes	1 carrot, chopped
1 lb boneless pork shoulder	½ cup dry red wine
Salt and black pepper to taste	⅛ tsp red pepper flakes
2 tbsp olive oil	2 tbsp tomato paste
1 onion, chopped	2 tsp dried Italian herb mix
2 garlic cloves, minced	16 oz rigatoni

DIRECTIONS and total time: approx. 40 minutes

Heat olive oil on Sauté. Season the pork with salt and brown for 4 minutes on both sides. Add in sausages, onion, garlic, celery, and carrot and sauté for 2 minutes. Stir in red wine and scrape the bottom of any browned bits. Cook for 3 minutes until it has reduced by half. Add pepper flakes, tomatoes, tomato paste, salt, herbs, and 1 cup of water; stir to combine. Seal the lid, select Manual at High and set the timer to 20 minutes. After cooking, do a quick pressure release. Shred the pork with 2 forks and break the sausages. Add 2 cups of water and the rigatoni. Seal the lid, press Pressure Cook at High, and cook for 4 minutes. After cooking, do a quick release. Sprinkle with Parmesan and serve.

Spaghetti Carbonara with Broccoli

INGREDIENTS for 4 servings

1 head broccoli, cut into florets	4 eggs
1 lb spaghetti	8 oz bacon
1 garlic clove, minced	1 cup Pecorino cheese, grated
Salt to taste	1 tbsp butter

DIRECTIONS and total time: approx. 20 minutes

Cover spaghetti with salted water in your IP. Seal the lid, select Manual, and cook for 4 minutes at High. Do a quick release. Remove pasta with slotted spoon to a bowl. Fit a steamer basket in the pot and place broccoli on top. Seal the lid and cook for 2 minutes at High. Do a quick pressure release. In a bowl, whisk eggs with cheese. Wipe the pot clean and set to Sauté. Add in bacon and garlic and cook for 5 minutes. Melt in the butter. Return pasta to the pot and reheat it for 30 seconds. Add in egg mixture and stir until the eggs thicken into a sauce. Top with the broccoli and serve.

Guajillo Chili Beans with Bacon

INGREDIENTS for 4 servings

4 oz smoked bacon, cooked and crumbled
4 dried Guajillo chilies, soaked, liquid reserved
1 cup black beans, soaked | Salt to taste
2 tbsp avocado oil | ½ tsp dried oregano
1 yellow onion, chopped | 3 cups tomatoes, chopped
5 cloves garlic | 4 cups vegetable broth
1 ½ tsp ground cumin | 1 bell pepper, chopped

DIRECTIONS and total time: approx. 50 minutes

Cut the stems of the Guajillo chilies and deseed. Put in a blender along with garlic and onion, and process until finely chopped. Mix all the spices in a bowl. Set your IP to Sauté and heat avocado oil. Place in the chili mixture and sauté for 5 minutes, stirring frequently. Stir in spices and cook for 30 seconds. Pour in the reserved chili liquid, black beans, tomatoes, vegetable broth, and bell pepper and stir to combine. Seal the lid, select Bean/Stew at High, and set time to 30 minutes. When done, perform a natural pressure release for 10 minutes. Stir in bacon and serve immediately.

Serrano Ham & Cheese Cups

INGREDIENTS for 4 servings

2 serrano ham slices, halved widthwise
1 tbsp olive oil | ½ oregano
4 large eggs | Salt and black pepper to taste
1 oz cottage cheese | ¼ cup grated Emmental
¼ cup half and half | ¼ cup caramelized onions

DIRECTIONS and total time: approx. 20 minutes

Heat olive oil on Sauté and cook ham for 2 minutes, turning once; reserve. Rush the inside of 4 ramekins with ham fat. Crack eggs into a bowl and add cottage cheese, half and half, oregano, salt, and pepper. Use a hand mixer to whisk the ingredients until combined. Stir in Emmental cheese and mix again to incorporate the cheese. Lay a piece of ham on the bottom of each cup. Share the onions among the cups as well as the egg mixture. Pour 1 cup of water in the pot and fit in a trivet. Arrange the ramekins on top. Seal the lid, select Manual at High for 7 minutes. When ready, do a quick release. Remove the cups and let chill before serving.

Lemon Apple Pies

INGREDIENTS for 4 servings

1 refrigerated pie crust, at room temperature
1 apple, chopped | ½ lemon, juiced
2 tbsp sugar | 1 tsp cornstarch

DIRECTIONS and total time: approx. 50 minutes

In a bowl, combine apple, sugar, and lemon juice. Let stand for 10 minutes, then drain and reserve the liquid.

In a bowl, whisk cornstarch into the reserved liquid and mix with the apple mixture. Put the piecrust on a floured surface and cut into 4 circles. Spoon a tbsp of apple mixture in the center of the circle. Brush the edges with some water and fold the dough over the filling. Press the edges to seal. Cut 3 small slits on top of each pie and grease with cooking spray. Arrange the pies on a greased baking pan. Pour 1 cup of water into your IP. Fit in a trivet and place the pan on top. Seal, select Manual and cook for 30 minutes at High. After cooking, do a quick pressure release. Serve cooled.

Grandma's Vanilla Cheesecake

INGREDIENTS for 6 servings

1 ½ cups finely crushed graham crackers
2 tbsp sugar | ¼ cup sour cream
4 tbsp butter, melted | 1 tbsp all-purpose flour
16 oz cream cheese | 1 ½ tsp vanilla extract
½ cup brown sugar | 2 eggs

DIRECTIONS and total time: approx. 45 min + chilling time

Grease a springform pan with cooking spray, then line with parchment paper. In a bowl, mix crumbs, sugar, and butter. Spoon the mixture into the pan and press firmly with a spoon. In a deep bowl, beat the cream cheese and brown sugar with a hand mixer. Whisk in sour cream to be smooth and stir in flour, and vanilla. Crack in the eggs and beat, but not to be overly smooth. Pour the mixture over the crumbs. Pour 1 cup of water into your IP and fit in a trivet. Put the springform pan on the trivet. Seal the lid, select Manual at High and set the timer to 35 minutes. Once ready, do a natural release for 10 minutes. Allow the cheesecake to cool for 1 hour. Cover with foil and refrigerate for 4 hours.

Cinnamon Plum Clafoutis

INGREDIENTS for 4 servings

2 tsp butter, softened | ½ cup flour
1 cup plums, chopped | 2 large eggs
1 cup whole milk | ¼ tsp cinnamon
½ cup half and half | ½ tsp vanilla extract
¼ cup sugar | 2 tbsp confectioners' sugar

DIRECTIONS and total time: approx. 25 minutes

Grease 4 ramekins with butter and divide the plums among them. Pour milk, half and half, sugar, flour, eggs, cinnamon, and vanilla in a bowl and whisk with a hand mixer until smooth. Pour the mixture over the plums. Pour 1 cup of water in your IP. Fit in a trivet and put the ramekins on top. Seal the lid, select Manual and cook for 11 minutes at High. When ready, do a quick release. Remove the ramekins onto a flat surface. Let cool and dust with confectioners' sugar.

Cinnamon Berry Cobbler

INGREDIENTS for 4 servings

2 bags mixed berries	¼ tsp almond extract
3 tbsp arrowroot starch	5 tbsp powdered sugar
1 cup sugar	1 cup crème fraiche
1 cup self-rising flour	1 tbsp melted butter
¼ tsp cinnamon powder	1 tbsp whipping cream

DIRECTIONS and total time: approx. 25 min + cooling time

Pour the berries into your IP along with arrowroot starch and sugar; mix to combine. Select Sauté and cook for 3 minutes. In a bowl, whisk flour, cinnamon powder, and powdered sugar. In a separate bowl, whisk crème fraiche, almond extract, and butter. Mix cream mixture with the dry ingredients. Spread the dough over the berries. Brush the topping with whipping cream. Seal the lid, select Manual and cook for 10 minutes at High. When ready, do a quick pressure release. Serve cooled.

Banana Bread with Frangelico Liqueur

INGREDIENTS for 4 servings

4 bananas, mashed	½ cup sugar
6 tbsp butter, melted	1 tsp baking powder
2 small eggs, beaten	2 cups flour
1 tbsp Frangelico liqueur	1 cup water

DIRECTIONS and total time: approx. 45 minutes

In a bowl, combine butter, eggs, bananas, and Frangelico liqueur. Whisk in sugar, baking powder and flour until combined. Pour the mixture in a greased baking pan. Pour water in your Instant Pot and fit in a trivet. Place the pan on top, seal the lid, select Manual at High, and set timer to 25 minutes. When ready, do a natural pressure release for 10 minutes. Remove the bread from the pan and let cool. Slice and serve.

Berry Mascarpone Cake

INGREDIENTS for 6 servings

1 large egg	2 tsp baking soda
1 cup butter, soften	¾ cup sugar
16 oz mascarpone cheese	¾ cup milk
2 cups flour	3 cups fresh berries

DIRECTIONS and total time: approx. 45 minutes

In a bowl, mix mascarpone, flour, and baking soda. In a separate bowl, beat butter, sugar, and egg until creamy. Add to the flour mixture and stir in the milk and berries. Pour into a greased baking pan. Pour 1 cup of water in IP and fit in a trivet. Place the pan on top. Seal the lid, select Manual at High and set timer to 25 minutes. When done, perform a natural release for 10 minutes. Let cool for a few minutes. Serve sliced.

Classic Caramel-Walnut Brownies

INGREDIENTS for 4 servings

8 oz white chocolate, melted	2 large eggs
8 tbsp butter, melted	¾ cup all-purpose flour
1 cup sugar	½ cup caramel sauce
2 tsp almond extract	½ cup walnuts, chopped

DIRECTIONS and total time: approx. 35 min + chilling time

In a bowl, mix chocolate with butter. Stir in almond extract and sugar. Whisk in eggs. Mix in flour and stir in walnuts. Pour batter into a greased cake pan. Place a trivet in IP and pour in 1 cup of water. Lay the pan on top. Seal the lid, select Manual, and cook for 25 minutes. When ready, do a quick pressure release. Remove the pan, drizzle the sauce on top and let cool. Cut into squares to serve.

Index

1. Adobo Chicken in Roasted Pepper Sauce 46
2. Almond Butter Bars 122
3. Apple & Brazil Nut Porridge 28
4. Apple-Butternut Squash Soup 102
5. Apple Cacao Dessert 123
6. Apple & Cinnamon Cake 126
7. Apple Coconut Dessert 122
8. Apple & Honey Chicken Drumsticks 55
9. Apple Oatmeal 22
10. Apples in Cranberry Sauce 94
11. Apricots & Pecans with Mascarpone 124
12. Apricot Wild Rice Pudding 31
13. Arroz con Leche with Prunes 34
14. Asian-Style Chicken Thighs 48
15. Authentic Spanish Crema Catalana 120
16. Awesome Candied Potatoes 93
17. Awesome Chocolate Lava Cake 122
18. Bacon Asparagus Wraps 113
19. Bacon & Cheese Eggs with Chives 111
20. Bacon & Mozzarella Egg Bites 135
21. Balls of Zucchini in Ginger Sauce 96
22. Balsamic Pork Tenderloin 61
23. Banana Bread with Frangelico Liqueur 137
24. Barbecued Brisket with Tagliatelle 79
25. Barley & Potato Soup 26
26. Basil Buttered Corn on the Cob 90
27. Basil Cherry Tomato Soup 101
28. Basil Chicken Casserole 52
29. Basil Infused Avocado Dip 118
30. Basil Infused Salmon with Chickpeas 40
31. Basil Lentil & Barley with Mushrooms 107
32. Basil Pork Meatballs 63
33. Basmati Rice with Pumpkin 33
34. BBQ Chicken Wings with Shallots 48
35. BBQ Pulled Pork 64
36. Bean Soup with Pork & Vegetables 23
37. Beat Lamb Stew with Kale & Peaches 85
38. Beef & Bean Goulash 82
39. Beef Brisket with Vegetables 84
40. Beef & Cavolo Nero Pot 83
41. Beef & Jalapeño Curry 83
42. Beef & Pancetta Bourguignon 77
43. Beef Paprikash 81
44. Beef & Portobello Stew 108
45. Beef, Potato & Carrot Soup 104
46. Beef Ribs Texas BBQ Style 115
47. Beef & Rice Stuffed Cabbage Leaves 32
48. Beef Roast with Red Potatoes 73
49. Beef & Rutabaga Stew 81
50. Beef & Sauerkraut German Dinner 72
51. Beef Sausage & Bean Tagliatelle 72
52. Beef Sausage & Spinach Stew 84
53. Beef Sloppy Joes with BBQ Sauce 134
54. Beef Sloppy Joes with Coleslaw 72
55. Beef Soup with Red Potatoes & Pancetta 84
56. Beef Spaghetti Bolognese 76
57. Beef Stew with Bacon & Avocado 110
58. Beef Stew with Carrots & Parsnips 110
59. Beef Stew with Fennel & Red Wine 134
60. Beef Stew with Tomatoes 83
61. Beef & Vegetable Casserole 79
62. Beef with Chestnuts & Pearl Onions 74
63. Beef with Garlic & Honey 78
64. Beef with Lemon-Grapefruit Sauce 73
65. Beef with Pearl Onions & Mushrooms 79
66. Beer Cheese Potato Soup 104
67. Beery Chocolate Cups 127
68. Bell Pepper & Salmon One-Pot 39
69. Bell Pepper & Zucchini Salmon 41
70. Berry Mascarpone Cake 137
71. Best Bacon Wrapped Mini Smokies 113
72. Best Black Bean Chili 25
73. Best Crab Patties 36
74. Black Bean & Green Chili con Queso 27
75. Black Bean & Quinoa Stew 23
76. Black-Eyed Pea & Sweet Potato Bowl 15
77. Blueberry Clafoutis 125
78. Blue Cheese Potatoes 90
79. Bok Choy & Tomato Side 21
80. Bolognese Sauce Vegan-Style 95
81. Braised Red Cabbage & Cherry Stew 100
82. Broccoli, Cauliflower & Zucchini Cakes 88
83. Broccoli & Potatoes with Gruyere 129
84. Brown Rice and Kidney Beans Casserole 100
85. Brussel Sprout & Beef with Red Sauce 76
86. Brussel Sprouts & Apple Lunch 95
87. Brussel Sprouts with Onions & Apples 16
88. Buckwheat with Vegetables & Ham 25
89. Buffalo Chicken Wings with Cheese Dip 114
90. Buffalo Turkey & Squash Casserole 56
91. Bulgur with Vegetables 28
92. Burgundy Beef Rice Stew 32
93. Burrito Beef 80
94. Buttered Trout 39
95. Butter-Lemon Pears 121
96. Butternut Squash & Carrot Egg Casserole 12
97. Cabbage & Carrot Soup with Bacon 104
98. Cajun Beef Ribeye 77
99. Cajun Chicken with Snow Beans 46
100. Camembert Root Vegetable Mix 117
101. Canadian-Style Succotash with Fish 130
102. Canned Tuna Casserole 38
103. Cannellini Bean & Chili Salad 114
104. Cannellini Beans Ragout 94
105. Caraway Chicken with Vegetables 43
106. Caribbean Beef Roast 77
107. Caribbean Black-Eyed Pea Stew 110
108. Carrot & Nut Cakes 11
109. Carrot & Onion Crabmeat 35
110. Carrot & Potato Crispy Chicken 131
111. Carrot & Zucchini Spirals with Avocado 95
112. Cashew Flavored Chicken 54
113. Catalan Vegetable Samfaina 93
114. Cauliflower Mac & Cheese 98
115. Cauliflower Popcorn 113
116. Cauliflower "Risotto" with Mushrooms 87
117. Celery & Chicken Casserole 114
118. Cheddar Cheese & Broccoli Soup 102

119. Cheeseburger Soup 106
120. Cheese, Egg & Sausage Casserole 22
121. Cheese Fondue 112
122. Cheese Sweet Corn 118
123. Cheesy Beef Tortilla Pie 79
124. Cheesy Bulgur with Spring Onions 27
125. Cheesy Chicken Piccata with Olives 50
126. Cheesy Grits with Crispy Pancetta 11
127. Cheesy Hamburger Tortillas 115
128. Cheesy Mushroom Cakes 128
129. Cheesy Mushroom Risotto 128
130. Cheesy Pancetta Penne with Green Peas 67
131. Cheesy Porcini Mushroom Risotto 33
132. Cheesy Potatoes with Chicken Sausage 49
133. Cheesy Potato Hash Brown 113
134. Cheesy Pumpkin Chutney 91
135. Cheesy Sausage & Pepperoni Linguine 29
136. Cheesy Sausage with Potatoes 116
137. Cheesy Shrimp Risotto 33
138. Cheesy Spinach with Eggs 90
139. Cheesy Tomato Soup 105
140. Cherry Tomato & Summer Squash Delight 18
141. Chicken Alfredo 51
142. Chicken Cordon Bleu 52
143. Chicken Enchilada Soup 102
144. Chicken Garam Masala 47
145. Chicken in Honey & Habanero Sauce 45
146. Chicken in Roasted Red Pepper Sauce 43
147. Chicken Jambalaya 47
148. Chicken Marrakesh 52
149. Chicken Meatballs in Tomato Sauce 132
150. Chicken & Mushrooms in Wine Sauce 53
151. Chicken & Mushroom Stew with Spinach 108
152. Chicken Stew with Potatoes & Barley 55
153. Chicken Tikka Masala 50
154. Chicken & Veggie Gumbo 33
155. Chicken Wings in Hot Sauce 131
156. Chicken with Baby Carrots & Mushrooms 45
157. Chicken with Brown Rice 51
158. Chicken with Carrot & Brown Rice 32
159. Chicken with Farfalle & Enchilada Sauce 29
160. Chicken with Green Beans & Potatoes 43
161. Chicken with Green Chilies 45
162. Chicken with Spicy Honey-Orange Sauce 54
163. Chicken with Vegetables & Salad 48
164. Chickpea & Bean Hummus 88
165. Chickpea & Spinach Chili 109
166. Chili Beef Brisket with Chives 71
167. Chili Chicken Breasts with Bell Peppers 49
168. Chili Chicken Carnitas 130
169. Chili Lamb with Carrots & Celery 86
170. Chili Pancetta Hash 22
171. Chili Pork with Pinto Beans 70
172. Chili Rice with Vegetables 32
173. Chipotle Beef Curry 76
174. Chipotle Beef with Wild Rice 76
175. Chipotle Chicken with Chives & Avocado 53
176. Chipotle Shredded Beef 82
177. Chipotle Soybeans 89
178. Chocolate Pudding Cake 124
179. Chocolate-Strawberry Bars 119
180. Chorizo & Black Bean Stew with Potatoes 107
181. Chorizo & Cheese Rice 34
182. Chorizo Sausage Sandwiches with Gravy 64
183. Chorizo with Bell Peppers & Onions 62
184. Christmas Banana Bread 121
185. Cilantro Cauli Rice with Carrots & Kale 97
186. Cilantro Vegetable Beef Soup 79
187. Cinnamon Berry Cobbler 137
188. Cinnamon-Flavored Apple Sauce 126
189. Cinnamon Plum Clafoutis 136
190. Cinnamon & Raisin Muffins 127
191. City Pork with Celery & Carrots 65
192. Clams a la Marinera 37
193. Classic Caramel-Walnut Brownies 137
194. Classic Vanilla Cheesecake 125
195. Coconut Pumpkin Soup 104
196. Coconut Stuffed Apples 125
197. Coconut White Chocolate Fondue 127
198. Colby Asparagus with Anchovy Dressing 117
199. Colby Cheese Chicken Drumsticks 43
200. Colorful Pasta with Pine Nuts 128
201. Coq Au Vin 44
202. Cottage Cheese Deviled Eggs 88
203. Country Beef Stew with Sweet Potatoes 80
204. Couscous with Cherries & Macadamia 28
205. Creamy Blue Cheese Broccoli 16
206. Creamy Chicken Legs 46
207. Creamy Chicken with Quinoa 28
208. Creamy Chicken with Tomato Sauce 44
209. Creamy Leek Potatoes 90
210. Creamy Potatoes with Pancetta Crisps 20
211. Creamy Pumpkin & Ginger Soup 128
212. Creamy Ranch Pork Chops 66
213. Creamy Shrimp Risotto 35
214. Creamy Turkey & Cauliflower Tortellini 29
215. Creole Seafood Gumbo 42
216. Crispy Sweet Potato Sticks 114
217. Crunchy Cod with Quinoa 129
218. Crunchy Pancetta & Egg Burgers 13
219. Cuban Mojo Pork 62
220. Cucumber, Pepper & Quinoa Salad 20
221. Cumin Chicken with Salsa Verde 50
222. Curried Beef Stew with Green Peas 80
223. Curried Pork Stew with Green Peas 63
224. Curry Chicken with Edamame 49
225. Curry Pinto Beans 24
226. Curry Spaghetti Squash 98
227. Curry Zucchini Soup 102
228. Date & Almond Rice Pudding 34
229. Date & Coconut Granola 22
230. Delicious Cod with Cherry Tomatoes 38
231. Delicious Pork Loin with Turnips & Apples 63
232. Delightful Tiramisu Cake 119
233. Dijon Chicken with Mushrooms & Kale 49
234. Dijon Deviled Eggs 116
235. Dilled Salmon with Fennel & Lemon 40
236. Dill Mackerel & Pasta Stew 31
237. Dill & Potato Salmon Chowder 40
238. Dinner Ribs with Beets & Potatoes 79
239. Drunken Mussels 37
240. Duck Legs with Serrano Pepper Sauce 111
241. Easy Barley Pilaf with Cashews 26
242. Easy Beef & Rice Kaiser rolls 75

243. Easy Beef Stew.................................... 82
244. Easy Citrus Fish................................... 39
245. Easy Mac'n'Cheese with Sriracha Sauce........ 130
246. Easy Mango-Teriyaki Chicken.................. 134
247. Easy Monkey Bread.............................. 22
248. Easy Peach Cobbler............................ 123
249. Easy Vegetable Roast........................... 96
250. "Eat-me" Ham & Pea Soup..................... 102
251. Effortless Lamb with Green Onions............. 85
252. Effortless Pork Chops............................ 67
253. Egg Noodles with Sausage & Pancetta......... 132
254. Egg Noodles with Tuna & Peas................. 36
255. Eggplant Caponata.............................. 21
256. Eggplant Caviar................................ 114
257. Eggplant & Tilapia Curry....................... 40
258. Eggs Florentine Casserole....................... 19
259. Emmental Baked Eggs.......................... 89
260. Empanadas Filled with Beef & Olives.......... 135
261. European Stew................................... 69
262. Fall Bean Chili................................. 109
263. Fall Pork Stew.................................. 58
264. Favorite "Ever" Cornbread..................... 26
265. Fennel & Potato Salad.......................... 13
266. Fennel-Scented Fish Stew....................... 41
267. Fennel White Bean Stew........................ 26
268. Fennel & Zucchini with Mushrooms............ 97
269. Flavorful Pork Roast in Beer Sauce............ 60
270. French Cheesy Beef Baguettes................. 135
271. French Toast.................................... 19
272. Fresh Fig & Banana Barley..................... 25
273. Fruit Mix with Almonds....................... 126
274. Fruit-Stuffed Pork Loin......................... 68
275. Garbanzo Beans & Mixed Vegetable Stew...... 24
276. Garden Vegetable Spaghetti.................... 88
277. Garlic Balsamic Steak.......................... 71
278. Garlic Basil Chicken with Carrots.............. 48
279. Garlic Buttered Almonds...................... 115
280. Garlic & Chili Crab Legs....................... 42
281. Garlic & Chili Prawns.......................... 41
282. Garlic Green Peas with Zucchini............... 99
283. Garlic Kale Hummus............................ 92
284. Garlicky BBQ Pork Butt........................ 62
285. Garlicky Chicken Wings with Herbs............ 50
286. Garlicky Chicken with Mushrooms............. 44
287. Garlicky Potato & Rutabaga Mash............ 118
288. Garlicky Sweet Pork with Rice................. 65
289. Garlic Mushrooms with Wine & Parsley........ 96
290. Garlic & Paprika Chicken....................... 54
291. Garlic Red Potatoes............................. 18
292. Garlic Tilapia in Tomato-Olives Sauce........ 130
293. German Pork with Cabbage & Tomatoes........ 64
294. Ginger Lime Salmon............................ 36
295. Ginger Mustard Greens with Bacon............. 21
296. Ginger & Scallion Chicken...................... 44
297. Gingery Sweet Potato & Kale Bowl............. 94
298. Gnocchi with Zucchini & Tomatoes............ 17
299. Golden Beets with Green Olives................. 18
300. Grana Padano Green Risotto.................... 87
301. Grana Padano Grits with Ham & Eggs.......... 24
302. Grandma's Beef with Apple & Vegetables....... 73
303. Grandma's Cabbage with Apples................ 21
304. Grandma's Pear & Peach Compote............ 125

305. Grandma's Sweet Pork Roast................... 63
306. Grandma's Vanilla Cheesecake................ 136
307. Grandma's Veggie Ground Pork................ 59
308. Grapefruit Potatoes with Walnuts.............. 17
309. Greek Chicken Soup with Olive Tapenade..... 103
310. Greek Kakavia Fish Soup....................... 38
311. Greek-Style Pulled Pork........................ 70
312. Green Beans with Fresh Garlic................. 98
313. Green Chili Buttered Corn...................... 93
314. Green Chili & Cheese Frittata.................. 97
315. Green Chili Pork................................ 61
316. Green Onion Pork Ribs......................... 66
317. Green Onion & Walnut Salmon Pilaf.......... 132
318. Ground Beef & Egg Casserole.................. 12
319. Ground Beef & Tomato Chili.................. 110
320. Ground Beef with Zucchini Noodles........... 74
321. Gruyère Cheese & Lobster Pasta............... 36
322. Guajillo Chili Beans with Bacon.............. 136
323. Habanero Beef Tortilla Tart................... 129
324. Halibut with Mango Sauce...................... 39
325. Hard-Boiled Eggs............................. 113
326. Harissa Potato & Spinach Stew............... 108
327. Hazelnut & Apple Delight..................... 123
328. Hazelnut Banana & Date Millet................ 28
329. Healthy Salmon with Broccoli.................. 35
330. Hearty Sausage Soup......................... 106
331. Heavenly Black Bean & Bell Pepper Chili...... 99
332. Heavenly Coconut Pancakes.................... 14
333. Heavenly Spinach with Ricotta Cheese......... 18
334. Herb Chicken with Potatoes & Green Beans..... 47
335. Herby Beef Stroganoff.......................... 81
336. Herby Cavatappi Pasta Siciliana.............. 130
337. Herby Chicken Thighs.......................... 49
338. Herby Chicken with Tomatoes.................. 54
339. Herby Cipollini Onions....................... 112
340. Herby Clams in White Wine.................... 35
341. Herby Lamb with Vegetables................... 85
342. Herby Pork Butt with Potatoes................. 59
343. Herby Vegetables.............................. 88
344. Hispanic Chicken & Rice..................... 134
345. Holiday Almond Cake........................ 119
346. Holiday Beef Meatloaf......................... 71
347. Homemade Asian-Style Tomato Chutney....... 20
348. Homemade Bean Dip........................... 24
349. Homemade Beef Minestrone.................... 75
350. Homemade Duck & Snow Pea Soup............ 56
351. Homemade Grits with Shrimp.................. 40
352. Homemade Raspberry Compote............... 119
353. Honey-Dijon Pork Chops....................... 68
354. Honey Garlic Chicken.......................... 53
355. Honey Quinoa with Walnuts.................... 25
356. Hot Buffalo Chicken Balls.................... 112
357. Hot Chicken Dip.............................. 113
358. Hot Chicken & Leek Cassoulet................. 43
359. Hot Chicken Wings with Sage.................. 48
360. Ice Cream Topped Brownie Cake.............. 121
361. Inviting Potatoes & Snow Beans................ 15
362. Italian Beef Stew with Root Vegetables......... 78
363. Italian Chicken Breasts......................... 46
364. Italian Sausage with Beans & Chickpeas........ 25
365. Italian-Style Chicken......................... 131
366. Italian-Style Mushrooms with Sausage........ 111

367. Italian-Style Pancetta & Potato Casserole........................ 57
368. Jalapeño Chicken Dip.. 113
369. Jalapeño Chicken Quesadillas with Kale 133
370. Jalapeño Chicken with Herbs.. 55
371. Jalapeño Haddock with Samfaina 128
372. Jalapeño Pork Stew 63
373. Jalapeño Pork with Pico de Gallo 70
374. Jalapeño Seafood Jambalaya... 41
375. Jalapeño Tofu Stew with Vegetables 100
376. Jamaican-Style Jerk Chicken... 53
377. Jamón Serrano & Parmesan Egg Muffins 111
378. Japanese-Style Tofu Soup.. 102
379. Juicy Chili Orange Wings.. 46
380. Juicy Chorizo Sausage with Tater Tots........................... 62
381. Juicy Sweet Pork Ribs.. 59
382. Juicy & Tender Pork Loin.. 58
383. Juicy Turkey with Mushrooms 56
384. Juniper Beef Ragu 77
385. Kalamata & Zucchini Toast... 92
386. Kale Pesto Tagliatelle with Green Beans 30
387. Kidney Bean & Shiitake Spread..................................... 23
388. Korean Beef Brisket 81
389. Korean-Style Pork 65
390. Lamb & Bok Choy Curry 85
391. Lamb Cacciatore 86
392. Lamb & Mushroom Ragout 86
393. Lamb Roast with Turnips.. 86
394. Lamb Shanks in Port Wine 85
395. Lamb Shanks & Root Vegetable Stew.......................... 110
396. Lamb Stew.. 85
397. Lamb with Green Onions 86
398. Lazy-Morning Eggs in Hollandaise Sauce...................... 11
399. Leftover Turkey Stew.. 109
400. Lemon Apple Pies 136
401. Lemon Artichokes.. 99
402. Lemon Asparagus... 87
403. Lemon & Cinnamon Braised Pork 57
404. Lemon & Cinnamon Poached Pears............................. 121
405. Lemony Berry Cream 119
406. Lemony Carrot Sticks with Nuts 112
407. Lemony Chicken with Thyme & Garlic........................... 44
408. Lemony Grana Padano Broccoli 18
409. Lentil & Bacon Soup 103
410. Lentil Soup with Persillade Topping 105
411. Lima Bean & Spinach Stew 23
412. Lime Chicken with Pesto Sauce.................................... 48
413. Lime & Ginger Eggplants 96
414. Malaysian Beef Curry 80
415. Mango Okra Gumbo.. 96
416. Mango Pork Roast with Dijon Mustard 61
417. Mango Pork Sandwiches... 68
418. Mango Tarts.. 126
419. Mango & Walnut French-Style Toast 11
420. Manhattan-Style Clam Chowder 42
421. Maple Barbecued Chicken 52
422. Marsala Wine Chicken with Mushrooms 53
423. Mashed Garlic Cauliflower Dish.................................. 118
424. Mashed Potatoes & Celeriac with Chives 130
425. Mayonnaise & Bacon Stuffed Eggs...............................111
426. Meat-Free Lasagna with Mushrooms 18
427. Meatless Mexican Rice... 31
428. Mediterranean Chicken.. 50

429. Mediterranean Cod.. 36
430. Mediterranean Pork Meatballs 69
431. Mediterranean Pork Roast.. 68
432. Mediterranean Vegetable Stew 110
433. Melt-in-Your-Mouth Beef with Vegetables 84
434. Mexican Chicken & Corn Chowder 105
435. Mexican-Style Green Chili Chicken 132
436. Mexican-Style Ropa Vieja.. 77
437. Minestrone al Pesto with Cheese Bread 129
438. Mint & Cilantro Infused Pork 64
439. Mint & Parmesan Zucchini 95
440. Minty Barley Bowls.. 16
441. Mirin Tofu Bowl.. 99
442. Mom's Banana Cake 125
443. Mom's Carrots with Walnuts & Berries 87
444. Mom's Rump Roast with Potatoes 74
445. Mom's Vegetable Soup... 101
446. Monterey Jack Vegetable Casserole.............................. 89
447. Moo-Shu Wraps... 67
448. Morning Blueberry Oatmeal with Peaches 95
449. Moroccan Chicken Soup... 101
450. Mount-Watering Beef Ribs with Shiitakes 71
451. Mozzarella Broccoli with Hazelnuts 97
452. Mushroom & Bell Pepper Bruschettas 91
453. Mushroom & Cheese Buckwheat.................................. 24
454. Mushroom & Eggplant Mix 98
455. Mushroom & Green Onion Chicken 49
456. Mushroom Lentil Stew... 108
457. Mushroom Pâté 17
458. Mushroom & Potato Beef Stew................................... 133
459. Mushroom & Sesame Pâté 111
460. Mustard & Sweet Zucchini 20
461. Mustardy Beef Steaks with Beer Gravy 73
462. Niçoise-Style Ratatouille.. 89
463. North African Chicken Stew 109
464. Nut & Apple Breakfast... 12
465. Nut Crusted Tilapia.. 37
466. Nutmeg Cauliflower Potato Mash................................. 15
467. Nutmeg Chicken Gnocchi Soup 105
468. One-Pot Beef with Beans 24
469. One-Pot Colby Cheese, Ham & Eggs............................. 12
470. One-Pot Fennel & Parsnip Beef.................................... 75
471. Onion Apple Goose 56
472. Onion & Potato Frittata 14
473. Orange Cheesecake 126
474. Orange Cinnamon Ribs.. 61
475. Orange Crème Caramel 122
476. Orange Glazed Chicken.. 55
477. Orange Pork Carnitas 64
478. Orange Tofu & Broccoli Cups...................................... 116
479. Oregano Chicken with Garlic & Tomatoes 45
480. Oregano & Parmesan Zucchini Noodles 94
481. Oregano Pearl Barley & Chorizo Soup 103
482. Oregano Pork with Egg Noodles.................................. 65
483. Palak Paneer 97
484. Paleo Crusted Veggie Quiche....................................... 96
485. Papaya & Honey Quinoa.. 28
486. Paprika Chicken in White Wine Sauce........................... 48
487. Paprika & Garlic Shrimp... 40
488. Paprika & Leek Chicken Pilaf...................................... 132
489. Paprika Lima Bean Dip with Pancetta 27
490. Parmesan Chicken with Rice.. 54

491. Parmesan Zoodle Soup 87
492. Parsley Beef Roast with Mushrooms 83
493. Parsley Buttered Beef 81
494. Parsley & Carrot Chicken Stew 44
495. Parsley Haddock with Potatoes 36
496. Parsley Pork Breakfast Biscuits 13
497. Party Cherry Pie 122
498. Party Cinnamon & Yogurt Cheesecake 121
499. Party Dark Chocolate Bread Pudding 14
500. Party Egg Custard 112
501. Party Mix 113
502. Peach & Golden Raisin Porridge 27
503. Peach Short Ribs 61
504. Peanut Pear Wedges 127
505. Pear & Cherry Pork Tenderloin 58
506. Pear, Coconut & Pecan Porridge 14
507. Pearl Barley & Black Olive Salad 26
508. Pearl Onion & Squash Beef Stew 134
509. Peas, Sweet Potatoes & Spinach Pot 91
510. Pecan & Mashed Potato Bake 92
511. Penne with Mixed Peppers & Beans 31
512. Penne with Pepperoncini Sauce 90
513. Penne with Sage & Pancetta 29
514. Peppered Pork Tenderloin with Rice 70
515. Perfect Mediterranean Asparagus 18
516. Picante Beef Stew with Barley 78
517. Picante Chicken Thighs 51
518. Picante Red Bean & Corn Dip 24
519. Pineapple Chocolate Pudding 120
520. Pineapple & Soda-Glazed Ham 118
521. Pineapple Upside Down Cake 123
522. Pink Beans with Pancetta & Tomatoes 23
523. Pinto Bean & Sweet Potato Chili 100
524. Pizza Marguerite with Cauliflower Crust 116
525. Poached Trout with Pomegranate 38
526. Poblano Pepper & Sweet Corn Side Dish 98
527. Polish-Style Beef & Cabbage Pot 82
528. Poppy Seed & Lemon Bars 120
529. Pork and Sauerkraut Goulash 60
530. Pork & Canadian Bacon Soup 106
531. Pork Chops in Honey & Apple Sauce 67
532. Pork Chops in Onion Sauce 66
533. Pork Chops Teriyaki Style 67
534. Pork Chops with Broccoli 57
535. Pork Chops with Shallots & Carrots 62
536. Pork Chops with Veggies 61
537. Pork Goulash with Spaghetti 70
538. Pork in Tomato Buttermilk Sauce 60
539. Pork Loin with Mustard Sauce 69
540. Pork Meatballs with Sour Mushroom Sauce ... 62
541. Pork Ragu with Rigatoni 135
542. Pork Rib Chops with Carrots & Parsnips 60
543. Pork Ribs with Wine Pecan Sauce 66
544. Pork & Rice Stuffed Peppers 65
545. Pork & Shallot Frittata 57
546. Pork Shoulder in BBQ Sauce 59
547. Pork Steaks with Apricot Sauce 60
548. Pork Stew with Sun-Dried Tomatoes 69
549. Pork Tenderloin in Sweet Ginger Sauce 58
550. Pork with Brown Rice 31
551. Pork with Mushrooms & Tomato Sauce 133
552. Pork with Prune Sauce 62
553. Pork with Shallots & Mushrooms 59
554. Portobello Mushroom & Leek Delight 19
555. Potato Balls with Walnut-Yogurt Sauce 117
556. Potato & Parsnip Mix 117
557. Power Green Minestrone Stew with Lemon 99
558. Prawn & Tuna Skewers with Soy Sauce 35
559. Provençal Meatballs with Cheese Sauce 76
560. Prune & Peach Barley 19
561. Pulled Pork Mexican-Style 68
562. Pumpkin Cake 124
563. Pumpkin Custard 120
564. Pumpkin Granola 22
565. Pumpkin Hummus 112
566. Pumpkin & Lentil Dhal 92
567. Pumpkin & Pearl Barley Soup 103
568. Pumpkin Spice Oatmeal 21
569. Quick Cilantro Salmon 14
570. Quick & Easy Beef Meatloaf 74
571. Quick Ginger-Carrot Puree 15
572. Quick Indian Creamy Eggplants 99
573. Quick Pork Chops with Brussels Sprouts 57
574. Quick Rum Egg Custard 127
575. Quick Veggie Meal 90
576. Quinoa Energy Bars 124
577. Raclette Soup with Tortillas 100
578. Raisin Chocolate Cookies 122
579. Ramen Noodles with Beef Meatballs 31
580. Red Cabbage & Beet Borscht 107
581. Red Cabbage & Bell Pepper Side 20
582. Red Cabbage with Coconut 15
583. Red Lentil Soup 107
584. Reuben Dip 114
585. Ribs with Plum Sauce 68
586. Rich Parsnip & Mushroom Pork 59
587. Ricotta Stuffed Potatoes 100
588. Risotto with Green Peas & Mushrooms 32
589. Rolled Chicken with Asparagus & Prosciutto . 115
590. Rosemary Beef Stew 108
591. Rosemary Butter Beans 25
592. Rosemary Butternut Squash Stew 108
593. Rosemary Flank Steak 75
594. Rosemary Salmon Soup with Rice 33
595. Rosemary Salmon with Spinach 37
596. Rotini with Beef & Monterey Jack Cheese 29
597. Rutabaga Salad with Honey Dressing 17
598. Sage Drumsticks with Red Sauce 47
599. Sage Zucchini & Navy Bean Soup 102
600. Salmon & Asparagus Frittata 42
601. Salmon Loaf with Cucumber Sauce 38
602. Salmon with Hot-Garlic Sauce 131
603. Salmon with Parsley-Lemon Sauce 38
604. Saucy Basmati Rice 32
605. Saucy Beef Short Ribs 83
606. Saucy Chicken Teriyaki 46
607. Saucy Corned Beef Brisket 72
608. Saucy Mustard Pork 66
609. Saucy Seafood Penne with Chorizo 129
610. Saucy Turkey with Green Peas 133
611. Sausage and Kale Casserole with Eggs 13
612. Sausage & Cheese Frittata 13
613. Sausage & Cream Cheese Dip 115
614. Sausage Pilaf with Sun-Dried Tomatoes 34

615. Sausage with Beer & Sauerkraut............................ 70
616. Sausage with Fusilli Pasta & Cheese 31
617. Sauteed Spinach With Bacon & Chickpeas............ 60
618. Savory Baby Spinach & Carrot Side..................... 17
619. Savory Beef Roast in Passion Fruit Gravy............ 84
620. Savory Blueberry Curd..................................... 120
621. Savory Faro Breakfast... 22
622. Savory Lemon Zesty Toast.................................. 14
623. Savory Mushroom & Squash Platter..................... 20
624. Savory Nutmeg Yam Mash................................... 17
625. Savory Spinach & Leek Relish.............................. 87
626. Savory Tomato Bell Peppers................................ 19
627. Savoy Cabbage with Pancetta.............................. 59
628. Scallion & Tofu Bowl... 92
629. Scrumptious Stuffed Pears 123
630. Seafood Paella with Broccoli................................ 39
631. Serrano Chili Chicken... 45
632. Serrano Ham & Cheese Cups.............................. 136
633. Serrano Pepper Bulgur.. 28
634. Shallot Turkey with Apricot Gravy...................... 55
635. Sherry Pork Chops with Artichoke Hearts 67
636. Shiitake & Baby Carrot Beef Stew........................ 81
637. Shiitake Mushroom Oats with Garlic.................... 12
638. Shrimp Paella with Andouille Sausage 131
639. Silky Lemon Cheesecake with Blueberries........... 119
640. Simple Basil & Haddock with Capers.................... 37
641. Simple Celery Jasmine Rice................................. 34
642. Simple Cranberry Peach Biscuits........................ 123
643. Simple Herby Potatoes.. 92
644. Simple Poached Apricots.................................... 121
645. Simple Pumpkin Soup.. 107
646. Simple Sage Whole Chicken................................ 47
647. Simple Softboiled Eggs....................................... 11
648. Simple Sweet Potatoes.. 91
649. Sirloin Steak with Gorgonzola Cheese.................. 72
650. Slow-Cooked Honey-Mustard Chicken 51
651. Smoked Beef Steak... 78
652. Smoked Paprika Potato Chips............................. 112
653. Smoked Paprika Spiced Squash Hash................... 16
654. Smoked Paprika Squid with Green Beans.............. 37
655. Smoked Turkey & Bean Soup............................. 104
656. Snow Pea & Raisin Salad.................................... 93
657. South American Chicken & Lentil Soup............... 105
658. Spaghetti Carbonara with Broccoli 135
659. Spaghetti Squash with Kale & Broccoli................. 97
660. Spanish Pisto Manchego.................................... 107
661. Spanish Rice with Chicken Legs.......................... 34
662. Speedy Meatballs.. 80
663. Speedy Nectarines with Blueberry Sauce............. 122
664. Spelt & Red Beans with Mushrooms.................... 27
665. Spiced Pork Ribs... 69
666. Spiced Sweet Potato Soup................................. 103
667. Spicy Baby Back Ribs.. 132
668. Spicy Beef with Chickpeas.................................. 77
669. Spicy Broccoli with Peas & Potatoes.................... 15
670. Spicy Chicken & Mixed Vegetable Stew 109
671. Spicy Chicken Soup... 51
672. Spicy Coconut Salmon Curry.............................. 41
673. Spicy Eggplants.. 95
674. Spicy Haricot Vert & Potato Curry..................... 106
675. Spicy Mashed Pinto Beans.................................. 27
676. Spicy Pork Chops.. 65
677. Spicy Pork Sausage Meatloaf.............................. 58
678. Spicy Red Lentils with Yogurt............................ 94
679. Spicy Roasted Whole Chicken............................. 51
680. Spicy-Sweet Meatballs...................................... 115
681. Spinach Dip.. 114
682. Spinach & Feta Pie Sandwiches.......................... 91
683. Spinach & Gnocchi Chicken Sausage Pot............. 55
684. Split Pea Beef Stew... 26
685. Sriracha Pulled Turkey with Ale Beer................... 56
686. Steamed Artichokes with Parsley Aioli................. 17
687. Steamed Pollock... 40
688. Steamed Salmon with Caper Sauce...................... 39
689. Steamed Tabasco Potatoes.................................. 16
690. Steamed Tilapia with Radicchio Salad.................. 42
691. Stewed Beef Oxtails... 80
692. Stewed Beef with Vegetables............................... 74
693. Stewed Vegetables... 98
694. Sticky BBQ Chicken Drumsticks........................ 116
695. Sticky Ginger Ale Short Ribs.............................. 75
696. Sticky Sweet Chicken Wings.............................. 115
697. Strawberry & White Chocolate Porridge.............. 15
698. Summer Berry Cobbler..................................... 124
699. Summer Garden Quiche..................................... 11
700. Sunday Beef Garam Masala................................ 72
701. Sunday Crab Legs with White Wine..................... 36
702. Sunday Paprika Potatoes with Herbs.................... 14
703. Sweet Chicken Drumsticks................................. 46
704. Sweet Corn & Onion Eggs.................................. 12
705. Sweet Ginger Beef Ribs...................................... 71
706. Sweet Milk Balls... 121
707. Sweet Potatoes with Brussel Sprouts.................... 20
708. Sweet Potatoes with Zucchini............................. 16
709. Sweet Rice Pudding with Hazelnuts..................... 34
710. Sweet Shredded Pork... 64
711. Sweet & Sour Pork.. 66
712. Sweet & Sour Shrimp... 42
713. Sweet & Spicy Chicken Mole.............................. 53
714. Sweet & Spicy Chicken Thighs............................ 47
715. Sweet Tomato Sauce.. 91
716. Swiss Chard Crisps with Orange Juice................. 118
717. Swiss Chard, Zucchini & Mushroom Rice............ 32
718. Tahini Tofu with Cauliflower & Potatoes.............. 89
719. Tarragon Beef & Prune Casserole........................ 82
720. Tarragon Pork with Mushroom Sauce.................. 63
721. Tasty Apple Risotto... 126
722. Tasty Beef with Carrot-Onion Gravy................... 75
723. Tasty Beef with Rotini Pasta.............................. 78
724. Tasty Honey Pumpkin Pie................................. 120
725. Tasty Mac & Cheese.. 94
726. Tasty Onion Frittata with Bell Peppers................. 13
727. Tasty Pork with Carrots & Shallots..................... 57
728. Tasty Potato & Carrot Mash............................... 21
729. Tasty Trout with Spiralized Vegetables................. 37
730. Tempeh Stir-Fry with Sherry & Parsley................ 90
731. Tender BBQ Ribs.. 58
732. Teriyaki Chicken in Lettuce Wrap...................... 116
733. Teriyaki-Style Chicken Thighs........................... 50
734. Thai Chicken 52
735. The Best Ever Pineapple Pork Meatballs............... 60
736. Three-Meat Mozzarella Quiche........................... 12
737. Thyme & Bell Pepper Chicken............................ 52
738. Thyme Braised Lamb... 86

739. Thyme Chicken Soup 47
740. Thyme Chicken with Red Currant Sauce 43
741. Thyme Creamy Beef Roast 71
742. Thyme & Frascati Cauliflower 19
743. Thyme & Green Onion Pork Chops 69
744. Thyme Potato & Cannellini Bean Pottage 19
745. Thyme Potato & Pumpkin Cream Soup 103
746. Thyme Pot Roast with Potatoes 73
747. Thyme Tomato Dip Sauce 117
748. Tiger Prawns with Red Lentils 25
749. Tomato Beans with Tuna 39
750. Tomato & Broccoli Casserole 94
751. Tradicional Indian Chicken Curry 106
752. Traditional Catfish Chowder 35
753. Traditional Italian Peperonata 30
754. Tuna & Artichoke Egg Noodles 30
755. Turkey with Broccoli & Carrots 56
756. Turmeric Chicken & Broccoli Soup 105
757. Turmeric Vegan Sausage Casserole 89
758. Turnip & Chickpea Stew 109
759. Tuscan Turkey Breast with Beans 45
760. Tuscan Vegetable Tortellini Soup 101
761. Two-Bean & Chickpea Stew 23
762. Udon Noodle Chicken Soup 104
763. Vanilla & Fruit Compote 125
764. Vanilla Sweet Potato Oatmeal 21
765. Vegan Broccoli with Tahini Sauce 98
766. Vegan Burrito Bowls 92
767. Vegan Shepherd's Pie 88
768. Vegan White Bean & Avocado Salad 26
769. Vegetable Lasagna with Mushrooms 29
770. Vegetable Medley with Brazil Nuts 95

771. Vegetable One-Pot 99
772. Vegetable & Peanut Pilaf 87
773. Vegetable Soup with Parsley Croutons 106
774. Veggie Flax Patties 93
775. Walnut Fudge 124
776. Whiskey-Glazed Meatloaf 74
777. White Bean & Pancetta Soup 101
778. White Beans with Tuna 28
779. White Chocolate Cake in a Cup 127
780. White Wine Pasta Bolognese 30
781. Wild Rice & Salmon Soup 41
782. Wild Rice with Three-Color Bell Peppers 33
783. Winter Beef with Vegetables 84
784. Winter Chicken Hotpot 54
785. Winter Pork Belly with Red Cabbage 66
786. Winter Root Vegetable Pot 93
787. Winter Squash & Cauliflower Bowl 16
788. Winter Squash & Chickpea Soup 101
789. Yellow Lentil Dip 27
790. Yellow Split Peas with Cilantro & Spinach 96
791. Yummy Beef with Vegetables 76
792. Yummy Lamb Stew 108
793. Yummy Smoked Sausage Bites 117
794. Zesty Carrots with Pistachios 118
795. Ziti Pasta with Pork Balls & Vegetables 30
796. Zucchini & Beef Lasagna 30
797. Zucchini Pomodoro Pasta 91
798. Zucchini & Potato Beef Stew 82
799. Zucchini & Potato Patties 118
800. Zucchini Rump Steak 78